Modern Approach to Artificial Intelligence

Volume II

Preface

Artificial intelligence is the term given to the intelligence that is seen to be exhibited by machines or software. It has emerged as an independent academic field of study. One can define this arena as the study and design of intelligent agents, where an intelligent agent is a system that comprehends its environment and takes actions that increase its chances of success. The term is also applicable to the task of developing systems gifted with the logical processes that are characteristic of humans, such as the ability to discover meaning, reason, generalize and learn from experience. The field is based on the foundational claim that the central property of humans, that is, intelligence, can be so accurately expressed that a machine can be made to simulate and imitate it. Artificial Intelligence research is a highly technical and specialized field, and can be divided into various branches. The goals of AI research include planning, learning, reasoning, natural language processing or communication, knowledge, perception as well as the ability to move and manipulate objects. The field of artificial intelligence is an interdisciplinary one, in which numerous scientific and social science disciplines converge such as psychology, computer science, linguistics, neuroscience, philosophy as well as other specialized fields such as artificial psychology. This is a highly scientific field that is undergoing constant and rapid changes and thus needs skilled researchers and engineers in its ranks.

This book lists and discusses the research compiled on the advances that artificial intelligence has undergone recently. I am thankful to those scientists and researchers whose toil and hard work helped make this effort a success as well as those outside the scientific community who have been unwavering in their support.

Editor

Artificial-Intelligence-Based Techniques to Evaluate Switching Overvoltages during Power System Restoration

Iman Sadeghkhani,[1] **Abbas Ketabi,**[2] **and Rene Feuillet**[3]

[1] *Department of Electrical Engineering, Islamic Azad University, Najafabad Branch, Najafabad 85141-43131, Iran*
[2] *Department of Electrical Engineering, University of Kashan, Kashan 87317-51167, Iran*
[3] *Grenoble Electrical Engineering Lab (G2ELab), Grenoble INP, BP46, 38402 Saint Martin d'Hères Cedex, France*

Correspondence should be addressed to Iman Sadeghkhani; i.sadeghkhani@ec.iut.ac.ir

Academic Editor: Richard Mitchell

This paper presents an approach to the study of switching overvoltages during power equipment energization. Switching action is one of the most important issues in the power system restoration schemes. This action may lead to overvoltages which can damage some equipment and delay power system restoration. In this work, switching overvoltages caused by power equipment energization are evaluated using artificial-neural-network- (ANN-) based approach. Both multilayer perceptron (MLP) trained with Levenberg-Marquardt (LM) algorithm and radial basis function (RBF) structure have been analyzed. In the cases of transformer and shunt reactor energization, the worst case of switching angle and remanent flux has been considered to reduce the number of required simulations for training ANN. Also, for achieving good generalization capability for developed ANN, equivalent parameters of the network are used as ANN inputs. Developed ANN is tested for a partial of 39-bus New England test system, and results show the effectiveness of the proposed method to evaluate switching overvoltages.

1. Introduction

In recent years, due to economic competition and deregulation, power systems are being operated closer and closer to their limits. At the same time, power systems have increased in size and complexity. Both factors increase the risk of major power outages. After a blackout, power needs to be restored as quickly and reliably as possible, and, consequently, detailed restoration plans are nec [1–4].

One of the major concerns in power system restoration is the occurrence of overvoltages as a result of switching procedures. These can be classified as transient overvoltages, sustained overvoltages, harmonic resonance overvoltages, and overvoltages resulting from ferroresonance. Steady-state overvoltages occur at the receiving end of lightly loaded transmission lines as a consequence of line-charging currents (reactive power balance). Excessive sustained overvoltages may lead to damage of transformers and other power system equipment. Transient overvoltages are a consequence

of switching operations on long transmission lines, or the switching of capacitive devices, and may result in arrester failures. Ferroresonance is a nonharmonic resonance characterized by overvoltages whose waveforms are highly distorted and can cause catastrophic equipment damages [1, 5].

Overvoltage will put the transformer into saturation, causing core heating and copious harmonic current generation. Circuit breaker called upon to operate during periods of high voltage will have reduced interrupting capability. At some voltage, even the ability to interrupt line-charging current will be lost [6–8].

This paper presents the artificial neural network (ANN) application for estimation of peak and duration of overvoltages under switching transients during transformer, shunt reactor, and transmission lines energization.

In [6], switching overvoltages during single-phase transformer have been evaluated using multilayer perceptron (MLP) trained with Levenberg-Marquardt (LM) algorithm. In this paper, three-phase transformer has been analyzed.

Many time-domain simulations are required to train ANN resulting in a large amount of simulation time. For the transformer and shunt reactor energization study, this paper uses a harmonic index which can calculate overvoltages for the worst case of switching time and remanent flux [6]. This index reduces ANN training time effectively. Also, there is no need to specify switching time and remanent flux. A tool such as proposed in this paper that can give the maximum switching overvoltage and its duration will be helpful to the operator during system restoration. Also it can be used as a training tool for the operators. Developed ANN is tested for a partial of 39-bus New England test system to illustrate the proposed approach.

2. Study System Modelling

The electrical components of the network are modeled using the Power System Blockset (PSB) (MATLAB/Simulink-based simulation tool [9, 10]). These models should be adapted for the desired frequency range (here the frequencies up to $f = 10f_0$ are considered to be sufficient). The generator is represented by an ideal voltage source behind the subtransient inductance in series with the armature winding resistance that can be as accurate as the Park model [11]. Phase of voltage source is determined by the load flow results. Transmission lines are described by distributed line models. The circuit breaker is represented by an ideal switch. The transformer model takes into account the winding resistances (R_1, R_2), the leakage inductances (L_1, L_2), and the magnetizing characteristics of the core, which is modeled by a resistance, R_m, simulating the core active losses and a saturable inductance, L_{sat}. The shunt reactor model takes into account the leakage inductance as well as the magnetizing characteristics of the core, which is modeled by a resistance, R_m, simulating the core active losses and a saturable inductance, L_{sat}. The saturation characteristic is specified as a piecewise linear characteristic [12]. All of the loads are modeled as constant impedances.

3. Training Artificial Neural Network

In this paper, two ANN structures have been used: multilayer perceptron (MLP) trained with Levenberg-Marquardt (LM) algorithm and radial basis function (RBF). Detailed structures of MLP-LM and RBF are presented in [13] and [14], respectively.

Percentage error is calculated as follows:

$$\text{error} (\%) = \frac{|\text{ANN} - \text{PSB}|}{\text{PSB}} \times 100. \tag{1}$$

The sample system considered for explanation of the proposed methodology and ANN training is a 400 kV extra-high-voltage (EHV) network shown in Figure 1. The equivalent circuit parameters are added to ANN inputs to achieve good generalization capability for trained ANN. In fact, in this approach ANN is trained just once for sample system of Figure 1. Since ANN training is based on equivalent circuit parameters, developed ANN can be used for every studied

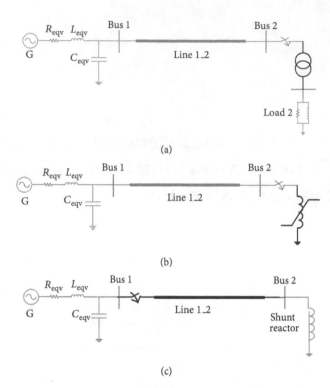

FIGURE 1: Sample systems for power components energization study. (a) Transformer energization, (b) shunt reactor energization, and (c) transmission line energization. G: generator, R_{eqv}: equivalent resistance, L_{eqv}: equivalent inductance, and C_{eqv}: equivalent capacitance.

system. In other words, it is just sufficient to convert every studied system to the equivalent system of Figure 1, then it is possible to use developed ANN to estimate overvoltages.

4. Transformer Energization Study

The major cause of harmonic resonance overvoltage problems is the switching of lightly loaded transformers at the end of transmission lines. The harmonic-current components of the same frequency as the system resonance frequencies are amplified in case of parallel resonance, thereby creating higher voltages at the transformer terminals. This leads to a higher level of saturation, resulting in higher harmonic components of the inrush current that again results in increased voltages. This can happen particularly in lightly damped systems, common at the beginning of a restoration procedure when a path from a black-start source to a large power plant is being established and only a few loads are restored yet [1, 5].

Normally for harmonic overvoltages analysis during transformer energization, the worst case of the switching angle and remanent flux must be considered, which is a function of switching time, transformer characteristics and its initial flux condition, and impedance characteristics of the switching bus [12]. Using the worst switching angle and remanent flux, the number of simulations for each case can be reduced significantly.

TABLE 1: Effect of switching time and remanent flux on the maximum of overvoltages and duration of $V_{peak} > 1.3$ p.u.

Switching angle (deg.)	Remanent flux (p.u.)	V_{peak} (p.u.)	Duration of ($V_{peak} > 1.3$ p.u.) (s)
Transformer study			
39	0.65	2.1961	0.7544
80	0.62	1.8095	0.4627
87	0.09	1.8831	0.8469
60	0.42	2.0482	0.5134
15	0.3	1.5319	0.2753
Shunt reactor study			
20	0.27	1.9205	0.5628
20	0.65	1.5841	0.3394
75	0.27	1.6537	0.3064
60	0.5	1.5293	0.2675

In order to determine the worst-case switching time and remanent flux, the following index is defined as

$$W = \sum_{h=2}^{10} Z_{jj}(h) \cdot I_j(h, t_0, \phi_r), \qquad (2)$$

where t_0 is the switching time, ϕ_r is the initial transformer flux, and h is the harmonic order. This index can be a definition for the worst-case switching condition and remanent flux. Using a numerical algorithm, one can find the switching time and remanent flux for which W is maximal (i.e., harmonic overvoltages are maximal).

Figure 2(a) shows the result of the PSB frequency analysis at bus 2 in Figure 1(a). The magnitude of the Thévenin impedance, seen from bus 2, $Z_{bus\,2}$, shows a parallel resonance peak at 246 Hz. Figures 2(b), 2(c), and 2(d) show changes of W index with respect to the current starting angle and remanent flux for three phases. As shown in Figure 2, $W_{max,B}$ is bigger than $W_{max,A}$ and $W_{max,C}$. Therefore, if simulation is performed based on switching angle and remanent flux related to $W_{max,B}$, maximum overvoltages are achieved. Table 1 summarizes the results of overvoltages simulation for five different switching angles and remanent flux that includes $W_{max,A}$ (80° and 0.62 p.u.), $W_{max,B}$ (39° and 0.65 p.u.), and $W_{max,C}$ (87° and 0.09 p.u.). Results verify the effectiveness of W index.

As mentioned in [6], the most important aspects which influence the transformer overvoltages are voltage at transformer bus before switching, line length, switching angle, saturation curve slope, and remanent flux. This information will help the operator to select the proper sequence of transformer to be energized safely with transients appearing safe within the limits. As mentioned in a previous section, equivalent resistance, equivalent inductance, and equivalent capacitance have been added to ANN inputs to enhance generalization capability. Based on (2) and Figure 2, switching angle and remanent flux are omitted from ANN inputs; thus, ANN training procedure time is reduced significantly. Therefore, in this paper for training ANN, the following parameters are considered as ANN inputs:

(i) voltage at transformer bus before switching,

(ii) equivalent resistance of the network,

(iii) equivalent inductance of the network,

(iv) equivalent capacitance of the network,

(v) line length,

(vi) saturation curve slope.

The steps for harmonic overvoltages assessment and estimation are listed as follows:

(1) determine the characteristics of transformer that should be energized,

(2) calculate the $Z_{ii}(h)$ at the transformer bus for $h = 2f_0, \ldots, 10f_0$,

(3) compute the worst switching angle and remanent flux for simulation,

(4) run PSB simulation,

(5) determine the overvoltage peak and duration,

(6) repeat the steps 1 to 5 with various system parameters to learn artificial neural network,

(7) test the artificial neural network with different system parameters.

Schematic diagram of transformer energization study during power system restoration is illustrated in Figure 3.

5. Study of Shunt Reactor Energization

Long EHV transmission lines are generally compensated by means of shunt reactor sets. Reactor failures have directed attention to the transient overvoltages generated by reactor switching. Shunt reactors are applied to regulate the reactive power balance of a system by means of compensating for the surplus reactive power generation of transmission lines. Reactors are normally disconnected at heavy load and are connected to the lines at periods of low load. Consequently, frequent switching is a significant characteristic of shunt reactors in order that they can react to the changing system load condition [15].

Transients caused by shunt reactor switching have been an important parameter in the design of the relevant equipment (reactor, circuit breaker, and insulation) of power systems [16]. Based on considered model for shunt reactor, it is possible to use harmonic index which is defined in a previous section. Table 1 summarizes the results of overvoltages simulation for four different switching angles and remanent flux that verify the effectiveness of W index for shunt reactor energization study.

The most important parameters which influence the shunt reactor overvoltages are voltage at shunt reactor bus before switching, line length, switching angle, saturation curve slope, remanent flux, and shunt reactor capacity. Using W index, switching angle and remanent flux have been omitted from ANN inputs. Also, equivalent circuit parameters are added to ANN inputs to increase generalization capability. Consequently, in this case, the following parameters are selected as ANN inputs:

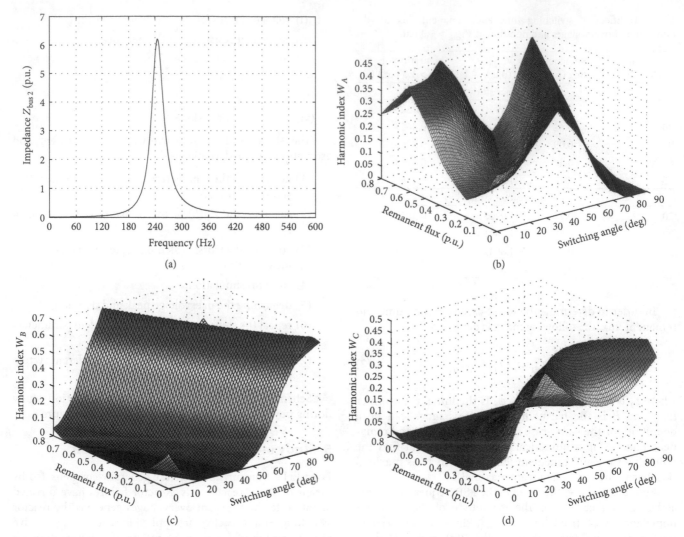

FIGURE 2: (a) Impedance at bus 2 and changes of W index with respect to current starting angle and remanent flux in (b) phase A, (c) phase B, and (d) phase C.

(i) voltage at shunt reactor bus before switching,

(ii) equivalent resistance of the network,

(iii) equivalent inductance of the network,

(iv) equivalent capacitance of the network,

(v) line length,

(vi) shunt reactor capacity,

(vii) saturation curve slope.

The steps of overvoltages assessment and estimation follow:

(1) determine the characteristics of shunt reactor that should be energized,

(2) calculate the $Z_{ii}(h)$ at the shunt reactor bus for $h = 2f_0, \ldots, 10f_0$,

(3) compute the worst switching angle and remanent flux for simulation,

(4) run PSB simulation,

(5) determine the overvoltage peak and duration,

(6) repeat the steps 1 to 5 with various system parameters to learn artificial neural network,

(7) test the artificial neural network with different system parameters.

6. Transmission Line Energization Study

In most countries, the main step in the process of power system restoration, following a complete/partial blackout, is energization of primary restorative transmission lines. Switching overvoltage is of a primary importance in insulation coordination for extra-high-voltage (EHV) lines. The objective of simulating switching overvoltage is to help for a proper insulation coordination and would lead to minimize damage and interruption to service as a consequence of steady-state, dynamic, and transient overvoltage [17].

During the early stages of restoring high-voltage overhead and underground transmission lines, concerns are with three

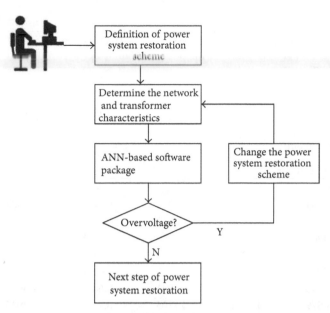

FIGURE 3: ANN-based approach to analyze harmonic overvoltages during transformer energization.

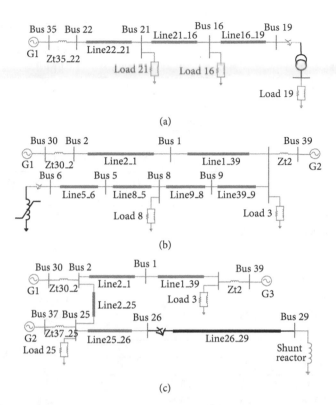

FIGURE 4: Portions of 39-bus New England test systems: (a) transformer energization, (b) shunt reactor energization, and (c) transmission line energization.

related overvoltages: sustained power frequency overvoltages, switching transients (surges), and harmonic resonance. In the early stages of the restoration, the lines are lightly loaded; resonance therefore is lightly damped, which in turn means that the resulting resonance voltages may be very high [1].

In order to reduce the steady-state overvoltage of no-load transmission lines, a shunt reactor is connected at the receiving end of transmission line.

In practical system, a number of factors affect the overvoltages factors due to energization or reclosing. The most important factors are voltage at sending-end bus of transmission line before switching, switching angle, line length, line capacitance, and shunt reactor capacity. Equivalent circuit parameters are added to ANN inputs to increase generalization capability. Consequently, in this case, following parameters are considered as ANN inputs:

(i) voltage at the sending-end bus of the transmission line before switching,

(ii) equivalent resistance of the network,

(iii) equivalent inductance of the network,

(iv) equivalent capacitance of the network,

(v) closing time of the circuit breaker poles,

(vi) line length,

(vii) line capacitance,

(viii) shunt reactor capacity.

The steps for transient overvoltages estimation are listed as follows:

(1) determine the characteristics of transmission line that should be energized,

(2) run PSB simulation,

(3) determine the overvoltage peak and duration,

(4) repeat the steps 1 to 3 with various system parameters to learn artificial neural network,

(5) test the artificial neural network with different system parameters.

7. Case Study

In this section, the proposed algorithm is demonstrated for three case studies that are a portion of 39-bus New England test system which is shown in Figure 4, and its parameters are listed in [18].

For training ANNs (three cases), all experiments have been repeated for different system parameters which form 2000 sets. For producing these sets, ANN inputs have been varied in proper range for each parameter. 1000 sets were used to train each ANN, and 1000 sets were used to test each ANN. Table 2 shows specifications of developed ANNs.

Figure 4(a) shows a one-line diagram of a portion of 39-bus New England test system which is in restorative state. The generator at bus 35 is a black-start unit. The load 19 shows cranking power of the later generator that must be restored by the transformer of bus 19. When the transformer is energized, harmonic overvoltages can be produced because the transformer is lightly loaded. The equivalent circuit of this system that is seen behind bus 16 is determined, and values of equivalent resistance, equivalent inductance, and

TABLE 2: Specifications of trained ANNs.

	Number of hidden layers		Number of neurons in hidden layers		Training time (epochs)	
	LM	RBF	LM	RBF	LM	RBF
Transformer energization	2	2	8	10	45	72
Shunt reactor energization	2	2	8	10	61	95
Transmission line energization	2	2	7	9	53	68

TABLE 3: Some sample testing data and output for LM algorithm.

Transformer energization							
V	L.L.	V_{PSB}	V_{LM}	$Error_V$	T_{PSB}	T_{LM}	$Error_T$
0.9314	155	1.3252	1.3684	3.2576	0.1264	0.1237	2.1682
0.9668	182	1.4577	1.4324	1.7386	0.3819	0.3644	4.5937
0.9812	200	1.5031	1.4807	1.4928	0.3285	0.3378	2.8406
1.0435	215	1.6602	1.6498	0.6239	0.5094	0.5143	0.9571
1.0752	237	1.8535	1.9076	2.9175	0.6673	0.6438	3.5194
1.1373	256	1.9892	1.9396	2.4916	0.5961	0.6039	1.3058
1.1781	288	2.0545	2.0879	1.6271	0.7105	0.7197	1.2935
1.2098	310	2.0361	2.0934	2.8132	0.9254	0.9457	2.1962

Shunt reactor energization								
V	L.L.	S.R.	V_{PSB}	V_{LM}	$Error_V$	T_{PSB}	T_{LM}	$Error_T$
1.1442	150	70	1.5011	1.4497	3.4218	0.1936	0.1904	1.6459
1.1561	165	45	1.5453	1.5857	2.6149	0.2375	0.2351	1.0246
1.2302	178	30	1.6769	1.7241	2.8137	0.3469	0.3628	4.5728
1.2514	200	30	1.7481	1.7194	1.6424	0.3952	0.4043	2.3071
1.3326	215	23	1.9507	2.0117	3.1295	0.5104	0.5195	1.7915
1.3326	215	17	1.9914	1.9749	0.8261	0.5536	0.5571	0.6248
1.4165	230	17	2.1652	2.1759	0.4936	0.6742	0.6594	2.1963
1.4327	242	10	2.2479	2.2172	1.3674	0.7593	0.7395	2.6134

Transmission line energization									
V	L.L.	S.R.	S.A.	V_{PSB}	V_{LM}	$Error_V$	T_{PSB}	T_{LM}	$Error_T$
0.9491	375	40	30	2.3508	2.4024	2.1962	0.3652	0.3704	1.4328
0.9127	240	40	30	2.2769	2.2328	1.9381	0.3107	0.3159	1.6649
0.9973	240	55	60	2.3016	2.3849	3.6172	0.3496	0.3458	1.0793
0.9754	195	12	75	2.3882	2.4523	2.6835	0.4073	0.4034	0.9458
1.0719	315	23	15	2.4195	2.4071	0.5124	0.4217	0.4257	0.9426
1.0592	282	45	5	2.3725	2.3413	1.3157	0.3846	0.3948	2.6419
1.0946	137	63	45	2.3596	2.3902	1.2984	0.3378	0.3424	1.3674
1.1123	346	10	53	2.8537	2.7944	2.0791	0.5449	0.5543	1.7204

V: voltage at power component bus before switching (p.u.), L.L.: line length (km), S.R.: shunt reactor capacity (MVAR), S.A.: switching angle (deg.), V_{PSB}: overvoltage peak calculated by PSB (p.u.), V_{LM}: overvoltage peak calculated by LM (p.u.), T_{PSB}: overvoltage duration calculated by PSB (s), T_{LM}: overvoltage duration calculated by LM (s), $error_V$: voltage error (%), and $error_T$: duration time error (%).

equivalent capacitance are calculated. In other words, the case study system is converted to equivalent system as in Figure 1(a). Values of equivalent resistance, equivalent inductance, and equivalent capacitance are 0.00326 p.u., 0.02793, and 1.8561 p.u., respectively. For testing trained ANN, values of voltage at transformer bus (bus 19) and line length are varied, and overvoltage peak and duration are calculated using developed ANN. Table 3 contains the same sample result of test data of transformer energization for LM algorithm, and Table 4 has these data for RBF structure.

As another example, the system in Figure 4(b) is examined. In the next step of the restoration, unit at bus 6 must be restarted. In order to reduce the steady-state overvoltage of no-load transmission lines, the reactor at bus 6 should be energized. In this condition, harmonic overvoltages can be produced. After calculating equivalent circuit seen from bus 5, various cases of shunt reactor energization are taken into account, and corresponding overvoltages peak and duration are computed from PSB program and trained ANN. In this case, values of equivalent resistance, equivalent inductance,

TABLE 4: Some sample testing data and output for RBF structure.

		Transformer energization						
V	L.L.		V_{PSB}	V_{RBF}	Error$_V$	T_{PSB}	T_{RBF}	Error$_T$
0.9314	155		1.3252	1.3496	1.8426	0.1264	0.1274	0.8255
0.9668	182		1.4577	1.4526	0.3479	0.3819	0.3694	3.2697
0.9812	200		1.5031	1.4759	1.8103	0.3285	0.3356	2.1762
1.0435	215		1.6602	1.6156	2.6851	0.5094	0.5183	1.7531
1.0752	237		1.8535	1.8772	1.2794	0.6673	0.6802	1.9357
1.1373	256		1.9892	2.0191	1.5008	0.5961	0.5929	0.5374
1.1781	288		2.0545	2.0150	1.9217	0.7105	0.6911	2.7264
1.2098	310		2.0361	2.0791	2.1135	0.9254	0.9386	1.4215
		Shunt reactor energization						
V	L.L.	S.R.	V_{PSB}	V_{RBF}	Error$_V$	T_{PSB}	T_{RBF}	Error$_T$
1.1442	150	70	1.5011	1.5268	1.7135	0.1936	0.1881	2.8214
1.1561	165	45	1.5453	1.5356	0.6281	0.2375	0.2268	4.5184
1.2302	178	30	1.6769	1.6141	3.7428	0.3469	0.3557	2.5369
1.2514	200	30	1.7481	1.7206	1.5746	0.3952	0.3902	1.2657
1.3326	215	23	1.9507	1.9955	2.2974	0.5104	0.5214	2.1624
1.3326	215	17	1.9914	1.9295	3.1108	0.5536	0.5612	1.3751
1.4165	230	17	2.1652	2.2251	2.7659	0.6742	0.6407	4.9752
1.4327	242	10	2.2479	2.2811	1.4782	0.7593	0.7809	2.8395
		Transmission line energization						
V	L.L.	S.R.	S.A.	V_{PSB}	V_{RBF}	Error$_V$	T_{PSB}	T_{RBF}	Error$_T$
0.9491	375	40	30	2.3508	2.3126	1.6245	0.3652	0.3748	2.6184
0.9127	240	40	30	2.2769	2.3064	1.2951	0.3107	0.3051	1.7963
0.9973	240	55	60	2.3016	2.3363	1.5084	0.3496	0.3421	2.1507
0.9754	195	12	75	2.3882	2.3757	0.5219	0.4073	0.4126	1.2985
1.0719	315	23	15	2.4195	2.3328	3.5826	0.4217	0.4297	1.9046
1.0592	282	45	5	2.3725	2.3924	0.8397	0.3846	0.3691	4.0293
1.0946	137	63	45	2.3596	2.2892	2.9841	0.3378	0.3306	2.1266
1.1123	346	10	53	2.8537	2.8927	1.3682	0.5449	0.5399	0.9157

V: voltage at power component bus before switching (p.u.), L.L.: line length (km), S.R.: shunt reactor capacity (MVAR), S.A.: switching angle (deg.), V_{PSB}: overvoltage peak calculated by PSB (p.u.), V_{RBF}: overvoltage peak calculated by RBF (p.u.), T_{PSB}: overvoltage duration calculated by PSB (s), T_{RBF}: overvoltage duration calculated by RBF (s), error$_V$: voltage error (%), and error$_T$: duration time error (%).

and equivalent capacitance are 0.00577 p.u., 0.02069, and 0.99 p.u., respectively. The summary of few results is presented in Table 3 for LM algorithm and Table 4 for RBF structure.

For testing developed ANN for transmission lines energization study, the system in Figure 4(c) is examined, that is, another portion of 39-bus New England test system. In the next step of the restoration, line 26_29 must be restarted. As mentioned before, first this system is converted to equivalent circuit of Figure 1(c). In this case, values of equivalent resistance, equivalent inductance, and equivalent capacitance are 0.00792 p.u., 0.0247, and 1.1594 p.u., respectively. For testing developed ANN, various cases of transmission line energization are taken into account, and corresponding peak and duration of overvoltages are computed from PSB program and trained ANN. The summary of few results is presented in Table 3 for LM algorithm and Table 4 for RBF structure. It can be seen from the results that the LM algorithm and RBF structure are able to estimate overvoltage

peak and duration with good accuracy. Maximum voltage and duration time error for LM algorithm are 3.6172% and 4.5937%, respectively. These errors are proper for power systems because the acceptable range for voltage variation is ±5%. Also, maximum voltage and duration time error for RBF structure are 3.7428% and 4.9752%, respectively, which are within the acceptable range.

8. Conclusion

This paper introduced an ANN-based method to evaluate switching overvoltages during power equipment energization. Both MLP-LM and RBF structures have been used to train ANN. To achieve good generalization capability for developed ANN, its training is performed using equivalent circuit parameters of the network. For transformer and shunt reactor studies, a harmonic index has been used which evaluates switching overvoltages for the worst case of switching time and remanent flux. This index reduces training time of ANN effectively. Also, there is no need to specify switching time and remanent flux. The results from both LM and RBF schemes are close to results from the conventional method and can assist prediction of the overvoltage of other case studies within the range of training set. Simulation results for a partial 39-bus New England test system show that the proposed method can evaluate switching overvoltages properly, and it can be used as an operator-training tool during power system restoration.

References

[1] M. M. Adibi, R. W. Alexander, and B. Avramovic, "Overvoltage control during restoration," *IEEE Transactions on Power Systems*, vol. 7, no. 4, pp. 1464–1470, 1992.

[2] A. Ketabi, A. M. Ranjbar, and R. Feuillet, "Analysis and control of temporary overvoltages for automated restoration planning," *IEEE Transactions on Power Delivery*, vol. 17, no. 4, pp. 1121–1127, 2002.

[3] S. A. Taher and I. Sadeghkhani, "Estimation of magnitude and time duration of temporary overvoltages using ANN in transmission lines during power system restoration," *Simulation Modelling Practice and Theory*, vol. 18, no. 6, pp. 787–805, 2010.

[4] A. Ketabi, I. Sadeghkhani, and R. Feuillet, "Using artificial neural network to analyze harmonic overvoltages during power system restoration," *European Transactions on Electrical Power*, vol. 21, no. 7, pp. 1941–1953, 2011.

[5] G. Morin, "Service restoration following a major failure on the hydro-quebec power system," *IEEE Transactions on Power Delivery*, vol. 2, no. 2, pp. 454–463, 1987.

[6] A. Ketabi, I. Sadeghkhani, and R. Feuillet, "Using artificial neural network to analyze harmonic overvoltages during power system restoration," *European Transactions on Electrical Power*, vol. 21, no. 7, pp. 1941–1953, 2011.

[7] D. Thukaram, H. P. Khincha, and S. Khandelwal, "Estimation of switching transient peak overvoltages during transmission line energization using artificial neural network," *Electric Power Systems Research*, vol. 76, no. 4, pp. 259–269, 2006.

[8] I. Sadeghkhani, A. Ketabi, and R. Feuillet, "Radial basis function neural network application to power system restoration studies," *Computational Intelligence and Neuroscience*, vol. 2012, Article ID 654895, 2012.

[9] G. Sybille, P. Brunelle, L. Hoang, L. A. Dessaint, and K. Al-Haddad, "Theory and applications of power system blockset, a MATLAB/Simulink-based simulation tool for power systems," in *Proceedings of IEEE Power Engineering Society Winter Meeting*, pp. 774–779, 2000.

[10] A. Ketabi and I. Sadeghkhani, *Electric Power Systems Simulation Using MATLAB*, Morsal Publications, 2011.

[11] M. M. Duró, "Damping modelling in transformer energization studies for system restoration: some standard models compared to field measurements," in *Proceedings of IEEE Bucharest PowerTech: Innovative Ideas Toward the Electrical Grid of the Future*, Bucharest, Romania, July 2009.

[12] G. Sybille, M. M. Gavrilovic, J. Belanger, and V. Q. Do, "Transformer saturation effects on EHV system overvoltages," *IEEE Transactions on Power Apparatus and Systems*, vol. 104, no. 3, pp. 671–680, 1985.

[13] M. T. Hagan and M. B. Menhaj, "Training feedforward networks with the Marquardt algorithm," *IEEE Transactions on Neural Networks*, vol. 5, no. 6, pp. 989–993, 1994.

[14] A. Karami and M. S. Mohammadi, "Radial basis function neural network for power system load-flow," *International Journal of Electrical Power and Energy Systems*, vol. 30, no. 1, pp. 60–66, 2008.

[15] L. Prikler, G. Bán, and G. Bánfai, "EMTP models for simulation of shunt reactor switching transients," *International Journal of Electrical Power and Energy Systems*, vol. 19, no. 4, pp. 235–240, 1997.

[16] I. Sadeghkhani, A. Ketabi, and R. Feuillet, "Radial basis function neural network application to measurement and control of shunt reactor overvoltages based on analytical rules," *Mathematical Problems in Engineering*, vol. 2012, Article ID 647305, 2012.

[17] T. Keokhoungning, S. Premrudeepreechacharn, and K. Ngamsanroaj, "Evaluation of switching overvoltage in 500 kV transmission line interconnection Nam Theun 2 power plant to Roi Et 2 substation," in *Proceedings of the Asia-Pacific Power and Energy Engineering Conference (APPEEC '09)*, March 2009.

[18] S. Wunderlich, M. M. Adibi, R. Fischl, and C. O. D. Nwankpa, "Approach to standing phase angle reduction," *IEEE Transactions on Power Systems*, vol. 9, no. 1, pp. 470–478, 1994.

2

A Novel Reinforcement Learning Architecture for Continuous State and Action Spaces

Víctor Uc-Cetina

Facultad de Matemáticas, Universidad Autónoma de Yucatán, Periférico Norte Tablaje 13615, Apartado Postal 192, C.P. 97119 Mérida, Yucatán, Mexico

Correspondence should be addressed to Víctor Uc-Cetina; uccetina@uady.mx

Academic Editor: Farouk Yalaoui

We introduce a reinforcement learning architecture designed for problems with an infinite number of states, where each state can be seen as a vector of real numbers and with a finite number of actions, where each action requires a vector of real numbers as parameters. The main objective of this architecture is to distribute in two actors the work required to learn the final policy. One actor decides what action must be performed; meanwhile, a second actor determines the right parameters for the selected action. We tested our architecture and one algorithm based on it solving the robot dribbling problem, a challenging robot control problem taken from the RoboCup competitions. Our experimental work with three different function approximators provides enough evidence to prove that the proposed architecture can be used to implement fast, robust, and reliable reinforcement learning algorithms.

1. Introduction

Applying reinforcement learning (RL) to solve real-world robotic problems is certainly not so common nowadays mainly because most RL methods require several training episodes to learn an optimal policy. This condition supposes having a robot performing a task several thousand times, as it learns through reinforcement learning. In addition to the time required for the training process, we must also consider the time we must spend calibrating sensors and actuators, and the possible damage the robots may suffer. Therefore, one common approach is to first try to solve difficult problems with continuous states and actions in simulated environments, where even the noise of real sensors and actuators can be simulated.

In this paper we propose a novel RL architecture for continuous state and actions spaces. Such an architecture was tested with a difficult control problem in the official simulator of the RoboCup [1]. The Robot World Cup or RoboCup for short is an international tournament taking place every year since 1997, each year in a different country. The RoboCup is known up to date as a standard and challenging problem for artificial intelligence and robotics. The most important goal of RoboCup is to advance the overall technological level of society, and as a more pragmatic goal to achieve the following.

By mid-twenty-first century, a team of fully autonomous humanoid robot soccer players shall win the soccer game, complying with the official rule of the FIFA, against the winner of the most recent World Cup.

One of the competitions in this tournament is the simulation league. In this category two teams of eleven virtual soccer players each play for ten minutes. The main advantage of this league is that it allows us to focus more on higher level concepts and less on the hardware problems related to working with real robots. In general, the simulator provides a challenging testbed due to its nondeterministic behavior with real-time demands and semistructured conditions. The robot dribbling problem, a challenging control problem taken from this competition, is perfect for our purpose. It is difficult to solve and it requires handling continuous states and actions. Solutions to the dribbling problem using reinforcement learning were first provided by Gollin [2].

As we have already mentioned, RoboCup has become a popular testbed for new artificial intelligence methods in general and for machine learning methods in particular. For instance, Riedmiller and Gabel [3] have been working on the application of reinforcement learning to solve problems in the RoboCup, especially in the simulation league. Other recent research works related to RL and robot soccer are presented by Cherubini et al. [4] and Leng and Lim [5]. In the former, the authors compare two learning algorithms based on policy gradient to solve the humanoid walking gait problem, which is not a trivial issue addressed in humanoid robotic soccer. In the latter, a simulation testbed is introduced and it is used to analyze the effectiveness of different RL algorithms, specially in a competitive and cooperative learning framework, involving several goal-oriented agents. Some other researchers have proposed simplified versions of the RoboCup simulator. This is the case of Stone and his research group, who proposed the keepaway domain [6].

Reinforcement learning methods for problems with continuous state and action spaces have become more and more important, as an increasing number of researchers try to solve real-world problems. In a recently published work, Montazeri et al. [7] present a novel algorithm based on growing self-organizing maps, which is shown to be effective in solving the continuous state-action problem in RL. However, among the most promising RL methods for continuous state and action spaces are the ones based on the actor-critic architecture [8]. Crites and Barto [9] introduced an actor-critic algorithm that is equivalent to Q-learning constrained by a particular exploration strategy. In this method, Q-values are encoded within the policy and value function of the actor and critic. In general, it updates the critic only when the most probable action is performed from any given state, and it rewards the actor taking into account the relative probability of the action that was executed. The authors provided a convergence proof for the case where the state and action sets are finite. Algorithms based on the standard actor-critic architecture are structured in 2 main modules. One module known as the actor which implements a policy that maps states to actions, and a second module known as the critic which attempts to estimate the value of each state in order to provide useful feedback to the actor. In such methods the actor adapts to the critic and the critic adapts to the actor. Learning in both modules is obtained through the computation of the temporal difference error.

In the next section, we provide a basic background on reinforcement learning and the standard actor-critic architecture. Then, in Section 3 we introduce our proposed A^2C architecture and one RL algorithm based on it. Section 4 gives details about our experimental work, as well as some discussions about the main results we obtained. Finally, Section 5 presents our conclusions and gives suggestions for possible extensions of our research work.

2. Background

In reinforcement learning [8, 10, 11], the central idea is that of an agent learning to accomplish a goal through its interaction with an environment. Such a problem is commonly approached using the Markov decision process (MDP) framework [12–15]. The agent interacts with the environment several times and gather, information about the rewards obtained and the states visited, after performing different actions in different states.

Formally, a Markov decision process (MDP) is a tuple (S, A, P, γ, R), where

(i) S is a set of states,

(ii) A is a set of actions,

(iii) $P(s_{t+1} \mid s_t, a_t)$ are the state transition probabilities for all states $s_t, s_{t+1} \in S$ and actions $a \in A$,

(iv) $\gamma \in [0, 1)$ is a discount factor,

(v) $R : S \times A \rightarrow \Re$ is the reward function.

The MDP dynamics is follows. An agent in state $s_t \in S$ performs an action a_t selected from the set of actions A. As a result of performing action a_t, the agent receives a reward with expected value $R(s_t, a_t)$, and the current state of the MDP transitions to some successor state s_{t+1}, according to the transition probability $P(s_{t+1} \mid s_t, a_t)$. Once in state s_{t+1} the agent chooses and executes an action a_{t+1}, receiving reward $R(s_{t+1}, a_{t+1})$ and moving to state s_{t+2}. The agent keeps choosing and executing actions, creating a path of visited states $s_t, s_{t+1}, s_{t+2}, \ldots$ and obtaining the following rewards:

$$R(s_0, a_0) + \gamma R(s_1, a_1) + \gamma^2 R(s_2, a_2) + \cdots \quad (1)$$

The reward at timestep t is discounted by a factor of γ^t. By doing so, the agent gives more importance to those rewards obtained sooner. In an MDP, we try to maximize the sum of expected rewards obtained by the agent

$$E\left[R(s_0, a_0) + \gamma R(s_1, a_1) + \gamma^2 R(s_2, a_2) + \cdots\right]. \quad (2)$$

A policy is defined as any function $\pi : S \rightarrow A$ mapping states to the actions. A value function $V(s)$ for a policy π is defined as the expected sum of discounted rewards, obtained by performing always the actions provided by π as

$$V^\pi(s) = E\left[R(s_0, \pi(s_0)) + \gamma R(s_1, \pi(s_1)) \right.$$
$$\left. + \gamma^2 R(s_2, \pi(s_2)) + \cdots \mid s_0 = s, \pi\right]. \quad (3)$$

V^π is the expected sum of discounted rewards that the agent would receive if it starts in state s and takes actions given by π. Given a fixed policy π, its value function V^π satisfies the following Bellman equation:

$$V^\pi(s) = R(s, \pi(s)) + \gamma \sum_{s' \in S} P(s' \mid s, \pi(s)) V^\pi(s'). \quad (4)$$

The optimal value function is defined as

$$V^*(s) = \max_\pi V^\pi(s). \quad (5)$$

This function gives the best possible expected sum of discounted rewards that can be obtained using any policy π. Using (4) and (5), we can obtain the Bellman equation for the optimal value function as

$$V^*(s) = \max_{a \in A}\left[R(s, a) + \gamma \sum_{s' \in S} P(s' \mid s, a) V^*(s')\right]. \quad (6)$$

The Bellman equation is fundamental in the design of RL algorithms. In general, using the data collected by the agent, RL algorithms compute estimates of the state or action value function.

Value functions could be stored using lookup tables. However, interesting problems have a large number of states and actions, sometimes, an infinite number of them. For such cases, we need to replace the lookup table with a function approximator. Using a function approximator naturally complicates the learning process, since we need to deal with more parameters. However, it is the most effective way that we have so far to deal with the curse of dimensionality. Another promising way to deal with complex state and action spaces is based on the exploitation of temporal abstractions, through the use of hierarchical reinforcement learning methods, as explained by Barto and Mahadevan [16].

One of the main developments in reinforcement learning was the introduction of the temporal difference (TD) methods, which are a class of incremental learning procedures specialized for prediction problems [17]. They are driven by the error or difference between temporally successive predictions of the states. Learning occurs whenever there is a change in the prediction over time.

The simplest TD method known as TD(0) updates the estimate of the value function, after going from state s to state s' and receiving the reward r, using the following rule:

$$V_{t+1}(s) \longleftarrow V_t(s) + \alpha \left[r + \gamma V_t(s') - V_t(s) \right]. \quad (7)$$

Based on this rule, several popular RL methods such as SARSA [8] and the actor-critic [8] methods were developed. SARSA is an on-policy temporal difference control algorithm which continually estimates the state-action value function Q^π for the behavior policy π, and at the same time changes π toward greediness with respect to Q^π. If the policy is such that each action is executed infinitely often in every state, every state is visited infinitely often, and it is greedy with respect to the current action-value function in the limit, and then by decaying α, the algorithm converges to Q^* [18].

Actor-critic methods are TD methods that have a separate memory structure to explicitly represent the policy independent of the value function. The policy structure is known as the actor, because it is used to select actions, and the estimated value function is known as the critic, because it criticizes the actions made by the actor. Learning is always on-policy: the critic must learn about and critique whatever policy is currently being followed by the actor. The critique takes the form of a TD error. This scalar is the only output of the critic and guides the learning occurring in both actor and critic as illustrated in Figure 1.

Typically, the critic is a state-value function. After each action selection, the critic evaluates the new state to determine whether things have gone better or worse than expected. That evaluation is the TD error as

$$\delta_t = r_{t+1} + \gamma V(s_{t+1}) - V(s_t), \quad (8)$$

where V is the current value function implemented by the critic. This TD error can be used to evaluate the action just

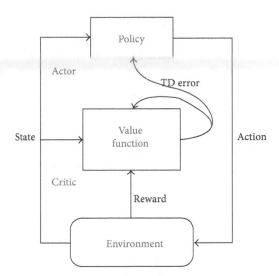

FIGURE 1: The actor-critic architecture.

selected, the action a_t taken in state s_t. If the TD error is positive, it suggests that the tendency to select a_t should be strengthened for the future, whereas if the TD error is negative it suggests that the tendency should be weakened. Under batch updating, TD converges deterministically to a single answer independent of the step-size parameter α, when α is sufficiently small [8].

Actor-critic methods have two significant apparent advantages.

(i) They require minimal computation in order to select actions. Consider a case where there are an infinite number of possible actions, for example, a continuous-valued action. Any method learning just action values must search through this infinite set in order to pick an action. If the policy is explicitly stored, then this extensive computation may not be needed for each action selection.

(ii) They can learn an explicitly stochastic policy; that is, they can learn the optimal probabilities of selecting various actions.

3. Architecture and Algorithm

The A^2C architecture, illustrated in Figure 2, is the result of our search for a robust reinforcement learning architecture specifically designed to tackle intelligent control problems with continuous state and action spaces, where the computation of the final policy must be performed very fast.

The key part of this architecture design is the idea of distributed policy learning, which allows the agent to learn and store the information of the final policy using only two modules, instead of only one. Sometimes trying to use one structure to store the policy of a complex reinforcement learning problem is simply not enough. We need to distribute the amount of information required to store the policy in more than one module. Therefore, the proposed architecture increases the number of modules used to store the final policy

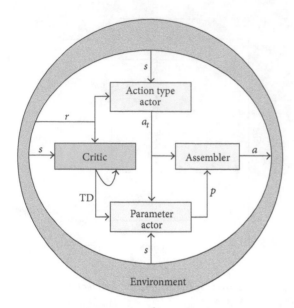

FIGURE 2: The A²C architecture.

from one to two: the *action type actor* and the *parameter actor*. During the learning phase, a third module known as the assembler is used to assemble one action type and one vector of parameters into one executable action. The functions of each of the three modules are as follows.

(i) Action type actor learns from the scalar reward r which action type a_t is the best one to be executed by the agent in the next time stage.

(ii) Parameter actor learns from the temporal difference error TD which parameter vector p is the best for the action type a_t provided by the action type actor.

(iii) Assembler takes the action type a_t and the parameter vector p and assembles the action a to be executed by the agent.

The action type actor implements SARSA learning [8]. This module focuses on learning the best action type at each moment. Given that the number of actions is finite and small, the learning process in this module is fast and robust, even when the states are expressed as continuous vectors.

The parameter actor learns from the temporal difference error computed after each execution of an action. At each time, the parameter action suggests what it believes is the best parameter for the action type chosen by the action type actor. Then, it observes the TD error generated after applying the action formed by the action type and the parameters. If the TD error is greater than zero, it means that the action type and the parameters vector selected are good, and its selection in the future must be reinforced. In this algorithm reinforcing the use of a specific parameters vector means that we should train the function approximators with the supervised training example (s, p), where s is the current state and p is the vector of parameters.

If the TD error is zero or less than zero, it means that one out of three possibilities is happening: (1) the action type selected is incorrect and the parameter vector is correct; (2)

the action type selected is correct and the parameter vector is incorrect; (3) both the action type and the parameter vector are incorrect. Only in the first case we should reinforce the selection of such parameters vector; however, it is impossible to determine in which of these three cases we have fallen. Therefore, we simply jump to the next state without experimenting any learning within the parameter actor.

Note that the parameter actor is responsible only for the selection of the parameters; however, it is evaluated taking into account both the action type and the parameters. Under this condition, it is only possible to guarantee the correct learning of the parameters if we can guarantee that the action type actor will eventually learn the correct action types; otherwise, the parameter actor will fail to learn the right parameters.

As in the standard actor-critic architecture, we also employed the typical critic module, which learns from the temporal difference error TD the value function $V(s)$ used to evaluate the quality of each state s. This evaluation is used by the critic itself to improve its estimation of $V(s)$ and it is also used by the parameter actor to improve its estimation of the best parameters for the action types.

To implement our architecture, a number of function approximators are required. The number of function approximators is determined by the number of action types and the number of parameters required by each action type. Figure 3 illustrates the function approximators used in our experimental work. We employed 4 function approximators for the action type actor, 7 for the parameter actor, and 1 for the critic.

The algorithm we propose to implement our architecture is the SARSA A²C.

(1) Initialize the *action type actor*, the *parameter actor*, and the *critic*. This step refers to randomly choosing the initial values of all the parameters used by all the function approximators.

(2) From current state s, select the best action type a_t and parameter vector $\vec{p}_{a_t}$. To select the best action type, we simply evaluate all the function approximators used by the action type actor, with the current state s, and we pick the action type whose function approximator gives the greatest evaluation. Once we have selected the best action type for the current state s, we evaluate the function approximators assigned to that action type, to get $\vec{p}_{a_t}$.

(3) Assembly action a with action type a_t and parameter vector $\vec{p}_{a_t}$. This step is a plain call to the code function used internally by our agent to get ready to execute the chosen action.

(4) For each training episode, use learning rate α and discount factor γ to do the following.

   (a) Execute action a and observe next state s' and the scalar reward r.

   (b) Compute the TD error as $\varepsilon = [r + \gamma \widehat{V}(s')] - \widehat{V}(s)$, where $\widehat{V}(s)$ is the state value function stored by the critic.

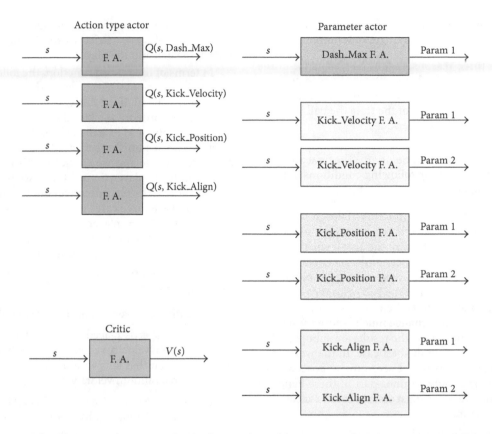

FIGURE 3: 12 function approximators used to implement the action type actor, the parameter actor, and the critic.

(c) Update the critic using the TD error with $\widehat{V}(s) \leftarrow \widehat{V}(s) + \alpha\varepsilon$.

(d) If ($\varepsilon > 0$) then reinforce the use of $\vec{p}_{a_t}$ by retraining the function approximator of action type a_t with the example $(s, \vec{p}_{a_t})$.

(e) From the next state s', compute the next action type a'_t and parameter vector $\vec{p}_{a'_t}$.

(f) Assemble the next action a' with action type a'_t and parameter vector $\vec{p}_{a'_t}$.

(g) Update the action type actor with $Q(s, a_t) \leftarrow Q(s, a_t) + \alpha[r + \gamma Q(s', a'_t) - Q(s, a_t)]$, where $Q(s, a_t)$ is the state-action value function implemented as a function approximator.

(h) Update the current state with $s \leftarrow s'$ and the current action with $a \leftarrow a'$.

4. Experimental Results

In the RoboCup simulation league, one of the most difficult skills that the robots can perform is dribbling. Dribbling can be defined as the skill that allows a player to run on the field while keeping the ball always within its kickable margin, as illustrated in Figure 4. In order to accomplish this skill, the player must alternate *dash* and *kick* actions.

There are three factors that make this skill a difficult one to accomplish.

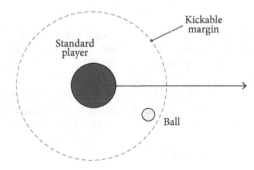

FIGURE 4: The dribbling problem.

(1) The simulator adds noise to the movement of objects and to the parameters of commands.

(2) Since the ball must remain close to the robot without collisioning with it, and at the same time it must be kept in the kick range, the margin for error is small.

(3) The most challenging factor is the use of heterogeneous players during competitions. Using heterogeneous players means that for each game the simulator generates seven different player types at startup, and the eleven players of each team are selected from this set of seven types. Given that each player type has different "physical" capacities, an optimal policy learned with one type of player is simply suboptimal

when followed by another player of different type. In theory, the number of player types is infinite.

Due to these three reasons, a good performance in the dribbling skill is very difficult to obtain. Up to date, even the best teams perform only a reduced number of dribbling sequences during a game. Most of the time the ball is simply passed from one player to another.

4.1. Desired Characteristics of the Solution. The final policy we are looking for must fulfill the following conditions if it is to be used during competitions.

(i) The final policy, seen as a function of the current state, must be easy to evaluate. During competitions, many decisions must be taken by the team, such as computing positions, velocities, and accelerations, and deciding what kicks and dashes must be performed to keep the possession of the ball or to recover it. All these computations must be done as fast as possible so the state does not change much before the actions are executed; otherwise, the results are suboptimal or completely useless in the best case. In the worst case, the adversary team might score many goals against us. Dribbling is only a minor part of these bunch of computations and we must assure that its execution is as fast as possible.

(ii) It must have a high performance with heterogeneous players. Solving the dribbling problem with standard players could be achieved easily. However, getting a competitive performance with the heterogeneous players is a different story.

(iii) The generation of such policy must be done with few manual adjustments. The RoboCup Simulator is being continuously improved, if the learning algorithm depends strongly on some parameters of the players or the server, and those parameters are removed in the future due to major changes in the simulator software, then major changes will be required in the learning algorithm to keep it useful, especially if we require several manual adjustments.

(iv) Performance at least around 20 meters with high reliability is required. This is a self-imposed condition by our team based on the experience accumulated during several years of experimentation and competitions. We have seen that after 20 meters the policies that push the players to run faster can be successful with fast players, but terrible with the slow ones who tend to lose the ball very often.

4.2. Experiments. The state is seen by the player as a parameter vector which consists of the following 10 variables: (1) player decay, (2) dash power rate, (3) kickable margin, (4) kick rand, (5) ball position x—player position x, (6) ball position y—player position y, (7) ball velocity x—player velocity x, (8) ball velocity y—player velocity y, (9) player velocity x, and (10) player velocity y. The first 4 variables are some of the parameters that define a type of player, and for this problem,

they were the most useful during our experimentation. The other 6 variables are needed to specify the current physical state of the ball and the player.

In terms of the reward function, the following is applied. If the ball is in the way of the player, the player receives only a punishment of -10. If the first case is not true, we check if the ball is in the border of the kickable margin which means that the player is about to lose the ball, and in that case the player receives only a punishment of -10. If the first and second cases are not true and we check the third case. If the ball is very close, to the player, there is the possibility of collisioning, and in that case the player receives only a punishment of -10. If none of these three cases is true, then the player receives a positive reward r = player position x + ball position x + [$50 *$ (player velocity x + ball velocity x)], where 50 is a weight parameter chosen experimentally.

The results presented next were obtained under the following experimental settings.

(i) Both the player and the ball are initially in movement.

(ii) The player is placed at the center of the field with a random velocity vector v_p and the ball is placed in any position that falls within the kick range of the player with a random velocity vector v_b.

(iii) The player has 4 actions: Dash Max, Kick Velocity, Kick Position, and Kick Align.

(iv) At each training episode we let the player try 35 actions at most.

(v) If the ball goes out of the kickable margin of the player, the current training episode is finished.

(vi) During training and testing, a new set of players is generated every 7 episodes. In this way we basically train with a different player each episode. By doing so, we pretend to improve the generalization of our learned model.

We used 3 different function approximators to implement the actors and the critic.

(i) Multilayer perceptrons.

(ii) Multilayer perceptrons with one layer of radial basis functions [19].

(iii) Arrays of radial basis functions.

In Figure 5, we see the performance of the SARSA A^2C algorithm using only multilayer perceptrons with 3 different numbers of hidden units: 2, 10, and 20. After 50,000 training episodes, all three configurations of the networks managed to learn a policy that allows a performance of 15 meters at least, being the configuration with 2 hidden units slightly better with a performance of 16 meters. From the graph, we can also see that as we increase the number of hidden units, the learning curve becomes less smooth. Based on these results, the configuration of the multilayer perceptron with 2 hidden units was the most reliable.

We modified the multilayer perceptrons networks adding a layer of radial basis functions between the input and the

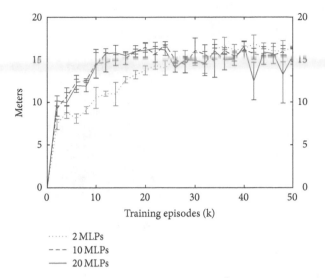

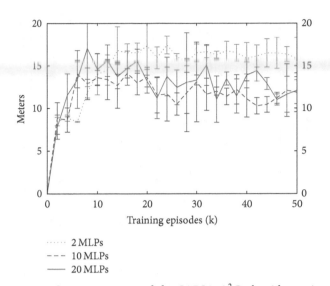

FIGURE 5: Learning curves of the SARSA A²C algorithm using different numbers of multilayer perceptrons.

FIGURE 6: Learning curves of the SARSA A²C algorithm using different numbers of multilayer perceptrons and 10 radial basis functions for each multilayer perceptron.

hidden layer that works as a filter layer. Each input unit was connected to 10 gaussian radial basis functions. The idea was to try to localize the learning. The resulting learning curves are shown in Figure 6. We can see that in the case of using 10 and 20 hidden units, the performance obtained is not more than 12 meters, being worse than that obtained using only the multilayer perceptrons without radial basis functions. It is also clear that the learning curves become less smooth. However, we can notice that the configuration of 2 hidden units keeps its performance of 16 meters and it is able to reach this performance in less training time than the simple multilayer perceptron network. The network with radial basis function using 2 hidden units gets its best performance in 15,000 training episodes; meanwhile, the network without radial basis functions needs at least 40,000 episodes.

For the third implementation of the SARSA A²C algorithm, we used n arrays of gaussian radial basis functions, one array per input. In Figure 7, we can see the learning curves obtained with 10, 30, and 50 radial basis functions. The final performance of 25 meters is much better than that obtained with the previous function approximators. This performance is obtained in less than 10,000 training episodes, which is very fast compared to the results shown in the two previous graphs. Also, we can notice that as we increase the number of radial basis functions, the learning curves need a little more time to go up. All three learning curves are smooth and with small variance, which means that we are finding very reliable policies.

Figure 8 shows the best learning curves found together with each function approximator. It is clear that the best performance in terms of training time and reliability is obtained using only radial basis functions.

4.3. Final Policy Performance. Table 1 shows a comparison of the two best reinforcement learning methods found so far to solve the dribbling problem.

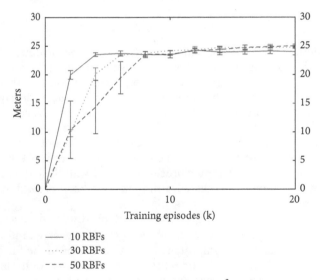

FIGURE 7: Learning curves of the SARSA A²C algorithm using different numbers of radial basis functions.

TABLE 1: Comparison of the best policies for the dribbling problem.

	SARSA A²C	$Q(\lambda)$-learning
Algorithm type	Actor-Critic	$Q(\lambda)$-learning
Function approx.	RBFs	CMACs
States	Continuous	Continuous
Actions	Continuous	Discrete
Total learning time	10 minutes	24 hours 30 minutes
Average distance	25.45 meters	29.21 meters
Maximum distance	36.23 meters	39.0 meters

From Table 1, we can see the following. Both methods employed linear function approximators. The states are handled continuously by both methods. The SARSA A²C

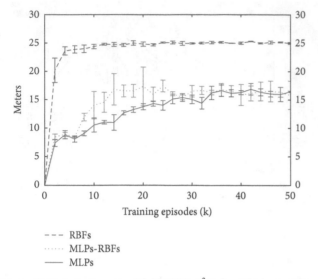

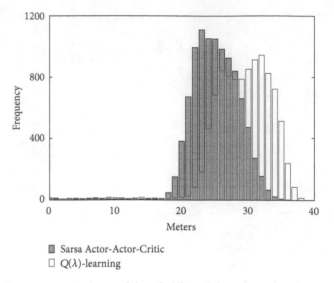

FIGURE 8: Learning curves of the SARSA A^2C algorithm using three different function approximators: radial basis functions, multilayer perceptrons, and multilayer perceptrons with a layer of radial basis functions.

FIGURE 9: Comparison of the reliability of the policies found with the SARSA Actor-Actor-Critic algorithm and the $Q(\lambda)$-learning algorithm.

method handles the actions continuously; meanwhile, in $Q(\lambda)$-learning, a finite set of actions with continuous parameters is employed. However, it is important to consider that in $Q(\lambda)$-learning, a finite set of actions is generated randomly at the beginning of the training process. Then, an algorithm is used during 24 hours to discover and delete the less useful actions. After this reduction process, the final set of actions contains about 30 action with continuous parameters. At this point, the policy learning process is started with the reduced set of actions. The policy learning process takes around 30 minutes.

In terms of average distance and maximum distance, $Q(\lambda)$-learning is superior to SARSA A^2C. However, we must realize that a more important factor to consider in the final policy performance is the reliability. By reliability we mean how much we can trust our policy during a game. In other words, we are interested in knowing how often the player will manage to run at least a given number of meters before it loses the ball due to a wrong action selection. Therefore, in order to study the reliability of the policies found with the SARSA A^2C algorithm in comparison with $Q(\lambda)$-learning, we performed the following experiment. Using one of the best policies obtained, we let 10,000 different players run with the ball from the center of the soccer field. We wrote down how many meters each player managed to run before losing the ball. Then, using this statistics we plotted the graphs in Figures 9 and 10.

From Figure 9, we can see that with $Q(\lambda)$-learning policy most of the players managed to run at least 20 meters; meanwhile, with the SARSA A^2C policy they run at least 18 meters. Now, if we make a closeup of this graph and focus on the first 20 meters as an accumulated frequency histogram, the image we see is the one in Figure 10. In this figure, something interesting is evident. With $Q(\lambda)$-learning policy,

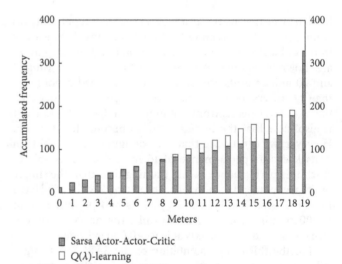

FIGURE 10: Accumulated frequency: Comparison of the reliability of the policies found with the SARSA Actor-Actor-Critic algorithm and the $Q(\lambda)$-learning algorithm.

the players lose the ball more often than with the SARSA A^2C policy. Notice that a perfect policy will not allow the player to lose the ball before running at least 20 meters. And if we were working with a perfect policy, all the frequency columns from meter 0 to 19 would be of size 0, meaning that the players always run at least 20 meters. We can see that from meter 0 to 8, $Q(\lambda)$-learning policy is more reliable, and between meters 9 and 18, the SARSA A^2C policy is more reliable.

In competitions, the time required to compute each of the decisions taken by the players must be reduced as much as possible. Once the final policy has been learned, during competition we need to compute the following.

(1) We need to compute he type of action to be executed and the parameters of such action. To select

the action, we need to compute the Q values corresponding to each type of action. The cost of this computation is $4(c_1 + c_2 + \cdots + c_n)$, where n is the number of radial basis functions and c_i is the cost of computing the output of the gaussian function r_i and multiplying this output by the corresponding weight w_i. We multiply the cost by 4, since we have to perform these operations for each type of action.

(2) Then, we must find the maximum of such 4 Q values. We need to perform 3 comparisons to find the greatest Q value. Therefore, the cost is $3c$, where c is the cost of each logic comparison.

(3) Finally, we need to compute the parameters of the chosen type of action. In the worst case we would need to compute the values of two parameters. The cost of this computation is $2(c_1 + c_2 + \cdots + c_n)$, where n is the number of radial basis functions and c_i is the cost of computing the output of the gaussian function r_i and multiplying this output by the corresponding weight w_i. We multiply the cost by 2, since we have to perform these operations for each parameter of the selected action.

5. Conclusions and Future Work

We have introduced the Actor-Actor-Critic architecture and explained its benefits in problems with continuous state and action spaces. Based on such architecture, we presented the SARSA Actor-Actor-Critic algorithm or SARSA A^2C for short. Such an algorithm generate reliable policies for the dribbling problem in short training times. We have also presented and described the experimental results obtained when applying the SARSA A^2C algorithm to the most difficult test scenario considered in this research. Finally, we have made a comparison of our method and the current best method to solve the dribbling problem.

We have shown through experimentation that an algorithm with two actors and one critic, where the action type actor is trained using Q values through SARSA learning and the parameter actor and the critic are trained using the standard temporal difference error, is capable of learning policies with good performance and the learning process is fast and completely reliable.

We have also seen that the array of radial basis functions works better than the multilayer perceptron and the multilayer perceptron with one layer of radial basis functions.

The results obtained for a specially challenging task in the RoboCup framework suggest that the implementation of our A^2C architecture may also lead to outstanding performance in other RL problems with continuous state and action spaces.

Among our future work involving the A^2C architecture, we consider the solution of other problems with continuous state and action spaces, the development of other algorithms based on it, and the study of ways of implementing hierarchical A^2C methods.

Acknowledgments

The author would like to express his gratitude to Professor Hans-Dieter Burkhard for his advice and support, and Ralf Berger for his experimental work with the $Q(\lambda)$ algorithm.

References

[1] RoboCup, "The goals of robocup.robocup federation on," 2001, http://www.robocup.org/about-robocup/objective/.

[2] M. Gollin, *Implementation einer bibliothek für reinforcement learning und anwendung in der robocup simulationsliga [M.S. thesis]*, Humboldt University of Berlin, Berlin, Germany, 2005.

[3] M. Riedmiller and T. Gabel, "On experiences in a complex and competitive gaming domain: reinforcement learning meets RoboCup," in *Proceedings of the 3rd IEEE Symposium on Computational Intelligence and Games (CIG '07)*, pp. 17–23, April 2007.

[4] A. Cherubini, F. Giannone, L. Iocchi, M. Lombardo, and G. Oriolo, "Policy gradient learning for a humanoid soccer robot," *Robotics and Autonomous Systems*, vol. 57, no. 8, pp. 808–818, 2009.

[5] J. Leng and C. P. Lim, "Reinforcement learning of competitive and cooperative skills in soccer agents," *Applied Soft Computing Journal*, vol. 11, no. 1, pp. 1353–1362, 2011.

[6] P. Stone, G. Kuhlmann, M. E. Taylor, and Y. Liu, "Keepaway soccer: from machine learning testbed to benchmark," in *RoboCup-2005: Robot Soccer World Cup IX*, I. Noda, A. Jacoff, A. Bredenfeld, and Y. Takahashi, Eds., pp. 93–105, Springer, Berlin, Germany, 2006.

[7] H. Montazeri, S. Moradi, and R. Safabakhsh, "Continuous state/action reinforcement learning: a growing self-organizing map approach," *Neurocomputing*, vol. 74, no. 7, pp. 1069–1082, 2011.

[8] R. S. Sutton and A. G. Barto, *Reinforcement Learning: An Introduction*, The MIT Press, Cambridge, Mass, USA, 1998.

[9] R. H. Crites and A. G. Barto, "An actor/critic algorithm that is equivalent to q-learning," in *Advances in Neural Information Processing Systems*, 1995.

[10] L. P. Kaelbling, M. L. Littman, and A. W. Moore, "Reinforcement learning: a survey," *Journal of Artificial Intelligence Research*, vol. 4, pp. 237–285, 1996.

[11] V. Heidrich-Meisner, M. Lauer, C. Igel, and M. Riedmiller, "Reinforcement learning in a nutshell," in *Proceedings of the 15th European Symposium on Artificial Neural Networks*, 2007.

[12] R. A. Howard, *Dynamic Programming and Markov Processes*, The MIT Press, Cambridge, Mass, USA, 1960.

[13] S. Ross, *Introduction to Stochastic Dynamic Programming*, Academic Press, New York, NY, USA, 1983.

[14] D. P. Bertsekas and J. N. Tsitsiklis, *Neuro-Dynamic Programming*, Athena Scientific, 1996.

[15] M. Puterman, *Markov Decision Processes*, John Wiley & Sons, New York, NY, USA, 1994.

[16] A. G. Barto and S. Mahadevan, "Recent advances in hierarchical reinforcement learning," *Discrete Event Dynamic Systems*, vol. 13, no. 1-2, pp. 41–77, 2003.

[17] R. S. Sutton, "Learning to predict by the methods of temporal differences," *Machine Learning*, vol. 3, no. 1, pp. 9–44, 1988.

[18] S. Singh, T. Jaakkola, M. L. Littman, and C. Szepesvári, "Convergence results for single-step on-policy reinforcement-learning algorithms," *Machine Learning*, vol. 38, no. 3, pp. 287–308, 2000.

[19] V. Uc-Cetina, "Multilayer perceptrons with radial basis functions as value functions in reinforcement learning," in *Proceedings of the European Symposium on Artificial Neural Networks*, 2008.

3

A Novel Approach to Improve the Performance of Evolutionary Methods for Nonlinear Constrained Optimization

Alireza Rowhanimanesh and Sohrab Efati

Center of Excellence on Soft Computing and Intelligent Information Processing (SCIIP), Ferdowsi University of Mashhad, Mashhad, Iran

Correspondence should be addressed to Alireza Rowhanimanesh, rowhanimanesh@ieee.org

Academic Editor: Joanna Józefowska

Evolutionary methods are well-known techniques for solving nonlinear constrained optimization problems. Due to the exploration power of evolution-based optimizers, population usually converges to a region around global optimum after several generations. Although this convergence can be efficiently used to reduce search space, in most of the existing optimization methods, search is still continued over original space and considerable time is wasted for searching ineffective regions. This paper proposes a simple and general approach based on search space reduction to improve the exploitation power of the existing evolutionary methods without adding any significant computational complexity. After a number of generations when enough exploration is performed, search space is reduced to a small subspace around the best individual, and then search is continued over this reduced space. If the space reduction parameters (red_gen and red_factor) are adjusted properly, reduced space will include global optimum. The proposed scheme can help the existing evolutionary methods to find better near-optimal solutions in a shorter time. To demonstrate the power of the new approach, it is applied to a set of benchmark constrained optimization problems and the results are compared with a previous work in the literature.

1. Introduction

A significant part of today's engineering problems are constrained optimization problems (COP). Although there exist efficient methods like Simplex for solving linear COP, solving nonlinear COP (NCOP) is still open for novel investigations. Different methods have been proposed for solving NCOP. Among them, natural optimization and especially population-based schemes are the most general and promising ones. These methods can be applied to all types of COP including convex and nonconvex, analytical and non-analytical, real-, integer- and mixed-valued problems. One of the most applied techniques for solving NCOP are evolutionary methods.

Various techniques have been introduced for handling nonlinear constrains by evolutionary optimization (EO) methods. These approaches can be grouped in four major categories [1, 2]: (1) methods based on penalty functions that are also known as indirect constraint handling, (2) methods based on a search of feasible solutions including repairing unfeasible individuals [3, 4], superiority of feasible points [5], and behavioral memory [6], (3) methods based on preserving feasibility of solutions like preserving feasibility by designing special crossover and mutation operators [7], the GENOCOP system [8], searching the boundary of feasible region [9], and homomorphous mapping [10], and (4) Hybrid methods [11–13]. Also, decoding such as transforming the search space can be considered as the fifth category which is less common. None of these approaches are complete and each of them has both advantages and weak-points. For example, although the third method (preserving feasibility) might perform very well, it is usually problem dependent and designing such a method for a given problem may be difficult, computationally expensive, and sometimes impossible. Among these approaches, the most general one is the first technique.

Penalty-based constraint handling incorporates constraints into a penalty function that is added to the main fitness function. By this work, the main constrained problem is converted to an unconstrained problem. The main advantage of this method is its generality and simplicity (problem-independent penalty functions). Thus, this method is known as the most common approach for handling nonlinear constraints in EO.

Adding a penalty function to a fitness (objective) function creates a new unconstrained problem that might have further complexity. The introduction of penalties may transform a smooth objective function into a rugged one and the search may then become more easily trapped in local optimum [14]. Therefore, several penalty-based constraint handling methods have been proposed to improve the performance of penalty-based constrained evolutionary optimization. In [2], a survey has been performed on several types of these methods including death penalty [2, 15], static penalty [16, 17], dynamic penalty [18, 19], annealing penalty [20, 21], adaptive penalty [22–24], segregated GA [25], and coevolutionary penalty [26]. In addition to these types, other hybrid (e.g., niched-penalty approach [27]) and heuristic techniques (e.g., stochastic ranking [28]) could be found in the literature.

Due to its generality and applicability, this paper focuses on penalty-based constraint handling without loss of generality. However, the proposed approach is independent from the type of constraint handling and optimization technique. This paper demonstrates how the power of exploitation of constrained EO (CEO) can be increased by reducing the search space after enough exploration is performed. The proposed approach is simple and general and does not add any computational complexity to the original algorithm. Also, it could be applied to other optimization techniques like constrained PSO and hybrid methods.

This paper is organized as follows. In Section 2, the proposed approach is described and the details are explained and illustrated over a specific constrained optimization problem introduced in [29]. In Section 3, the performance of the proposed scheme is tested on eleven well-known test problems and the results are compared with [10].

2. Proposed Approach

A general constrained nonlinear programming problem is formulated as follows:

$$\begin{aligned}
\text{minimize} \quad & f(x) \\
\text{subject to} \quad & g_i(x) \leq 0, \quad i = 1, 2, \ldots, p \\
& h_i(x) = 0, \quad i = p + 1, \ldots, m \\
& l_j \leq x_j \leq u_j, \quad j = 1, \ldots, n,
\end{aligned} \tag{1}$$

where $x = (x_1, x_2, \ldots x_n)$ is the vector of decision variables, $f(x)$ is a scalar lower-bounded objective function, $\{g_i(x), i = 1, \ldots, p\}$ is a set of p inequality constraints, $\{h_i(x), i = p + 1, \ldots, m\}$ is a set of m- p equality constraints, and $[l_j, u_j]$ is the domain of the ith variable. $f(x)$, $g_i(x)$, and $h_i(x)$ are allowed to be either linear or nonlinear, convex or nonconvex, differentiable or nondifferentiable, continuous or discrete, and analytical or nonanalytical. Also, x can be

either discrete or continuous or mixed-valued. Without loss of generality, the problem is considered minimization since $\max f(x)$ is equivalent to $-\min(-f(x))$. As mentioned in [10], it is a common practice to replace equation $h_i(x) = 0$ by the inequality $|h_i(x)| \leq \delta$ for some small $\delta > 0$. This replacement is considered in the rest of this paper, and, consequently, the above problem consists of m inequality constraints. For simplicity, all of the constraints are shown by $g_i(x) \leq 0$ where $i = 1, 2, \ldots, m$. Note that bound constraints $l_j \leq x_j \leq u_j$ can be directly handled in most of the population-based optimization methods such as EO. Thus, only $g_i(x) \leq 0$ $(i = 1, 2, \ldots, m)$ are considered as the constraints. Without loss of generality, to simplify the understanding of the proposed idea, its details are explained over a specific constrained optimization problem as an illustrative example chosen from the literature.

2.1. An Illustrative Example. Consider the following constrained nonlinear programming problem [29]:

$$\begin{aligned}
\text{Minimize} \quad & f(x) = (x_1^2 + x_2 - 11)^2 + (x_1 + x_2^2 - 7)^2 \\
\text{s.t.} \quad & -4.84 + (x_1 - 0.05)^2 + (x_2 - 2.5)^2 \leq 0 \longrightarrow g_1(x) \leq 0 \\
& -x_1^2 - (x_2 - 2.5)^2 + 4.84 \leq 0 \longrightarrow g_2(x) \leq 0 \\
& 0 \leq x_i \leq 6, \quad i = 1, 2.
\end{aligned} \tag{2}$$

The feasible space and the global minimum of this problem are displayed in Figure 1. In this paper, a simple constrained GA (CGA) has been used for solving constrained optimization problems. This CGA is composed of a simple real-valued GA introduced in [30] and a static penalty function that is added to the original objective (fitness) function as follows:

$$f_p(x) = f(x) + p \sum_{i=1}^{m} \max\{0, g_i(x)\}. \tag{3}$$

In this equation, $\max\{0, g_i(x)\}$ gives the violation value of the constraint $g_i(x) \leq 0$, and p is the penalty coefficient that must be determined by the designer. In some cases, assigning a proper value to p is difficult and this is known as the main disadvantage of static penalty functions. As an alternative, adaptive [22–24] and dynamic [18, 19] penalty functions have been proposed. By defining $f_p(x)$, the constrained nonlinear programming problem of (2) is converted to the following unconstrained nonlinear programming problem:

$$\begin{aligned}
\text{Minimize} \quad & f_p(x) = f(x) + p \sum_{i=1}^{2} \max\{0, g_i(x)\} \\
\text{s.t.} \quad & 0 \leq x_i \leq 6, \quad i = 1, 2.
\end{aligned} \tag{4}$$

This problem (4) is solved by the above-mentioned CGA. The CGA routine utilizes a simple real-valued GA introduced in [30] with population size of 50, selection rate of 0.5, elitism with elite rate of 0.05, single-point crossover, and uniform mutation with mutation rate of 0.2. The value of penalty coefficient is 10 and the maximum number of

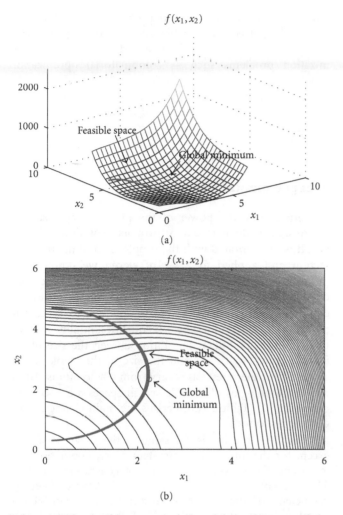

(a)

(b)

FIGURE 1: The feasible space and the global minimum of the problem of (2).

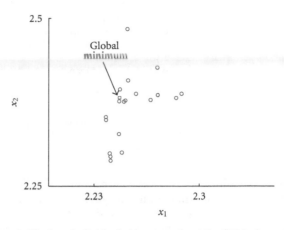

FIGURE 2: The best individuals (at generation 10) of 20 independent runs and the global minimum.

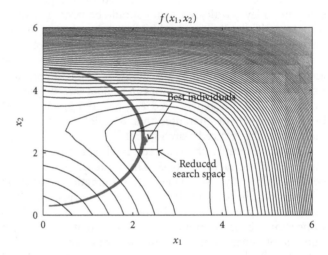

FIGURE 3: The original search space can be reduced to a small subspace around the global optimum after a number of generations when enough exploration has been performed.

generations is allowed to be 10. Figure 2 indicates the best individuals (solutions) of 20 independent runs. Regarding this figure, all of these individuals have been converged to the global minimum through 10 generations. Figure 3 illustrates these individuals on the original search space. A new idea is emerged from considering these figures, that is, the best individual will converge to the global optimum after a number of generations. In other words, the global optimum will locate in a small neighborhood of the best individual after a number of generations. Consequently, after a number of generations when enough exploration has been performed, the search space can be reduced to a small subspace around the best individual, and then the search can be continued over this reduced space. The experimental study of the next section demonstrates that if the space reduction parameters (red_gen and red_factor) are adjusted properly, the reduced space will include the global optimum. Here, the reduced search space is defined as follows:

$$\text{reduced}\_l_i = \max\{\text{best\_ind}(\text{red\_gen})$$

$$-\text{red\_factor} \cdot (u_i - l_i), l_i\}, \quad i = 1, \dots, n,$$

$$\text{reduced}\_u_i = \min\{\text{best\_ind}(\text{red\_gen})$$

$$+\text{red\_factor} \cdot (u_i - l_i), u_i\}, \quad i = 1, \dots, n. \tag{5}$$

In these equations, $[l_i, u_i]$ and $[\text{reduced}\_l_i, \text{reduced}\_u_i]$ are the original and reduced domains of variables, respectively. best_ind(red_gen) is the best individual of the generation red_gen. red_gen specifies the generation in which the reduction of search space is performed. Here, this search space reduction is done only one time at generation red_gen. The size of the reduced search space is determined by red_factor that varies between 0 and 1. Also, the value of mutation rate can be changed after this reduction.

Indeed, the value of red_gen determines the total number of generations in CGA (constrained GA) that are devoted to exploration in order to find a region around of the global minimum. The value of red_gen determines a tradeoff between exploration and exploitation and highly depends on the general characteristics of the given optimization problem.

TABLE 1: A comparison between the proposed approach, [22] and [29] for the same number of function evaluations in solving the problem of (2). The best results are indicated in boldface.

	Best	Mean	Worst
Proposed approach	**13.590846**	**13.61073**	**13.84861**
[29]	13.59658	—	244.11616
[22]	13.59085	30.74880	152.54840

If the global minimum is inside a narrow (sharp) valley, CGA usually needs more time to find the global valley, and thus a large value of red_gen should be considered. Also, since the valley is narrow, red_factor could be set to a small value. In contrast, if the global minimum is inside a wide (flat) valley, CGA usually needs less time to find the global valley, and therefore smaller values can be used for red_gen. Also, since the valley is wide, red_factor should be large. The value of red_gen is usually increased by increasing the number of decision variables. In most of the optimization problems, since the general characteristics of the given problem can be approximately identified by the designer, some appropriate values for red_gen and red_factor can be heuristically guessed by the designer. In general, red_gen and red_factor should be large enough to guarantee that the global optimum is included in the reduced search space.

For this example, the reduced search space is shown in Figure 3 for red_factor = 0.05. The value of red_gen must be determined by user. However, systematic or adaptive schemes can be developed in further investigations. The value of red_gen influences the power of exploration. This value should be large enough to guarantee that after red_gen number of generations, the best individual and the global optimum are close together. Moreover, the size of the reduced search space (the value of red_factor) must be large enough to include the global optimum.

This example has been solved by the proposed approach using the above-mentioned CGA. Here, the value of penalty coefficient is 20, the maximum number of generations is 50, red_factor = 0.05, and and red_gen = 5. The mutation rate is 0.2 for the first five generations and after Generation 5 (red_gen), it is changed into 0.05. The results of 50 independent runs are displayed in Table 1. The same experiment has been also done by [22, 29] with the same number of function evaluations. Table 1 compares the results of the proposed approach with these two references where the best results are indicated in boldface.Although the proposed approach has been incorporated with a simple method of CEO which is trivial in contrast to the other existing techniques of CEO in the literature, it could get better results in this example for the same number of function evaluations in comparison with [22, 29].

According to the above-mentioned explanations, the proposed method and formulation of this paper can be directly applied to different continuous (real-valued) optimization problems and incorporated with different optimization methods. Moreover, since the main contribution of this paper is the notion of search space reduction, that is general and problem-independent, the proposed approach is flexible enough to be generalized (with minor changes) to discrete and mixed-valued optimization problems such as combinatorial optimization problems where the domain is not continuous. In the next section, the performance of the new scheme is examined by a set of eleven well-known continuous test problems.

3. Experimental Study

To demonstrate the power of the proposed approach to improve the performance of constrained evolutionary methods, it is incorporated with the simple CEO of the previous section and applied to a set of eleven well-known test problems introduced in [1, 10]. These test problems consist of objective functions of different types (linear, quadratic, cubic, polynomial, and nonlinear) and various types and numbers of constraints (linear inequalities, nonlinear equations, and inequalities). The ratio between the size of the feasible search space $|F|$ and the size of the whole search space $|S|$ for these test cases vary from 0% to almost 100% and the topologies of feasible search spaces are also quite different [10]. Table 2 summarizes the main characteristics of these test cases.

The CGA routine is the same as the previous section except for the following parameters. Here, population size is 70 and the maximum number of generations is 5000. The values of mutation rate, red_gen, red_factor, and penalty coefficient are different for each test case as shown in Table 3. Equality constraints ($h(x) = 0$) were converted into inequality constraints by $\delta = 0.0001$ ($|h(x)| \leq \delta$). For each test case, 20 independent runs were performed. The same experiment has been done on this test set in [10]. It should be mentioned that the authors in [10] utilizes the third method of constraint handling (preserving feasibility by homomorphous mapping). Table 4 indicates the results of the proposed approach and its comparison with [10] for the same number of function evaluations. The best results are indicated in Boldface. For problem G5, we could not find any suitable static penalty coefficient for handling the constraints. This is due to the inadequacy of static penalty functions. However, this problem could not be solved by [10] too. It should be mentioned that this test case (G5) has been solved in some other references [22, 28].

According to comparative results of Table 4, although the proposed approach had been incorporated with a simple method of CEO which is trivial in contrast to the other existing techniques of CEO in the literature, its performance (finding a better near-optimal solution) is better than [10] in 70% of cases in this benchmark experimental study. Since the number of function evaluations is the same in this study and in the study of [10], it can be concluded that the proposed approach can also improve the efficiency (convergence speed) of the CEO in 70% of cases in contrast to [10].

TABLE 2: Summary of eleven test problems [10].

	Type of problem	n	Type of f	Linear inequality	Nonlinear equality	Nonlinear inequality	$|F|/|S|$	Optimum value
G1	Minimum	13	Quadratic	9	0	0	0.0111%	−15.0
G2	Maximum	20	Nonlinear	0	0	2	99.8474%	0.803553
G3	Maximum	10	Polynomial	0	1	0	0.0000%	1.0
G4	Minimum	5	Quadratic	0	0	6	52.1230%	−30655.5
G5	Minimum	4	Cubic	2	3	0	0.0000%	5126.4981
G6	Minimum	2	Cubic	0	0	2	0.0066%	−6961.8
G7	Minimum	10	Quadratic	3	0	5	0.0003%	24.306
G8	Maximum	2	Nonlinear	0	0	2	0.8560%	0.0958250
G9	Minimum	7	Polynomial	0	0	4	0.5121%	680.63
G10	Minimum	8	Linear	3	0	3	0.0010%	7049.33
G11	Minimum	2	Quadratic	0	1	0	0.0000%	0.75

TABLE 3: The values of mutation rate, red_gen, red_factor, and penalty coefficient for each test problem.

	Mutation rate (before and after red_gen)	red_gen	red_factor	Penalty coefficient
G1	0.2–0.05	1000	0.05	10
G2	0.2–0.05	1500	0.1	10
G3	0.2–0.1	2000	0.1	1000
G4	0.2–0.05	1000	0.05	1500
G5	—	—	—	—
G6	0.2–0.1	1000	0.02	10000
G7	0.2–0.05	2000	0.05	10
G8	0.2–0.05	1000	0.05	1000
G9	0.2–0.05	1000	0.05	10
G10	0.2–0.1	2500	0.2	15000
G11	0.2–0.05	1000	0.05	10

TABLE 4: The performance of the proposed approach in comparison with [10] on eleven test problems. The number of function evaluations is the same in both studies. The best results are indicated in boldface.

		Best	Mean	Worst	Optimal
G1	Proposed approach	**−14.99145**	**−14.96119**	**−14.81634**	−15.0
	[10]	−14.7207	−14.4609	−14.0566	
G2	Proposed approach	0.78727	0.74244	0.67530	0.803553
	[10]	**0.79506**	**0.79176**	**0.78427**	
G3	Proposed approach	0.98704	0.92063	0.72812	1.0
	[10]	**0.9983**	**0.9965**	**0.9917**	
G4	Proposed approach	**−30665.259**	**−30662.639**	**−30648.807**	−30655.5
	[10]	−30662.5	−30643.8	−30617.0	
G5	Proposed approach	—	—	—	5126.4981
	[10]	—	—	—	
G6	Proposed approach	**−6917.85904**	**−6862.02084**	**−6425.38018**	−6961.8
	[10]	−6901.5	−6191.2	−4236.7	
G7	Proposed approach	**24.52525**	**26.12999**	**29.24032**	24.306
	[10]	25.132	26.619	38.682	
G8	Proposed approach	**0.09582504**	**0.09582504**	**0.095825036**	0.0958250
	[10]	0.095825	0.0871551	0.0291434	
G9	Proposed approach	**680.74163**	**681.00480**	**681.53181**	680.63
	[10]	681.43	682.18	682.88	
G10	Proposed approach	7132.98320	7543.48592	8845.85330	7049.33
	[10]	7215.8	9141.7	11894.5	
G11	Proposed approach	**0.75**	0.75085	0.75655	0.75
	[10]	**0.75**	**0.75**	**0.75**	

4. Conclusions

This paper proposes a general and computationally simple approach to improve the performance of evolution-based optimization methods for solving nonlinear constrained optimization problems. After a number of generations when enough exploration is performed, the search space is reduced to a small subspace around the best individual, and the search is continued over this reduced space. If the reduction parameters (red_gen and red_factor) are adjusted properly, the reduced search space will include the global optimum. Here, this method was incorporated with a simple constrained GA and its performance was tested and compared with the method in [10] on a set of eleven benchmark test problems. The comparative results of the experimental study demonstrate that the proposed approach can considerably improve the performance (finding better near-optimal solutions) and efficiency (convergence speed) of the simple constrained GA in comparison with [10] without adding any considerable computational complexity to the original algorithm. The proposed scheme is general and can be incorporated with other population-based optimization methods for solving nonlinear programming problems.

References

[1] Z. Michalewicz and M. Schoenauer, "Evolutionary algorithms for constrained parameter optimization problems," *Evolutionary Computation*, vol. 4, no. 1, pp. 1–32, 1996.

[2] Ö. Yeniay, "Penalty function methods for constrained optimization with genetic algorithms," *Mathematical and Computational Applications*, vol. 10, no. 1, pp. 45–56, 2005.

[3] Z. Michalewicz and G. Nazhiyath, "Genocop III: a co-evolutionary algorithm for numerical optimization problems with nonlinear constraints," in *Proceedings of the 2nd IEEE International Conference on Evolutionary Computation*, pp. 647–651, December 1995.

[4] A. Rowhanimanesh, A. Khajekaramodin, and M.-R. Akbarzadeh-T, "Evolutionary constrained design of seismically excited buildings, actuators placement," in *Proceedings of the 1st Joint Congress on Intelligent and Fuzzy Systems (ISFS '07)*, pp. 297–304, Mashhad, Iran, 2007.

[5] K. Deb, "An efficient constraint handling method for genetic algorithms," *Computer Methods in Applied Mechanics and Engineering*, vol. 186, no. 2–4, pp. 311–338, 2000.

[6] M. Schouenauer and S. Xanthakis, "Constrained GA optimization," in *Proceedings of the 5th International Conference on Genetic Algorithms*, pp. 473–580, 1993.

[7] A. Rowhanimanesh, A. Khajekaramodin, and M.-R. Akbarzadeh-T, "Evolutionary constrained design of seismically excited buildings: sensor placement," *Applications of Soft Computing*, vol. 58, pp. 159–169, 2009.

[8] Z. Michalewicz and C. Z. Janikow, "Handling constraints in genetic algorithms," in *Proceedings of the 4th International Conference on Genetic Algorithms*, pp. 151–157, 1993.

[9] M. Schoenauer and Z. Michalewicz, "Evolutionary computation at the edge of feasibility," in *Proceedings of the 4rth International Conference on Parallel Problem Solving from Nature*, pp. 22–27, 1996.

[10] S. Koziel and Z. Michalewicz, "Evolutionary algorithms, homomorphous mappings, and constrained parameter optimization," *Evolutionary Computation*, vol. 7, no. 1, pp. 19–44, 1999.

[11] H. Adeli and N. T. Cheng, "Augmented lagrangian genetic algorithm for structural optimization," *Journal of Aerospace Engineering*, vol. 7, no. 1, pp. 104–118, 1994.

[12] B. W. Wah and Y. Chen, "Hybrid constrained simulated annealing and genetic algorithms for nonlinear constrained optimization," in *Proceedings of the Congress on Evolutionary Computation*, vol. 2, pp. 925–932, May 2001.

[13] J. H. Kim and H. Myung, "Evolutionary programming techniques for constrained optimization problems," *IEEE Transactions on Evolutionary Computation*, vol. 1, no. 2, pp. 129–140, 1997.

[14] T. P. Runarsson and X. Yao, "Constrained evolutionary optimization: the penalty function approach," in *Evolutionary Optimization*, R. Sarker, M. Mohammadian, and X. Yao, Eds., pp. 87–113, Kluwer Academic Publishers, 2002.

[15] T. Bäck, F. Hoffmeister, and H. P. Schwell, "A survey of evolution strategies," in *Proceedings of the 4th International Conference on Genetic Algorithms*, pp. 2–9, 1991.

[16] A. Homaifar, S. H. Y. Lai, and X. Qi, "Constrained optimization via genetic algorithms," *Simulation*, vol. 62, no. 4, pp. 242–254, 1994.

[17] M. A. Kuri and C. C. Quezada, "A universal eclectic genetic algorithm for constrained optimization," in *Proceedings of the 6th European Congress on Intelligent Techniques & Soft Computing*, pp. 518–522, 1998.

[18] J. A. Joines and C. R. Houck, "On the use of non-stationary penalty functions to solve nonlinear constrained optimization problems with GA's," in *Proceedings of the 1st IEEE Conference on Evolutionary Computation*, pp. 579–584, June 1994.

[19] S. Kazarlis and V. Petridis, "Varying fitness functions in genetic algorithms: studying the rate of increase in the dynamic penalty terms," in *Proceedings of the 5th International Conference on Parallel Problem Solving from Nature*, pp. 211–220, 1998.

[20] F. Mendivil and R. Shonkwiler, "Annealing a genetic algorithm for constrained optimization," *Journal of Optimization Theory and Applications*, vol. 147, no. 2, pp. 395–410, 2010.

[21] Z. Michalewicz and N. Attia, "Evolutionary optimization of constrained problems," in *Proceedings of the 3rd Annual Conference on Evolutionary Programming*, pp. 98–108, 1994.

[22] H. J. C. Barbosa and A. C. C. Lemonge, "An adaptive penalty scheme in genetic algorithms for constrained optimization problems," in *Proceedings of the Genetic and Evolutionary Computation Conference (GECCO '02)*, pp. 287–294, 2002.

[23] M. Gen and R. Cheng, "A survey of penalty techniques in genetic algorithms," in *Proceedings of the IEEE International Conference on Evolutionary Computation*, pp. 804–809, May 1996.

[24] A. Smith and D. Tate, "Genetic optimization using a penalty function," in *Proceedings of the 5th International Conference on Genetic Algorithms*, pp. 499–503, 1993.

[25] R. Le Riche, C. Knopf-Lenior, and R. T. Haftka, "A segregated genetic algorithm for constrained structural optimization," in *Proceedings of the 6th International Conference on Genetic Algorithms*, pp. 558–565, 1995.

[26] C. A. C. Coello, "Use of a self-adaptive penalty approach for engineering optimization problems," *Computers in Industry*, vol. 41, no. 2, pp. 113–127, 2000.

[27] K. Deb and S. Agarwal, "A niched-penalty approach for constraint handling in genetic algorithms," in *Proceedings of*

the *International Conference on Adaptive and Natural Computing Algorithms (ICANNGA '99)*, Portoroz, Slovenia, 1999.

[28] T. P. Runarsson and X. Yao, "Stochastic ranking for constrained evolutionary optimization," *IEEE Transactions on Evolutionary Computation*, vol. 4, no. 3, pp. 284–294, 2000.

[29] K. Deb, "An efficient constraint handling method for genetic algorithms," *Computer Methods in Applied Mechanics and Engineering*, vol. 186, no. 2–4, pp. 311–338, 2000.

[30] R. L. Haupt and S. E. Haupt, *Practical Genetic Algorithms*, John Wiley & Sons, 2004.

4

Radial-Basis-Function-Network-Based Prediction of Performance and Emission Characteristics in a Bio Diesel Engine Run on WCO Ester

Shiva Kumar,[1] P. Srinivasa Pai,[2] and B. R. Shrinivasa Rao[2]

[1] Department of Mechanical Engineering, MIT, Manipal 576104, India
[2] Department of Mechanical Engineering, NMAMIT, Nitte 574110, India

Correspondence should be addressed to Shiva Kumar, shiva_katipalla@yahoo.co.in

Academic Editor: Jun He

Radial basis function neural networks (RBFNNs), which is a relatively new class of neural networks, have been investigated for their applicability for prediction of performance and emission characteristics of a diesel engine fuelled with waste cooking oil (WCO). The RBF networks were trained using the experimental data, where in load percentage, compression ratio, blend percentage, injection timing, and injection pressure were taken as the input parameters, and brake thermal efficiency (BTE), brake specific energy consumption (BSEC), exhaust gas temperature (T_{exh}), and engine emissions were used as the output parameters. The number of RBF centers was selected randomly. The network was initially trained using variable width values for the RBF units using a heuristic and then was trained by using fixed width values. Studies showed that RBFNN predicted results matched well with the experimental results over a wide range of operating conditions. Prediction accuracy for all the output parameters was above 90% in case of performance parameters and above 70% in case of emission parameters.

1. Introduction

The world is presently confronted with a twin crisis of fossil fuel depletion and environmental degradation. Indiscriminate extraction and lavish consumption of fossil fuels have led to a reduction in underground-based carbon resources. The search for an alternative fuel which promises a harmonious correlation with the sustainable development, energy conservation, and management has become highly pronounced in the present context. The fuels of bio-origin like vegetable oils can provide a feasible solution to this crisis. The energy density, cetane number, and heat of vaporization of vegetable oils are comparable to diesel values. It is renewable, available everywhere, and has proved to be a cleaner fuel and more environment friendly than the fossil fuels [1–3]. Also from the literature, it is revealed that the emissions from the biodiesel engines are comparatively lesser from the engines with the petroleum-based fuels [4–6]. But the higher viscosity of vegetable oils affects the flow

properties of fuel such as spray, atomization, and consequent vaporization and air fuel mixing.

Heating and blending of vegetable oils may reduce the viscosity and improve the volatility of the vegetable oils, but its molecular structure remains unchanged. Literature survey revealed that converting vegetable oils into methyl esters will overcome all problems related with vegetable oils [7, 8].

However, high cost of biodiesel is the major obstacle for its commercialization. The biodiesel produced from vegetable oil or animal fat is usually more expensive than petroleum-based diesel fuel from 10 to 50%. Moreover during 2010, the prices of virgin vegetable oils have nearly doubled in relation to the early 2000. This is of great concern to biodiesel producers, since the cost of feedstock comprises approximately 70–95% of total operating costs at a biodiesel plant. Compared to neat vegetable oils, the cost of waste cooking oils (WCO) is anywhere from 60% less to free, depending on the source and availability. WCOs constitute a major waste generated in hotels and other public eateries.

Radial-Basis-Function-Network-Based Prediction of Performance and Emission Characteristics in a Bio Diesel Engine Run on WCO Ester

27

FIGURE 1: Photograph of the experimental setup.

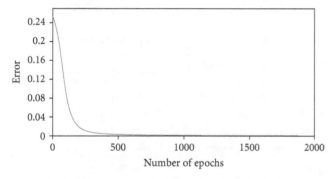

FIGURE 2: General architecture of RBF network.

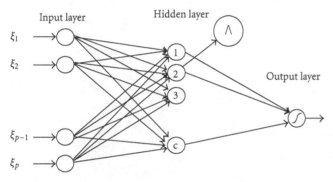

FIGURE 3: Variation of error during RBF training with 275 hidden neurons for the WCO methyl ester model.

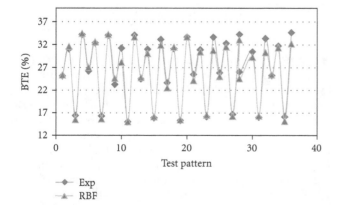

FIGURE 4: Comparison of experimental and network predicted values for BTE.

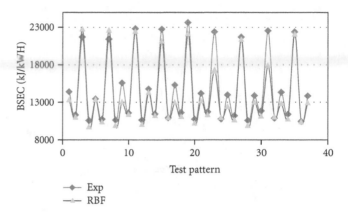

FIGURE 5: Comparison of experimental and network predicted values for BSEC.

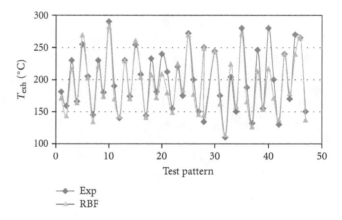

FIGURE 6: Comparison of experimental and network predicted values for T_{exh}.

This will be more often recycled for human consumption. The chemicals present in the recycled oil may cause health problems to human beings.

An alternative way for disposal of WCO is by recycling it. The main use of recycled WCO is in the production of animal feeds and in a much smaller proportion in the manufacture of soaps and biodegradable lubricants. Some health risks can be traced from the use of recycled cooking oils in animal feeding. Alternatively, WCO can be used as a fuel in CI engines after suitably modifying the fuel properties [9–12].

Manufacturers and engine application engineers usually want to know the performance of a C.I engine for various proportions of blends, for various compression ratios, and at different injection timings and injection pressures. This requirement can be met either by conducting comprehensive tests or by modeling the engine operation. Testing the engine under all possible operating conditions and fuel cases are both time consuming and expensive. On the other hand, developing an accurate model for the operation of a C.I engine fuelled with blends of biodiesel is too difficult due to the complex nature of the processes involved. As an alternative, engine performance and exhaust emissions can be modeled using Artificial Neural Networks (ANNs). This technique can be applied to predict the desired output

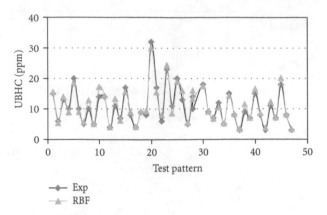

FIGURE 7: Comparison of experimental and RBF predicted values for test data for UBHC.

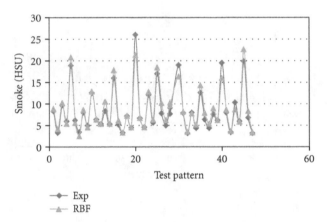

FIGURE 8: Comparison of experimental and network predicted values for smoke.

TABLE 1: Specifications of the engine.

Engine	Four stroke, single cylinder, water cooled, and constant speed diesel engine.
Rated power	3.2 KW
Speed	1500 rpm
Bore	87.5 mm
Stroke	110 mm
Compression ratio	12 to 18 : 1
Crank angle sensor	Resolution 1°
Engine indicator	For data scanning and interfacing with Pentium III processor
Swept volume	661cc
Temperature indicator	Digital PT-100

parameters when enough experimental data is made available.

ANNs are used to solve a variety of problems in science and engineering particularly in some areas where conventional modeling fail. The predictive capability of ANN results from training on experimental data and then validation by independent data. Various authors have investigated the

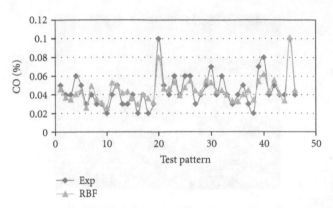

FIGURE 9: Comparison of experimental and network predicted values for CO.

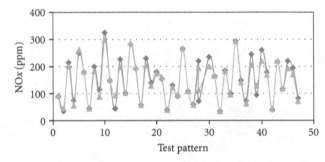

FIGURE 10: Comparison of experimental and network predicted values for NO_x.

TABLE 2: Experimental conditions using WCO methyl ester blends.

S. No	Operating parameters	Variations				
1	Engine load (%)	0	25	50	75	100
2	WCO blend (%)	10	15	20	25	
3	Compression ratio	16	17.5	18		
4	Injection timing (°BTDC)	24	27	30		
5	Injection pressure (bar)	160	190	220		

TABLE 3: Variation of MSE with the number of centers.

Number of centers	100	150	200	250	275	280
MSE	0.001985	0.00163	0.00149	0.0011	0.00100	0.0011

application of ANN to different thermal systems including internal combustion engines [13–17]. In a study carried out by Alonso et al. [18], ANN were employed as predicting tools for prediction of brake specific fuel consumption (BSFC), NO_x, and CO emissions. They developed individual models for emissions using the experimental data. Best prediction was obtained for BSFC and NO_x emissions. Ghobadian et al. [19] developed an ANN model to predict the engine emissions from a diesel engine using WCO as a fuel. They found fairly good results for the prediction of torque, specific fuel consumption, carbon monoxide (CO), and unburnt hydrocarbon (UBHC) emission. Yusaf et al. [20] used ANN to predict the engine torque, power, BSFC,

Radial-Basis-Function-Network-Based Prediction of Performance and Emission Characteristics in a Bio
Diesel Engine Run on WCO Ester

29

TABLE 4: Performance of RBF network with fixed centers selected at random for variable width.

S No	Variable	Training accuracy (%)	Test accuracy (%)
1	BTE	100	96
2	BSEC	99	94
3	T_{exh}	98	90
4	NO_x	88	82
5	Smoke	85	77
6	CO	72	69
7	UBHC	73	69

TABLE 5: Variation of MSE with the RBF width.

Width value	0.02	0.05	0.08	0.09	0.12	0.15
MSE	0.0015	0.0012	0.0010	0.0010	0.008	0.2977

TABLE 6: Performance of the network for optimized number of centers and width.

S No	Variable	Training accuracy	Test accuracy
1	BTE	100	96
2	BSEC	99	94
3	T_{exh}	98	90
4	NO_x	91	81
5	Smoke	85	78
6	CO	72	69
7	UBHC	72	70

and emissions from a diesel engine fuelled with CNG and diesel. ANN modeling was done with multilayer perceptron (MLP). They observed that the model was able to predict the performance and emission characteristics with a correlation coefficient of more than 0.9. Sayin et al. [21] developed ANN models to predict engine emissions from a SI engine. They observed that developed ANN models were able to predict accurately the emission parameters. Arcaklioğlu and Çelikten [22] demonstrated that ANN models accurately predict the performance parameters and emissions from a diesel engine when the engine was run on neat diesel. They took engine operating parameters as the inputs and the corresponding performance parameters and emissions as outputs for the network. The literature review reveals that use of MLP for modeling engine performance and emission characteristics is common [18–22]. But the application of radial basis function (RBF) networks for modeling of thermal systems is very limited [23–26]. In this context RBF technique has been used for modeling performance and emission characteristics of a biodiesel engine. RBFNN was developed based on the random selection of centers of the RBF units. The widths of RBF units were calculated using two approaches and a comparison has been carried out with regard to their prediction accuracy.

TABLE 7: Test pattern numbers corresponding to the specific engine loading condition.

Loading condition	Test patterns
25%	3, 7, 11, 15, 19, 23, 27, 31, 35
50%	1, 5, 9, 13, 17, 21, 25, 29, 33, 37
75%	2, 6, 10, 14, 16, 18, 22, 24, 26, 30, 32, 34
100%	4, 8, 12, 20, 28, 36

2. Experimental Setup

Since the direct use of vegetable oil poses problems during the running of the engines because of its higher viscosity, it is subjected to a process called as transesterification which reduces the viscosity and improves its volatility. Biodiesel is prepared from waste cooking oil using the transesterification process. Prepared biodiesel is mixed with neat diesel in various concentrations (10%, 15%, 20%, and 25%) by volume which has been termed as B10, B15, B20, and B25, respectively, and used as fuel to run the engine.

The performance and emission tests were conducted on a computerized 5.2 kW single cylinder, four stroke, naturally aspirated, direct injection, variable compression ratio, and water cooled diesel engine test rig. Figure 1 shows the photograph of the experimental setup. It is a single cylinder, four stroke compression ignition engine connected to an eddy current dynamometer. It is provided with temperature sensors for the measurement of temperatures of jacket water, calorimeter water, calorimeter exhaust gas inlet, and outlet temperature. It is also provided with pressure sensors for the measurement of combustion gas pressure and fuel injection pressure. An encoder is fixed for crank angle record. The signals from these sensors were interfaced with a computer to display P-θ, P-V, and fuel injection pressure versus crank angle plots. There is also a provision for the measurement of volumetric fuel flow. The built in software in the system calculated indicated power, brake power, thermal efficiency, volumetric efficiency, and heat balance. An AVL Digas 444 exhaust gas analyzer was used to measure the CO, HC, and NO_x emissions in the engine exhaust. An AVL 437C smoke meter was used to measure the smoke intensity in the engine exhaust. Specifications of the engine are given in Table 1. Experiments were conducted initially by using neat diesel at various loads and then with WCO methyl ester blends. Experiments were repeated by changing the compression ratios, injection timings, and injection pressures as shown in Table 2.

3. Neural Network Modeling

A neural network is a massively parallel distributed processor made up of simple processing units, which has a natural propensity for strong experimental knowledge and making it available for use. They can learn from examples and are fault tolerant in the sense that they are able to handle noisy and incomplete data. They are able to deal with nonlinear problems and once trained can perform prediction and generalization at high speeds [27]. They differ from conventional modeling approaches in their ability to learn about the system without the prior knowledge of the process relationships. The prediction by a well-trained ANN is much faster than the conventional simulation programs or mathematical models as no lengthy iterative calculations are needed to solve differential equations using numerical methods. One of the advantages is their ability to model complex nonlinear relationships between multiple input variables and required outputs. In the case of diesel engine modeling using blends of biodiesel, where complex interactions between the different variables are not yet completely understood, ANN approach for modeling is well suited. It consists of large number of neurons and interconnections between them. According to the structure of the connections, they have been identified as feed forward and recurrent networks. Feed forward networks have one-way connections, from the input to the output layer. They are most commonly used for prediction and nonlinear function fitting. Here the neurons are arranged in the form of layers. Neurons in one layer get inputs from previous layer and feed their outputs to the next layer. The last layer is called the output layer. Layers between the input and output layers are called hidden layers and are termed as multilayered networks. In the present study, modeling has been done by using radial basis function neural networks (RBFNNs), which is a feed forward network.

4. Radial Basis Function Neural Networks (RBFNNs)

RBF networks, a class of feed forward networks have universal approximation capabilities. The design of this network is viewed as a curve fitting approximation problem in a high dimensional space. According to this view point, learning is equivalent to finding a surface in a multidimensional space that provides the best fit to the training data. In its most basic form it involves 3 layers with entirely different roles. Input layer is made of source nodes that connect the network to its environment. Second is the hidden layer which applies a nonlinear transformation from the input space to the hidden space, which is of high dimensionality. Output layer is linear, supplying the response of the network to the activation patterns applied to the input layer. Figure 2 shows the general architecture of the RBF network. An RBF is symmetrical about a given mean or center in a multidimensional space. Each RBF unit has two parameters, a center x_j, and a width σ_j. This center is used to compare the network input vector to produce a radially symmetrical response. The width controls the smoothness properties of the interpolating function. Response of the hidden layer are scaled by the connection weights of the output layer and then combined to produce the network output. In the classical approach to RBF network implementation, the basic functions are usually chosen as Gaussian and the number of hidden units is fixed based on some properties of the input data. The weights connecting the hidden and output units are estimated by linear least squares method (LMS) [27].

There are different learning strategies available for the design of an RBF network, depending on how centers of the radial basis functions of the network are specified [28, 29]. In the present study, Random initialization method has been used for RBF modeling.

The simplest approach is to design RBFNN. In this, the number of radial-basis functions defining the activation functions of the hidden units are fixed. Specifically, the locations of the centers may be chosen randomly from the training data set. The RBFs use Gaussian activation function which is defined as $\phi_j(x) = \exp(-\|x_j - \xi_i\|^2/2\sigma_j^2)$, where x_j is the center and σ_j is the width (standard deviation), $j = 1, 2, \ldots, c$, where c is the number of centers. The only parameter that would need to be learned in this approach is the linear weights in the output layer of the network. The weights are learned using a simple LMS algorithm. The algorithm to train the network by using random initialization method is the following.

(1) Select the number of RBF centers arbitrarily.

(2) Initialize their centers from input data randomly.

(3) Set $E_{\text{tot}} = 0$.

(4) Choose the input output pair (ξ_i^μ, ζ_k^μ), where $\mu = 1, 2, 3, \ldots n$ are the number of patterns and $i = 1, 2, 3, \ldots p$ are the number of input features, k is the output feature.

(5) Compute the hidden layer output $v_j = e^{\|x_j - \xi_i\|^2}/2\sigma_j^2$, where x_j is the center and σ_j is width of the RBF unit.

(6) Compute the output using $O_k = 1/(1 + e^{-\sum w_{kj} V_j})$.

(7) Compute the square error $E = (O_k - \zeta_k) \times (O_k - \zeta_k)$ and $E_{\text{tot}} = E_{\text{tot}} + E$.

(8) The change in the output layer weights are calculated as

$$\partial_k = (O_k - \zeta_k) \times O_k \times (O_k - \zeta_k)$$
$$\Delta w_{kj} = \partial_k \times v_j \times \alpha \times \eta, \tag{1}$$

where η and α are learning rate and momentum parameters, and

$$w_{kj}^{\text{new}} = w_{kj}^{\text{old}} + \Delta w_{kj}. \tag{2}$$

(9) If $E_{\text{tot}} > E_{\text{min}}$ then go to step 4.

(10) Save weights, centers, widths, and exit [29].

For training the networks, load percentage, compression ratio, blend percentage, injection timing, and injection pressure were taken as the input parameters and brake thermal efficiency, brake specific energy consumption, exhaust gas temperature and engine emissions NO_x, smoke, and CO and UBHC were used as the output parameters. The training of the network has been done with different number of RBF units. The widths of the RBF units were determined using a P-nearest neighbor heuristic (each RBF unit has a different width value) [28] and studies have been carried out. The simulation parameters η and α were fixed as 0.85 and 0.05, respectively, and were maintained constant for all the studies. The data set was divided into two groups—training data set, used for training the network with about 85% of the data selected randomly, and test data set with the remaining data used for testing the network performance. For the different number of selected centers MSE have been tabulated in Table 3. It is clear from the table that the error decreases as the number of centers increased and reached a minimum for 275 beyond which the error increased. Hence, 275 was selected as the optimum number of centers. The variation of error with the number of epochs during training with 275 RBF units is shown in Figure 3.

Mean square error (MSE) has been used for evaluating the network performance. Error limit of 5% was considered for performance parameters and 10% for emission parameters [20–22]. Based on these values the prediction accuracy of the network for both training and test data is as shown in Table 4.

In another study, widths have been kept (fixed) constant for all the RBF units and the network was trained for different values of widths. Table 5 shows the MSE of RBF network with different values of widths, for 275 RBF units. It is clear from the table that the error decreased with the increase in the value of the width. The optimum value of width has been chosen as 0.08, since the MSE was least corresponding to this width. Beyond this value of the width the error started to increase. Using the above width, the network was trained and network results so obtained have been tabulated in Table 6.

On comparing the prediction accuracy of the network results, fixed widths for RBF units gave better performance prediction than variable width. The prediction accuracy for the emission parameters are relatively lower than that for the performance parameters. This could be attributed to the error made during the emission measurements and the complexity involved in the combustion process. Figures 4, 5, 6, 7, 8, 9, and 10 shows the plot of experimental and RBF network predicted results for the test data selected randomly from the entire experimental data. The results indicate that ANN predicted values are very close to the experimental values for the test data under different loading conditions (25%, 50%, 75%, and 100%). Table 7 shows the test pattern number and the corresponding loading condition with respect to BSEC. Hence RBFNN can be used for effectively predicting the performance and emission parameters of a biodiesel engine fuelled with WCO methyl ester.

5. Conclusions

In this paper an attempt has been made to model engine performance parameters and emissions using RBF neural network. Experiments were conducted on a four stroke CI engine using different biodiesel blends. Load percentage, compression ratio, blend percentage, injection timing, and injection pressure were taken as the input parameters. Brake thermal efficiency, brake specific energy consumption, exhaust gas temperature and engine emissions NO_x, smoke, UBHC, and CO were used as the output parameters. RBF neural networks which are a new class of networks not very widely used for these applications have been used in this work. Centers of the RBF units were selected randomly.

Fixing the widths of RBF units rather than using variable widths calculated using P-nearest neighbor heuristic gave better results. RBF network results matched closely with the experimental results for the test data with the prediction accuracy of more than 90% for performance parameters and around 70% for emission parameters. Hence, it can be concluded that RBFNN can be effectively used for modeling a biodiesel engine.

References

[1] J. Huang, Y. Wang, S. Li, A. P. Roskilly, H. Yu, and H. Li, "Experimental investigation on the performance and emissions of a diesel engine fuelled with ethanol-diesel blends," *Applied Thermal Engineering*, vol. 29, no. 11-12, pp. 2484–2490, 2009.

[2] K. Sureshkumar, R. Velraj, and R. Ganesan, "Performance and exhaust emission characteristics of a CI engine fueled with Pongamia pinnata methyl ester (PPME) and its blends with diesel," *Renewable Energy*, vol. 33, no. 10, pp. 2294–2302, 2008.

[3] A. K. Agarwal and K. Rajamanoharan, "Experimental investigations of performance and emissions of Karanja oil and its blends in a single cylinder agricultural diesel engine," *Applied Energy*, vol. 86, no. 1, pp. 106–112, 2009.

[4] T. Venkateshwara Rao, G. Prabhakar Rao, and K. Hema Chandra Reddy, "Experimental investigation of pongamia, Jatropha, Neem metyl esters as biodiesel in C.I. Engine," *Jordan Journal of Mechanical and Industrial Engineering*, vol. 2, no. 2, pp. 117–122, 2008.

[5] A. P. Roskilly, S. K. Nanda, Y. D. Wang, and J. Chirkowski, "The performance and the gaseous emissions of two small marine craft diesel engines fuelled with biodiesel," *Applied Thermal Engineering*, vol. 28, no. 8-9, pp. 872–880, 2008.

[6] A. K. Hossain and P. A. Davies, "Plant oils as fuels for compression ignition engines: a technical review and life-cycle analysis," *Renewable Energy*, vol. 35, no. 1, pp. 1–13, 2010.

[7] A. K. Babu and G. Devaradjane, "Vegetable oils and their derivatives as fuel for CI engines—an overview," SAE Technical Paper 2003-01-0767, SAE International.

[8] A. S. Ramadhas, S. Jayaraj, and C. Muraleedharan, "Use of vegetable oils as I.C. Engine fuels—a review," *Renewable Energy*, vol. 29, no. 5, pp. 727–742, 2004.

[9] S. Zheng, M. Kates, M. A. Dubé, and D. D. McLean, "Acid-catalyzed production of biodiesel from waste frying oil," *Biomass and Bioenergy*, vol. 30, no. 3, pp. 267–272, 2006.

[10] A. V. Tomasevic and S. S. Siler-Marinkovic, "Methanolysis of used frying oil," *Fuel Processing Technology*, vol. 81, no. 1, pp. 1–6, 2003.

[11] M. Canakci and A. Necati Özsezen, "Evaluating waste cooking oils as alternative diesel fuel," *Gazi University Journal of Science*, vol. 18, no. 1, pp. 81–91, 2005.

[12] Z. Utlu and M. S. Koçak, "The effect of biodiesel fuel obtained from waste frying oil on direct injection diesel engine performance and exhaust emissions," *Renewable Energy*, vol. 33, no. 8, pp. 1936–1941, 2008.

[13] M. L. Traver and R. J. Atkinson, "Neural network based diesel engine emission prediction using in cylinder combustion pressure," SAE Technical Paper 1999-01-1532, SAE International.

[14] D. Yuanwang, Z. Meilin, X. Dong, and C. Xiaobei, "An analysis for effect of cetane number on exhaust emissions from engine with the neural network," *Fuel*, vol. 81, no. 15, pp. 1963–1970, 2002.

[15] M. Gölcü, Y. Sekmen, P. Erduranli, and M. S. Salman, "Artificial neural-network based modeling of variable valve-timing in a spark-ignition engine," *Applied Energy*, vol. 81, no. 2, pp. 187–197, 2005.

[16] M. M. Prieto, E. Montanes, and O. Menendez, "Power plant condenser performance forecasting using a non-fully connected artificial neural network," *Energy*, vol. 26, no. 1, pp. 65–79, 2001.

[17] H. Bechtler, M. W. Browne, P. K. Bansal, and V. Kecman, "Neural networks—a new approach to model vapour-compression heat pumps," *International Journal of Energy Research*, vol. 25, no. 7, pp. 591–599, 2001.

[18] J. M. Alonso, F. Alvarruiz, J. M. Desantes, L. Hernández, V. Hernández, and G. Moltó, "Combining neural networks and genetic algorithms to predict and reduce diesel engine emissions," *IEEE Transactions on Evolutionary Computation*, vol. 11, no. 1, pp. 46–55, 2007.

[19] B. Ghobadian, H. Rahimi, A. M. Nikbakht, G. Najafi, and T. F. Yusaf, "Diesel engine performance and exhaust emission analysis using waste cooking biodiesel fuel with an artificial neural network," *Renewable Energy*, vol. 34, no. 4, pp. 976–982, 2009.

[20] T. F. Yusaf, D. R. Buttsworth, K. H. Saleh, and B. F. Yousif, "CNG-diesel engine performance and exhaust emission analysis with the aid of artificial neural network," *Applied Energy*, vol. 87, no. 5, pp. 1661–1669, 2010.

[21] C. Sayin, H. M. Ertunc, M. Hosoz, I. Kilicaslan, and M. Canakci, "Performance and exhaust emissions of a gasoline engine using artificial neural network," *Applied Thermal Engineering*, vol. 27, no. 1, pp. 46–54, 2007.

[22] E. Arcaklioğlu and I. Çelikten, "A diesel engine's performance and exhaust emissions," *Applied Energy*, vol. 80, no. 1, pp. 11–22, 2005.

[23] Z. T. Liu and S. M. Fei, "Study of CNG/diesel dual fuel engine's emissions by means of RBF neural network," *Journal of Zhejiang University*, vol. 5, no. 8, pp. 960–965, 2004.

[24] R. Johnsson, "Cylinder pressure reconstruction based on complex radial basis function networks from vibration and speed signals," *Mechanical Systems and Signal Processing*, vol. 20, no. 8, pp. 1923–1940, 2006.

[25] K. K. Botros, G. Kibrya, and A. Glover, "A demonstration artificial neural-networks-based data mining for gas-turbine-driven compressor stations," *Journal of Engineering for Gas Turbines and Power*, vol. 124, no. 2, pp. 284–297, 2002.

[26] N. Roy and R. Ganguli, "Filter design using radial basis function neural network and genetic algorithm for improved operational health monitoring," *Applied Soft Computing*, vol. 6, no. 2, pp. 154–169, 2006.

[27] S. Haykin, *Neural Networks, A Comprehensive Foundation*, Macmillan, New York, NY, USA, 1984.

[28] P. Srinivasa Pai, T. N. Nagabhushan, P. K. Ramakrishna Rao et al., "Radial basis function neural networks for tool wear monitoring," *International Journal of COMADEM*, vol. 5, no. 3, pp. 21–30, 2003.

[29] P. Srinivasa Pai, *Acoustic emission based tool wear monitoring using some improved neural network methodologies [Ph.D. thesis]*, S.J. College of Engineering, University of Mysore, Mysore, India, 2004.

5

Basin Hopping as a General and Versatile Optimization Framework for the Characterization of Biological Macromolecules

Brian Olson,[1] Irina Hashmi,[1] Kevin Molloy,[1] and Amarda Shehu[1, 2]

[1] Department of Computer Science, George Mason University, Fairfax, VA 22030, USA
[2] Department of Bioengineering, George Mason University, Fairfax, VA 22030, USA

Correspondence should be addressed to Amarda Shehu, amarda@gmu.edu

Academic Editor: Zhiyuan Luo

Since its introduction, the basin hopping (BH) framework has proven useful for hard nonlinear optimization problems with multiple variables and modalities. Applications span a wide range, from packing problems in geometry to characterization of molecular states in statistical physics. BH is seeing a reemergence in computational structural biology due to its ability to obtain a coarse-grained representation of the protein energy surface in terms of local minima. In this paper, we show that the BH framework is general and versatile, allowing to address problems related to the characterization of protein structure, assembly, and motion due to its fundamental ability to sample minima in a high-dimensional variable space. We show how specific implementations of the main components in BH yield algorithmic realizations that attain state-of-the-art results in the context of ab initio protein structure prediction and rigid protein-protein docking. We also show that BH can map intermediate minima related with motions connecting diverse stable functionally relevant states in a protein molecule, thus serving as a first step towards the characterization of transition trajectories connecting these states.

1. Introduction

Global optimization is an objective of many disciplines, both in academic and industrial settings [1, 2]. Characterization of complex systems often poses very hard global optimization problems with many variables [3, 4]. Algorithms that target such problems largely build on or combine four main approaches: deterministic, stochastic, heuristic, and smoothing [3, 5–7]. All these algorithms are challenged by systems where the variable space contains multiple distinct minima. While most algorithms can efficiently find a minimum, not all can feasibly locate the global minimum.

Some of the most successful applications of global optimization algorithms on characterizing physical and biological systems build on the stochastic Monte Carlo (MC) procedure and its Metropolis variant [8]. For instance, simulated annealing is one of the most widely used algorithms for finding the global minimum of a multivariable function for different complex systems [4, 9, 10]. Adaptations that build on deterministic and stochastic numerical procedures, such as molecular dynamics (MD) and MC, are abundant in computational biology for the structural characterization of biological macromolecules (cf. [11, 12]).

Basin hopping (BH) is a global optimization framework that is particularly suited for multivariable multimodal optimization problems [13], and it is our thesis in this paper that BH is an effective framework for the characterization of biological macromolecules. The basic BH framework is well studied and understood, but modifications to its core components are necessary for application to complex biological systems. In what follows, we first summarize the basic BH framework and some of its salient properties before proceeding to identify modifications necessary for application to biological macromolecules.

BH combines heuristic procedures with local searches to enhance its exploration of the given variable space, conducted as a series of perturbations followed by local optimization. As shown in pseudocode in Algorithm 1,

```
(1) i ← 0
(2) Xᵢ ← random initial point in variable space
(3) Yᵢ ← LOCALSEARCH (Xᵢ)
(4) while STOP not satisfied do
(5)     Xᵢ₊₁ ← PERTURB (Yᵢ)
(6)     Yᵢ₊₁ ← LOCALSEARCH (Xᵢ₊₁)
(7)     if f(Yᵢ₊₁) < f(Yᵢ) then
(8)         i ← i + 1
```

ALGORITHM 1: Basic BH framework in pseudocode.

the framework can be described in terms of a local search procedure LOCALSEARCH that maps a point X_i in variable space to its nearest minimum Y_i, a perturbation move PERTURB that modifies a current minimum Y_i to obtain a new point X_{i+1} in variable space, and a stopping criterion STOP that terminates these repeated applications of a structural perturbation followed by a local optimization. The repeated applications result in a trajectory of local minima Y_i. As shown in Algorithm 1, only the lowest minimum needs to be retained in memory when seeking the global minimum of some function f. It is important to note that Algorithm 1 shows a specific realization of the BH framework, known as monotonic BH (MBH), where the current minimum is not accepted if it does not lower the lowest value obtained for the function f so far. In this case, another perturbation is attempted in order to obtain a new starting point for the local optimization that follows.

While this basic framework is easy to describe and employ for global optimization, effective implementations exploit specific domain expertise about the system at hand [14–19]. Heuristics are designed based on specific system knowledge to implement an effective perturbation component. Domain-specific expertise is also employed for an effective implementation of the local search component. The stopping criterion is often implemented in terms of a maximum number of function evaluations or in terms of no improvements over a window of the last sampled minima. It is important to note that the stochasticity in BH is mainly due to the implementation of the perturbation component, which seeks to take the exploration out of the current local minimum. The local optimization component, on the other hand, can employ deterministic numerical techniques to locate the local minimum with arbitrary accuracy [20].

The core advantage of the BH framework over a multistart method that essentially samples local minima at random is that BH moves between adjacent local minima in the variable space. This strategy is more effective when exploring high-dimensional variable spaces associated with complex physical systems, where the addition of new dimensions can result in an exponential increase in the number of minima in the space [21]. The adjacency is a result of a deep connection between the perturbation and local optimization. Despite the application setting, a good general rule is for the perturbation to preserve some structural characteristics of the local minimum Y_i it is disrupting to obtain a new starting point X_{i+1} for the next application of the local optimization.

If the magnitude of the perturbation jump in the variable space, measured through some distance function $d(Y_i, X_{i+1})$, is small, then X_{i+1} may remain in the basin of attraction of Y_i, and the local optimization will bring X_{i+1} back to Y_i. On the other end of the spectrum, the perturbation can completely disrupt Y_i and obtain an X_{i+1} that could have essentially been obtained at random. While the local optimization will yield a new local minimum $Y_{i+1} \neq Y_i$, the BH will degenerate to a multistart method in this case. Different studies have shown that the perturbation needs to preserve some of the structure of the current minimum for BH to be more effective than the multistart method [20, 22]. It is the careful implementation of the perturbation component that allows BH to organize the local minima it samples according to an adjacency relationship [21].

The BH framework is sometimes referred to as a funnel-descent method, because its core behavior of iterating over adjacent local minima has turned out to be an effective optimization strategy for functions with a funnel landscape [21]. The generality of the framework and its ease of adaption for different systems has resulted in diverse applications, which span from geometry problems, such as packing circles in circular containers [20], to statistical physics problems of characterizing low-energy states of small atomic clusters [3].

The BH framework originated in the computational biology community dating back to the pioneering work of Wales [3], where the objective was to characterize the minima of the Lennard-Jones energy function in small atomic clusters. The term basin hopping was coined in this work, though to an extent, the stated motivation for the BH framework was from related optimization algorithms in the evolutionary search community. In fact, BH can be viewed as a special case of Iterated Local Search, which is popular for solving discrete combinatorial optimization problems [23]. An algorithmic realization of the BH framework was available prior to the work of Wales, most notably in Scheraga's MC with minimization algorithm [9, 24].

The BH framework is particularly suited to deal with molecular spaces, where the function sought for optimization is a complex nonconvex potential energy function summing over the interactions among atoms in a 3-dimensional molecular structure. The global minimum of the function corresponds to the structural state of the molecule that is most stable under equilibrium conditions and so relevant for biological activity. Structural characterization of the biologically active (native) state of biological macromolecules is an important problem in computational structural biology. A grand-standing challenge nowadays is to characterize such states for protein molecules, which are central in many chemical pathways in the cell and are the focus of this paper.

Proteins are complex systems with hundreds to thousands of atoms. These atoms are organized in amino-acid building blocks which connect serially to form a polypeptide chain (the N-terminus of one amino acid connects to the C-terminus of the other to form a peptide). Figure 1(a) shows a short polypeptide chain. Depending on the representation employed, a spatial arrangement of the atoms that constitute a polypeptide chain, also referred to as a conformation, may require the specification of a prohibitive number of variables. A popular representation in computational structural biology employs only the angles shown in Figure 1(a). These angles can be used to define the variable space, as their modification gives rise to different conformations.

The variable, or conformational, space of a polypeptide chain is associated with a funnel-like energy surface [25, 26]. The size and ruggedness of this surface, illustrated in Figure 1(b), are the primary reasons why obtaining structural information on native state of a protein polypeptide chain based on the chain's amino-acid sequence alone is an outstanding challenge in computational structural biology [27]. Meeting this challenge, often known as ab initio protein structure prediction, is needed, however, to close the gap between the wealth of protein sequence data and the scarce information on their native structures. Obtaining structural information ab initio promises to elucidate the structure-function relationship and advance structure-driven studies and applications on protein molecules [28–30].

The funnel-like but rugged energy surface of protein molecules seems suitable for the BH framework. In general, it is challenging to locate the global minimum in this surface and so elucidate the native structure of a protein. One of the main reasons relates to imperfect modeling. The energy functions currently available to probe the protein energy surface are semiempirical and contain inherent errors [31]. Due to the specific process undertaken in computational chemistry to design such functions, the actual global minimum of a designed protein energy function may deviate significantly from the true global minimum (the native structure obtained by experiment in the wet laboratory). Studies report deviations in the 2–4 Å range [32]. Due to these deviations, computational approaches that aim to obtain a broad view of the energy surface are more appropriate, particularly if they are to be followed by detailed heavy-duty optimization techniques on select conformations.

A common strategy among protocols for ab-initio protein structure prediction is the sampling of a large number of low-energy conformations. These are end points of many independent MD or MC trajectories optimizing some chosen energy function [28, 33–39]. Alternatively, the trajectories can be integrated in a tree to better control the exploration and use online analysis to bias the tree away from high-energy oversampled regions [40, 41]. The conformations are then grouped by structural similarity to reveal local minima from which it is worth continuing the exploration at higher

representational detail. The goal then becomes obtaining convergence to a region of the space that can be predicted to represent the native state.

In the context of ab-initio protein structure prediction, BH can be employed to explicitly sample local minima in the protein energy surface. At a superficial level, this would require the retainment of an ensemble of local minima and not just the current one. In addition, while the pseudocode in Algorithm 1 shows a simple realization of the BH framework, MBH, applications of BH on molecular spaces often make probabilistic decisions on whether to accept a current minimum. Procedurally, the framework still consists of repeated applications of a structural perturbation followed by an energy minimization. However, a Metropolis criterion [42] biases the sampling of local minima towards lower energy ones over time. Essentially, the decision to accept Y_{i+1} is made with probability $\exp(-[E(Y_{i+1})-E(Y_i)]/[K_B T])$, where E refers to the energy function, K_B is the Boltzmann constant, and T is temperature. Temperature does not need a physical meaning, as its main role is to scale the height of an energy barrier.

The appeal of the BH framework is that it transforms the protein energy surface into a collection of interpenetrating staircases, as illustrated in Figure 1(c). A succinct discrete representation is obtained for this surface in terms of local minima. It is important to note that BH does not modify the energy surface in any way. Instead, it projects each point (conformation) to its closest local minimum to effectively reveal a map of the energy surface in terms of local minima. The details of the energy surface between local minima are lost, but this degree of resolution is still very useful for a structural characterization of protein molecules.

Given its ease of implementation, BH is starting to gain popularity as an optimization framework for biological systems. Current applications of BH for structural characterization of biological molecules essentially differ in the specific implementations for the perturbation and local optimization components. Local optimization, for instance, is implemented as gradient descent or Metropolis MC at low temperature, whereas the perturbation component, on the other hand, directly modifies atomic coordinates in existing work. These implementation choices have allowed BH algorithms to capture local minima of small atomic clusters and even map energy surfaces of polyalanines and other small proteins [14, 32, 43, 44]. However, applications to structure prediction [45] have been limited to small proteins, mainly because representation of conformations through atomic coordinates results in a prohibitive variable space. In particular, the BH algorithm in [45] succeeds in locating conformations closer to the experimentally determined native structure than MD with simulated annealing, but its efficiency drops on sequences longer than 75 amino acids.

In this paper, we show that BH is a useful framework for structural characterization beyond structure prediction. We recognize that BH is general and can be employed to map the equilibrium conformational space of a biological system. For instance, we show that with suitable modifications to the perturbation and local optimization components, BH can be applied to protein-protein docking to reveal native

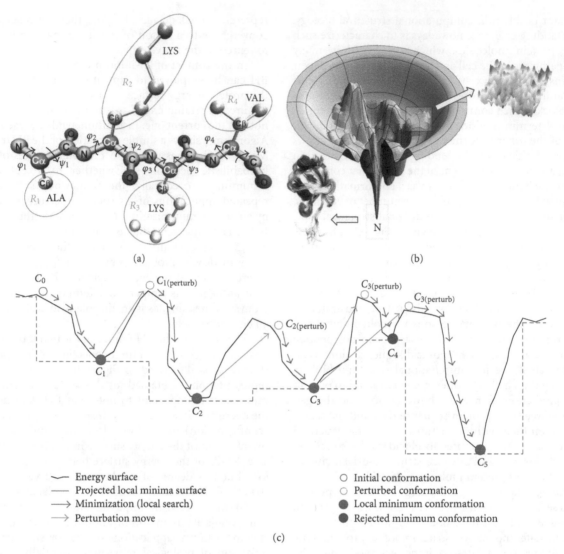

FIGURE 1: (a) A short polypeptide chain of 4 amino acids, alanine, lysine, lysine, and valine, is shown. The backbone atoms shared by all amino acids are N, C_α, C, and O. Side-chain atoms unique to 20 types of amino acids are in gray. The backbone (ϕ, ψ) dihedral angles are annotated over the chain. (b) A model energy surface is illustrated, adapted from [25]. The surface is funnel-like but rugged. The native state at the bottom is denoted by N. Conformations associated with it (obtained from experiment) are illustrated for a particular protein molecule. (c) The BH framework essentially converts the function into a stepwise one. The perturbation and local optimization components are illustrated here with differently colored arrows. A minimum is shown here which fails the Metropolis criterion and is thus not accepted, prompting a new perturbation move.

lowest-energy configurations of protein molecules resulting from the assembly of various polypeptide chains. Specifically, in the context of ab-initio protein structure prediction, we show that implementations of the main components in BH that employ domain-specific knowledge result in increased efficiency and allow application to longer protein chains.

We also show that the ability of BH to provide a map of the energy surface in terms of minima is useful not only when the goal is to locate the global minimum (whether that minimum corresponds to the native structure of one protein polypeptide chain or of a complex resulting from assembly of multiple chains), but also when the objective is to characterize proteins with more than one functionally relevant state. Such proteins are abundant in biology as

effective biological machines that can tune their biological function through molecular motions [46–49]. A map of the minima surrounding the functionally relevant states is useful for understanding how the protein hops between minima in transition trajectories connecting these states [33, 49, 50].

The presentation in this paper of BH as a general, versatile framework builds over our recent work on ab-initio structure prediction and rigid protein-protein docking [22, 51]. In particular, in the context of structure prediction, we show that employment of the molecular fragment replacement technique allows BH to efficiently capture the native structure. In the context of protein-protein docking, we incorporate geometric hashing to efficiently obtain structural perturbations of a dimeric configuration.

Additional information from evolutionary sequence analysis allows restricting the variable space. Finally, we provide here a proof-of-concept demonstration that BH can be applied to understand the connectivity between functionally relevant states in a protein in terms of the minima surrounding these states. Obtaining a view of minima in the equilibrium conformational space of a protein molecule is the first step into elucidating motions and transition trajectories that take a protein between the states it uses for biological function.

2. Methods

The basic BH framework was showcased in Algorithm 1 in Section 1. Our algorithmic treatment in this section focuses on modifications to the basic components of BH which allow its application to the three different problems on which we focus in this paper. As described in Section 1, two modifications that allow application to these problems concern accepting a newly obtained local minimum according to the Metropolis criterion (unlike the basic MBH algorithm) and adding that minimum to a growing ensemble of BH-obtained local minima (unlike recording only the last one as in the basic MBH framework). The description of BH below is organized according to the three different applications showcased in this paper in Sections 2.1, 2.2, and 2.3, respectively. The treatment of BH in each application is limited to description of four main components: (1) representation of the system being modeled, which allows defining the variable space; (2) description of the energy function being optimized by BH; (3) implementation of the structural perturbation move; and (4) implementation of the local search procedure for the local optimization.

2.1. BH for Sampling Decoy Conformations for Ab Initio Protein.
As described above, the BH framework can be employed to obtain a broad view of the energy surface in terms of low-energy local minima. This can be done efficiently at a coarse-grained level of detail, employing an energy function that sacrifices detail and some accuracy to save computational time. The sampled conformations corresponding to the local minima are low-energy decoy conformations, which can then be fed to any structure prediction protocol for further analysis and refinement of select conformations with dedicated computational resources. The refinement will allow adding further detail, discriminating between decoy conformations, and making a prediction on which refined conformation can be considered to represent the native structure.

2.1.1. Employed Representation.
As illustrated in Figure 1(a), a polypeptide chain of n amino acids contains $2n$ backbone (ϕ, ψ) dihedral angles. Our representation of a protein conformation employs only these angles, which constitute the variable space. Side chains are sacrificed, as any structure prediction protocol can pack them as part of the ensuing refinement of decoy conformations [52]. The representation here is essentially the idealized geometry model, which fixes bond lengths and angles to idealized (native) values. Forward kinematics allows computing Cartesian coordinates of the backbone atoms (on which the energy function described below operates) from the ϕ, ψ angles in the representation [53].

2.1.2. Energy Function.
The energy function is a modification of the associative memory Hamiltonian with water (AMW) [54]. This function has been used previously by us and others in the context of ab-initio structure prediction [40, 41, 55–57]. AMW sums nonlocal terms (local interactions are kept at ideal values in the idealized geometry model): $E_{AMW} = E_{Lennard-Jones} + E_{H-Bond} + E_{contact} + E_{burial} + E_{water} + E_{Rg}$. The $E_{Lennard-Jones}$ term is implemented after the 12–6 Lennard-Jones potential in AMBER9 [58] but allows a soft penetration of van der Waals spheres. The E_{H-Bond} term allows modeling hydrogen bonds and is implemented as in [59]. The other terms, $E_{contact}$, E_{burial}, and E_{water}, allow formation of nonlocal contacts, a hydrophobic core, and water-mediated interactions, and are implemented as in [39].

The listed energy terms of E_{AMW} sum over pairwise interactions. For instance, the 12–6 functional form of the Lennard-Jones term is $-4\epsilon_{ij}[(\sigma_{ij}/r_{ij})^{12} - (\sigma_{ij}/r_{ij})^{6}]$, where ϵ_{ij} is a constant characteristic of the types of atoms at positions i and j, σ_{ij} is the average diameter of the atoms, and r_{ij} is their distance. This functional form illustrates the quadratic running time of a typical energy function modeling pairwise interactions. More importantly, the terms summed together in an energy function are competing; minima of one term are obtained by suboptima of the other. This competition is known as frustration and refers to the fact that slight changes in atomic positions may lower the value of one term but increase that of another term. The result of summing competing terms in an energy function is a complex multimodal function, whose optimization is nontrivial. More details on the functional form of the other terms of the AMW energy function can be found in [33, 54].

2.1.3. Implementation of Structural Perturbation.
The realization of the BH framework we describe here hops between two conformations representing two consecutive minima C_i and C_{i+1} through an intermediate $C_{perturb,i}$ conformation. The perturbation modifies C_i to obtain a higher-energy conformation $C_{perturb,i}$ to escape the current minimum. Essentially, 6 backbone dihedral angles of a fragment of the polypeptide chain associated with three consecutive amino acids in the current conformation C_i are modified simultaneously. This process is referred to as the molecular fragment replacement technique, because it allows replacing the current configuration (in terms of angles) of a selected fragment with another fragment configuration [60].

Molecular Fragment Replacement. The fragment replacement technique has allowed ab-initio structure prediction methods to make great advancements [28, 34–37]. Its key advantage is that it allows obtaining physically realistic modifications if the fragment configurations are sampled from a library of actual native structures obtained in the wet laboratory. The basic idea is that a subset of nonredundant protein structures are obtained from the Protein Data Bank [61], and configurations of all fragments that can be defined for k consecutive amino acids are excised from these structures and stored in a library. We direct the reader to [28, 41] for a detailed description of how the library is constructed. In this work, we employ a fragment of length 3 rather than a longer fragment, so that the magnitude of the jump resulting from the fragment replacement in variable space is limited.

The perturbation component is implemented as follows. Given a conformation C_i, a fragment of length 3 is selected at random over the polypeptide chain ($n - 2$ fragments can be defined with overlap over a chain of n amino acids). Once the fragment is selected, a configuration for that fragment is then sampled at random over those available for the fragment from the fragment configuration library. The replacement of the angles of the fragment in C_i with those of the configuration obtained from library results in $C_{\text{perturb},i}$.

Since low-energy conformations tend to be compact and leave little room for movement without raising energy (a concept known as frustration in protein biophysics), this implementation of the perturbation component is sufficient to obtain a high-energy conformation through which to escape the current local minimum. Additionally, $C_{\text{perturb},i}$ will share nearly all of its local structural features with C_i, but the new conformation will have a higher energy and a different overall global structure. We note that the first conformation to initiate BH is obtained after $n - 2$ fragment configuration replacements over an extended conformation.

2.1.4. Implementation of Local Optimization.

Our implementation of the local optimization conducts a series of modifications starting from $C_{\text{perturb},i}$ to reach a new minimum C_{i+1}. While numerical techniques can be used here, they tend to be inefficient [45]. We employ instead a greedy search, which essentially attempts a maximum of m consecutive fragment replacements (as described above for the perturbation component) until k consecutive attempts fail to lower energy. The resulting C_{i+1} conformation is added to the trajectory according to the Metropolis criterion based on the energetic difference with C_i.

Our implementation of the local optimization is probabilistic due to the fragment replacement technique. Moreover, the true bottom of a current basin may not be found. A working definition of a local minimum is employed instead in terms of the parameter k. Finding true local minima in the energy surface can be computationally intensive while unnecessary. For instance, analysis of the AMW surface in related work in [22] shows that the native structure is near but not at a minimum. In addition, the results in Section 3 make the case that a working definition of a local minimum is sufficient to discover near-native conformations.

2.2. BH for Sampling Decoy Configurations for Rigid Protein-Protein Docking.

In this application, the native structures of two protein polypeptide chains (referred to as monomers) are known atomic coordinates obtained for each of the chains from experiment or structure prediction protocols.

The objective is to find the native quaternary structure that brings the two monomers together. The assumption here is that the monomers do not change structure upon docking but bind rigidly with each other. Under this assumption, the objective is to find the spatial arrangement that brings one monomeric structure over the other and results in a dimeric configuration of lowest energy.

2.2.1. Employed Representation.

In rigid docking, the only variables of interest are those that allow representing a spatial arrangement of one monomeric structure over another. A natural way to do so is through rigid-body transformations, which can be represented as vectors of 6 variables (3 for translation and 3 for rotation in 3-dimensional space). Hence, the variable space here is the 6-dimensional SE(3) space consisting of rigid-body motions or transformations.

The variable space we consider here is not the entire SE(3) but is constrained to rigid-body motions that align geometrically complementary and evolutionary conserved regions of the molecular spaces associated with each of the monomers. This builds upon earlier work by us on rigid docking which makes use of geometric hashing [51, 62]. Geometric hashing is a popular technique that essentially discretizes the space of rigid-body transformations by defining these transformations as alignments of geometrically complementary regions on monomeric molecular surfaces [63–66]. In recent work [51, 62] we show that the number of regions relevant for alignment can be further reduced by focusing on regions with high evolutionary conservation. Such regions are often found to be on contact interfaces [67].

While details of the process through which rigid-body transformations are defined are available in previous work [51, 62], we provide here a brief summary. The Connolly representation is first obtained for each monomeric surface [68]. The representation stores geometrical information for points on the surface, including whether the point represents a convex, saddle, or concave region. The representation is made less dense by only storing key locations on the molecular surface, known as critical points [69]. Triangles can be defined over these points. Associating evolutionary information with a critical point (through an analysis of related biological sequences [67]) allows focusing on triangles with high sequence conservation. We refer to these as active triangles. Once two geometrically complementary (e.g., concave with convex) active triangles T_A and T_B are obtained (from the molecular surfaces of monomers A and B, resp.), a rigid body transformation is easily defined as the one that aligns the local coordinate frame associated with T_B over that associated with T_A.

2.2.2. Energy Function.

Each rigid-body motion can be represented as a transformation, a vector of 3 translation and 3 rotation components (details below) that when applied to the moving monomer (one monomer is designated as moving and the other as reference or base) move that monomer in space and bring it over the reference monomer. Atomic coordinates are then obtained for the resulting dimeric configuration, which can now be evaluated in terms of the interaction energy. The energy function we employ combines three nonlocal terms useful for contact interfaces: $E = E_{\text{VdW}} + E_{\text{electrostatic}} + E_{\text{hydrogen-bonding}}$. The first term implements the standard 12–6 Lennard-Jones potential as in the CHARMM force field [70]. The electrostatic term implements Coulomb's law, also as in the CHARMM force field [70]. The hydrogen-bonding term is calculated as in [71] through the 12–10 hydrogen potential: $E_{\text{hydrogen-bonding}} = 5 \times [(r_0/d_{ij})^{12} - 6 \times (r_0/d_{ij})^{10}]$, where d_{ij} is the distance between acceptor and donor atoms i and j, and $r_0 = 2.9\,\text{Å}$ is the optimal distance for hydrogen bonding. Energy is computed only for the contact interface, which is defined over pairs of atoms in one monomer in contact with the atoms in the other monomer. Two atoms are in contact if their Euclidean distance is not higher than $4.0\,\text{Å}$.

2.2.3. Implementation of Structural Perturbation.

The exposition above describes that a rigid-body motion is obtained by aligning an active triangle T_B on the surface of monomer B with a geometrically complementary active triangle T_A on the surface of the base monomer A. Let the current minimum C_i be the configuration corresponding to the transformation aligning T_B with T_A. In other words, the contact interface in C_i is that obtained by aligning T_B with T_A. As described in Section 1, an effective structural perturbation needs to preserve the adjacency relationship. For this reason, an effective perturbation in this context needs to modify the contact interface in C_i but limit the magnitude of the perturbation. The implementation we pursue here seeks a new pair of triangles, T'_A and T'_B, to perturb C_i and obtain $C_{\text{perturb},i}$. In order to limit the magnitude of the perturbation and preserve some of the contact interface of C_i in $C_{\text{perturb},i}$, T'_A needs to be close to T_A, and T'_B needs to be close to T_B.

This is implemented as follows. The molecular surface of each monomer is precomputed and represented in terms of a finite list of active triangles. The center of mass of each triangle is computed, and reverse indexing is used in order to sample a triangle T'_A and a triangle T'_B whose center of mass is within $d\,\text{Å}$ of the center of mass of triangles T_A and T_B, respectively. The process repeats until a pair T'_A and T'_B are found which are geometrically complementary. A new rigid-body transformation aligning T'_B with T'_A is then defined, resulting in the perturbed configuration $C_{\text{perturb},i}$. Sampling in a d-radius neighborhood allows controlling and limiting the extent to which $C_{\text{perturb},i}$ perturbs the structural features of C_i (in this context, the contact interface).

2.2.4. Implementation of Local Optimization.

As in the realization of the BH framework for protein structure prediction, the local optimization here also attempts at most m structural modifications starting with $C_{\text{perturb},i}$. The optimization terminates early if k consecutive modifications fail to lower energy. A naive implementation of the local optimization could employ the same structural modifications as the perturbation component; that is, new pairs of geometrically complementary active triangles are sought, but using a smaller d value. Our recent work on docking shows, however, that it becomes difficult to find

geometrically complementary active triangles with smaller values of d [72]. A more effective alternative is to sample new rigid-body transformations directly rather than through new pairs of geometrically complementary active triangles and to do so in a continuous small neighborhood of an initial transformation.

Let the vector $\langle t, u, \theta \rangle$ be a rigid-body transformation, where t refers to the translation component, and $\langle u, \theta \rangle$ is an axis-angle representation of the orientation component (implemented through quaternions). In each move in the local optimization, a new random transformation is sampled in a small neighborhood of the transformation representing the configuration resulting from the previous modification. A new translation component t' is sampled in a δ_t neighborhood of t. A new axis u' is sampled by rotating around u by a sampled angle value δ_ϕ; a new angle θ' for the rotation component is obtained by sampling in a δ_θ neighborhood around θ. The result is that each move is a small modification of the contact interface to project a configuration onto its nearest local minimum. We note that, as before in the context of structure prediction, a working definition is employed here for the local minimum.

The result is a trajectory of low-energy dimeric configurations that are useful as decoys for the purpose of docking protocols. As in protein structure prediction, protein-protein docking protocols rely on first obtaining low-energy decoy configurations. Structural and energetic analysis then allows selecting a subset for further refinement in order to make a prediction on the native quaternary structure.

2.3. BH for Mapping Minima Connecting Diverse Stable States of a Protein Molecule.

Many proteins employ motions to access different structures that allow them to tune their biological function [73, 74]. An important problem is to understand how a protein transitions between different functionally relevant states [50, 75, 76]. The problem of obtaining transition trajectories is directly related to that of obtaining the connectivity of the space around stable states. Computing transition trajectories is challenging [77], as such trajectories can connect structural states far away in the variable space. By taking into account a system's dynamics, the typical MD framework is in principle desirable to provide information on the time scales associated with conformational changes in a transition trajectory. However, its practical application is limited. Long simulation times may be needed to observe a transition trajectory to go over energy barriers.

In this proof-of-concept application, we propose that the BH framework can be a valuable tool as a first step towards elucidating transition trajectories. BH can be employed to map the minima connecting two given structural states and thus elucidate energetically credible conformational paths. Treating conformations in the path as important milestones, MD-based techniques can then be employed to locally deform a conformational path into an actual transition trajectory that incorporates dynamics [78].

In this application, the representation, energy function, and the implementations of the perturbation and local search components of BH are as in Section 2.1. Here we pursue a proof-of-principle demonstration as follows. Let us suppose we are given two stable structural states of a protein, A and B. One of them can be regarded as the initial conformation to initiate a BH trajectory of local minima, and the other as the goal. A given number, let us say h, of BH trajectories can be initiated from the initial structure. The trajectories are allowed to grow for a fixed number of energy evaluations. In the unbiased scenario, the trajectories do not employ information about the location of the goal conformation in variable space. The results in Section 3 show that with sufficient sampling, if the initial and goal conformations are low-energy (i.e., stable), even unbiased BH trajectories are successful at approaching the goal conformation.

In a second scenario, the trajectories can be biased. Let us define an ϵ-radius ball around the goal conformation. As long as a BH trajectory stays outside this volume of the variable space (i.e., no minima are ϵ or closer to the goal), the BH exploration proceeds unbiased. When the trajectory enters the designated goal region of the variable space, say through its current minimum C_i, the exploration is biased towards obtaining minima that stay within the goal region. Given C_i, multiple perturbations followed by local optimization are attempted until a C_{i+1} is found which remains in the goal region. While the number of attempts is limited to a maximum of l consecutive failures before the BH exploration returns to its unbiased setting, in practice it is possible to remain in a goal region for a sufficiently large ϵ. The exploration terminates when the goal conformation is approached within some determined tolerance.

The value of ϵ is related to that of l. Moreover, a meaningful value for ϵ depends on the distance metric used and its effectiveness on a particular system. For instance, on small proteins, lRMSD can be used to determine the radius of the goal region. On other systems, instead, other measurements allow circumventing some of the issues with lRMSD. For instance, the TM-score [79] and GDT_TS [80] allow better capturing structural similarities than lRMSD when motions are localized to specific regions. The two are also less sensitive to noise. Familiarity with the system to be modeled allows better determining which measurement should be used and what values will be effective for ϵ and l. As the goal in this paper is to show a proof-of-concept demonstration that BH can be useful to obtain information on minima connecting diverse stable states in the equilibrium conformational space of a protein, we do not devote time to fine tuning parameters. The results in Section 3 show that values exist for these parameters that allow BH to come in closer proximity to the goal structural state in the biased over the unbiased implementation. Further tuning of the parameters is expected to improve the results and provide interesting directions for researchers to explore the viability of BH in this application context.

3. Results

Experimental Setup. The stopping criterion in each experimental setting to evaluate the performance of BH is set to a fixed number of energy evaluations. This number is 10^7 energy evaluations for the application of BH on structure prediction and 10^6 on our last application of connecting between different stable states. Results for the protein-protein docking do not change after $10,000$ conformations, so this number is employed as a stopping criterion. Additionally, m and k are set to 100 and 20, respectively. In the application on docking, different values are tried for δt, $\delta \phi$, $\delta \theta$, and the ones employed for the experiments presented below are 1.5 Å, 10°, and 30°, respectively. On the last application of BH, h is set to 10 trajectories, ϵ is set to a TM-score of 0.4, $l = 100$, and the exploration terminates earlier than 10^6 energy evaluations when the current minimum is within a TM-score of 0.9 of the goal conformation.

We present three main sets of results according to the three different BH applications analyzed here. Where possible, results are compared to those reported by other state-of-the-art structure prediction or protein-protein docking methods (Tables 1 and 2 in the results presented in Sections 3.1 and 3.2, resp.). In addition, analysis of the BH-obtained minima is conducted, and distributions of the distances between consecutive minima are shown. This allows evaluating whether the implementations for the perturbation and local optimization in each application setting preserve the adjacency relationship between consecutively obtained minima. The comparison with state-of-the-art methods and the adjacency analysis employ the least Root-Mean-Squared Deviation (lRMSD) semimetric. Analysis of results obtained on the third application of BH on connecting stable states of a protein molecule employs additional measurements, such as GDT_TS and TM-score (Tables 3 and 4 in the results presented in Section 3.3). The minima sampled by BH in the context of this third application are also visualized on a low-dimensional projection of the variable space (the projection coordinates are detailed below) that reveals where the BH sampling focuses.

The main measurement used in the analysis below is lRMSD. Briefly, lRMSD measures the weighted Euclidean distance between corresponding atoms after optimal superposition of the two conformations under comparison (or configurations, if consisting of more than one polypeptide chain). The optimal superposition refers to the rigid-body motion or transformation in SE(3) minimizing this weighted Euclidean distance [81]. lRMSD captures structural dissimilarity, but it is not a Euclidean metric, as it does not obey the triangle inequality. Low values indicate high similarity, and high values indicate high dissimilarity, but interpretation of intermediate values is difficult. Interpretation has been the subject of many studies [82]. For instance, lRMSD has been found to depend on system size. A 5 Å lRMSD between a computed conformation and the native structure of a short protein chain of no more than 30 amino acids is considered a large deviation, but the same dissimilarity is less significant for a medium-size protein of 100 amino acids or more. Working interpretations abound. In general, for medium-size proteins, if the lowest lRMSD obtained over computed conformations to the known native structure is more than 6-7 Å, the native structure is not considered to have been captured in silico.

TABLE 1: Comparison of the lowest lRMSDs obtained by BH to those obtained by other methods on the protein dimers studied here. MBH refers to monotonic BH. lRMSDs reported by BH, MBH, and the work in [56] in columns 5–7 are over backbone atoms, whereas those reported by the work in [36, 84] in columns 8-9 are over alpha carbons of the backbone chain.

Number	PDB ID	Length	Fold	BH (Å)	MBH (Å)	[56] (Å)	[36] (Å)	[84] (Å)
1	1dtdB	61	α/β	6.9	6.6	7.5	6.5	5.7
2	1isuA	62	α/β	6.3	6.5	6.5	6.5	6.9
3	1c8cA	64	α/β	6.5	5.7	7.2	3.7	5.0
4	1sap	66	α/β	6.5	6.0	7.36	4.6	6.6
5	1hz6A	67	α/β	5.7	6.0	6.6	3.8	3.4
6	1wapA	68	β	7.4	8.1	7.3	8.0	7.7
7	1fwp	69	α/β	6.3	6.7	7.1	8.1	7.3
8	1ail	70	α	3.2	4.2	4.0	5.4	6.0
9	1aoy	78	α/β	5.7	6.1	5.8	5.7	5.7
10	1cc5	83	α	5.8	5.6	5.8	6.5	6.2
11	2ezk	93	α	4.3	5.8	6.0	5.5	6.6
12	1hhp	99	β	10.4	10.5	11.0	NA	NA
13	2hg6	106	α/β	8.8	9.3	9.7	NA	NA
14	3gwl	106	α	4.9	4.9	6.3	NA	NA
15	2h5nD	123	α	7.5	7.8	8.6	NA	NA

TABLE 2: Comparison of the lowest lRMSDs obtained by BH to those obtained by other methods. Systems that are CAPRI targets are denoted by an asterisk.

Number	PDB ID (chains)	Size	BH (Å)	[66] (Å)	[91] (Å)
1	1c1y (A,B)	1376, 658	1.8	1.2	N/A
2	1ds6 (A,B)	1413, 1426	3.4	1.2	N/A
3	1tx4 (A,B)	1579, 1378	2.4	1.4	N/A
4	1www (W,Y)	862, 782	2.6	11.4	N/A
5	1flt (V,Y)	770, 758	2.7	1.5	N/A
6	1vcb (A,B)	755, 692	3.4	0.8	N/A
7	1vcb (B,C)	692, 1154	2.7	13.1	N/A
8	1ohz* (A,B)	1027, 416	2.7	1.7	0.6
9	1t6g* (A,C)	2628, 1394	3.6	1.7	3.8
10	1zhi* (A,B)	1597, 1036	4.6	25.3	3.4
11	2hqs* (A,C)	3127, 856	2.6	29.1	2.5
12	1qav (A,B)	663, 840	2.6	1.4	N/A
13	1g4y (B,R)	682, 1156	4.1	0.8	N/A
14	1cse (E,I)	1920, 522	2.4	0.7	N/A
15	1g4u (R,S)	1398, 2790	3.2	1.0	N/A

However, high values of lRMSD cannot be automatically interpreted to indicate significant structural dissimilarity. Since lRMSD weighs each atom equally, it cannot capture global topology changes and overly penalizes cases where the differences are localized to a specific region of the molecule due to, say, a large-scale motion. For instance, the lRMSD of two conformations can be high even if structural deviations are limited to a loop that has a different orientation in the two conformations under comparison [83]. In such cases, other measurements, such as GDT_TS and TM-score, can be more appropriate. While different in implementation details, these

two scores essentially locate a maximum subset of atoms between two conformations under comparison which are close in space after optimal superposition and minimizes an overall lRMSD-based error. While GDT_TS is reported in %, TM-score is unitless. Both capture similarity, so higher values are better. While lRMSD and GDT_TS depend on system size, TM-scores are found to be more reliable [83], which is why we employ them here in the analysis in Section 3.3 on the third BH application on connecting diverse stable states.

3.1. Analysis of BH-Obtained Decoy Conformations of a Protein Polypeptide Chain. Our realization of the BH framework for the purpose of ab-initio structure prediction is applied to a comprehensive list of 15 target protein systems. These systems, listed in Table 1, range from 61–123 amino acids in length and cover the α, β, and α/β folds. Many of them are selected due to the availability of data reported on them by structure prediction protocols. On these systems, computing 10^7 energy function evaluations takes 1–4 days of CPU time on a 2.4 Ghz Core i7 processor, depending on chain length.

3.1.1. Comparison with State-of-the-Art Methods. Table 1 shows comparisons to state-of-the-art methods in ab-initio structure prediction in terms of lRMSD. Over all minima obtained from each amino acid sequence by BH, the conformation with the lowest lRMSD to the known native structure of that sequence (experimentally obtained structure with PDB ID shown in this table) is recorded, and that value is reported in column 5 in Table 1. To take into account stochasticity, we report in Table 1 the average lowest lRMSD obtained over 3 independent runs. This value is compared to lowest lRMSDS reported by methods that are popular in ab-initio structure prediction [36, 84]. We also compare to data obtained with our previous work on ab-initio structure prediction with a robotics-inspired tree-based exploration

TABLE 3: Initial conformations of calmodulin are in the rows, whereas goal conformations are denoted in the columns. Three measurements, lowest lRMSD, highest TM-score, and highest GDT_TS scores to any of the goal conformations, are reported over the 10 trajectories started from each initial conformation.

PDB	1cfd			1cll			2f3y		
ID	lRMSD (Å)	TM-score	GDT_TS (%)	lRMSD (Å)	TM-score	GDT_TS (%)	lRMSD (Å)	TM-score	GDT_TS (%)
1cfd	6.70	0.57	56	6.48	0.60	50	8.20	0.44	38
1cll	5.84	0.50	43	2.38	0.84	78	6.24	0.53	54
2f3y	6.7	0.47	40	2.50	0.82	74	2.87	0.77	73

TABLE 4: Initial conformations of adenylate kinase are in the rows, whereas goal conformations are denoted in the columns. Three measurements, lowest lRMSD, highest TM-score, and highest GDT_TS scores to any of the goal conformations, are reported over the 10 trajectories started from each initial conformation.

PDB	1dvr		2aky		2ak3		4ake	
ID	TM-score	GDT_TS (%)	TM-score	GDT_TS (%)	TM-score	GDT_TS (%)	TM-score	GDT_TS (%)
1dvr	0.99	99	0.83	74	0.41	25	0.32	20
2aky	0.84	76	1.00	100	0.44	28	0.31	18
2ak3	0.41	25	0.44	28	0.99	99	0.39	25
4ake	0.31	18	0.29	17	0.41	26	1.00	100

method [40, 41]. Monotonic BH (MBH) is also included in the comparisons (column 6).

The results in Table 1 make the case that BH performs just as well as state-of-the-art methods in structure prediction in terms of its ability to obtain low-lRMSD conformations in an ab-initio setting. The role of the energy function may partially explain some differences among the methods, as they employ different energy functions (MBH and [41] also employ AMW). It is interesting to note that, while our realization of BH (which uses a Metropolis criterion to add the next minimum to its trajectory) obtains lower lowest lRMSDs on more proteins than MBH, the performance of MBH is comparable to the other methods in many cases. MBH can be regarded as a special case of the BH framework with the Metropolis criterion, where temperature $T = 0$. The T value we use here for our realization of BH allows a 2.6 kcal/mol energy increase between two consecutive local minima with probability 0.1.

3.1.2. Evaluation of Adjacency Relationship. Adjacency between local minima obtained consecutively by BH is often stated as important for global optimization. Here we show concretely, in the context of ab-initio structure prediction, how this adjacency correlates with the lowest lRMSD reported by BH to the known native structure of each of the protein systems studied. The lRMSD between two consecutive local minima is computed, and the average is recorded for a given protein system. This value is plotted against the lowest lRMSD from the native structure obtained by BH on each protein system in Figure 2. A strong correlation of 94% is observed in Figure 2 between the average consecutive local minima distance and the lowest lRMSD to the native structure. This result suggests that adjacency of consecutively sampled local minima is related to the ability of BH to locate the native structure. Figure 2 shows that, in cases where the average consecutive local

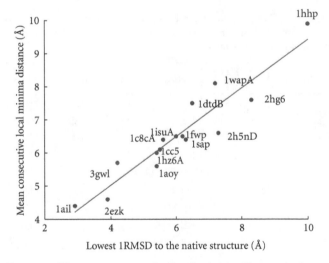

FIGURE 2: The mean consecutive local minima distance is drawn against the lowest lRMSD obtained for each protein.

minima distance is large, BH does not come close to the native structure.

Further detail is provided in Figure 3 on two protein systems. These systems are selected to represent two diametrical cases that correspond to the bottom left and top right portions in Figure 2. The lowest lRMSD structures obtained for each of these two systems by BH are superimposed over their respective native structures in Figures 3(a)-3(b). The entire distribution of consecutive local minima distances is shown for these two proteins in Figures 3(c)-3(d). Figures 3(c)-3(d) further show that, in cases where the majority of consecutive minima are not adjacent in variable space, the overall performance of BH in terms of lowest lRMSD to the native structure suffers. One reason for the poor adjacency is that the fragment replacement may perturb too much

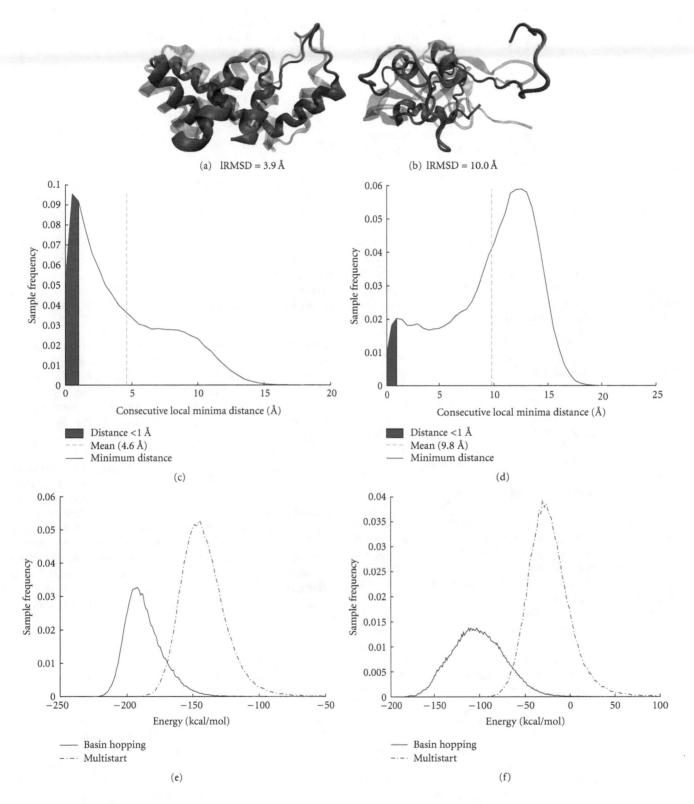

(a) lRMSD = 3.9 Å

(b) lRMSD = 10.0 Å

(c)

(d)

(e)

(f)

FIGURE 3: (a and b) The lowest-lRMSD conformation (in opaque red) is superimposed over the known native structure (in transparent blue) for the protein with native PDB ID 2ezk in (a) and 1hhp in (b). (c and d) The distribution of consecutive local minima distances in terms of lRMSD is shown in (c and d) for the two proteins, respectively. (e and f) The distribution of energies obtained by BH is superimposed over that obtained by the multistart method on each of the two proteins.

of a conformation. In a recent analysis [85], we show that this can be controlled by biasing the sampling of fragment replacements towards those that will result in small structural changes in terms of lRMSD between C_i and $C_{perturb,i}$.

Comparison of BH with Multistart Sampling. Adjacency of consecutive local minima in BH is often stated as a key distinguishing characteristic over a multistart method, where initial points for local optimization are essentially sampled at random over the variable space. Here we show the effect of the adjacency relationship in a concrete setting in terms of the energetic quality of the sampled minima. On the same two protein systems where the above analysis highlights consecutive local minima distances, we show in Figures 3(e)-3(f) the distribution of energies. Figures 3(e)-3(f) superimposes the distribution obtained by BH over that obtained by the multistart method. The results show that BH obtains lower-energy minima than the multistart method. In the context of ab-initio structure prediction, the quality of decoy conformations obtained by BH is superior over that obtained by a multistart method.

Sampling Redundancy in BH. It is interesting to determine how often our realization of the BH framework here comes close to the native structure. We show this visually through a projection of the variable space in a few dimensions. The projection coordinates we choose are based on the ultrafast shape recognition (USR) features [86], which we have employed in previous work to guide a tree-based exploration of the variable space with measurements taken over a low-dimensional projection [40, 56]. These coordinates give a coarse representation of the molecular shape. They are first momenta of distance distributions of atoms in a molecule from selected points on the molecule. The selected (reference) points are the centroid (ctd), point closest to centroid (cst), point farthest from centroid (cfd), point farthest from cfd, and so on. More reference points can be defined this way, but the ones we employ for the visual representation here use only ctd and cfd. It is worth noting that, while coarse, the USR-based projection is fast to compute for each conformation, unlike PCA- or ISOMAP-based decompositions [87–89], which are time consuming and hard to use in an online setting and contain several other shortcomings noted for conformational space [90].

Figure 4 shows the projection of BH-sampled minima over the two USR-based coordinates measured using the ctd and cfd reference points. The projection is discretized so that cells can be defined in a 2d grid for the purpose of measuring how often BH samples similar minima in terms of their coarse 2d USR-based representation. The 2d grid in Figure 4 is color coded with a blue-to-red color scheme that corresponds to cells with low-to-high number of minima projected to them. The cell that contains the projection of the native structure is marked with an ×.

The projection of the sampled minima in this USR-based 2-dimensional space allows visualizing highly sampled regions by BH. The representation is coarse (e.g., cell widths used here for visualization can be made smaller), as

conformations that map to the same cell may be several Å apart, but the projection is useful to draw two conclusions. First, compared to the vast variable space (sea of blue in Figure 4), BH sampling seems to focus in regions near the native structure. These regions represent the equilibrium conformational space. Second, sampling can be redundant; some regions are more populated than others. Future research can address redundancy in order to enhance the capability of BH to sample the equilibrium conformational space of a protein molecular in terms of local minima.

3.2. Analysis of BH-Obtained Decoy Configurations of Protein-Protein Dimers. Our realization of the BH framework for the purpose of protein-protein docking is applied to a comprehensive list of 15 different dimers. These vary in size, represent diverse functional classes, and have been tested by other protein-protein docking methods, and some are even CAPRI targets. Testing is carried out on a 2.66 GHz Opteron processor with 8 GB of memory. Depending on system size, obtaining 10, 000 conformations takes 6–12 CPU hours.

3.2.1. Comparison with State-of-the-Art Methods. Table 2 shows the lowest lRMSD from the known native structure (with PDB ID shown in column 1) obtained by BH in column 3. Lowest lRMSDs reported on these systems by other methods are shown in columns 4-5. System size in terms of number of atoms in each of the chains is shown in column 2. Table 2 shows that BH achieves low lRMSDs to the native structure on each system. Moreover, these are comparable to the lRMSDs reported by other related methods. In particular, the method presented in [66] employs geometric hashing, whereas that in [91] uses long optimizations with a carefully designed energy function that employs information on evolutionary conservation to sample low-energy conformations. In addition to a comparable performance with these methods, BH samples many configurations within 5 Å lRMSD of the native structure (data not shown). These configurations, if selected and further refined in the course of a multistage docking protocol, will allow obtaining the native structure in great detail.

3.2.2. Evaluation of Adjacency Relationship. We investigate here the adjacency between consecutively sampled local minima. Figure 5(a) plots the mean consecutive local minima distance in terms of lRMSD for each protein against the lowest lRMSD obtained to the native structure. A positive correlation of 73% is observed. The mean consecutive local minima distance is less than 15 Å for about half of the systems. While this may seem like a large number compared to the related results on ab-initio structure prediction, the range is larger due to the size of the dimeric systems (lRMSD depends on size). The strong correlation suggests that adjacency of consecutively sampled minima directly relates with the ability of BH to locate a global minimum. Lower lowest lRMSDs (<5 Å) are obtained here compared to the ab-initio structure prediction setting. This is not surprising, as the variable space here is 6-dimensional, whereas the space

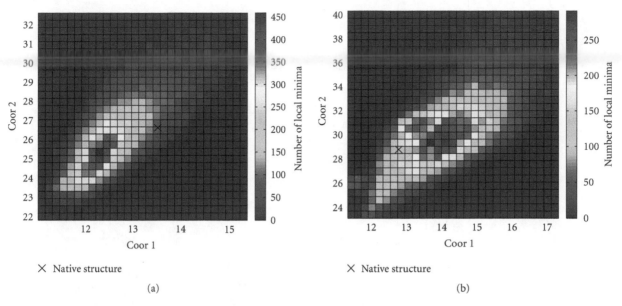

× Native structure

(a)

× Native structure

(b)

FIGURE 4: The 2d grids show projections of BH-sampled minima using two USR-based coordinates (with ctd and cfd as reference points). The projection for the protein with native PDB ID 2ezk is shown in (a), and that for the protein with native PDB ID 1hhp is shown in (b). The grids are color coded with a blue-to-red color scheme to show cells with low-to-high number of minima projected to them. The cell that contains the projection of the native structure is marked with an ×. The range of values of each of the coordinates is estimated as in [40]. Maximum values are based on an extended chain, and minimum values are based on the Flory compact self-excluding model of a chain of n amino acids. To improve visualization, the ranges are limited here, and the grids are clipped to allow focusing to regions with some minimal population.

in the ab-initio structure prediction application contains hundreds of dimensions.

Further detail is provided in Figures 5(d)-5(e), which shows the distribution of lRMSDs between consecutively sampled local minima on two protein systems. These systems are selected to represent two diametrical cases that correspond to the bottom left and top right portions in Figure 5(a). The actual lowest-lRMSD structures obtained on these systems are shown in Figures 5(b)-5(c), super-imposed over the corresponding native structures of these proteins. The distributions in Figures 5(d)-5(e) show that more pairs of consecutive minima with low lRMSDs are obtained for the protein where BH also obtains a lower lowest lRMSD to the native structure.

3.3. Analysis of BH Trajectories in Connecting Diverse Stable States of a Protein.
The unbiased setting of BH is tested here in detail on two proteins, calmodulin and adenylate kinase. Some encouraging results are shown for the biased setting as well, but a detailed investigation of the biased implementation and parameter tuning is beyond the purpose of this work.

3.3.1. Mapping Minima between Stable States in Calmodulin.
Calmodulin is a 144 amino-acid long EF-hand protein that binds calcium and regulates more than 100 proteins, including kinases, phosphodiesterases, calcium pumps, and motility proteins [46–48]. The protein resembles a dumbbell, with the terminal domains linked by a flexible α-helix and the termini in a transorientation from each other on either

side of the central linker. The partial unfolding of the central linker around position 77 gives calmodulin flexibility.

Calmodulin has been captured in three different functionally relevant structural states in the wet laboratory [92–94]. These states are documented in the PDB as X-ray structures under PDB IDs 1cfd (apo state), 1cll (calcium-binding state), and 2f3y (collapsed peptide-binding state). The central helix is fully formed in the calcium-binding state, unfolds in the middle in the apo state, and bends in the collapsed state. Transitions between the apo and collapsed states have been observed both in experiment and simulation [49, 50].

In order to test the unbiased setting of BH in this application, the following experiment is conducted. Each of the structures is obtained from the PDB and employed as an initial conformation. $h = 10$ Bh trajectories are launched independently from any of them. The proximity to any of the other two structures is reported in Table 3. Entry at row i and column j reports the best proximity over the 10 trajectories initiated from structure i to goal structure j.

Proximity to the goal is measured in three ways. Table 3 shows lowest lRMSD, highest TM-score [79], and highest GDT_TS [80]. The results in Table 3 show that BH is able to capture the structure with PDB ID 1cfd (apo) when initiated from 1cll (semicollapsed state) and vice versa (TM-scores above 0.5 are found to capture significant structural similarity [83]). BH also captures the structure with PDB ID 1cll (semicollapsed state) when initiated from 2f3y (collapsed state) and vice versa. A very low lRMSD and very high TM-score and GDT_TS score are obtained from 2f3y to 1cll.

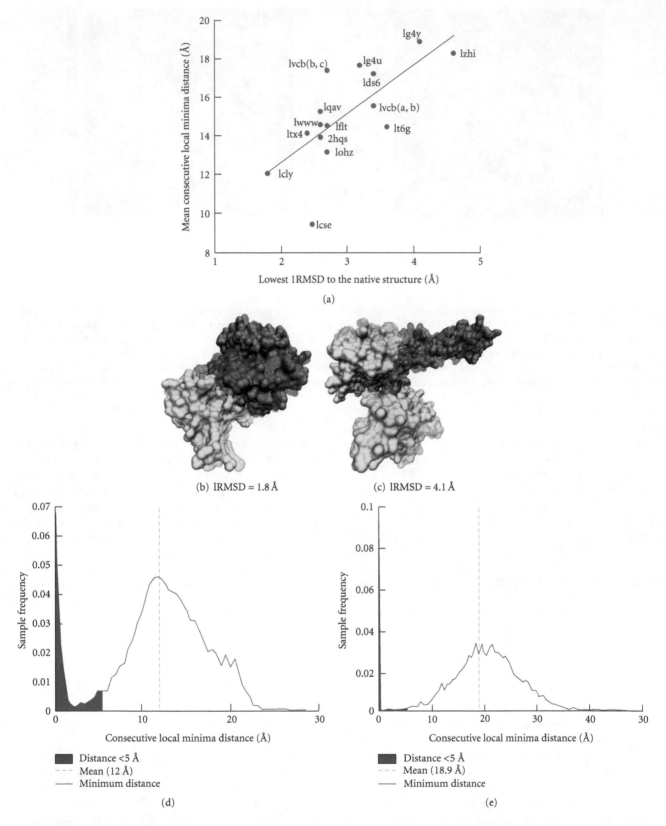

FIGURE 5: (a) The mean consecutive local minima distance is drawn against the lowest lRMSD obtained for each protein. (b and c) The lowest-lRMSD dimeric configuration (in opaque, with chains in different colors) is superimposed over the known native structure (in transparent) for the protein with native PDB ID 1c1y in (b) and 1g4y in (c). (d and e) The distribution of consecutive local minima distances in terms of lRMSD is shown in (d and e) for each of the proteins, respectively.

This is an encouraging result, since 1cll captures a partially closed state, whereas 2f3y captures calmodulin in its close state. Structurally, 1cfd, the apo state, is further away from the semicollapsed and collapsed states. Indeed, all three measurements in Table 3 indicate that BH has not captured state 1cfd from 2f3y and vice versa.

Table 3 also shows values along the main diagonal, which record the closest that a BH trajectory comes to its initial conformation. While this is achieved often through the very first minimum, the structure with PDB ID 1cfd is the only exception. This indicates that this structure is not at a local minimum, and BH quickly steers away from this initial conformation. This may also explain the difficulty of capturing that state when initiated from any of the other two. In addition, analysis of the biased setting for calmodulin reveals that when an ϵ value of 0.4 in terms of TM-score is used, BH is able to come closer to the goal structures. Improvements are around 0.5 Å (data not shown).

3.3.2. Mapping Minima between Stable States in Adenylate Kinase. Adenylate kinase is a 214 amino-acid long phosphotransferase enzyme that maintains energy balance in cells by catalyzing the reversible reaction $Mg^{2+} \cdot ATP + AMP \rightleftharpoons Mg^{2+} \cdot ADP + ADP$ [95]. The protein consists of a CORE domain and two substrate-binding (AMP- and ATP-) domains. The binding domains move and bind substrates independently, resulting in different functional states.

Adenylate kinase has been found in four different structural states in the wet laboratory [96–99]: the apo state, where both substrate-binding domains are open (available in the PDB under PDB ID 4ake), the collapsed state, where both domains are closed (available under PDB ID 2aky), and two intermediate states, where one of the domains is open and the other closed (PDB IDs 1dvr and 2ak3). Transitions between the apo and collapsed states have been observed both in experiment and simulation [76, 100, 101].

Unbiased BH trajectories are initiated from each of the four structures, and the best proximity to any of the other three is reported in Table 4 in terms of TM-score and GDT_TS. lRMSD is not employed, as the chains deposited under the PDB IDs listed above are of different lengths (due to differences in the setup of the structure resolution protocol in the wet laboratory). The results in Table 4 show that adenylate kinase is indeed a challenging system. The BH trajectories manage to come close only to the structure with PDB ID 2aky when initiated from the structure with PDB ID 1dvr and vice versa. This is an encouraging result, nonetheless, because the structures with PDB ID 1dvr and 2aky are structurally closer to each other.

Outstanding Challenges. Calmodulin and adenylate kinase are considered challenging systems for computational investigation due to their large size [33]. The results above support the fact that size limits sampling capability in BH. The upper bound of 10^6 energy evaluations limits BH to sample around $1,500$ minima for calmodulin and $1,000$ minima for adenylate kinase. Considering the small number of minima sampled, the results above are encouraging. They suggest

that, with improvements to enhance the sampling capability, BH is a promising tool for mapping the equilibrium conformational space of a protein and elucidating the connectivity between different stable states.

4. Conclusion

We have shown that BH is a general, versatile framework that allows structural characterization of important biological macromolecules, such as proteins. We have selected three different applications of importance in computational structural biology on which to show the power and promise of the BH framework. Domain-specific expertise is used to implement effective perturbation and local optimization components. Important generally recognized characteristics of the BH framework, such as adjacency of local minima and its relation to the quality of the reported global minimum, are demonstrated in the applications selected in this paper.

Taken together, the results show that BH is an effective framework for structural characterization of protein systems. It is more effective than the multistart method, and the adjacency of consecutively sampled local minima is directly related with the ability of BH to come close to the global minimum. The presented results make the case that BH can be an effective tool for generating good-quality decoys for ab-initio structure prediction and protein-protein docking and a promising framework for mapping the connectivity of functionally relevant states in flexible proteins.

We note that the implementations we offer here for the key components in BH are a first step, and further tuning can result in better performance. Further analysis into different implementations is necessary to obtain a better understanding of the BH framework and its capability to enhance sampling of molecular spaces. We are currently pursuing such a comparative analysis. For instance, in recent work [85] we show that the implementation of the perturbation component employed here is sufficient to escape a current minimum and that the greedy search employed for the local optimization is just as effective but more efficient than Metropolis MC searches at low temperature [22, 102].

The application on proteins with diverse stable states serves as a proof of concept that BH can be employed to map the intermediate minima that connect stable states. The results presented here show that the framework is promising and merits further investigation in this context. The trajectory of minima obtained by BH in connecting two stable states can be considered a coarse conformational path. This path can be transformed into an actual trajectory that takes the protein through specific molecular motions from one state to another. The process is not dissimilar from how paths in robotics motion sampling are converted to actual execution trajectories with dynamics constraints [103]. The coarse transition paths can be refined through, for instance, short steered MD simulations connecting adjacent minima. Other path deformation techniques are available, and this is a direction we will explore in future research.

We believe the exposition of BH in this paper will bring more attention to this framework as a powerful global optimization tool for biological systems. Its versatility, as we show here in the context of three different yet related applications on proteins, merits further investigation. In particular, different implementations for the main components in BH can be investigated to balance between accuracy and efficiency. Moreover, related ideas from the evolutionary computing community on population-based strategies can be employed to promote diversity of minima, as proposed in recent work on geometrical problems [20]. Related ideas from our robotics-inspired search of molecular conformational spaces [40] can be exploited to organize the BH-sampled minima, steer the exploration away from over-populated regions in the variable space, and so enhance the sampling capability in BH.

Acknowledgments

This work is supported in part by NSF CCF no. 1016995 and NSF IIS CAREER Award no. 1144106.

References

[1] C. A. Floudas and P. M. Pardalos, *Encyclopedia of Optimization*, Kluwer Academic Publishers, Norwell, Mass, USA, 2001.

[2] "Nonconvex optimization and its applications," in *Global Optimization: Scientific and Engineering Case Studies*, J. Pinter, Ed., vol. 85 of *Mathematics and Statistics*, Springer Science and Business Media, New York, NY, USA, 2006.

[3] D. J. Wales and J. P. K. Doye, "Global optimization by basin-hopping and the lowest energy structures of Lennard-Jones clusters containing up to 110 atoms," *Journal of Physical Chemistry A*, vol. 101, no. 28, pp. 5111–5116, 1997.

[4] A. Tiano, F. Pizzochero, and P. Venini, "A global optimization approach to nonlinear system identification," in *Conference on Control and Automation*, pp. 752–761, 1999.

[5] A. R. Leach, "A survey of methods for searching the conformational space of small and medium-sized molecules," in *Reviews in Computational Chemistry*, vol. 2, pp. 1–55, VCH Publishing, New York, NY, USA, 1991.

[6] H. A. Scheraga, "Predicting three-dimensional structures of oligopeptides," in *Reviews in Computational Chemistry*, K. B. Lipkowitz and D. B. Boyd, Eds., vol. 3, pp. 73–142, VCH Publishing, New York, NY, USA, 1992.

[7] R. V. Pappu, R. K. Hart, and J. W. Ponder, "Analysis and application of potential energy smoothing and search methods for global optimization," *Journal of Physical Chemistry B*, vol. 102, no. 48, pp. 9725–9742, 1998.

[8] S. Kirkpatrick, C. D. Gelatt, and M. P. Vecchi, "Optimization by simulated annealing," *Science*, vol. 220, no. 4598, pp. 671–680, 1983.

[9] A. Nayeem, J. Vila, and H. A. Scheraga, "A comparative study of the simulated-annealing and monte carlowith-minimization approaches to the minimum-energy structures of polypeptides: [Met]-enkephalin," *Journal of Computational Chemistry*, vol. 12, no. 5, pp. 594–605, 1991.

[10] R. C. Brower, G. Vasmatzis, M. Silverman, and C. Delisi, "Exhaustive conformational search and simulated annealing for models of lattice peptides," *Biopolymers*, vol. 33, no. 3, pp. 329–334, 1993.

[11] W. F. van Gunsteren, D. Bakowies, R. Baron et al., "Biomolecular modeling: goals, problems, perspectives," *Angewandte Chemie*, vol. 45, no. 25, pp. 4064–4092, 2006.

[12] A. Shehu, "Conformational search for the protein native state," in *Protein Structure Prediction: Method and Algorithms*, Rangwala and G. Karypis, Eds., Wiley Book Series on Bioinformatics, chapter 21, Fairfax, VA, USA, 2010.

[13] R. H. Leary, "Global optimization on funneling landscapes," *Journal of Global Optimization*, vol. 18, no. 4, pp. 367–383, 2000.

[14] M. Iwamatsu and Y. Okabe, "Basin hopping with occasional jumping," *Chemical Physics Letters*, vol. 399, no. 4–6, pp. 396–400, 2004.

[15] M. A. Miller and D. J. Wales, "Novel structural motifs in clusters of dipolar spheres: knots, links, and coils," *Journal of Physical Chemistry B*, vol. 109, no. 49, pp. 23109–23112, 2005.

[16] J. M. Carr and D. J. Wales, "Global optimization and folding pathways of selected alpha-helical proteins," *The Journal of Chemical Physics*, vol. 123, no. 23, p. 234901, 2005.

[17] T. James, D. J. Wales, and J. Hernández-Rojas, "Global minima for water clusters $(H_2O)n$, $n \leq 21$, described by a five-site empirical potential," *Chemical Physics Letters*, vol. 415, no. 4–6, pp. 302–307, 2005.

[18] R. Gehrke and K. Reuter, "Assessing the efficiency of first-principles basin-hopping sampling," *Physical Review B*, vol. 79, no. 8, Article ID 085412, 10 pages, 2009.

[19] D. J. Wales, *Energy Landscapes and Structure Prediction Using Basin-Hopping*, Wiley-VCH Verlag GmbH and Co. KGaA, 2010.

[20] A. Grosso, A. R. M. J. U. Jamali, M. Locatelli, and F. Schoen, "Solving the problem of packing equal and unequal circles in a circular container," *Journal of Global Optimization*, vol. 47, no. 1, pp. 63–81, 2010.

[21] M. Locatelli, "On the multilevel structure of global optimization problems," *Computational Optimization and Applications*, vol. 30, no. 1, pp. 5–22, 2005.

[22] B. Olson and A. Shehu, "Evolutionary-inspired probabilistic search for enhancing sampling of local minima in the protein energy surface," *Proteome Science*, vol. 10, no. supplement 1, p. S5, 2012.

[23] O. M. H. R. Lourenco and T. Stutzle, "Iterated local search," in *Handbook of Metaheuristics*, F. Glover and G. Kochenberger, Eds., vol. 57, no. 513 of *Operations Research & Management Science*, pp. 321–353, Kluwer Academic Publishers, 2002.

[24] Z. Li and H. A. Scheraga, "Monte Carlo-minimization approach to the multiple-minima problem in protein folding," *Proceedings of the National Academy of Sciences of the United States of America*, vol. 84, no. 19, pp. 6611–6615, 1987.

[25] K. A. Dill and H. S. Chan, "From levinthal to pathways to funnels," *Nature Structural Biology*, vol. 4, no. 1, pp. 10–19, 1997.

[26] J. N. Onuchic and P. G. Wolynes, "Theory of protein folding," *Current Opinion in Structural Biology*, vol. 14, no. 1, pp. 70–75, 2004.

[27] J. Moult, K. Fidelis, A. Kryshtafovych, and A. Tramontano, "Critical assessment of methods of protein structure prediction (CASP) round IX," *Proteins*, vol. 79, supplement 10, pp. 1–5, 2011.

[28] P. Bradley, K. M. S. Misura, and D. Baker, "Toward high-resolution de novo structure prediction for small proteins," *Science*, vol. 309, no. 5742, pp. 1868–1871, 2005.

[29] S. Yin, F. Ding, and N. V. Dokholyan, "Eris: an automated estimator of protein stability," *Nature Methods*, vol. 4, no. 6, pp. 466–467, 2007.

[30] T. Kortemme and D. Baker, "Computational design of protein-protein interactions," *Current Opinion in Chemical Biology*, vol. 8, no. 1, pp. 91–97, 2004.

[31] V. Hornak, R. Abel, A. Okur, B. Strockbine, A. Roitberg, and C. Simmerling, "Comparison of multiple amber force fields and development of improved protein backbone parameters," *Proteins*, vol. 65, no. 3, pp. 712–725, 2006.

[32] A. Verma, A. Schug, K. H. Lee, and W. Wenzel, "Basin hopping simulations for all-atom protein folding," *The Journal of Chemical Physics*, vol. 124, no. 4, p. 044515, 2006.

[33] A. Shehu, L. E. Kavraki, and C. Clementi, "Multiscale characterization of protein conformational ensembles," *Proteins*, vol. 76, no. 4, pp. 837–851, 2009.

[34] R. Bonneau, C. E. M. Strauss, C. A. Rohl et al., "De novo prediction of three-dimensional structures for major protein families," *Journal of Molecular Biology*, vol. 322, no. 1, pp. 65–78, 2002.

[35] T. J. Brunette and O. Brock, "Guiding conformation space search with an all-atom energy potential," *Proteins*, vol. 73, no. 4, pp. 958–972, 2008.

[36] J. DeBartolo, A. Colubri, A. K. Jha, J. E. Fitzgerald, K. F. Freed, and T. R. Sosnick, "Mimicking the folding pathway to improve homology-free protein structure prediction," *Proceedings of the National Academy of Sciences of the United States of America*, vol. 106, no. 10, pp. 3734–3739, 2009.

[37] J. Debartolo, G. Hocky, M. Wilde, J. Xu, K. F. Freed, and T. R. Sosnick, "Protein structure prediction enhanced with evolutionary diversity: SPEED," *Protein Science*, vol. 19, no. 3, pp. 520–534, 2010.

[38] A. Shehu, L. E. Kavraki, and C. Clementi, "Unfolding the fold of cyclic cysteine-rich peptides," *Protein Science*, vol. 17, no. 3, pp. 482–493, 2008.

[39] M. C. Prentiss, C. Hardin, M. P. Eastwood, C. Zong, and P. G. Wolynes, "Protein structure prediction: the next generation," *Journal of Chemical Theory and Computation*, vol. 2, no. 3, pp. 705–716, 2006.

[40] A. Shehu and B. Olson, "Guiding the search for native-like protein conformations with an Ab-initio tree-based exploration," *International Journal of Robotics Research*, vol. 29, no. 8, pp. 1106–1127, 2010.

[41] B. Olson, K. Molloy, and A. Shehu, "In search of the protein native state with a probabilistic sampling approach," *Journal of Bioinformatics and Computational Biology*, vol. 9, no. 3, pp. 383–398, 2011.

[42] N. Metropolis, A. W. Rosenbluth, M. N. Rosenbluth, A. H. Teller, and E. Teller, "Equation of state calculations by fast computing machines," *The Journal of Chemical Physics*, vol. 21, no. 6, pp. 1087–1092, 1953.

[43] R. Abagyan and M. Totrov, "Biased probability Monte Carlo conformational searches and electrostatic calculations for peptides and proteins," *Journal of Molecular Biology*, vol. 235, no. 3, pp. 983–1002, 1994.

[44] P. N. Mortenson, D. A. Evans, and D. J. Wales, "Energy landscapes of model polyalanines," *Journal of Chemical Physics*, vol. 117, no. 3, pp. 1363–1376, 2002.

[45] M. C. Prentiss, D. J. Wales, and P. G. Wolynes, "Protein structure prediction using basin-hopping," *The Journal of Chemical Physics*, vol. 128, no. 22, Article ID 225106, 9 pages, 2008.

[46] A. S. Manalan and C. B. Klee, "Calmodulin," *Advances in Cyclic Nucleotide and Protein Phosphorylation Research*, vol. 18, pp. 227–278, 1984.

[47] A. R. Means, "Molecular mechanisms of action of calmodulin," *Recent Progress in Hormone Research*, vol. 44, pp. 223–262, 1988.

[48] K. T. O'Neil and W. F. DeGrado, "How calmodulin binds its targets: sequence independent recognition of amphiphilic α-helices," *Trends in Biochemical Sciences*, vol. 15, no. 2, pp. 59–64, 1990.

[49] B. E. Finn, J. Evenas, T. Drakenberg, J. P. Waltho, E. Thulin, and S. Forsen, "Calcium-induced structural changes and domain autonomy in calmodulin," *Nature Structural Biology*, vol. 2, no. 9, pp. 777–783, 1995.

[50] B. W. Zhang, D. Jasnow, and D. M. Zuckermann, "Efficient and verified simulation of a path ensemble for conformational change in a united-residue model of calmodulin," *Proceedings of the National Academy of Sciences of the United States of America*, vol. 104, no. 46, pp. 18043–18048, 2007.

[51] I. Hashmi, B. Akbal-Delibas, N. Haspel, and A. Shehu, "Guiding protein docking with geometric and evolutionary information," *Journal of Bioinformatics and Computational Biology*, vol. 10, no. 3, Article ID 1242008, 16 pages, 2012.

[52] A. A. Canutescu, A. A. Shelenkov, and R. L. Dunbrack Jr., "A graph-theory algorithm for rapid protein side-chain prediction," *Protein Science*, vol. 12, no. 9, pp. 2001–2014, 2003.

[53] M. Zhang and L. E. Kavraki, "A new method for fast and accurate derivation of molecular conformations," *Journal of Chemical Information and Computer Sciences*, vol. 42, no. 1, pp. 64–70, 2002.

[54] G. A. Papoian, J. Ulander, M. P. Eastwood, Z. Luthey-Schulten, and P. G. Wolynes, "Water in protein structure prediction," *Proceedings of the National Academy of Sciences of the United States of America*, vol. 101, no. 10, pp. 3352–3357, 2004.

[55] A. Shehu, "An ab-initio tree-based exploration to enhance sampling of low-energy protein conformations," in *Robotics: Science and Systems*, pp. 241–248, Seattle, Wash, USA, 2009.

[56] B. S. Olson, K. Molloy, S. F. Hendi, and A. Shehu, "Guiding search in the protein conformational space with structural profiles," *Journal of Bioinformatics and Computational Biology*, vol. 10, no. 3, Article ID 1242005, 2012.

[57] J. A. Hegler, J. Laetzer, A. Shehu, C. Clementi, and P. G. Wolynes, "Restriction vs. guidance: fragment assembly and associative memory hamiltonians for protein structure prediction," *Proceedings of the National Academy of Sciences of the United States of America*, vol. 106, no. 36, pp. 15302–15307, 2009.

[58] D. A. Case, T. A. Darden, T. E. I. Cheatham et al., *Amber 9*, University of California, San Francisco, Calif, USA, 2006.

[59] H. Gong, P. J. Fleming, and G. D. Rose, "Building native protein conformations from highly approximate backbone torsion angles," *Proceedings of the National Academy of Sciences of the United States of America*, vol. 102, no. 45, pp. 16227–16232, 2005.

[60] K. F. Han and D. Baker, "Global properties of the mapping between local amino acid sequence and local structure in proteins," *Proceedings of the National Academy of Sciences of the United States of America*, vol. 93, no. 12, pp. 5814–5818, 1996.

[61] H. M. Berman, K. Henrick, and H. Nakamura, "Announcing the worldwide Protein Data Bank," *Nature Structural Biology*, vol. 10, no. 12, p. 980, 2003.

[62] I. Hashmi, B. Akbal-Delibas, N. Haspel, and A. Shehu, "Protein docking with information on evolutionary conserved

interfaces," in *Bioinformatics and Biomedicine Workshops (BIBMW '11)*, pp. 358–365, November 2011.

[63] G. Terashi, M. Takeda-Shitaka, K. Kanou, M. Iwadate, D. Takaya, and H. Umeyama, "The SKE-DOCK server and human teams based on a combined method of shape complementarity and free energy estimation," *Proteins*, vol. 69, no. 4, pp. 866–872, 2007.

[64] D. Schneidman-Duhovny, Y. Inbar, R. Nussinov, and H. J. Wolfson, "PatchDock and SymmDock: servers for rigid and symmetric docking," *Nucleic Acids Research*, vol. 33, no. 2, pp. W363–W367, 2005.

[65] Y. Inbar, H. Benyamini, R. Nussinov, and H. J. Wolfson, "Combinatorial docking approach for structure prediction of large proteins and multi-molecular assemblies," *Physical Biology*, vol. 2, no. 4, pp. S156–S165, 2005.

[66] Y. Inbar, H. Benyamini, R. Nussinov, H. J. Wolfson, and B. Honig, "Prediction of multimolecular assemblies by multiple docking," *Journal of Molecular Biology*, vol. 349, no. 2, pp. 435–447, 2005.

[67] S. Engelen, L. A. Trojan, S. Sacquin-Mora, R. Lavery, and A. Carbone, "Joint evolutionary trees: a large-scale method to predict protein interfaces based on sequence sampling," *PLoS Computational Biology*, vol. 5, no. 1, Article ID e1000267, 2009.

[68] M. L. Connolly, "Analytical molecular surface calculation," *Applied Crystallography*, vol. 16, no. 5, pp. 548–558, 1983.

[69] R. Norel, S. L. Lin, H. J. Wolfson, and R. Nussinov, "Examination of shape complementarity in docking of unbound proteins," *Proteins*, vol. 36, no. 3, pp. 307–317, 1999.

[70] B. R. Brooks, R. E. Bruccoleri, B. D. Olafson, D. J. States, S. Swaminathan, and M. Karplus, "CHARMM: a program for macromolecular energy, minimization, and dynamics calculations," *Journal of Computational Chemistry*, vol. 4, no. 2, pp. 187–217, 1983.

[71] T. Kortemme and D. Baker, "A simple physical model for binding energy hot spots in protein-protein complexes," *Proceedings of the National Academy of Sciences of the United States of America*, vol. 99, no. 22, pp. 14116–14121, 2002.

[72] I. Hashmi and A. Shehu, "A basin hopping algorithm for protein-protein docking," in *Proceedings of the IEEE International Conference on Bioinformatics and Biomedicine (IEEE BIBM '12)*, J. Gao, W. Dubitzky, C. Wu et al., Eds., pp. 466–469, Philadelphia, Pa, USA, 2012.

[73] J. R. Schnell, H. J. Dyson, and P. E. Wright, "Structure, dynamics, and catalytic function of dihydrofolate reductase," *Annual Review of Biophysics and Biomolecular Structure*, vol. 33, pp. 119–140, 2004.

[74] E. Z. Eisenmesser, O. Millet, W. Labeikovsky et al., "Intrinsic dynamics of an enzyme underlies catalysis," *Nature*, vol. 438, no. 7064, pp. 117–121, 2005.

[75] K. I. Okazaki, N. Koga, S. Takada, J. N. Onuchic, and P. G. Wolynes, "Multiple-basin energy landscapes for large-amplitude conformational motions of proteins: structure-based molecular dynamics simulations," *Proceedings of the National Academy of Sciences of the United States of America*, vol. 103, no. 32, pp. 11844–11849, 2006.

[76] Q. Lu and J. Wang, "Single molecule conformational dynamics of adenylate kinase: energy landscape, structural correlations, and transition state ensembles," *Journal of the American Chemical Society*, vol. 130, no. 14, pp. 4772–4783, 2008.

[77] P. Majek, H. Weinstein, and R. Elber, *Pathways of Conformational Conformational Transitions in Proteins*, chapter 13, Taylor and Francis group, 2008.

[78] D. R. Weiss and M. Levitt, "Can morphing methods predict intermediate structures?" *Journal of Molecular Biology*, vol. 385, no. 2, pp. 665–674, 2009.

[79] Y. Zhang and J. Skolnick, "Scoring function for automated assessment of protein structure template quality," *Proteins*, vol. 57, no. 4, pp. 702–710, 2004.

[80] A. Zemla, "LGA: a method for finding 3D similarities in protein structures," *Nucleic Acids Research*, vol. 31, no. 13, pp. 3370–3374, 2003.

[81] A. D. McLachlan, "A mathematical procedure for superimposing atomic coordinates of proteins," *Acta Crystallographica A*, vol. 26, no. 6, pp. 656–657, 1972.

[82] V. N. Maiorov and G. M. Crippen, "Significance of root-mean-square deviation in comparing three-dimensional structures of globular proteins," *Journal of Molecular Biology*, vol. 235, no. 2, pp. 625–634, 1994.

[83] J. Xu and Y. Zhang, "How significant is a protein structure similarity with TM-score = 0.5?" *Bioinformatics*, vol. 26, no. 7, pp. 889–895, 2010.

[84] J. Meiler and D. Baker, "Coupled prediction of protein secondary and tertiary structure," *Proceedings of the National Academy of Sciences of the United States of America*, vol. 100, no. 21, pp. 12105–12110, 2003.

[85] B. Olson and A. Shehu, "Efficient basin hopping in the protein energy surface," in *Proceedings of the IEEE International Conference on Bioinformatics and Biomedicine (BIBM '12)*, J. Gao, W. Dubitzky, C. Wu et al., Eds., pp. 119–124, Philadelphia, Pa, USA, 2012.

[86] P. J. Ballester and W. G. Richards, "Ultrafast shape recognition to search compound databases for similar molecular shapes," *Journal of Computational Chemistry*, vol. 28, no. 10, pp. 1711–1723, 2007.

[87] M. L. Teodoro, G. N. Phillips, and L. E. Kavraki, "Understanding protein flexibility through dimensionality reduction," *Journal of Computational Biology*, vol. 10, no. 3-4, pp. 617–634, 2003.

[88] P. Das, M. Moll, H. Stamati, L. E. Kavraki, and C. Clementi, "Low-dimensional, free-energy landscapes of protein-folding reactions by nonlinear dimensionality reduction," *Proceedings of the National Academy of Sciences of the United States of America*, vol. 103, no. 26, pp. 9885–9890, 2006.

[89] H. Stamati, C. Clementi, and L. E. Kavraki, "Application of nonlinear dimensionality reduction to characterize the confonrmational landscape of small peptides," *Proteins*, vol. 78, no. 2, pp. 223–235, 2010.

[90] M. A. Rohrdanz, W. Zheng, M. Maggioni, and C. Clementi, "Determination of reaction coordinates via locally scaled diffusion map," *Journal of Chemical Physics*, vol. 134, no. 12, Article ID 124116, 2011.

[91] E. Kanamori, Y. Murakami, Y. Tsuchiya, D. M. Standley, H. Nakamura, and K. Kinoshita, "Docking of protein molecular surfaces with evolutionary trace analysis," *Proteins*, vol. 69, no. 4, pp. 832–838, 2007.

[92] H. Kuboniwa, N. Tjandra, S. Grzesiek, H. Ren, C. B. Klee, and A. Bax, "Solution structure of calcium-free calmodulin," *Nature Structural Biology*, vol. 2, no. 9, pp. 768–776, 1995.

[93] R. Chattopadhyaya, W. E. Meador, A. R. Means, and F. A. Quiocho, "Calmodulin structure refined at 1.7 Å resolution," *Journal of Molecular Biology*, vol. 228, no. 4, pp. 1177–1192, 1992.

[94] J. L. Fallon, D. B. Halling, S. L. Hamilton, and F. A. Quiocho, "Structure of calmodulin bound to the hydrophobic IQ domain of the cardiac Cav1.2 calcium channel," *Structure*, vol. 13, no. 12, pp. 1881–1886, 2005.

[95] D. G. Rhoads and J. M. Lowenstein, "Initial velocity and equilibrium kinetics of myokinase," *Journal of Biological Chemistry*, vol. 243, no. 14, pp. 3963–3972, 1968.

[96] G. W. Müller, G. J. Schlauderer, J. Reinstein, and G. E. Schulz, "Adenylate kinase motions during catalysis: an energetic counterweight balancing substrate binding," *Structure*, vol. 4, no. 2, pp. 147–156, 1996.

[97] U. Abele and G. E. Schulz, "High-resolution structures of adenylate kinase from yeast ligated with inhibitor Ap5A, showing the pathway of phosphoryl transfer," *Protein Science*, vol. 4, no. 7, pp. 1262–1271, 1995.

[98] G. J. Schlauderer, K. Proba, and G. E. Schulz, "Structure of a mutant adenylate kinase ligated with an ATP-analogue showing domain closure over ATP," *Journal of Molecular Biology*, vol. 256, no. 2, pp. 223–227, 1996.

[99] K. Diederichs and G. E. Schulz, "The refined structure of the complex between adenylate kinase from beef heart mitochondrial matrix and its substrate AMP at 1.85 Å resolution," *Journal of Molecular Biology*, vol. 217, no. 3, pp. 541–549, 1991.

[100] J. Ådén and M. Wolf-Watz, "NMR identification of transient complexes critical to adenylate kinase catalysis," *Journal of the American Chemical Society*, vol. 129, no. 45, pp. 14003–14012, 2007.

[101] C. Snow, G. Qi, and S. Hayward, "Essential dynamics sampling study of adenylate kinase: comparison to citrate synthase and implication for the hinge and shear mechanisms of domain motions," *Proteins*, vol. 67, no. 2, pp. 325–337, 2007.

[102] B. Olson and A. Shehu, "Populating local minima in the protein conformational space," in *IEEE International Conference on Bioinformatics and Biomedicine (BIBM '11)*, pp. 114–117, November 2011.

[103] H. Choset, K. M. Lynch, S. Hutchinson et al., *Principles of Robot Motion: Theory, Algorithms, and Implementations*, MIT Press, Cambridge, Mass, USA, 1st edition, 2005.

6

A Stochastic Hyperheuristic for Unsupervised Matching of Partial Information

Kieran Greer

Distributed Computing Systems, Belfast, UK

Correspondence should be addressed to Kieran Greer, kgreer@distributedcomputingsystems.co.uk

Academic Editor: Thomas Mandl

This paper (Revised version of a white paper "Unsupervised Problem-Solving by Optimising through Comparisons," originally published on DCS and Scribd, October 2011.) describes the implementation and functionality of a centralised problem solving system that is included as part of the distributed "licas" system. This is an open source framework for building service-based networks, similar to what you would do on a Cloud or SOA platform. While the framework can include autonomous and distributed behaviour, the problem-solving part can perform more complex centralised optimisation operations and then feed the results back into the network. The problem-solving system is based on a novel type of evaluation mechanism that prefers comparisons between solution results, over maximisation. This paper describes the advantages of that and gives some examples of where it might perform better, including possibilities related to a more cognitive system.

1. Introduction

This paper describes the implementation and functionality of a centralised problem-solving system that is included as part of the distributed "licas" service-based framework [1]. The licas (lightweight (internet-based) communication for autonomic services) system is an open source framework for building service-based networks, similar to what you would do on a Cloud or SOA platform. The framework comes with a server for running the services on, mechanisms for adding services to the server, mechanisms for linking services with each other, and mechanisms for allowing the services to communicate with each other. The default communication protocol inside of licas itself is an XML-RPC mechanism, but dynamic invocation of external Web Services is also possible. The main server package is now completely J2ME compatible, meaning that porting to a mobile device should be possible. The architecture and adaptive capabilities through dynamic linking add something new that is not available in other similar systems.

While the framework is built around distributed and autonomous objectives, the system is also useful as a test platform for more general AI problems. As such, a centralised component has been added, allowing for heuristic searches to evaluate the situation and feedback the results. The centralised problem solver uses a hyperheuristic with a matching process at its core. The algorithm and novel nature of the process can be briefly described as follows. The solutions and the problem datasets are randomly placed into a grid and then a game is played to try and optimise the total cost over the whole grid. This is done by matching values across rows or columns. For the current problem only solution evaluations are matched, where to match any two solutions the algorithm must remove any rows that are in-between the two to be matched. The algorithm therefore also removes solutions as well as trying to keep other ones. While matching does not maximise, the algorithm tries to produce the largest overall score and therefore prefers to match higher valued solutions over lower valued ones. The philosophy behind the algorithm is described more completely in [2]. It would work particularly well for problems that might require some sort of symbolic evaluation instead of a numerical one. In that case, an exact evaluation of what value is "better" might not be possible and so some sort of matching evaluation would be required instead.

With regards to licas running information-based services, the purpose of the problem solver is to try to combine distributed sources of information through heuristic search to generate more meaning over the information sources as a whole. The information to be combined can be partial in nature, or change over time. It is therefore difficult to evaluate accurately what pieces of information would belong together. Additional data could make an evaluation better or worse and so some sort of comparison or matching process might be preferred. The hyperheuristic is able to control this process and feed the results back into the network, so that the distributed information sources that are most likely to contain related information can be combined in an efficient and accurate manner. The problem solver itself can actually solve problems using either a hill-climbing approach or the new matching process, but this paper is concerned with the matching process only. This paper describes the new heuristic and considers the system integration details in particular. It also considers the scenarios where the new heuristic would work particularly well and describes how this differs from the more traditional clustering methods. The conclusions will also try to tie this in with a more cognitive model, which is something that the author is currently working on.

The rest of this paper is organised as follows. Section 2 summarises the main features of hyperheuristics and why they are useful. Section 3 discusses the problem of variable selection and some other heuristic algorithms that are commonly used for categorisation. Section 4 describes the new hyperheuristic framework in more detail, including implementation details. Section 5 describes some tests results that show the heuristic working in an unsupervised manner. Section 6 gives some conclusions on the work and Section 7 describes future possibilities in the area of a more cognitive model.

2. Hyperheuristics

Most of this section has been taken from the literature review on hyperheuristics [3]. Many real-world problems that require some level of intelligence are difficult to solve. If all of the potential solutions can be realised, then the best one will be available and can be selected. Often, there are too many potential solutions and so heuristic search is required to estimate what the best solution might be. This is where intelligence is required, to help the heuristic to select what potential solutions should be explored further. The problem solving process is restricted to the information that is available in any potential solution. The search process can then reveal more information that was not originally known, but if the search space is very large, any solution will still only be an estimate or approximation of the true answer. The choice of heuristic that should be used to make this approximation then becomes very important, as different heuristics can evaluate certain concepts better than others. The main goal of hyperheuristics is to develop algorithms that are more generally applicable. Paper [4] is a recent survey of hyperheuristics. As noted in [5], a heuristic can be considered as a "rule of thumb" or "educated guess" that reduces the search required to find a solution. Allowing different types of evaluator to give a more complete picture of what the correct evaluation is. While a single heuristic can get stuck in locally optimal solutions, if several heuristics are compared, then

a more universal picture can be obtained. This can lead to better solutions somewhere else in the search space. The main drawback is that hyperheuristics need to be configured, or fine-tuned with the correct parameter settings, to work well. This is often a manual trial and error process.

The introductory sections in [4] make some interesting points. They note that hyperheuristics were initially developed as "heuristics to choose heuristics". They are not intended to operate on the problem data itself, as a meta-heuristic would do. Instead, they operate on the heuristics that do evaluate the data directly, to select what solutions should be considered at each evaluation stage. With the incorporation of genetic programming, there is also the option of using "heuristics to generate heuristics". The hyperheuristic can select which heuristics are mutated, or changed, for the next evaluation stage. The problem solving system of licas currently only uses heuristics to generate new heuristics, inside a genetic programming framework. Using heuristics to generate new heuristics not only involves selecting heuristics for the next evaluation stage, but also the ability to alter them resulting in a new heuristic not previously available. These sorts of problems can be solved by generating random solutions as part of a search process. Each solution is then changed in some way to improve it, until an optimal solution is obtained. The next stage of each search process is then directed by optimising the new solution set. Genetic programming itself is not inherently hyperheuristic, as it can also be used to represent the problem solutions. The hyperheuristic framework is more likely to use genetic programming principles to mutate existing solutions to generate better ones.

2.1. Hyperheuristics Related to the New Problem Solver Heuristic. This section looks at specific examples of heuristics that are directly related to the new hyperheuristic that is the core evaluator in the problem solver. The paper [6] describes a hyperheuristic framework that is self-organising by using reinforcement learning to order potential solutions. In this case, they apply each heuristic to a candidate solution to determine how it changes. If the solution changes positively, then the change is accepted. This is a perturbative approach, but includes both heuristic selection and heuristic creation or mutation. The low-level heuristics are evaluated through reinforcement learning into positive or negative ones. The positive ones are more likely to produce a positive evaluation and so are placed into a category of hill-climbing heuristics, to try to move directly to an optimal solution. The negative ones are placed into a category of mutational heuristics, which can then be changed to produce different ones.

Paper [7] would classify the new hyperheuristic as an evolutionary mechanism, because it contains a stochastic element and also allows for solution mutations. They note that while this can lead to mistrust in its use, it is also a more natural or bioinspired way of solving a problem. A key factor with this hyperheuristic, or for comparisons with other ones, is where in the process the randomness is applied. In most cases, the low-level heuristics can be changed in a random way, to generate new solutions that are then evaluated by the hyperheuristic for improvements to the current solution.

In this case, the randomness applies to the evaluation process of the hyperheuristic itself. Their own XCS algorithm uses the problem state to determine what heuristic to apply at some stage of the problem solving process. It also however, chooses randomly which problem to solve at each step, and randomness is also used as part of the problem-solving process itself. They also write.

> *"The key idea in hyper-heuristics is to use members of a set of known and reasonably understood heuristics to transform the state of a problem. The key observation is a simple one: the strength of a heuristic often lies in its ability to make some good decisions on the route to fabricating an excellent solution. Why not, therefore, try to associate each heuristic with the problem conditions under which it flourishes and hence apply different heuristics to different parts or phases of the solution process? The alert reader will immediately notice an objection to this whole idea. Good decisions are not necessarily easily recognisable in isolation. It is a sequence of decisions that builds a solution, and so there can be considerable epistasis involved— that is, a non-linear interdependence between the parts. However, many general search procedures such as evolutionary algorithms and, in particular, classifier systems, can cope with a considerable degree of epistasis, so the objection is not necessarily fatal."*

This appears to state that it is not always obvious or clear when a particular solution should be selected. As with nature, some level of randomness can be used to make an incorrect or imperfect selection process more robust. Paper [8] describes a hyperheuristic that also uses a simulated annealing approach for selecting which solutions to search further. The purpose of simulated annealing is also to add a stochastic element, to make the heuristic more generally applicable. The stochastic element can prevent a search from getting trapped in a local minimum, a place that a particular heuristic would naturally evaluate to, based on its limited knowledge. The stochastic element can help to make a decision that lies outside of the evaluation of the heuristic. The unpredictability however means that it can be hit-and-miss. Their algorithm adopts a simulated annealing acceptance criterion to alleviate the shortcomings of hill-climbing or exhaustive search. Their algorithm also uses stochastic heuristic selection mechanisms instead of deterministic ones, which has been shown to be superior for some evolutionary optimisation problems [9]. They evaluate a heuristic to get a score and then use simulated annealing to generate a probability threshold that the score must then match. The better solution score is more likely to meet the selection criteria. Paper [10] is also very interesting and tries to develop a hierarchical clustering algorithm that might be more applicable to the aims of the current project. It also describes other types of categorisation and matching functions not listed here.

3. Variable Selection

Before any entity can be analysed, it has to be determined what the most important features of that entity are. These features are then used to classify or evaluate the entity. This can be a difficult task because an entity could be composed of thousands of different features and so it is important to recognise the most important ones that make it different, or the same, as other entities. Paper [11] describes mechanisms for selecting variables or features from large repositories of unstructured data. These can act as filters, to select what variables or features from a potentially large dataset should be used to actually classify the dataset. It also notes that the most relevant variables are not necessarily the most useful when building a predictor or evaluator and so it is not simply a statistical matter of selecting the most popular variables. It is also possible to select subsets of variables that together have good predictive power. Papers [12, 13] discuss the difference between relevant and useful variables. In [12] they describe that at a conceptual level, one can divide the task of concept learning into two subtasks: deciding which features to use to describe the concept and deciding how to combine those features. The selection of relevant features, and the elimination of irrelevant ones, is one of the central problems in machine learning. Algorithms can range from something like nearest neighbour, which can calculate attribute distances based on all available information, to weighted feature selection, or even techniques for learning logical descriptions. The definition of relevance can mean [12] the following.

(1) Relevant to the target concept.

(2) Strongly or weakly relevant to a sample or distribution.

(3) Relevant as a complexity measure.

(4) Incremental usefulness.

Relevant to a target concept means that a change in the variable's value can change its classification allocated by the target concept. Relevant to a sample or distribution is the same, except for the fact that the variable is then required to be part of the sample, as well as relevant to the target concept. These notions are more important for an algorithm that is deciding which features to keep or ignore. Relevance to just the target concept can sometimes be used to try and prove the algorithm itself rather than its evaluating results. The new heuristic has potential for feature selection and would probably belong to category 2. In particular, for selecting the most appropriate values for certain variables or features from distributed or partial information. These evaluations can be better or worse than the true value and might vary around some distribution or mean of the true value. Each group of features or concepts can also be different in each solution part, but related or derived from a larger set. Sections 4 and 5 describe how the hyperheuristic can be used to try to select the best set of values for this type of scenario, in an unsupervised manner.

3.1. Feature Selection Equations. Existing feature selection usually involves categorising or clustering into distinct groups. This is also often a supervised process, with known clusters being used to train the classifier, so that it can then recognise these clusters in other datasets as well. There are a number of existing equations that can be used to categorise data. Most of these actually belong to clustering algorithms that would try to measure how similar two individual data objects are, although some individual objects can be represented by cluster means. This is not actually what the matching process described in this paper is trying to do and so it already shows a possible difference in the use of the new hyperheuristic algorithm. Some of these equations are as follows.

3.1.1. Euclidean Distance.

This is a linear measurement that is one of the simpler classification metrics. It sums the difference between all attributes of two different input objects to determine how similar they are to each other. The equation can look like [14]:

$$d_{12} = \sum_{j=1}^{k} \left(\pi_{1j} - \pi_{2j} \right)^2, \tag{1}$$

where d is the distance and π_1 or π_2 are the input objects.

3.1.2. Kullback-Leibler Information Divergence.

The Kullback-Leibler information divergence is a measure of the difference between two probability distributions. As described in Wikipedia: it can be used as a distance metric and measures the expected number of extra bits required to code samples from P when using a code based on Q, rather than using a code based on P. The equation can look like [14]:

$$D(p\|q) = \sum_{j=1}^{n} p_j \log\left(\frac{p_j}{q_j}\right) \quad \text{for } p = (p_1, p_2, \ldots, p_n),$$

$$q = (q_1, q_2, \ldots, q_n). \tag{2}$$

This measures distances between probability distributions, instead of single dataset values and is therefore probably more useful for measuring the distance between created cluster groups, than the individual data objects.

3.1.3. Jaccard Coefficient.

The Jaccard coefficient measures the similarity between datasets. It is a set theoretic measure and can be defined as the intersection of the datasets divided by the union of the datasets. For example,

the Jaccard coefficient between T_1 and T_2 can be defined as $|(T_1 \cap T_2)/(T_1 \cup T_2)|$.

Dividing by the intersection scales the result between 0 and 1. If the two sets are the same, for example, the equation computes to the value 1. If there are no elements the same, then it computes to 0. The Jaccard distance measure is then the opposite of this and measures the dissimilarity between two datasets. One drawback of the Jaccard coefficient is that it does not really consider negative input as well.

3.1.4. Rocchio Classifier.

The Rocchio classifier [15] is a similarity-based linear classifier that considers both positive and negative input. Equation [16] can be described as given a training dataset T_r, the Rocchio classifier directly computes a classifier $\vec{c_i} = \langle w_{1i}, w_{2i}, \ldots, w_{ri} \rangle$ for category c_i by means of the formula:

$$w_{ki} = \beta \cdot \sum_{\{d_j \in \text{POS}_i\}} \frac{w_{kj}}{|\text{POS}_i|} - \gamma \cdot \sum_{\{d_j \in \text{NEG}_i\}} \frac{w_{kj}}{|\text{NEG}_i|}, \tag{3}$$

where w_{kj} is the weight of dataset t_k in document d_j, and POS or NEG means that document d_j contained in the training dataset, does or does not belong to the classifier category c_i. A classifier built using the Rocchio method rewards the closeness of a test document to the centroid of the positive training examples and its distance from the centroid of the negative training examples.

3.1.5. Information Theoretic Ranking Using Probability Densities.

Paper [11] gives an example of a ranking equation that can be used with information theoretic criteria. Information theory has to do with data compression and also loss of information through noise. The following is an example of the sort of equation that would be used to evaluate that. This ranking equation can be used to determine the probability of one variable being associated with another one, or some target concept. This relies on probability densities that can be unknown or hard to estimate. With discrete or nominal variables however, it can be written as

$$I(i) = \sum_{x_i} \sum_{y} P(X = x_i, Y = y) \log \frac{P(X = x_i, Y = y)}{P(X = x_i)P(Y = y)}, \tag{4}$$

where $P(x_i)$ is the probability density for variable x at time i, $P(y)$ is the probability density for target y, and $P(x, y)$ is the probability of them occurring together. The value is therefore a measure of the dependency between the target and the variable in question.

3.1.6. Information Gain.

Paper [17] also describes information gain. With this method, both class membership and the presence/absence of a particular term are seen as random variables, and one computes how much information about the class membership is gained by knowing the presence/absence. Indeed, if the class membership is interpreted as a random variable C with two values, positive and negative, and a word is likewise seen as a random variable T with two values, present and absent, then using the information-theoretic definition of mutual information we may define Information Gain as

$$IG(t) = H(C) - H(C \mid T)$$

$$= S_{t,c} P(C = c, T = t) \ln\left[\frac{P(C = c, T = t)}{P(C = c)P(T = t)}\right]. \tag{5}$$

Here, t ranges over present, absent and c ranges over $\{c+, c-\}$. As pointed out above, this is the amount of information about C (the class label) gained by knowing T (the presence or absence of a given word).

3.1.7. Feature Selection Based on Linear Classifiers. As described in [17], both SVM and Perceptron, when used as linear classifiers, output predictions of the form:

$$\text{prediction}(x) = \text{sgn}\left(w^T x + b\right) = \text{sgn}\left(S_j w_j x_j + b\right). \quad (6)$$

Thus, a feature j with the weight w_j close to 0 has a smaller effect on the prediction than features with large absolute values of w_j. The weight vector w can also be seen as the normal to the hyperplane determined by the classifier, to separate positive from negative instances. Thus we often refer to the procedure as "normal based feature selection". One speculates that since features with small $|w_j|$ are not important for categorization they may also not be important for learning and, therefore, are good candidates for removal. A theoretical justification for retaining the highest weighted features is to consider the feature important if it significantly influences the width of the margin of the resulting hyperplane. This is described further in the paper.

4. New Stochastic Hyperheuristic Framework

The new hyperheuristic framework was first introduced in [2]. Essentially, it uses a matching evaluation over a maximising one. However, it also tries to maximise the matching score and so will favour higher scoring matches over lower scoring ones. It also uses a randomising procedure to place all potential solutions in a grid, where any solution can be placed in any position. The matching process then matches solutions by removing any solutions that are between them in the grid and grouping the matched ones together for evolving into a new solution. This process therefore also removes solutions as well as evolving the potentially better ones and in that sense is self-regulating. There are, however, other parameters that need to be set during configuration.

This sort of process might be preferable for the feature selection problem that has been described, or the heuristic might, in general, be more suitable for a different class or type of problem. The clustering heuristics that have been described in Section 3 are intended to categorise similar datasets through a matching process, where the datasets with the most similar characteristics are grouped together. This therefore requires several category types and then several datasets belonging to each category type. The aim of the new heuristic is to try to "optimise some global evaluation" through a similar matching process. This evaluation applies to the data or problem set more as a whole, rather than evaluating each solution as a separate entity. It is more similar to a neural network trying to realise a single evaluation function that maps its input to its output, than several evaluation functions, each mapping a different value set. It is not a case of categorising the different datasets individually into similar groups, but rather, trying to evolve all solutions in the most robust way, in order to arrive at an optimal collective solution value. The whole search space belongs to the same single problem. Some of the best potential solutions can be removed, if it means that other ones match better as a result. Each matching phase is probably also associated with an evolution of the related solutions, to produce offspring that would then more closely match or solve the problem. The correct evolutions are not known beforehand and so it is consistency through matching that is used to decide which solutions to evolve. The idea is that a more robust solution pool will be created, even at the cost of some very good ones and this will lead the search to a better global optimum, when keeping locally good solutions might lead to getting stuck in a local optimum.

4.1. Implementation Details. The problem solving framework has now been implemented as part of the licas system [1]. Licas provides a framework for building distributed service-based networks of information sources, for example. The individual services can self-organise through a novel linking mechanism and can also display autonomous behaviours. The self-organising mechanism is relatively lightweight and essentially stores links from one service or node to another represented by a weight strength. The links are made more accurate through a path description made up of metadata or concepts that relate to the association between the linked services or nodes. So there is not a great deal of computation that takes place to create these links. It is also a highly distributed solution, where one link or association does not have to relate to any other one. It is built up purely through the feedback of the system use and does not use any centralised or knowledgeable algorithm.

The problem solver is then more of a centralised solution. It can be sent the information from the network sources, use heuristic search and evaluations to perform a more complex problem-solving operation and then feed these results back into the network, to allow the sources to update themselves through the more complex search procedure. The problem solver can also be used by itself without the network, to solve any sort of problem using genetic algorithms, where the framework is very extendible with the user's own classes. Figure 1 is a schematic of the general problem solving framework. The problem solving is performed locally and not distributed throughout all of the network services or nodes.

Any test problem can be configured using a test script. The licas system also has a GUI that can be used to run the tests. An information mediator can be used to send and retrieve the information from the distributed sources. Each source can be used to create a service that is initialised with the information and then run on the network. The paths to the data sources can be specified in the script-currently file paths. The mediator then periodically asks the services for their recent evaluations or information and invokes the problem solver to cluster or solve the information set as best it can. The result of this can then be sent back to the services. It is currently turned into dynamic links, to update the network structure.

5. Testing

A set of tests have been created to test the problem solving framework for usefulness as a feature selector. The tests are designed mainly to determine if the problem-solving process

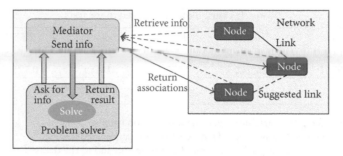

FIGURE 1: General problem-solving framework.

is constructive, that is, it is doing something in an intelligent manner and not simply trying to match things in a random way. The test was as follows: datasets of concepts or features were created. The features were just letters or letter combinations of the alphabet, where each dataset was assigned a random selection of these features. Each dataset therefore had a randomly selected subset of all of the features. Each feature was assigned a random score, but distributed around some mean value. There was a preferred or more common mean value, with a distribution of values either side of it. Each feature therefore had a random score, but more commonly, this score would be closer to the mean value of the distribution. The matching process therefore should match the more common scores and therefore choose those related solutions for evolving further. It would also naturally select certain groups of features for evolving as part of the process.

The evaluation and evolution process in simply an intersection of the dataset features. During the comparison, if both datasets have certain features in common, their distribution from the mean for those features only is calculated and this is taken to be the similarity score. It is also only those features that are then included in an evolved solution. The evolution algorithm evolves using an intersection and so the sums for single datasets will generally be larger than for evolved sets. A hill-climbing approach did not work as well for this type of problem, because maximising the count would prefer the original datasets with all of their features and largest values, over an evolved one with only subsets of those features. The hyperheuristic using a similarity approach, preferred combining datasets with the smallest difference in score, when the evaluation score could be any size. Other evaluation equations were also tried, such as Euclidean, Jaccard, or similarity, see Section 3.1, but the intersection of features proved to be a more suitable approach.

5.1. *Example Test Data.* One example test was as follows: 30 datasets were created randomly. Each dataset contained 20 random features selected from a possible 40 features. Each feature was assigned a random score taken from the distribution described in Table 1. This description shows that there was a mean value of 10 that would be selected 40% of the time. This is indicated by the 0.4 percentage value and the 1.0 distribution value in the centre of the script description.

There was then a distribution, either of values 11–13 or 7–9 that would be selected 17.5% of the time. Either side of the centre value are two sets with 0.175 percentages and then a distribution change of ±3.0. The next distribution was 14–16 or 4–6, selected 7.5% of the time. Finally, the distribution of either the values 17–19 or 1–3 would be selected 5% of the time.

A random process might be expected to produce an average, or 50% deviation, from the true mean value of 10, when selecting variable or feature values. If considering just the difference from the mean value, if 10 separate values are selected then this could be calculated on average as the mean value 10 is selected 4 times, 8 is selected 3.5 times, 5 is selected 1.5 times, and 2 is selected 1 time. Note that 8 selected 3.5 times relates to doubling up on either 8 or 12 (both sides), selected 1.75 times each, and so forth. The difference is being measured here and not the exact total. This gives a total average of

$$40 + 28 + 7.5 + 2 = \frac{77.5}{10} = 7.75. \tag{7}$$

This is a difference of 2.25 from the true mean value of 10. The success of the test was then calculated as follows. Some of the final clusters contained the original solution datasets, while others contained the evolved solution datasets. If the process is constructive or intelligent, then the evolved solutions should be closer to the mean value than the original ones. Therefore the stats calculated the difference to the mean for the original solutions that were part of the final solution set and also the evolved solutions that were part of the final solution set. The original solutions that were included actually had an average difference of possibly around 2.27, which is close to the random average value. The evolved solutions had an average difference of possibly 1.57, which is a 30% improvement on the random or single datasets value. A 30% improvement in something might be good or bad, depending on the particular application or problem. The test data, while random, is not from a real application. So while this might not be able to prove a better approach, it shows that the process is constructive and is doing something intelligent. It is unsupervised and therefore all of the evaluations are taken from the information that is presented at the time. Using the intersection method as the evaluator and evolver is again just for initial results, where further tests could find some improvement there as well.

TABLE 1: Distribution values used in the tests.

Percentage distribution	5%	7.5%	17.5%	40%	17.5%	7.5%	5%
Value distribution	1–3	4–6	7–9	10	11–13	14–16	17–19
Program script	0.05 : 3	0.075 : 3	0.175 : 3	0.4 : 1	0.175 : 3	0.075 : 3	0.05 : 3

---

(1) Read the variable set and the distribution values.
(2) Generate a number of datasets from the set of variables.
   (a) Randomly select variables from the set to add to the dataset.
   (b) Randomly select a count from the distribution, for each variable.
(3) Save the test dataset with a unique name.

ALGORITHM 1: Algorithm for generating the test data.

---

(1) Generate a number of datasets from the spec and random generator.
(2) Read each dataset and generate a test service (and solution) from it.
(3) Evaluate the fitness, or value, of each solution.
(4) Place the solution evaluations in the grid, in a random order, and try to match.
   (a) A match is determined by a pre-defined allowed amount of difference.
   (b) Only a specified number of final matches are kept.
   (c) Also, keep the matches with the larger values.
   (d) Matched solutions are stored as pairs to be evolved.
(5) Evolve the matched solutions to produce a new test set of original plus matched solutions.
(6) The evolved solution can be an intersection or mutation of the original two solutions.
(7) Measure the total average variable value of existing original solutions in the
   final set and the total average variable value of evolved solutions in the final set.
(8) The evolved solutions should have an average value closer to the mean.

ALGORITHM 2: Algorithm for evaluating the test data.

5.2. Test Algorithm. A more complete description of how the new hyper-heuristic framework works is given in [2]. This section includes algorithms specifically for the test that was carried out. The test data was created from Algorithm 1.

The datasets were evaluated and solutions generated based on the Algorithm 2.

6. Conclusions

This paper has described a new type of problem-solving framework, based more on corroborative or matching evidence, than on purely maximising some function. The aims of the current project are to develop a hyperheuristic framework for evaluating information sources, to try to combine sources that might be related. The problem itself however might not be a typical categorisation one, but one that tries to realise some global function over the whole set of problem data. It might be more similar to a neural network trying to realise a single evaluation function than several evaluation functions that each map a different thing. Tests have shown that it could be useful, for example, for selecting feature groups or best values out of partial information sets. Each dataset contains only parts of the whole solution or picture, when combining and evaluating these parts produce new solutions and parts that are closer to the whole picture.

While the data was random, it would still contain certain patterns, based on the created feature groups. This would be strengthened by the count and count additions, associated with each feature and new solution.

The work arose from looking at the problem of aggregating distributed information sources or concepts autonomously, to try to formulate more complex real-world entities. For example, can a sensorised system that is fed information from distributed sources, determine for itself, what concepts it receives are key and belong together as a more complete entity. If the underlying framework is unintelligent, relying more on statistical updates, then the stochastic element could help to provide more robust solutions. Also, because there is no inherent intelligence, there should be no bias towards any particular solution, where the statistical process should determine this for itself.

7. Future Work

The author also has an interest in developing a more brain-like or cognitive model. While the distributed part of this model has been written about recently [18], there is also possibly a centralised part to the model as well. This has been noted and could even be thought of as the consciousness part. If the neurons in the brain form in a purely mechanical way, without any real intelligence, then a more centralised and intelligent part that can interpret the firing neurons might be required. It is also known that the human brain does not store information only once, but duplicates it in different areas. When the neurons fire, either a stronger signal from one set of neurons, or possibly from duplication of the firing pattern in different areas, could determine what the correct thought or decision is. If several areas fire at the same time with parts related to the same problem, this would produce a stronger overall signal and could help to suggest what the correct interpretation is. This is especially useful if the search process is not particularly structured or constructive, that is without a clear search path, for example, when the duplication can help to confirm what the correct interpretation is. This also means that a matching process is more attractive as the decision maker. If the decision is based on a signal strength from one place only, then the actual measurement of this has to be interpreted slightly more accurately and the neuron would need to do more. Although, more inputs to the neuron would also simply change this. If the signal is stronger through duplication however, then a more simple matching process can possibly derive the same conclusion. The author therefore finds the hyperheuristic that uses comparisons more attractive as the centralised component for his current cognitive model. A decision would be formed through more neuronal areas firing relevant signals when the input is received.

References

[1] Licas, http://licas.sourceforge.net/.

[2] K. Greer, "A stochastic hyper-heuristic for optimising through comparisons," in *Proceedings of the 3rd International Symposium on Knowledge Acquisition and Modeling (KAM'10)*, pp. 325–328, IEEE, Wuhan, China, October 2010.

[3] K. Greer, "Literature review for the multi-source intelligence project called "a stochastic hyper-heuristic for optimising through comparisons,"" Distributed Computing Systems Research Report, 2011, http://www.scribd.com/doc/58227009/Hyper-Heuristic-Literature-Review.

[4] E. K. Burke, M. Hyde, G. Kendall, G. Ochoa, E. Ozcan, and R. Qu, "A survey of hyper-heuristics," Computer Science Technical Report NOTTCS-TR-SUB-0906241418-2747, University of Nottingham, 2009, (hhSurvey09).

[5] M. Bader-El-Den and R. Poli, "Generating SAT Local-Search Heuristics using a GP Hyper-Heuristic Framework," in *Proceedings of the 8th International Conference on Artificial Evolution (EA'07)*, pp. 37–49, 2007.

[6] E. Ozcan, M. Misir, and E. K. Burke, "A self-organising hyper-heuristic framework," in *Proceedings of the 4th Multidisciplinary International Scheduling Conference: Theory & Applications (MISTA'09)*, pp. 784–787, Dublin, Ireland, August 2009.

[7] J. G. Marín-Blázquez and S. Schulenburg, "Multi-step environment learning classifier systems applied to hyper-heuristics," in *Proceedings of the 8th Annual Genetic and Evolutionary Computation Conference*, pp. 1521–1528, Washington, DC, USA, July 2006.

[8] R. Bai, J. Blazewicz, E. K. Burke, G. Kendall, and B. McCollum, "A simulated annealing hyper-heuristic methodology for flexible decision support," Tech. Rep. NOTTCS-TR-2007-8, School of CSiT, University of Nottingham, 2007.

[9] T. P. Runarsson and X. Yao, "Stochastic ranking for constrained evolutionary optimization," *IEEE Transactions on Evolutionary Computation*, vol. 4, no. 3, pp. 284–294, 2000.

[10] N. Sahoo, J. Callan, R. Krishnan, G. Duncan, and R. Padman, "Incremental hierarchical clustering of text documents," in *Proceedings of the 15th ACM Conference on Information and Knowledge Management (CIKM'06)*, pp. 357–366, New York, NY, USA, November 2006.

[11] I. Guyon and A. Elisseeff, "An introduction to variable and feature selection," *Journal of Machine Learning Research*, vol. 3, pp. 1157–1182, 1993.

[12] A. L. Blum and P. Langley, "Selection of relevant features and examples in machine learning," *Artificial Intelligence*, vol. 97, no. 1-2, pp. 245–271, 1997.

[13] R. Kohavi and G. H. John, "Wrappers for feature subset selection," *Artificial Intelligence*, vol. 97, no. 1-2, pp. 273–324, 1997.

[14] S. McClean, B. Scotney, K. Greer, and R. Pairceir, "Conceptual clustering of heterogeneous distributed databases," in *Proceedings of the 12th Joint European Conference on Machine Learning (ECML'01) and 5th European Conference on Principles and Practice of Knowledge Discovery in Databases (PKDD'01), Workshop on Ubiquitous Data Mining for Mobile and Distributed Environments*, pp. 46–55, September 2001.

[15] J. J. Rocchio, "Relevance feedback in information retrieval," in *The SMART Retrieval System: Experiments in Automatic Document Processing*, G. Salton, Ed., pp. 313–323, Prentice Hall, Englewood Cliffs, NJ, USA, 1971.

[16] G. Guo, H. Wang, D. Bell, Y. Bi, and K. Greer, "An kNN model-based approach and its application in text categorization," in *Computational Linguistics and Intelligent Text Processing, 5th International Conference, Cicling 2004, Seoul, Korea*, A. Gelbukh, Ed., pp. 559–570, Springer, New York, NY, USA, 2004.

[17] D. Mladenić, J. Brank, M. Grobelnik, and N. Milic-Frayling, "Feature selection using linear classifier weights: Interaction with classification models," in *Proceedings of Sheffield SIGIR—27th Annual International ACM SIGIR Conference on Research and Development in Information Retrieval*, pp. 234–241, Sheffield, UK, July 2004.

[18] K. Greer, "Symbolic neural networks for clustering higher-level concepts," *NAUN International Journal of Computers*, vol. 5, no. 3, pp. 378–386, 2011.

7

Work Out the Semantic Web Search: The Cooperative Way

Dora Melo,[1,2] **Irene Pimenta Rodrigues,**[2,3] **and Vitor Beires Nogueira**[2,3]

[1] Iscac, Instituto Politécnico de Coimbra, Quinta Agrícola-Bencanta, 3040-316 Coimbra, Portugal
[2] Centre for Artificial Intelligence (CENTRIA) and Departamento de Informática, FCT/UNL, Quinta da Torre, 2829-516 Caparica, Portugal
[3] Departamento de Informática, Universidade de Évora, Rua Romão Ramalho, No. 59, 7000-671 Évora, Portugal

Correspondence should be addressed to Dora Melo, dmelo@iscac.pt

Academic Editor: Mladen Stanojević

We propose a Cooperative Question Answering System that takes as input natural language queries and is able to return a cooperative answer based on semantic web resources, more specifically DBpedia represented in OWL/RDF as knowledge base and WordNet to build similar questions. Our system resorts to ontologies not only for reasoning but also to find answers and is independent of prior knowledge of the semantic resources by the user. The natural language question is translated into its semantic representation and then answered by consulting the semantics sources of information. The system is able to clarify the problems of ambiguity and helps finding the path to the correct answer. If there are multiple answers to the question posed (or to the similar questions for which DBpedia contains answers), they will be grouped according to their semantic meaning, providing a more cooperative and clarified answer to the user.

1. Introduction

Ontologies and the semantic web [1] became a fundamental methodology to represent the conceptual domains of knowledge and to promote the capabilities of semantic question answering systems [2]. These systems by allowing search in the structured large databases and knowledge bases of the semantic web can be considered as an alternative or as a complement to the current web search.

There is a gap between users and the semantic web: it is difficult for end users to understand the complexity of the logic-based semantic web. Therefore, it is crucial to allow a common web user to profit from the expressive power of semantic web data models while hiding its potential complexity. There is a need for user-friendly interfaces that scale up to the web of data and support end-users in querying this heterogeneous information source.

Consistent with the role played by ontologies in structuring semantic information on the web, ontology-based question answering systems allow us to exploit the expressive power of ontologies and go beyond the usual "keyword-based queries".

Question answering systems provide concise answers to natural language question posed by users in their own terminology [3]. Those answers must also be in natural language in order to improve the system and provide a better user friendly interface.

In this paper, we propose a cooperative question-answering system that receives queries expressed in natural language and is able to return a cooperative answer, also in natural language, obtained from resources on the semantic web (Ontologies and OWL2 Descriptions). The system starts a dialogue whenever there is some question ambiguity or when it detects that the answer is not what the user expected. Our proposal includes deep parsing, (Deep parsing is directly based on property grammars. It consists, for a given sentence, in building all the possible subsets of overlapped elements that can describe a syntactic category. A subset is positively characterized if it satisfies the constraints of a grammar.) the use of ontologies, lexical and semantic repositories, such as the WordNet [4], and web resources, such as DBpedia [5].

Our goal is to provide a system that is independent of prior knowledge of the semantic resources by the user and is able to answer cooperatively to questions posed in natural language. The system maintains the structure of the dialogue and this structure provides a context for the interpretation of the questions and includes implicit context such as spatial and temporal knowledge, entities, and information useful for the semantic interpretation, like discourse entities used for anaphora resolution, on finding what an instance of an expression is being referred to. The implementation of the system is not complete, the components responsible for search in the knowledge base and interpretation of the questions are implemented, and the modules responsible for generating the semantic representation of the question, the construction of the answer, and the treatment of ambiguities are being developed.

This paper is organized as follows. First, in Section 2, we present an overview on cooperative question answering. In Section 3, we introduce the proposed system, describing the main components of its architecture. In parallel, we present an example as an illustration of the system functionality. Afterwards, in Section 4, we present related work, highlighting the main differences to the proposed system. Finally, in Section 5, we present the conclusions and the future work.

2. An Overview on Cooperative Question Answering

Question answering may be seen as the task of automatically answering a question posed in natural language. To find the answer to a question, a question answering system may use either a prestructured database or a collection of natural language documents. The domain of search could vary from small local document collections to internal organization documents, to compiled news wire reports, even to the World Wide Web. Therefore, we can say that a question answering system provides precise answers to user questions by consulting its knowledge base.

The first question-answering systems were developed in the 1960s and they were basically natural language interfaces to expert systems that were tailored to specific domains. The advent of internet has reintroduced the need for user-friendly querying techniques that reduce information overflow and poses new challenges to the research in automated question answering.

The most important question answering application areas are information extraction from the entire web, online databases, and inquiries on individual websites. Current question answering [3] systems use text documents as their underlying knowledge source and combine various natural language processing techniques to search for the answers. In order to provide users with accurate answers, question answering systems need to go beyond lexical-syntactic analysis to semantic analysis, processing of texts, and knowledge resources. Moreover, question answering systems equipped with reasoning capabilities can derive more adequate answers by resorting to knowledge representation and reasoning systems like description logic and ontologies. A survey on ontology-based question answering is presented in [6]. A study on the usability of natural language interfaces and natural language query languages, over ontology-based knowledge, for the end-users is presented in [7]. To that end, the authors introduce four interfaces each allowing a different query language and present a usability study benchmarking these interfaces. The results of the study reveal

a clear preference for full natural language query sentences with a limited set of sentence beginnings over keywords or formal query languages.

Several recent conferences and workshops have focused on aspects of the question answering research area. Starting in 1999, the Text Retrieval Conference (TREC) (http://trec.nist.gov/) has sponsored a question answering track which evaluates systems that answer factual questions by consulting the documents of the TREC corpus. A number of systems in this evaluation have successfully combined information retrieval and natural language processing techniques. In [8], the authors present some reviews and compare three main question answering approaches based on natural language processing, information retrieval, and question templates, eliciting their differences and the context of application that best suits each of them.

Cooperative question answering is an automated question answering in which the system, taking as the starting point an input query, tries to establish a controlled dialogue with its user, that is, the system collaborate automatically with users to find the information that they are seeking. These systems provide users with additional information, intermediate answers, qualified answers, or alternative queries. One form of cooperative behavior involves providing associated information that is relevant to a query. Relaxation generalizing a query to capture neighboring information is a means to obtain possibly relevant information. A cooperative answering system described in [9] uses relaxation to identify automatically new queries that are related to the original query. A study on adapting machine-learning techniques defined for information extraction tasks to the slightly different task of answer extraction in question answering systems is presented in [10]. The authors identified the specificities of the systems and also tested and compared three algorithms, assuming an increasing abstraction of natural language texts. A semantic representation formalism dedicated to cooperative question answering systems is presented in [11, 12], which is based on the lexical conceptual structure and represents in an homogeneous way web texts, natural language questions and their related answers, and a different mode of cooperative response are presented. The author also presents and analyzes the prerequisites to the construction of cooperative responses in term of resources, knowledge, and process. In order to enhance cooperative question answering the author in [13] presents a spectrum of techniques for improving question answering, and discusses their potential uses and impact.

A cooperative answer [14, 15] to a query is an indirect answer that is more helpful to the user than a direct, literal answer would be. A cooperative answer may explain the failure of a query to produce results and/or suggest follow-up queries. In the case where a query does produce results, a cooperative answer may provide additional information not explicitly requested by the user. Cooperative answers arose in the context of natural language question answering and they were originally motivated by the desire to follow the conventions of human conversation in human machine interactions performed in natural language. In fact, a cooperative answer generation is preferable to answer extraction for the purpose of answering: firstly, it humanizes the system; second, it permits the usage of adapted vocabulary; finally, it allows the introduction of information that the user did not explicitly request, but might be interested in.

There are some examples of works that try to build answers, instead of merely extract and retrieve. In [16], the authors proposed a model of question answering, where the system tries, from an input query, to establish a controlled dialogue with its user. In the dialogue, the system tries to identify and to suggest to the user new queries related to the input query. The dialogue control is based on the structure of the concepts stored in the knowledge base, on domain restrictions, and on specific constraining rules. The authors in [17] present a prototype system that gives cooperative answers, corrects misconceptions, and attempts to meet users' needs, which uses semantic information about the database to formulate coherent and informative answers. The main features of lexicalisation strategies deployed by humans in question answering tasks is presented in [18]. The authors also show how these strategies can be reproduced in automated question answering systems, in particular in Intelligent Cooperative Question-Answering Systems. A method to search for answers which are in the neighborhood of the user's original query could be used to produce responses that will serve the user's needs are presented in [19].

Advanced reasoning for question answering systems raises new challenges since answers are not only directly extracted from texts or structured databases but also constructed via several forms of reasoning in order to generate answer explanations and justifications. Integrating knowledge representation and reasoning mechanisms allows, for example, to respond to unanticipated questions and to resolve situations in which no answer is found in the data sources. Cooperative answering systems are typically designed to deal with such situations by providing useful and informative answers. These systems should identify and explain false presuppositions or various types of misunderstandings found in questions.

3. Proposed System

Very briefly, the proposed system receives a natural language question and translates it into a semantic representation using Discourse Representation Structures (DRS) (For us a DRS is a set of referents, universally quantified variables and a set of conditions (first-order predicates). The conditions are either atomic (of the type $P(u_1, \ldots, u_n)$ or $u_1 = u_2$) or complex (negation, implication, disjunction, conjunction or generalized quantifiers) . Then, after consulting the semantic sources of information, it provides a natural language answer. If there are multiple answers to the question posed (or to the similar questions for which DBpedia contains answers), they will be grouped according to their semantic meaning, providing a more cooperative, informative, and clear answer to the user. Therefore, we consider that our system provides a user friendly interface.

Our system implementation is based on logic programming, more specifically, Prolog with several extensions and libraries. Among the reasons for such choice is the fact that there is a wide range of libraries for querying and processing of OWL2 ontologies, WordNet has an export for Prolog, and there are extensions that allow us to incorporate the notion of context into the reasoning process. Moreover, Wielemaker [20] provides a study for query translation and optimization more specifically the SeRQL RDF query language, where queries are translated to Prolog goals, optimized by reordering literals. Finally, in [21], the authors describe how to develop a semantic web application entirely in Prolog.

At this moment, our system is under development. The modules that are implemented are the Ontology Discovery and the Semantic Evaluation and the components that are not completed are the Discourse Controller module and the DRS generator. Our system architecture is presented in Figure 1 and to help its understanding, we describe the main components in the following subsections.

3.1. Semantic Interpretation. Semantic analysis (or interpretation) is built using first-order logic [22] extended with generalized quantifiers [23]. We take special care with the discourse entities in order to have the appropriate quantifier introduced by the determinant interpretation. At this step, the syntactic structure of the question is rewritten into a DRS, that is supported by Discourse Representation Theory [24].

The implementation of this component follows an approach similar to the one for constructing a question answering system over documents databases proposed in [25]. The system consists of two separated modules: preliminary analysis of the documents (information extraction) and processing questions (information retrieval). The system is looking for processing the corpus and the questions, supported by theories of computational linguistics: syntactic analysis (grammatical restrictions) using deep parsing, followed by semantic analysis using the Theory of Discourse Representation, and finally the semantic (pragmatic) interpretation using ontology and logical inference. At this moment, the implementation of this module is still under development. Many of the parts are still done manually, such as the transformation of syntactic structure into its representation DRS. We use the C&C CCG parser (http://svn.ask.it.usyd.edu.au/trac/candc/) to obtain the syntactic structure of the question.

As an illustration, consider the question "All French romantic writers have died?." The syntactic analysis generates a derivation tree, obtained from grammatical interpretation, that is rewritten according to a set of rules and integrated into a DRS, expressed in Prolog facts. In our study, it is stated by the following representation structure:

```
drs ([all-X, exist-Y],[writer(Y),
french(Y), romantic(Y)],

[die(X), is(X,Y)]).
```

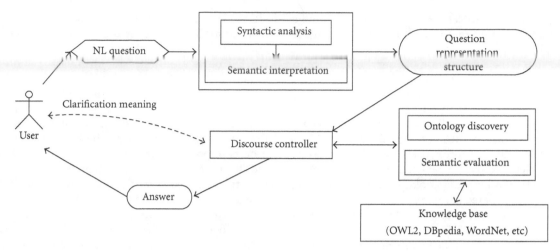

FIGURE 1: Question Answering System Architecture.

where the referent of the discourse is `all-X`, with `X` an universally quantified discourse entity, the main predications of the question are `die(X)`, `is(X,Y)` and the presupposed predications are `writer(Y)`, `French(Y)`, `romantic(Y)`, with `Y` an existential quantified discourse entity. The system has to find and check, for those entities `Y` that verify all the question presupposed conditions, if all entities `X` (that are entities `Y`) verify the main predication condition. If this is true, the answer to the question will be affirmative and, in order to provide a more informative answer, the system also may present a list with all French, romantic, writers resource entities that died.

3.2. Ontology Discovery. The Ontology Discovery is guided by the Discourse Controller to obtain the extension of sentence representation along with the reasoning process. The reasoning context and the question meaning will change whenever the Discourse Controller reaches a dead end.

This system module looks for similarities between labels according to their string-based, taking into account abbreviations, acronyms, domain, and lexical knowledge. To maximize recall, the ontology searches for classes, properties or instances that have labels matching a search term either exactly or partially and if an answer is not achieved, each term in the query is extended with its synonyms, hypernyms, and hyponyms obtained from WordNet [26]. Afterwards, we extract a set of semantic resources which may contain the information requested.

Continuing the example of the previous section, in order to obtain the extension of sentence representation along the reasoning process, the system has to find the classes, properties or instances that have labels matching the search terms "writer", "French", "romantic" and "died", either exactly or partially. So, the system has to find the answers to the following questions:

(i) Which Classes, Properties or Instances Represent the Concept 'Writer'? The system finds the DBpedia property

`Writer` (http://dbpedia.org/ontology/Writer), with property domain `Work` and property range `Person`. These domains inform the system about the class properties and can confirm whether this is related with the question, if not will be thrown away and a new search will be made. For instance, at the grammatical interpretation step, one of the presuppositions found was that the entities that verify the question have to be persons. So, if the class `Writer` has not a relation with the class `Person`, or can not be applied to persons, at the phase of semantic interpretation it would not be added to the set of facts that represent the information provided by the question and wouldn't be considered in the construction of the answer;

(ii) Which Classes, Properties or Instances Represent the Concept "French"? The DBpedia has a class `birthPlace` (http://dbpedia.org/ontology/birthPlace) (an entity of type `ObjectProperty`, with property domain `Person` and property range `Place`) that represents the place where some persons were born. The term "french" is also interpreted as a "person of France" and has as a direct hypernym the term "country" (obtain from WordNet), so the system also has to find the classes, properties or instances of all similar meanings to the initial term that could lead to the correct answer;

(iii) Which Classes, Properties or Instances Represent the Concept "Romantic"? The system finds the DBpedia resource Romanticism (http://dbpedia.org/resource/Romanticism) (an entity of type Thing, a value of property movement (http://dbpedia.org/property/movement)—value of triples with property movement);

(iv) Which Classes, Properties or Instances Represent the Concept 'Die'? The DBpedia has a class `deathDate` (http://dbpedia.org/ontology/deathDate) (an entity of type `DatatypeProperty`, with property domain `Person` and property range `date`) that represents the death date of a person. The relation between the terms "die" and "death" can

be made by searching WordNet, where the term "die" can be interpreted as a "decease," that in turn has as synonym the term "death".

The next step is the construction of query(ies) needed to verify the initial question. These queries are obtained using a set of inference rules translated in automated Prolog queries that allow the verification of the terms consistency. At this moment, we use only the DBpedia Ontology that covers over 320 classes which form a subsumption hierarchy and are described by 1,650 different properties. To make knowledge base more complete, we also use SPARQL endpoints to query the DBpedia RDF and DBpedia Lookup Service for looking up DBpedia URIs by related keywords.

The prolog queries have to find the RDF triples that allow to relate the terms found. The terms http://dbpedia.org/ontology/Writer and http://dbpedia.org/resource/Romanticism are related and could be considered valid to continuing the process because the knowledge base contains the resource http://dbpedia.org/page/Victor_Hugo, which is one resource entity that verifies the presuppositions and main predicates of the question, appears in the triples

```
<http://dbpedia.org/resource/
  Victor_Hugo>

 <http://dbpedia.org/property/
   movement>

  <http://dbpedia.org/resource/
   Romanticism>.


<http://dbpedia.org/resource/
  Victor_Hugo>

 <http://www.w3.org/1999/02/22-rdf-
  syntax-ns#type>

  <http://dbpedia.org/ontology/
   Writer>.
```

If the question does not have an answer, a set of similar questions is constructed. Querying the WordNet, the system obtains similar terms to those that compose the initial question. This set of similar questions will enrich the knowledge domain and helps the interpretation of the original question or in the construction of its answer. If this set of new questions leads the system to different answers, we are in the presence of an ambiguity and the user is invoked to clarify it. If the system did not find any correspondence to a word and its derivatives, the user is informed and can clarify the system by reformulating the question or presenting other query(ies).

3.3. Semantic Evaluation. Semantic evaluation is intended to be the pragmatic evaluation (The pragmatic evaluation is the capacity to judge or calculate the quality, importance, amount or value of problem solutions that are solved in a realistic way which suits the present conditions rather than obeying fixed theories, ideas or rules.) step of the system, where the semantic question is transformed into a constraint

satisfaction problem. This is achieved by adding conditions that constrain the discourse entities. Moreover, this extra information (regarding the question interpretation) can help the Discourse Controller to formulate a more objective answer.

The semantic evaluation must reinterpret the semantic representation of the sentence based on the ontology considered in order to obtain the set of facts that represent the information provided by the question. Therefore, the process responsible for the semantic interpretation receives the DRS of the question and interprets it in a knowledge base with rules derived from the ontology and the information contained in the knowledge base like DBpedia and WordNet.

Back to our example, to solve the constraint problem the Dialogue Controller generates and poses questions such "Who are the French romantic writers?" to the question answering system, whose representation structure is

```
drs([wh-X,exist-Y],[writer(Y),
french(Y), romantic(Y)],
[person(X), is(X,Y)]).
```

First and according to the domain knowledge, the interpreter will transform the conditions of the DRS into OWL, that is, constructs the related predicates based in the ontology. For instance, the condition ontology_writer(The condition ontology_term represents the class, property or instance in the ontology that is the meaning of the term. If the interpreter has more than one possible ontology conditions for each term then will get several DRS rewritten with the terms of the ontology.) represents the DRS condition writer. Therefore, the new representation structure for the question is

```
drs([wh-X,exist-Y],[ontology_writer(Y),
ontology_french(Y),
ontology_romantic(Y)],
[ontology_person(X), is(X,Y)]).
```

After obtaining this new set of DRS, the terms of the ontology will be interpreted as usual Prolog predicates. Then, by applying the unification mechanism of Prolog, the system will obtain the following set of entities that verify the question:

```
Francois-Rene de Chateaubriand,

Alphonse de Lamartine,

Alfred de Musset,

Victor Hugo

Henri-Marie Beyle, Stendhal.
```

The search is done thoroughly and with the aim of finding all entities that verify the question "Who are the French romantic writers?". These entities verify the presuppositions predicates of the original question, that is, entities that are French romantic writers. Afterwards, the system has to verify that which of these entities check the main predicate die. Then, each solution is added to the set of knowledge. On the other hand, if any of these entities do not verify the main predicates, means that the answer to the initial question is negative and the system must justify the answer to the user. Thus, these entities are also added to the set of knowledge, marked with the information that verifies only the predicates pressupositions.

When the system completes the process of finding an answer to the initial question, it will produce a response according to their type. The initial question "All French romantic writers have died?" is a yes/no question and since all entities that verify the presupposition predicates also verify the main predicates the answer to the question will be affirmative. To provide a more cooperative and informative question, the system will show the list of entities found that verify the question.

3.4. *Discourse Controller.* The Discourse Controller is a core component that is invoked after the natural language question has been transformed into its semantic representation. Essentially, the Discourse Controller tries to make sense of the input query by looking at the structure of the ontology and the information available on the semantic web, as well as using string similarity matching and generic lexical resources (such as WordNet).

In Figure 2, we represent the architecture of the Discourse Controller. In outline, after transforming the natural language question into its semantic representation, the Discourse Controller is invoked and controls all the steps until the end, that is, until the system can return an answer to the user. More specifically, the Ontology Discover, is invoked in order to provide the extension of sentence representation. If the ontology representation of a term is not found, the Discourse Controller is alerted and the user is called to clarify it. When the extension of the sentence representation is complete, the Discourse Controller adds to his knowledge a set of semantic resources. Afterwards, the Semantic Evaluation is invoked. In this step, the question semantic is transformed into a constraint satisfaction problem by adding conditions that constraint the discourse entities. This extra information can help the Discourse Controller to formulate a more objective answer. If in the interpretation of all the information leads the Discourse Controller to an empty answer or to multiple answers, the user is called to clarify it and may be necessary to reinvoke the Ontology Discover. The process is finalized when the Discourse Controller is able to return an answer to the question posed by the user.

The Dialogue Controller deals with the set of discourse entities and is able to compute the question answer. It has to verify the question presupposition, choose the sources of knowledge to be used, and decide when the answer has been achieved, or to iterate using new sources of knowledge. The decision of when to relax a question in order to justify the answer and when to clarify a question and how to clarify it also taken by in this module.

Whenever the Discourse Controller isn't sure how to disambiguate between two or more possible terms or relations in order to interpret a query, it starts a dialogue with the user and asks him for disambiguation. The clarification done by the user will be essential for the Discourse Controller; this way is used to obtain the right answer to the query posed by the user. For instance, the question "Where is the Taj Mahal?", "Taj Mahal" could be mapped into the name of a Mausoleum, a Casino Hotel or an Indian Restaurant and only the user can clarify about the intended meaning. The more cooperative and interactive the Discourse Controller is, the closer it will be to the correct answer.

Another important aspect of the Discourse Controller is to provide a friendly answer to the user. The answer should be as close as possible to the natural language. For instance, the question answering system has to respond "yes" or "no" when the user posed the query "Is Barack Obama the President of the USA?". In this case, the answer will be "yes". However, the answer must be more informative for the user. Some concepts are defined in the temporal context, even if implicitly, and the answer should be more clear and informative. For instance, the term "President", in the context of the question, is defined as the title of head of state in some republics and has an associated duration for the mandate, a start date (date of election, date of taking office), and an end date of the mandate. So the answer to the question "Is Barack Obama the President of the USA?" should be "Yes, Barack Obama is the actual President of USA," that is more cooperative and informative.

For the cases where the answer to a question of type Yes/No is "No", the Discourse Controller will return a complete answer, clarifying the negation. If we consider the question "All the capitals of Europe have more than 200,000 inhabitants?" that has a "No" as an answer, the system will construct the proper answer that clarifies the user and will return "No, 9 capitals of Europe have less than or equal to 200,000 inhabitants".

If there are multiple answers to the question posed by the user (or to the similar questions for which DBpedia contains answers), they will be grouped according to their semantic meaning, providing a more cooperative and clean answer to the user. To do so, the discourse controller has to reason over the question and constructs the answer, well constructed questions have always the right words that help in the answer construction. For the question "Where is the Taj Mahal?", the user is called to clarify the system about the ambiguity of the question: Taj Mahal is a Mausoleum, a restaurant or Casino Hotel; consider that the user is not able to clarify it or he simply wants that the system returns all possible answers. So, when the system has all the answers to all possible interpretations for the question posed by the user, the Discourse Controller will not list the answer in a random way, but will list the answer according to their semantic meaning. To this purpose, first the system rearranges the set of solutions by grouping them according to their semantic meaning. Then all solutions will be listed according to their natural order placed in the set of solutions. One possible output for the question "Where is the Taj Mahal?" might be

```
Mausoleum Taj Mahal is in Agra, India,

Casino hotel Taj Mahal is in Atlantic
City, NJ, USA,
```

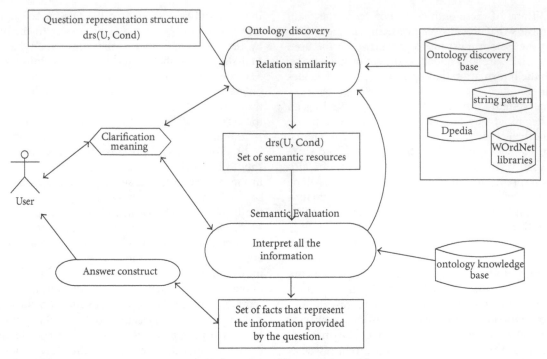

FIGURE 2: Discourse Controller Module Architecture.

Indian Restaurant Taj Mahal is in New Farm, Brisbane, Australia,

Indian Restaurant Taj Mahal is in 7315 3rd Ave., Brooklyn, NY, USA.

Our dialogue system has as main goal the use of interaction to obtain more objective and concrete answers. It is used not only to clarify the problems of ambiguity, but also to help finding the path to the correct answer. Making the dialogue system more cooperative makes one able to get closer to the answer desired by the user. In many cases, the user is the only one who can help the system in the deduction and interpretation of information.

4. Related Work

The representation of questions with generalized quantifiers as in [27] allows the use of various natural language quantifiers like all, at least 3, none, and so forth. Moreover, the question evaluation also resorts to logic programming with constraints.

A query language for OWL based on Prolog is presented in [28]. The author proposes a way of defining a query language based on a fragment of description logic and a way of mapping it into Prolog by means of logic rules.

An illustration of a question answering system for the Portuguese language that uses the web as a database, through metasearch on conventional search engines can be seen in [29]. This system uses surface text patterns to find answers in the documents returned by search engines. Another example of a question answering system where domain knowledge is represented by an ontology can be found in [30]: it is presented in an interface system for question

answering Chinese natural language that runs through a natural language parser.

In [31], we find a declarative approach to represent and reason about temporal contextual information. In this proposal, each question takes place in a temporal context and that context is used to restrict the answer.

The fundamental techniques for computing semantic representations for fragments of natural language and performing inference with the result are presented in [32]. The primary tools used are first-order logic and lambda calculus, where all the techniques introduced are implemented in Prolog. The authors also show how to use theorem provers and model builders in parallel to deal with natural language inference.

PowerAqua [33] is a multiontology-based question answering system that takes as input queries expressed in natural language and is able to return answers drawn from relevant distributed resources on the semantic web. PowerAqua allows the user to choose an ontology and then ask natural language queries related to the domain covered by the ontology. The system architecture and the reasoning methods are completely domain-independent, relying on the semantics of the ontology, and the use of generic lexical resources, such as WordNet.

An overview of cooperative answering in databases is presented in [34]. A logic-based model for an accurate generation of intensional responses within a cooperative question answering framework is proposed by the author of [35]. The author developed several categories of intensional forms and a variable depth intensional calculus that allows for the generation of intensional responses at the best level of abstraction and shows that it is possible to generate natural responses on a template basis. The same author in [36] presents an approach for designing a logic-based question answering system, WEBCOOP, that integrates knowledge representation and advanced reasoning procedures to generate cooperative responses to natural language queries on the web. This project was developed on a relatively limited domain that includes a number of aspects of tourism (transportation) and requires the development of a knowledge extractor from web pages (similarly to a knowledge extractor operating on passages resulting from an information retrieval component) and the elaboration of a robust and accurate question parser. The responses provided to users are built in web style by integrating natural language generation techniques with hypertexts in order to produce dynamic responses. Natural language responses are produced from semantic forms constructed from reasoning processes.

Our proposal is a friendly, simple, and cooperative question-answering system. The main difference is the cooperative way that answers the natural language questions posed by the user. We interact with the user in order to disambiguate and/or to guide the path to obtain the correct answer to the query posted, whenever this is possible to do by the reasoner. We also use cooperation to provide more informed answers. The answers are presented in natural language and have to clarify what the system can infer about the question from the knowledge domain. Therefore, the cooperative answer provided by our system has to explain the failure of a query to produce results and/or suggest follow-up queries. In the case where a query does produce results, the cooperative answer will provide additional information not explicitly requested by the user.

5. Conclusions and Future Work

We presented a cooperative semantic web question answering system that receives queries expressed in natural language and is able to return a cooperative answer, also in natural language, obtained from semantic web resources (Ontologies and OWL2 Descriptions). The system is able of dialoguing when the question has some ambiguity or when it detects that the answer is not what user expected. Our proposal includes deep parsing the use of ontologies, and other web resources such as the WordNet and the DBpedia.

As future work, clearly we need to conclude our prototype, and then make a test set for a quantitative evaluation of our system performance and also a test set for a qualitative evaluation of the dialogue performance. We intend to answer questions that are more elaborate and/or more difficult. Moreover, we also plan to extend to the Portuguese natural language. For this purpose, it will be necessary to enrich the knowledge domain with concepts that may be deduced from the initial domain. Although the system is intended to be domain independent, it will be tested in a number of domains, with special relevance to the wine and the movies, since for these fields there are many resources available in the semantic web. We also plan to build a DRS generator, that builds the question semantics and retains additional information that allows the Discourse Controller to provide a more adequate cooperative answer. We contemplate about enlarging the knowledge base with other ontologies in order to support open-domain question answering and take advantage of the vast amount of heterogeneous semantic data provided by the semantic web.

References

[1] I. Horrocks, "Ontologies and the semantic web," *Communications of the ACM*, vol. 51, no. 12, pp. 58–67, 2008.

[2] Q. Guo and M. Zhang, "Question answering based on pervasive agent ontology and Semantic Web," *Knowledge-Based Systems*, vol. 22, no. 6, pp. 443–448, 2009.

[3] L. Hirschman and R. Gaizauskas, "Natural language question answering: the view from here," *Natural Language Engineering*, vol. 7, pp. 275–300, 2001.

[4] C. Fellbaum, *WordNet: An Electronic Lexical Database*, The MIT Press, 1998.

[5] S. Auer, C. Bizer, G. Kobilarov, J. Lehmann, R. Cyganiak, and Z. Ives, "DBpedia: a nucleus for a Web of open data," *Lecture Notes in Computer Science*, vol. 4825, pp. 722–735, 2007.

[6] V. Lopez, V. Uren, M. Sabou, and E. Motta, "Is question answering fit for the semantic web? A survey," *Semantic Web*, vol. 2, no. 2, pp. 125–155, 2011.

[7] E. Kaufmann and A. Bernstein, "Evaluating the usability of natural language query languages and interfaces to Semantic Web knowledge bases," *Journal of Web Semantics*, vol. 8, no. 4, pp. 377–393, 2010.

[8] A. Andrenucci and E. Sneiders, "Automated question answering: review of the main approaches," in *Proceedings of the 3rd International Conference on Information Technology and Applications (ICITA '05)*, pp. 514–519, July 2005.

[9] T. Gaasterland, "Cooperative answering through controlled query relaxation," *IEEE Expert-Intelligent Systems and their Applications*, vol. 12, no. 5, pp. 48–59, 1997.

[10] F. Jousse, I. Tellier, M. Tommasi, and P. Marty, "Learning to extract answers in question answering: experimental studies," *Actes de CORIA*, pp. 85–100, 2005.

[11] F. Benamara, "A semantic representation formalism for cooperative question answering systems," in *Proceedings of the Knowledge Base Computer Systems*, 2002.

[12] F. Benamara, "A semantic representation formalism for cooperative question answering systems," in *Proceedings of the Knowledge Base Computer Systems (KBCS '08)*, 2008.

[13] D. L. McGuinness, "Question answering on the semantic web," *IEEE Intelligent Systems*, vol. 19, no. 1, pp. 82–85, 2004.

[14] F. Corella and K. Lewison, "A brief overview of cooperative answering," *Journal of Intelligent Information Systems*, vol. 1, pp. 123–157, 2009.

[15] T. Gaasterland, P. Godfrey, and J. Minker, "An overview of cooperative answering," *Journal of Intelligent Information Systems*, vol. 1, no. 2, pp. 123–157, 1992.

[16] G. J. de Sena and A. L. Furtado, "Towards a cooperative question-answering model," *Flexible Query Answering Systems*, vol. 1495, pp. 354–365, 1998.

[17] T. Gaasterland, P. Godfrey, J. Minker, and L. Novik, "A cooperative answering system," in *Logic Programming and Automated Reasoning*, pp. 478–480, Springer, 1992.

[18] F. Benamara and P. Saint-Dizier, "Lexicalisation strategies in cooperative question-answering systems," in *Proceedings of the 20th International Conference on Computational Linguistics. Number Cruse 1986 in COLING '04*, p. 1179, Association for Computational Linguistics, Stroudsburg, Pa, USA, 2004.

[19] T. Gaasterland, P. Godfrey, and J. Minker, "Relaxation as a platform for cooperative answering," *Journal of Intelligent Information Systems*, vol. 1, no. 3-4, pp. 293–321, 1992.

[20] J. Wielemaker, "An optimised semantic Web query language implementation in prolog," in *Proceedings of the 21st International Conference on Logic Programming (ICLP '05)*, pp. 128–142, October 2005.

[21] J. Wielemaker, M. Hildebrand, J. van Ossenbruggen et al., "Using Prolog as the fundament for applications on the semantic web," in *Proceedings of the International Workshop on Applications of Logic Programming in the Semantic Web and Semantic Web Services (ALPSWS '07)*, pp. 84–98, 2007.

[22] W. Hodges, Classical logic I: first-order logic. The Blackwell guide to philosophical logic, pp. 9–32, 2001.

[23] J. Barwise and R. Cooper, "Generalized quantifiers and natural language," *Linguistics and Philosophy*, vol. 4, pp. 159–219, 1981.

[24] H. Kamp and U. Reyle, *From Discourse to Logic. Volume 42 of Studies in Linguistics and Philosophy*, Kluwer, 1993.

[25] P. Quaresma, I. Rodrigues, C. Prolo, and R. Vieira, "Um sistema de Pergunta-Resposta para uma base de Documentos," *Letras de Hoje*, vol. 41, pp. 43–63, 2006.

[26] S. Witzig and A. Center, Accessing wordnet from prolog. Artificial Intelligence Centre, University of Georgia, pp. 1—18, 2003.

[27] I. Rodrigues, L. Quintano, and L. Ferreira, "Nl database dialogue question-answering as a constraint satisfaction problem," in *Proceedings of the 18th International Conference on Applications of Declarative Programming and Knowledge Management (INAP '09)*, pp. 97–108, University of Évora, 2009.

[28] J. M. Almendros-Jimenez, "A prolog-based query language for OWL," *Electronic Notes in Theoretical Computer Science*, vol. 271, pp. 3–22, 2011.

[29] J. Rabelo and F. Barros, *Pergunte! uma interface em português para pergunta-resposta na web [M.S. thesis]*, Informatics Center, Federal University of Per-nambuco, Brazil, 2004.

[30] Q. Guo, "Question answering system based on ontology," in *Proceedings of the 7th IEEE World Congress on Intelligent Control and Automation (WCICA '08)*, pp. 3347–3352, 2008.

[31] V. Nogueira and S. Abreu, "Temporal contextual logic programming," *Electronic Notes in Theoretical Computer Science*, vol. 177, pp. 219–233, 2007.

[32] P. Blackburn and J. Bos, Representation and inference for natural language: a first course in computational semantics. Center for the Study of Language and Information, 2005.

[33] V. Lopez and E. Motta, Poweraqua: Fishing the semantic web. Semantic Web: Research and Applications, 2006.

[34] J. Minker, "An overview of cooperative answering in databases," *Flexible Query Answering Systems*, pp. 282–285, 1998.

[35] F. Benamara, "Generating intensional answers in intelligent question answering systems," *Natural Language Generation*, pp. 11–20, 2004.

[36] F. Benamara, "Cooperative question answering in restricted domains: the WE-BCOOP experiment," in *Proceedings of the Workshop Question Answering in Restricted Domains, within ACL*, 2004.

8

Conservative Intensional Extension of Tarski's Semantics

Zoran Majkić

International Society for Research in Science and Technology, P.O. Box 2464, Tallahassee, FL 32316-2464, USA

Correspondence should be addressed to Zoran Majkić; majk.1234@yahoo.com

Academic Editor: Konstantinos Lefkimmiatis

We considered an extension of the first-order logic (FOL) by Bealer's intensional abstraction operator. Contemporary use of the term "intension" derives from the traditional logical Frege-Russell doctrine that an idea (logic formula) has both an extension and an intension. Although there is divergence in formulation, it is accepted that the "extension" of an idea consists of the subjects to which the idea applies, and the "intension" consists of the attributes implied by the idea. From the Montague's point of view, the meaning of an idea can be considered as particular extensions in different possible worlds. In the case of standard FOL, we obtain a commutative homomorphic diagram, which is valid in each given possible world of an intensional FOL: from a free algebra of the FOL syntax, into its intensional algebra of concepts, and, successively, into an extensional relational algebra (different from Cylindric algebras). Then we show that this composition corresponds to the Tarski's interpretation of the standard extensional FOL in this possible world.

1. Introduction

In "Über Sinn und edeutung," Frege concentrated mostly on the senses of names, holding that all names have a sense (meaning). It is natural to hold that the same considerations apply to any expression that has an extension. But two general terms can have the same extension and different cognitive significance; two predicates can have the same extension and different cognitive significance; two sentences can have the same extension and different cognitive significance. So, general terms, predicates, and sentences all have senses as well as extensions. The same goes for any expression that has an extension or is a candidate for extension.

The significant aspect of an expression's meaning is its extension. We can stipulate that the extension of a sentence is its truth-value, and that the extension of a singular term is its referent. The extension of other expressions can be seen as associated entities that contribute to the truth-value of a sentence in a manner broadly analogous to the way in which the referent of a singular term contributes to the truth-value of a sentence. In many cases, the extension of an expression will be what we intuitively think of as its referent, although this need not hold in all cases. While Frege himself is often interpreted as holding that a sentence's referent is its truth-value, this claim is counterintuitive and widely disputed. We

can avoid that issue in the present framework by using the technical term "extension." In this context, the claim that the extension of a sentence is its truth-value is a stipulation.

"Extensional" is most definitely a technical term. Say that the extension of a name is its denotation, the extension of a predicate is the set of things it applies to, and the extension of a sentence is its truth value. A logic is extensional if coextensional expressions can be substituted one for another in any sentence of the logic "salva veritate," that is, without a change in truth value. The intuitive idea behind this principle is that, in an extensional logic, the only logically significant notion of meaning that attaches to an expression is its extension. An intensional logics is exactly one in which substitutivity salva veritate fails for some of the sentences of the logic.

The first conception of intensional entities (or concepts) is built into the *possible-worlds* treatment of Properties, Relations, and Propositions (PRPs). This conception is commonly attributed to Leibniz and underlies Alonzo Church's alternative formulation of Frege's theory of senses ("*A formulation of the logic of sense and denotation*" in Henle, Kallen, and Langer, 3–24, and "*Outline of a revised formulation of the logic of sense and denotation*" in two parts, Nous, VII (1973), 24–33, and VIII, (1974), 135–156). This conception of PRPs is ideally suited for treating the *modalities* (necessity, possibility, etc.) and to Montague's definition of intension of a given virtual predicate $\phi(x_1, \ldots, x_k)$ (a FOL open-sentence with the tuple of free variables $(x_1, \ldots x_k)$), as a mapping from possible worlds into extensions of this virtual predicate. Among the possible worlds, we distinguish the *actual* possible world. For example, if we consider a set of predicates, of a given Database, and their extensions in different time-instances, then the actual possible world is identified by the current instance of the time.

The second conception of intensional entities is to be found in Russell's doctrine of logical atomism. In this doctrine, it is required that all complete definitions of intensional entities be finite as well as unique and noncircular: it offers an *algebraic* way for definition of complex intensional entities from simple (atomic) entities (i.e., algebra of concepts), conception also evident in Leibniz's remarks. In a predicate logics, predicates and open-sentences (with free variables) express classes (properties and relations), and sentences express propositions. Note that classes (intensional entities) are *reified*, that is, they belong to the same domain as individual objects (particulars). This endows the intensional logics with a great deal of uniformity, making it possible to manipulate classes and individual objects in the same language. In particular, when viewed as an individual object, a class can be a member of another class.

The distinction between intensions and extensions is important (as in lexicography [1]), considering that extensions can be notoriously difficult to handle in an efficient manner. The extensional equality theory of predicates and functions under higher-order semantics (e.g., for two predicates with the same set of attributes, $p = q$ is true iff these symbols are interpreted by the same relation), that is, the strong equational theory of intensions, is not decidable, in general. For example, the second-order predicate calculus and Church's simple theory of types, both under the standard semantics, are not even semi-decidable. Thus, separating intensions from extensions makes it possible to have an equational theory over predicate and function names (intensions) that is separate from the extensional equality of relations and functions.

Relevant recent work about the intension, and its relationship with FOL, has been presented in [2] in the consideration of rigid and *nonrigid* objects, with respect to the possible worlds, where the rigid objects, like "George Washington," are the same things from possible world to possible world. Nonrigid objects, like "the Secretary-General of United Nations," are varying from circumstance to circumstance and can be modeled semantically by functions from possible worlds to domain of rigid objects, like intensional entities. But in his approach, differently from that one, fitting changes also the syntax of the FOL, by introducing an "extension of" operator, $\downarrow$, in order to distinguish the intensional entity "gross-domestic-product-of-Denmark," and its use in "the gross domestic product of Denmark is currently greater than gross domestic product of Finland." In his approach, if x is an intensional variable, $\downarrow x$ is extensional, while $\downarrow$ is not applicable to extensional variables, differently from our where each variable (concept) has both intensional and extension. Moreover, in his approach the problem arises because the

action of letting x designate, that is, evaluating $\downarrow x$, and the action of passing to an alternative possible world, that is, of interpreting the existential modal operator $\diamond$, are not actions that commute. To disambiguate this, one more piece of machinery is needed as well, which substantially and ad-hock changes the syntax and semantics of FOL, introduces the Higher-order Modal logics, and is not a conservative extension of Tarski's semantics.

In most recent work in [3, 4] it is given an intensional version of first-order *hybrid* logic, which is also a hybridized version of Fitting's intensional FOL, by a kind of generalized models, thus, different from our approaches to conservative extension of Tarski's semantics to intensional FOL.

Another recent relevant work is presented by I-logic in [5], which combines both approach to semantics of intensional objects of Montague and Fitting.

We recall that Intensional Logic Programming is a new form of logic programming based on intensional logic and possible worlds semantics and is a well-defined practice in using the intensional semantics [6]. Intensional logic allows us to use logic programming to specify nonterminating computations and to capture the dynamic aspects of certain problems in a natural and problem-oriented style. The meanings of formulas of an intensional first-order language are given according to intensional interpretations and to elements of a set of possible worlds. Neighborhood semantics is employed as an abstract formulation of the denotations of intensional operators. The model-theoretic and fixpoint semantics of intensional logic programs are developed in terms of least (minimum) intensional Herbrand models. Intensional logic programs with intensional operator definitions are regarded as metatheories.

In what follows, we denote by B^A the set of all functions from A to B, and by A^n an n-folded cartesian product $A \times \cdots \times A$ for $n \geq 1$. By f, t we denote empty set $\emptyset$ and singleton set $\{\langle \rangle\}$, respectively (with the empty tuple $\langle \rangle$ i.e., the unique tuple of 0-ary relation), which may be thought of as falsity f and truth t, as those used in the relational algebra. For a given domain $\mathscr{D}$, we define that $\mathscr{D}^0$ is a singleton set $\{\langle \rangle\}$, so that $\{f, t\} = \mathscr{P}(\mathscr{D}^0)$, where $\mathscr{P}$ is the powerset operator.

2. Intensional FOL Language with Intensional Abstraction

Intensional entities are such concepts as propositions and properties. The term "intensional" means that they violate the principle of extensionality, the principle that extensional equivalence implies identity. All (or most) of these intensional entities have been classified at one time or another as kinds of Universals [7].

We consider a nonempty domain $\mathscr{D} = D_{-1} \bigcup D_I$, where a subdomain D_{-1} is made of particulars (extensional entities), and the rest $D_I = D_0 \bigcup D_1 \cdots \bigcup D_n \cdots$ is made of universals (D_0 for propositions (the 0-ary concepts)), and D_n, $n \geq 1$, for n-ary concepts.

The fundamental entities are *intensional abstracts* or so-called, that-clauses. We assume that they are singular terms; Intensional expressions like "believe," "mean," "assert," "know," are standard two-place predicates that take "that"-clauses as arguments. Expressions like "is necessary," "is true," and "is possible" are one-place predicates that take "that"-clauses as arguments. For example, in the intensional sentence "it is necessary that ϕ," where ϕ is a proposition, the "that ϕ" is denoted by the $< \phi >$, where $<>$ is the intensional abstraction operator, which transforms a logic formula into a *term*. Or, for example, "x believes that ϕ" is given by formula $p_i^2(x, < \phi >)$ (p_i^2 is binary "believe" predicate).

Here we will present an intensional FOL with slightly different intensional abstraction than that originally presented in [8].

Definition 1. The syntax of the first-order logic language with intensional abstraction $<>$, denoted by $\mathscr{L}$, is as follows:

logic operators $(\wedge, \neg, \exists)$, predicate letters in P (functional letters is considered as particular case of predicate letters), variables $x, y, z, \ldots$ in $\mathscr{V}$, abstraction $< \_ >$, and punctuation symbols (comma, parenthesis). With the following simultaneous inductive definition of *term* and *formula*,

(1) all variables and constants (0-ary functional letters in P) are terms;

(2) if $t_1, \ldots, t_k$ are terms, then $p_i^k(t_1, \ldots, t_k)$ is a formula ($p_i^k \in P$ is a k-ary predicate letter);

(3) if ϕ and ψ are formulae, then $(\phi \wedge \psi)$, $\neg\phi$, and $(\exists x)\phi$ are formulae;

(4) if $\phi(\mathbf{x})$ is a formula (virtual predicate) with a list of free variables in $\mathbf{x} = (x_1, \ldots, x_n)$ (with ordering from-left-to-right of their appearance in ϕ), and α is its sublist of *distinct* variables, then $< \phi >_\alpha^\beta$ is a term, where β is the remaining list of free variables preserving ordering in $\mathbf{x}$ as well. The externally quantifiable variables are the *free* variables not in α. When $n = 0$, $< \phi >$ is a term that denotes a proposition, for $n \geq 1$ it denotes an n-ary concept.

An occurrence of a variable x_i in a formula (or a term) is *bound* (*free*) if and only if it lies (does not lie) within a formula of the form $(\exists x_i)\phi$ (or a term of the form $< \phi >_\alpha^\beta$ with $x_i \in \alpha$). A variable is free (bound) in a formula (or term) if and only if it has (does not have) a free occurrence in that formula (or term).

A *sentence* is a formula having no free variables. The binary predicate letter p_1^2 for identity is singled out as a distinguished logical predicate, and formulae of the form $p_1^2(t_1, t_2)$ are to be rewritten in the form $t_1 \doteq t_2$. We denote by $R_=$ the binary relation obtained by standard Tarski's interpretation of this predicate p_1^2. The logic operators $\forall, \vee, \Rightarrow$ are defined in terms of $(\wedge, \neg, \exists)$ in the usual way.

Remark 2. The k-ary functional symbols, for $k \geq 1$, in standard (extensional) FOL are considered as $(k + 1)$-ary predicate symbols p^{k+1}: the function $f : \mathscr{D}^k \to \mathscr{D}$ is considered as a relation obtained from its graph $R = \{(d_1, \ldots, d_k, f(d_1, \ldots, d_k)) \mid d_i \in \mathscr{D}\}$, represented by a predicate symbol p^{k+1}.

The universal quantifier is defined by $\forall = \neg\exists\neg$. Disjunction and implication are expressed by $\phi \vee \psi = \neg(\neg\phi \wedge \neg\psi)$ and $\phi \Rightarrow \psi = \neg\phi \vee \psi$. In FOL with the identity $\doteq$, the formula $(\exists_1 x)\phi(x)$ denotes the formula $(\exists x)\phi(x) \wedge (\forall x)(\forall y)(\phi(x) \wedge \phi(y) \Rightarrow (x \doteq y))$. We denote by $R_=$ the Tarski's interpretation of $\doteq$.

In what follows, any open-sentence, a formula ϕ with nonempty tuple of free variables $(x_1, \ldots, x_m)$, will be called a m-ary *virtual predicate*, denoted also by $\phi(x_1, \ldots, x_m)$. This definition contains the precise method of establishing the *ordering* of variables in this tuple: such a method that will be adopted here is the ordering of appearance, from left to right, of free variables in ϕ. This method of composing the tuple of free variables is the unique and canonical way of definition of the virtual predicate from a given formula.

An *intensional interpretation* of this intensional FOL is a mapping between the set $\mathscr{L}$ of formulae of the logic language and intensional entities in $\mathscr{D}$, $I : \mathscr{L} \to \mathscr{D}$, which is a kind of "conceptualization", such that an open-sentence (virtual predicate) $\phi(x_1, \ldots, x_k)$ with a tuple of all free variables $(x_1, \ldots, x_k)$ is mapped into a k-ary *concept*, that is, an intensional entity $u = I(\phi(x_1, \ldots, x_k)) \in D_k$, and (closed) sentence ψ into a proposition (i.e., *logic* concept) $v = I(\psi) \in D_0$ with $I(\top) = Truth \in D_0$ for a FOL tautology $\top$. A language constant c is mapped into a particular (an extensional entity) $a = I(c) \in D_{-1}$ if it is a proper name, otherwise in a correspondent concept in $\mathscr{D}$.

An assignment $g : \mathscr{V} \to \mathscr{D}$ for variables in $\mathscr{V}$ is applied only to free variables in terms and formulae. Such an assignment $g \in \mathscr{D}^{\mathscr{V}}$ can be recursively uniquely extended into the assignment $g^* : \mathscr{T} \to \mathscr{D}$, where $\mathscr{T}$ denotes the set of all terms (here I is an intensional interpretation of this FOL, as explained in what follows), by

(1) $g^*(t) = g(x) \in \mathscr{D}$ if the term t is a variable $x \in \mathscr{V}$;

(2) $g^*(t) = I(c) \in \mathscr{D}$ if the term t is a constant $c \in P$;

(3) if t is an abstracted term $< \phi >_\alpha^\beta$, then $g^*(< \phi >_\alpha^\beta) = I(\phi[\beta/g(\beta)]) \in D_k, k = |\alpha|$ (i.e., the number of variables in α), where $g(\beta) = g(y_1, \ldots, y_m) = (g(y_1), \ldots, g(y_m))$ and $[\beta/g(\beta)]$ is a uniform replacement of each ith variable in the list β with the ith constant in the list $g(\beta)$. Notice that α is the list of all free variables in the formula $\phi[\beta/g(\beta)]$.

We denote by t/g (or ϕ/g) the ground term (or formula) without free variables, obtained by assignment g from a term t (or a formula ϕ), and by $\phi[x/t]$ the formula obtained by uniformly replacing x by a term t in ϕ.

The distinction between intensions and extensions is important especially because we are now able to have and *equational theory* over intensional entities (as $< \phi >$), that is, predicate and function "names," which is separate from the extensional equality of relations and functions. An *extensionalization function* h assigns to the intensional elements of $\mathscr{D}$ an appropriate extension as follows: for each proposition $u \in D_0, h(u) \in \{f, t\} \subseteq \mathscr{P}(D_{-1})$ is its extension (true or false value); for each n-ary concept $u \in D_n, h(u)$ is a subset of $\mathscr{D}^n$ (nth Cartesian product of $\mathscr{D}$); in the case of particulars $u \in D_{-1}, h(u) = u$.

The sets f, t are empty set $\{\}$ and set $\{\langle \rangle\}$ (with the empty tuple $\langle \rangle \in D_{-1}$, i.e., the unique tuple of 0-ary relation) which may be thought of as falsity and truth, as those used in the Codd's relational-database algebra [9], respectively, while $Truth \in D_0$ is the concept (intension) of the tautology.

We define that $\mathscr{D}^0 = \{\langle\rangle\}$, so that $\{f, t\} = \mathscr{P}(\mathscr{D}^0)$, where $\mathscr{P}$ is the powerset operator. Thus we have (we denote the disjoint union by "+"):

$$h = \left(h_{-1} + \sum_{i \geq 0} h_i\right) : \sum_{i \geq -1} D_i \longrightarrow D_{-1} + \sum_{i \geq 0} \mathscr{P}\left(D^i\right), \quad (1)$$

where $h_{-1} = id : D_{-1} \rightarrow D_{-1}$ is identity mapping, the mapping $h_0 : D_0 \rightarrow \{f, t\}$ assigns the truth values in $\{f, t\}$ to all propositions, and the mappings $h_i : D_i \rightarrow \mathscr{P}(D^i)$, $i \geq 1$, assign an extension to all concepts. Thus, the intensions can be seen as *names* of abstract or concrete entities, while the extensions correspond to various rules that these entities play in different worlds.

Remark 3 (Tarski's constraints). This intensional semantics has to preserve standard Tarski's semantics of the FOL. That is, for any formula $\phi \in \mathscr{L}$ with a tuple of free variables $(x_1, \ldots, x_k)$, and $h \in \mathscr{E}$, the following conservative conditions for all assignments $g, g\prime \in \mathscr{D}^{\mathscr{V}}$ have to be satisfied:

(T) $h(I(\phi/g)) = t$ if and only if $(g(x_1), \ldots, g(x_k)) \in h(I(\phi))$ and if ϕ is a predicate letter p^k, $k \geq 2$ which represents a $(k-1)$-ary functional symbol f^{k-1} in standard FOL,

(TF) $h(I(\phi/g)) = h(I(\phi/g')) = t$, and $\forall_{1 \leq i \leq k-1}(g'(x_i) = g(x_i))$ implies $g'(x_{k+1}) = g(x_{k+1})$.

Thus, intensional FOL has a simple Tarski first-order semantics, with a decidable unification problem, but we need also the actual world mapping which maps any intensional entity to its *actual world extension*. In what follows, we will identify a *possible world* by a particular mapping which assigns, in such a possible world, the extensions to intensional entities. This is a direct bridge between an intensional FOL and a possible worlds representation [10–15], where the intension (meaning) of a proposition is a *function*, from a set of possible $\mathscr{W}$ worlds into the set of truth values. Consequently, $\mathscr{E}$ denotes the set of possible *extensionalization functions* h satisfying the constraint (T). Each $h \in \mathscr{E}$ may be seen as a *possible world* (analogously to Montague's intensional semantics for natural language [12, 14]), as it has been demonstrated in [16, 17] and given by the bijection $is : \mathscr{W} \simeq \mathscr{E}$.

Now we are able to define formally this intensional semantics [15].

Definition 4. A two-step intensional semantics.

Let $\mathfrak{R} = \bigcup_{k \in \mathbb{N}} \mathscr{P}(\mathscr{D}^k) = \sum_{k \in \mathbb{N}} \mathscr{P}(D^k)$ be the set of all k-ary relations, where $k \in \mathbb{N} = \{0, 1, 2, \ldots\}$. Notice that $\{f, t\} = \mathscr{P}(\mathscr{D}^0) \in \mathfrak{R}$, that is, the truth values are extensions in $\mathfrak{R}$.

The intensional semantics of the logic language with the set of formulae $\mathscr{L}$ can be represented by the mapping

$$\mathscr{L} \xrightarrow{I} \mathscr{D} \Longrightarrow_{w \in \mathscr{W}} \mathfrak{R}, \quad (2)$$

where $\xrightarrow{I}$ is a *fixed intensional* interpretation $I : \mathscr{L} \rightarrow \mathscr{D}$ and $\Rightarrow_{w \in \mathscr{W}}$ is *the set* of all extensionalization functions $h = is(w) : \mathscr{D} \rightarrow \mathfrak{R}$ in $\mathscr{E}$, where $is : \mathscr{W} \rightarrow \mathscr{E}$ is the mapping from the set of possible worlds to the set of extensionalization functions.

We define the mapping $I_n : \mathscr{L}_{op} \rightarrow \mathfrak{R}^{\mathscr{W}}$, where $\mathscr{L}_{op}$ is the subset of formulae with free variables (virtual predicates), such that for any virtual predicate $\phi(x_1, \ldots, x_k) \in \mathscr{L}_{op}$ the mapping $I_n(\phi(x_1, \ldots, x_k)) : \mathscr{W} \rightarrow \mathfrak{R}$ is the Montague's meaning (i.e., *intension*) of this virtual predicate [10–14], that is, the mapping which returns with the extension of this (virtual) predicate in each possible world $w \in \mathscr{W}$.

We adopted this two-step intensional semantics, instead of well-known Montague's semantics (which lies in the construction of a compositional and recursive semantics that covers both intension and extension), because of a number of weakness of the second semantics:

Example 5. Let us consider the following two past participles: "bought" and "sold" (with unary predicates $p_1^1(x)$, "x has been bought", and $p_2^1(x)$, "x has been sold"). These two different concepts in the Montague's semantics would have not only the same extension but also their intension, from the fact that their extensions are identical in every possible world.

Within the two-step formalism, we can avoid this problem by assigning two different concepts (meanings) $u = I(p_1^1(x))$ and $v = I(p_2^1(x))$ in $\in D_1$. Note that we have the same problem in the Montague's semantics for two sentences with different meanings, which bear the same truth value across all possible worlds: in Montague's semantics, they will be forced to the *same* meaning.

Another relevant question with respect to this two-step interpretations of an intensional semantics is how in it the extensional identity relation $\doteq$ (binary predicate of the identity) of the FOL is managed. Here this extensional identity relation is mapped into the binary concept $Id = I(\doteq (x, y)) \in D_2$, such that $(\forall w \in \mathscr{W})(is(w)(Id) = R_=)$, where $\doteq (x, y)$ (i.e., $p_1^2(x, y)$) denotes an atom of the FOL of the binary predicate for identity in FOL, usually written by FOL formula $x \doteq y$.

Note that here we prefer to distinguish this *formal symbol* $\doteq \in P$ of the built-in identity binary predicate letter in the FOL, from the standard mathematical symbol "=" used in all mathematical definitions in this paper.

In what follows, we will use the function $f_{\langle\rangle} : \mathfrak{R} \rightarrow \mathfrak{R}$, such that for any relation $R \in \mathfrak{R}$, $f_{\langle\rangle}(R) = \{\langle\rangle\}$ if $R \neq \emptyset$; $\emptyset$ otherwise. Let us define the following set of algebraic operators for relations in $\mathfrak{R}$.

(1) Binary operator $\bowtie_S : \mathfrak{R} \times \mathfrak{R} \rightarrow \mathfrak{R}$, such that for any two relations $R_1, R_2 \in \mathfrak{R}$, the $R_1 \bowtie_S R_2$ is equal to the relation obtained by natural join of these two relations if S is a nonempty set of pairs of joined columns of respective relations (where the first argument is the column index of the relation R_1 while the second argument is the column index of the joined column of

the relation R_2); otherwise it is equal to the cartesian product $R_1 \times R_2$.

For example, the logic formula $\phi(x_i, x_j, x_k, x_l, x_m) \wedge \psi(x_l, y_i, x_j, y_j)$ will be traduced by the algebraic expression $R_1 \bowtie_S R_2$ where $R_1 \in \mathscr{P}(\mathscr{D}^5), R_2 \in \mathscr{P}(\mathscr{D}^4)$ are the extensions for a given Tarski's interpretation of the virtual predicate ϕ, ψ relatively, so that $S = \{(4,1),(2,3)\}$ and the resulting relation will have the following ordering of attributes: $(x_i, x_j, x_k, x_l, x_m, y_i, y_j)$.

(2) Unary operator $\sim: \mathfrak{R} \to \mathfrak{R}$, such that for any k-ary (with $k \geq 0$) relation $R \in \mathscr{P}(\mathscr{D}^k) \subset \mathfrak{R}$, we have that $\sim (R) = \mathscr{D}^k \setminus R \in \mathscr{D}^k$, where "$\setminus$" is the substraction of relations. For example, the logic formula $\neg\phi(x_i, x_j, x_k, x_l, x_m)$ will be traduced by the algebraic expression $\mathscr{D}^5 \setminus R$ where R is the extensions for a given Tarski's interpretation of the virtual predicate ϕ.

(3) Unary operator $\pi_{-m} : \mathfrak{R} \to \mathfrak{R}$, such that for any k-ary (with $k \geq 0$) relation $R \in \mathscr{P}(\mathscr{D}^k) \subset \mathfrak{R}$, we have that $\pi_{-m}(R)$ is equal to the relation obtained by elimination of the mth column of the relation R if $1 \leq m \leq k$ and $k \geq 2$; equal to $f_{\langle\rangle}(R)$ if $m = k = 1$; otherwise it is equal to R.

For example, the logic formula $(\exists x_k)\phi(x_i, x_j, x_k, x_l, x_m)$ will be traduced by the algebraic expression $\pi_{-3}(R)$ where R is the extensions for a given Tarski's interpretation of the virtual predicate ϕ and the resulting relation will have the following ordering of attributes: (x_i, x_j, x_l, x_m).

Notice that the ordering of attributes of resulting relations corresponds to the method used for generating the ordering of variables in the tuples of free variables adopted for virtual predicates.

Analogously to Boolean algebras, which are extensional models of propositional logic, we introduce now an intensional algebra for this intensional FOL, as follows.

Definition 6. Intensional algebra for the intensional FOL in Definition 1 is a structure $\mathscr{A}_{\text{int}} = (\mathscr{D}, f, t, Id, Truth, \{conj_S\}_{S \in \mathscr{P}(\mathbb{N}^2)}, neg, \{exists_n\}_{n \in \mathbb{N}})$, with binary operations $conj_S : D_I \times D_I \to D_I$, unary operation $neg : D_I \to D_I$, unary operations $exists_n : D_I \to D_I$, such that for any extensionalization function $h \in \mathscr{E}$, and $u \in D_k, v \in D_j, k, j \geq 0$,

(1) $h(Id) = R_=$ and $h(Truth) = \{\langle\rangle\}$.

(2) $h(conj_S(u,v)) = h(u) \bowtie_S h(v)$, where $\bowtie_S$ is the natural join operation defined above and $conj_S(u,v) \in D_m$ where $m = k+j-|S|$ if for every pair $(i_1, i_2) \in S$ it holds that $1 \leq i_1 \leq k, 1 \leq i_2 \leq j$ (otherwise $conj_S(u,v) \in D_{k+j}$).

(3) $h(neg(u)) = \sim (h(u)) = \mathscr{D}^k \setminus (h(u))$, where $\sim$ is the operation defined above and $neg(u) \in D_k$.

(4) $h(exists_n(u)) = \pi_{-n}(h(u))$, where π_{-n} is the operation defined above and $exists_n(u) \in D_{k-1}$ if $1 \leq n \leq k$ (otherwise $exists_n$ is the identity function).

Notice that for $u \in D_0$, $h(neg(u)) = \sim(h(u)) = \mathscr{D}^0 \setminus (h(u)) = \{\langle\rangle\} \setminus (h(u)) \in \{f, t\}$.

We define a derived operation union : $(\mathscr{P}(D_i) \setminus \emptyset) \to D_i$, $i \geq 0$, such that, for any $B = \{u_1, \ldots, u_n\} \in \mathscr{P}(D_i)$ we have that union$(\{u_1, \ldots, u_n\}) =_{\text{def}} u_1$ if $n = 1$; $neg(conj_S(neg(u_1), conj_S(\ldots, neg(u_n))\ldots)$, where $S = \{(l,l)|1 \leq l \leq i\}$, otherwise. Than we obtain that for $n \geq 2$,

$h(\text{union}(B))$

$$= h(neg(conj_S(neg(u_1), conj_S(\ldots, neg(u_n))\ldots))$$
$$= \mathscr{D}^i \setminus ((\mathscr{D}^i \setminus h(u_1)) \bowtie_S \cdots \bowtie_S (\mathscr{D}^i \setminus h(u_n))) \quad (3)$$
$$= \mathscr{D}^i \setminus ((\mathscr{D}^i \setminus h(u_1)) \bigcap \cdots \bigcap (\mathscr{D}^i \setminus h(u_n)))$$
$$= \bigcup \{h(u_j) \mid 1 \leq j \leq n\} = \bigcup \{h(u) \mid u \in B\}.$$

Intensional interpretation $I : \mathscr{L} \to \mathscr{D}$ satisfies the following homomorphic extension.

(1) The logic formula $\phi(x_i, x_j, x_k, x_l, x_m) \wedge \psi(x_l, y_i, x_j, y_j)$ will be intensionally interpreted by the concept $u_1 \in D_7$, obtained by the algebraic expression $conj_S(u,v)$ where $u = I(\phi(x_i, x_j, x_k, x_l, x_m)) \in D_5, v = I(\psi(x_l, y_i, x_j, y_j)) \in D_4$ are the concepts of the virtual predicates ϕ, ψ, relatively, and $S = \{(4,1),(2,3)\}$. Consequently, we have that for any two formulae $\phi, \psi \in \mathscr{L}$ and a particular operator $conj_S$ uniquely determined by tuples of free variables in these two formulae, $I(\phi \wedge \psi) = conj_S(I(\phi), I(\psi))$.

(2) The logic formula $\neg\phi(x_i, x_j, x_k, x_l, x_m)$ will be intensionally interpreted by the concept $u_1 \in D_5$, obtained by the algebraic expression $neg(u)$ where $u = I(\phi(x_i, x_j, x_k, x_l, x_m)) \in D_5$ is the concept of the virtual predicate ϕ. Consequently, we have that for any formula $\phi \in \mathscr{L}, I(\neg\phi) = neg(I(\phi))$.

(3) The logic formula $(\exists x_k)\phi(x_i, x_j, x_k, x_l, x_m)$ will be intensionally interpreted by the concept $u_1 \in D_4$, obtained by the algebraic expression $exists_3(u)$ where $u = I(\phi(x_i, x_j, x_k, x_l, x_m)) \in D_5$ is the concept of the virtual predicate ϕ. Consequently, we have that for any formula $\phi \in \mathscr{L}$ and a particular operator $exists_n$ uniquely determined by the position of the existentially quantified variable in the tuple of free variables in ϕ (otherwise $n = 0$ if this quantified variable is not a free variable in ϕ), $I((\exists x)\phi) = exists_n(I(\phi))$.

Once one has found a method for specifying the interpretations of singular terms of $\mathscr{L}$ (take in consideration the particularity of abstracted terms), the Tarski-style definitions of truth and validity for $\mathscr{L}$ may be given in the customary way. What is proposed specifically is a method for characterizing the intensional interpretations of singular terms of $\mathscr{L}$ in such a way that a given singular abstracted term $< \phi >_\alpha^\beta$ will denote an appropriate property, relation, or proposition, depending on the value of $m = |\alpha|$. Thus, the mapping of intensional abstracts (terms) into $\mathscr{D}$ will be defined differently from that given in the version of Bealer [18], as follows.

Definition 7. An intensional interpretation I can be extended to abstracted terms as follows: for any abstracted term $< \phi >_\alpha^\beta$, we define that

$$I\left(< \phi >_\alpha^\beta\right) = \text{union}\left(\left\{I\left(\phi\left[\frac{\beta}{g(\beta)}\right]\right) \mid g \in \mathcal{D}^{\overline{\beta}}\right\}\right), \quad (4)$$

where $\overline{\beta}$ denotes the set of elements in the list β, and the assignments in $\mathcal{D}^{\overline{\beta}}$ are limited only to the variables in $\overline{\beta}$.

Remark 8. Here we can make the question if there is a sense to extend the interpretation also to (abstracted) terms, because in Tarski's interpretation of FOL we do not have any interpretation for terms, but only the assignments for terms, as we defined previously by the mapping $g^* : \mathcal{T} \to \mathcal{D}$. The answer is positive, because the abstraction symbol $< \_ >_\alpha^\beta$ can be considered as a kind of the unary built-in functional symbol of intensional FOL, so that we can apply the Tarski's interpretation to this functional symbol into the fixed mapping $I(< \_ >_\alpha^\beta) : \mathcal{L} \to \mathcal{D}$, so that for any $\phi \in \mathcal{L}$ we have that $I(< \phi >_\alpha^\beta)$ is equal to the application of this function to the value ϕ, that is, to $I(< \_ >_\alpha^\beta)(\phi)$. In such an approach, we would introduce also the typed variable X for the formulae in $\mathcal{L}$, so that the Tarski's assignment for this functional symbol with variable X, with $g(X) = \phi \in \mathcal{L}$, can be given by

$$g^*\left(< \_ >_\alpha^\beta (X)\right)$$
$$= I\left(< \_ >_{-\alpha}^\beta\right)(g(X)) = I\left(< \_ >_\alpha^\beta\right)(\phi)$$
$$= \begin{cases} \langle \rangle \in D_{-1}, \\ \quad \text{if } \overline{\alpha} \bigcup \overline{\beta} \text{ is not equal to the set of free variables in } \phi; \\ = \text{union}\left(\left\{I\left(\phi\left[\frac{\beta}{g'(\beta)}\right]\right) \mid g' \in \mathcal{D}^{\overline{\beta}}\right\}\right) \in D_{|\overline{\alpha}|}, \\ \hspace{8cm} \text{otherwise.} \end{cases}$$

$$(5)$$

Notice than if $\beta = \emptyset$ is the empty list, then $I(< \phi >_\alpha^\beta) = I(\phi)$. Consequently, the denotation of $< \phi >$ is equal to the meaning of a proposition ϕ, that is, $I(< \phi >) = I(\phi) \in D_0$. In the case when ϕ is an atom $p_i^m(x_1, \ldots, x_m)$, then $I(< p_i^m(x_1, \ldots, x_m) >_{x_1, \ldots, x_m}) = I(p_i^m(x_1, \ldots, x_m)) \in D_m$, while $I(< p_i^m(x_1, \ldots, x_m) >^{x_1, \ldots, x_m}) = \text{union}(\{I(p_i^m(g(x_1), \ldots, g(x_m))) \mid g \in \mathcal{D}^{\{x_1, \ldots, x_m\}}\}) \in D_0$, with $h(I(< p_i^m(x_1, \ldots, x_m) >^{x_1, \ldots, x_m})) = h(I((\exists x_1) \cdots (\exists x_m) p_i^m(x_1, \ldots, x_m))) \in \{f, t\}$.

For example,

$$h\left(I\left(< p_i^1(x_1) \land \neg p_i^1(x_1) >^{x_1}\right)\right)$$
$$= h\left(I\left((\exists x_1)\left(< p_i^1(x_1) \land \neg p_i^1(x_1) >^{x_1}\right)\right)\right) = f. \quad (6)$$

The interpretation of a more complex abstract $< \phi >_\alpha^\beta$ is defined in terms of the interpretations of the relevant syntactically simpler expressions, because the interpretation

of more complex formulae is defined in terms of the interpretation of the relevant syntactically simpler formulae, based on the intensional algebra above. For example, $I(p_i^1(x) \land p_k^1(x)) = \text{conj}_{\{(1,1)\}}(I(p_i^1(x)), I(p_k^1(x)))$, $I(\neg\phi) = \text{neg}(I(\phi))$, $I(\exists x_i)\phi(x_i, x_j, x_i, x_k) = \text{exists}_3(I(\phi))$.

Consequently, based on the intensional algebra in Definition 6 and on intensional interpretations of abstracted terms in Definition 7, it holds that the interpretation of any formula in $\mathcal{L}$ (and any abstracted term) will be reduced to an algebraic expression over interpretations of primitive atoms in $\mathcal{L}$. This obtained expression is finite for any finite formula (or abstracted term) and represents the *meaning* of such finite formula (or abstracted term).

The *extension* of an abstracted term satisfy the following property.

Proposition 9. *For any abstracted term $< \phi >_\alpha^\beta$ with $|\alpha| \geq 1$, we have that*

$$h\left(I\left(< \phi >_\alpha^\beta\right)\right) = \pi_{-\beta}\left(h\left(I\left(\phi\right)\right)\right), \quad (7)$$

where $\pi_{-(y_1, \ldots, y_k)} = \pi_{-y_1} \circ \cdots \circ \pi_{-y_k}$, $\circ$ is the sequential composition of functions, and $\pi_{-\emptyset}$ is an identity.

Proof. Let $\mathbf{x}$ be a tuple of all free variables in ϕ, so that $\overline{\mathbf{x}} = \overline{\alpha} \bigcup \overline{\beta}$, $\alpha = (x_1, \ldots, x_k)$, then we have that $h(I(< \phi >_\alpha^\beta)) = h(\text{union}(\{I(\phi[\beta/g(\beta)]) \mid g \in \mathcal{D}^{\overline{\beta}}\}))$, from Definition 7 $= \bigcup\{h(I(\phi[\beta/g(\beta)])) \mid g \in \mathcal{D}^{\overline{\beta}}\} = \bigcup\{\{(g_1(x_1), \ldots, g_1(x_k)) \mid g_1 \in \mathcal{D}^{\overline{\alpha}} \text{ and } h(I(\phi[\beta/g(\beta)][\alpha/g_1(\alpha)])) = t\} \mid g \in \mathcal{D}^{\overline{\beta}}\} = \{g_1(\alpha) \mid g_1 \in \mathcal{D}^{\overline{\alpha} \cup \overline{\beta}} \text{ and } h(I(\phi/g_1)) = t\} = \pi_{-\beta}(\{g_1(\mathbf{x}) \mid g_1 \in \mathcal{D}^{\overline{\mathbf{x}}} \text{ and } h(I(\phi/g_1)) = t\}) = \pi_{-\beta}(\{g_1(\mathbf{x}) \mid g_1 \in \mathcal{D}^{\overline{\mathbf{x}}} \text{ and } g_1(\mathbf{x}) \in h(I(\phi))\})$, by (**T**) $= \pi_{-\beta}(h(I(\phi)))$. $\qquad\square$

We can correlate $\mathcal{E}$ with a possible-world semantics. Such a correspondence is a natural identification of intensional logics with modal Kripke-based logics.

Definition 10 (model). A model for intensional FOL with fixed intensional interpretation I, which expresses the two-step intensional semantics in Definition 4, is the Kripke structure $\mathcal{M}_{\text{int}} = (\mathcal{W}, \mathcal{D}, V)$, where $\mathcal{W} = \{is^{-1}(h) \mid h \in \mathcal{E}\}$, a mapping $V : \mathcal{W} \times P \to \bigcup_{n < \omega}\{t, f\}^{\mathcal{D}^n}$, with P a set of predicate symbols of the language, such that for any world $w = is^{-1}(h) \in \mathcal{W}$, $p_i^n \in P$, and $(u_1, \ldots, u_n) \in \mathcal{D}^n$ it holds that $V(w, p_i^n)(u_1, \ldots, u_n) = h(I(p_i^n(u_1, \ldots, u_n)))$. The satisfaction relation $\vDash_{w,g}$ for a given $w \in \mathcal{W}$ and assignment $g \in \mathcal{D}^{\mathcal{V}}$ is defined as follows:

(1) $\mathcal{M} \vDash_{w,g} p_i^k(x_1, \ldots, x_k)$ if and only if $V(w, p_i^k)(g(x_1), \ldots, g(x_k)) = t$,

(2) $\mathcal{M} \vDash_{w,g} \varphi \land \phi$ if and only if $\mathcal{M} \vDash_{w,g} \varphi$ and $\mathcal{M} \vDash_{w,g} \phi$,

(3) $\mathcal{M} \vDash_{w,g} \neg\varphi$ if and only if not $\mathcal{M} \vDash_{w,g} \varphi$,

(4) $\mathcal{M} \vDash_{w,g} (\exists x)\phi$ if and only if

(4.1) $\mathcal{M} \vDash_{w,g} \phi$, if x is not a free variable in ϕ;

(4.2) exists $u \in \mathcal{D}$ such that $\mathcal{M} \vDash_{w,g} \phi[x/u]$, if x is a free variable in ϕ.

It is easy to show that the satisfaction relation $\vDash$ for this Kripke semantics in a world $w = is^{-1}(h)$ is defined by $\mathcal{M} \vDash_{w,g} \phi$ if and only if $h(I(\phi/q)) = t$.

We can enrich this intensional FOL by another modal operators, as, for example, the "necessity" universal logic operator $\square$ with accessibility relation $\mathcal{R} = \mathcal{W} \times \mathcal{W}$, obtaining an S5 Kripke structure $\mathcal{M}_{int} = (\mathcal{W}, \mathcal{R}, \mathcal{D}, V)$. In this case, we are able to define the following equivalences between the abstracted terms without free variables $< \phi >^{\beta_1}_\alpha /g$ and $< \psi >^{\beta_2}_\alpha /g$, where all free variables (not in α) are instantiated by $g \in \mathcal{D}^{\mathcal{V}}$ (here $A \equiv B$ denotes the formula $(A \Rightarrow B) \wedge (B \Rightarrow A)$).

(i) (Strong) Intensional equivalence (or *equality*) "$\simeq$" is defined by $< \phi >^{\beta_1}_\alpha /g \simeq < \psi >^{\beta_2}_\alpha /g$ if and only if $\square(\phi [\beta_1/g(\beta_1)] \equiv \psi[\beta_2/g(\beta_2)])$, with $\mathcal{M} \vDash_{w,g'} \square \varphi$ if and only if for all $w' \in \mathcal{W}$, $(w,w') \in \mathcal{R}$ implies $\mathcal{M} \vDash_{w',g'} \varphi$. From Example 5, we have that $< p_1^1(x) >_x \simeq < p_2^1(x) >_x$, that is, "$x$ has been bought" and "x has been sold" are intensionally equivalent, but they have not the same meaning (the concept $I(p_1^1(x)) \in D_1$ is different from $I(p_2^1(x)) \in D_1$).

(ii) Weak intensional equivalence "$\approx$" is defined by $< \phi >^{\beta_1}_\alpha /g \approx < \psi >^{\beta_2}_\alpha /g$ if and only if $\Diamond \phi[\beta_1/g(\beta_1)] \equiv \Diamond \psi[\beta_2/g(\beta_2)]$. The symbol $\Diamond = \neg \square \neg$ is the correspondent existential modal operator. This weak equivalence is used for P2P database integration in a number of papers [16, 19–24].

Note that if we want to use the intensional equality in our language, then we need the correspondent operator in intensional algebra $\mathcal{A}_{int}$ for the "necessity" modal logic operator $\square$.

This semantics is equivalent to the algebraic semantics for $\mathcal{L}$ in [8] for the case of the conception where intensional entities are considered to be *equal* if and only if they are *necessarily equivalent*. Intensional equality is much stronger that the standard *extensional equality* in the actual world, just because it requires the extensional equality in *all* possible worlds; in fact, if $< \phi >^{\beta_1}_\alpha /g \simeq < \psi >^{\beta_1}_\alpha /g$, then $h(I(< A >^{\beta_1}_\alpha /g)) = h(I(< \psi >^{\beta_2}_\alpha /g))$ for all extensionalization functions $h \in \mathcal{E}$ (i.e., possible worlds $is^{-1}(h) \in \overline{\mathcal{W}}$).

It is easy to verify that the intensional equality means that in every possible world $w \in \overline{\mathcal{W}}$ the intensional entities u_1 and u_2 have the same extensions.

Let the logic modal formula $\square \phi[\beta_1/g(\beta_1)]$, where the assignment g is applied only to free variables in β_1 of a formula ϕ not in the list of variables in $\alpha = (x_1,\ldots,x_n)$, $n \geq 1$, represents an n-ary intensional concept such that $I(\square \phi[\beta_1/g(\beta_1)]) \in D_n$ and $I(\phi[\beta_1/g(\beta_1)]) = I(< \phi >^{\beta_1}_\alpha /g) \in D_n$. Then the extension of this n-ary concept is equal to (here

the mapping necess : $D_i \rightarrow D_i$ for each $i \geq 0$ is a new operation of the intensional algebra $\mathcal{A}_{int}$ in Definition 6)

$$h\left(I\left(\square\phi\left[\frac{\beta_1}{g(\beta_1)}\right]\right)\right)$$

$$= h\left(\text{necess}\left(I\left(\phi\left[\frac{\beta_1}{g(\beta_1)}\right]\right)\right)\right)$$

$$= \left\{ (g'(x_1),\ldots,g'(x_n)) \mid \right.$$

$$\left. \mathcal{M} \vDash_{w,g'} \square\phi\left[\frac{\beta_1}{g(\beta_1)}\right], \ g' \in \mathcal{D}^{\mathcal{V}} \right\}$$

$$= \left\{ (g'(x_1),\ldots,g'(x_n)) \mid g' \in \mathcal{D}^{\mathcal{V}}, \ \forall w_1 \right.$$

$$\left. \left((w,w_1) \in \mathcal{R} \text{ implies } \mathcal{M} \vDash_{w_1,g'} \phi\left[\frac{\beta_1}{g(\beta_1)}\right] \right) \right\}$$

$$= \bigcap_{h_1 \in \mathcal{E}} h_1\left(I\left(\phi\left[\frac{\beta_1}{g(\beta_1)}\right]\right)\right),$$

(8)

while

$$h\left(I\left(\Diamond\phi\left[\frac{\beta_1}{g(\beta_1)}\right]\right)\right)$$

$$= h\left(I\left(\neg\square\neg\phi\left[\frac{\beta_1}{g(\beta_1)}\right]\right)\right)$$

$$= h\left(\text{neg}\left(\text{necess}\left(I\left(\neg\phi\left[\frac{\beta_1}{g(\beta_1)}\right]\right)\right)\right)\right)$$

$$= \mathcal{D}^n \setminus h\left(\text{necess}\left(I\left(\neg\phi\left[\frac{\beta_1}{g(\beta_1)}\right]\right)\right)\right)$$

$$= \mathcal{D}^n \setminus \left(\bigcap_{h_1 \in \mathcal{E}} h_1\left(I\left(\neg\phi\left[\frac{\beta_1}{g(\beta_1)}\right]\right)\right)\right)$$

(9)

$$= \mathcal{D}^n \setminus \left(\bigcap_{h_1 \subset \mathcal{E}} h_1\left(\text{neg}\left(I\left(\phi\left[\frac{\beta_1}{g(\beta_1)}\right]\right)\right)\right)\right)$$

$$= \mathcal{D}^n \setminus \left(\bigcap_{h_1 \in \mathcal{E}} \mathcal{D}^n \setminus h_1\left(I\left(\phi\left[\frac{\beta_1}{g(\beta_1)}\right]\right)\right)\right)$$

$$= \bigcup_{h_1 \in \mathcal{E}} h_1\left(I\left(\phi\left[\frac{\beta_1}{g(\beta_1)}\right]\right)\right).$$

Consequently, the concepts $\square\phi[\beta_1/g(\beta_1)]$ and $\Diamond\phi[\beta_1/g(\beta_1)]$ are the *built-in* (or rigid) concept as well, whose extensions do not depend on possible worlds.

Thus, two concepts are intensionally *equal*, that is, $< \phi >_\alpha^{\beta_1}/g \approx < \psi >_\alpha^{\beta_2}/g$, if and only if $h(I(\phi[\beta_1/g(\beta_1)])) = h(I(\psi[\beta_2/g(\beta_2)]))$ for every h.

Analogously, two concepts are *weakly* equivalent, that is, $< \phi >_\alpha^{\beta_1}/g \approx < \psi >_\alpha^{\beta_2}/g$ if and only if $h(I(\Diamond\phi[\beta_1/g(\beta_1)])) = h(I(\Diamond\psi[\beta_2/g(\beta_2)]))$.

3. Application to the Intensional FOL without Abstraction Operator

In the case of the intensional FOL defined in Definition 1, without Bealer's intensional abstraction operator <>, we obtain the syntax of the standard FOL but with intensional semantics as presented in [15].

Such a FOL has a well-known Tarski's interpretation, defined as follows.

An interpretation (Tarski) I_T consists in a nonempty domain $\mathscr{D}$ and a mapping that assigns to any predicate letter $p_i^k \in P$ a relation $R = I_T(p_i^k) \subseteq \mathscr{D}^k$, to any functional letter $f_i^k \in F$ a function $I_T(f_i^k) : \mathscr{D}^k \to \mathscr{D}$, or, equivalently, its graph relation $R = I_T(f_i^k) \subseteq \mathscr{D}^{k+1}$ where the $k + 1$th column is the resulting function's value, and to each individual constant $c \in F$ one given element $I_T(c) \in \mathscr{D}$.

Consequently, from the intensional point of view, an interpretation of Tarski is a possible world in the Montague's intensional semantics, that is, $w = I_T \in \mathscr{W}$. The correspondent extensionalization function is $h = is(w) = is(I_T)$.

We define the satisfaction of a logic formulae in $\mathscr{L}$ for a given assignment $g : \mathscr{V} \to \mathscr{D}$ inductively, as follows.

If a formula ϕ is an atomic formula $p_i^k(t_1, \ldots, t_k)$, then this assignment g satisfies ϕ if and only if $(g^*(t_1), \ldots, g^*(t_k)) \in I_T(p_i^k)$; g satisfies $\neg\phi$ if and only if it does not satisfy ϕ; g satisfies $\phi \wedge \psi$ iff g satisfies ϕ and g satisfies ψ; g satisfies $(\exists x_i)\phi$ if and only if there exists an assignment $g' \in \mathscr{D}^{\mathscr{V}}$ that may differ from g only for the variable $x_i \in \mathscr{V}$, and g' satisfies ϕ.

A formula ϕ is true for a given interpretation I_T if and only if ϕ is satisfied by every assignment $g \in \mathscr{D}^{\mathscr{V}}$. A formula ϕ is valid (i.e., tautology) if and only if ϕ is true for every Tarksi's interpretation $I_T \in \mathfrak{I}_T$. An interpretation I_T is a model of a set of formulae Γ if and only if every formula $\phi \in \Gamma$ is true in this interpretation. We denote by FOL(Γ) the FOL with a set of assumptions Γ, and by $\mathfrak{I}_T(\Gamma)$ the subset of Tarski's interpretations that are models of Γ, with $\mathfrak{I}_T(\emptyset) = \mathfrak{I}_T$. A formula ϕ is said to be a *logical consequence* of Γ, denoted by $\Gamma \Vdash \phi$, if and only if ϕ is true in all interpretations in $\mathfrak{I}_T(\Gamma)$. Thus, $\Vdash \phi$ if and only if ϕ is a tautology.

The basic set of axioms of the FOL are that of the propositional logic with two additional axioms: (A1) $(\forall x)(\phi \Rightarrow \psi) \Rightarrow (\phi \Rightarrow (\forall x)\psi)$ (x does not occur in ϕ and it is not bound in ψ), and (A2) $(\forall x)\phi \Rightarrow \phi[x/t]$, (neither x nor any variable in t occurs bound in ϕ). For the FOL with identity, we need the *proper* axiom (A3) $x_1 \doteq x_2 \Rightarrow (x_1 \doteq x_3 \Rightarrow x_2 \doteq x_3)$.

The inference rules are Modus Ponens and generalization (G) "if ϕ is a theorem and x is not bound in ϕ, then $(\forall x)\phi$ is a theorem."

The standard FOL is considered as an extensional logic because two open sentences with the same tuple of variables $\phi(x_1, \ldots, x_m)$ and $\psi(x_1, \ldots, x_m)$ are equal if and only if they have the *same extension* in a given interpretation I_T, that is, if and only if $I_T^*(\phi(x_1, \ldots, x_m)) = I_T^*(\psi(x_1, \ldots, x_m))$, where I_T^* is the unique extension of I_T to all formulae, as follows.

(1) For a (closed) sentence ϕ/g, we have that $I_T^*(\phi/g) = t$ if and only if g satisfies ϕ, as recursively defined above.

(2) For an open-sentence ϕ with the tuple of free variables $(x_1, \ldots, x_m)$, we have that $I_T^*(\phi(x_1, \ldots, x_m)) =_{\text{def}} \{(g(x_1), \ldots, g(x_m)) \mid g \in \mathscr{D}^{\mathscr{V}} \text{ and } I_T^*(\phi/g) = t\}$.

It is easy to verify that for a formula ϕ with the tuple of free variables $(x_1, \ldots, x_m)$, $I_T^*(\phi(x_1, \ldots, x_m)/g) = t$ if and only if $(g(x_1), \ldots, g(x_m)) \in I_T^*(\phi(x_1, \ldots, x_m))$.

This extensional *equality* of two virtual predicates can be generalized to the extensional *equivalence* when both predicates ϕ, ψ have the same set of free variables but their ordering in the *tuples* of free variables is not identical: such two virtual predicates are equivalent if the extension of the first is equal to the proper permutation of columns of the extension of the second virtual predicate. It is easy to verify that such an extensional equivalence corresponds to the logical equivalence denoted by $\phi \equiv \psi$.

This extensional equivalence between two relations $R_1, R_2 \in \mathfrak{R}$ with the same arity will be denoted by $R_1 \cong R_2$, while the extensional identity will be denoted in the standard way by $R_1 = R_2$.

Let $\mathscr{A}_{\text{FOL}} = (\mathscr{L}, \doteq, \top, \wedge, \neg, \exists)$ be a free syntax algebra for "first-order logic with identity $\doteq$," with the set $\mathscr{L}$ of first-order logic formulae, with $\top$ denoting the tautology formula (the contradiction formula is denoted by $\neg\top$), with the set of variables in $\mathscr{V}$ and the domain of values in $\mathscr{D}$. It is well known that we are able to make the extensional algebraization of the FOL by using the *cylindric* algebras [25] that are the extension of Boolean algebras with a set of binary operators for the FOL identity relations and a set of unary algebraic operators ("projections") for each case of FOL quantification ($\exists x$). In what follows, we will make an analog extensional algebraization over $\mathfrak{R}$ but by interpretation of the logic conjunction $\wedge$ by a set of *natural join* operators over relations introduced by Codd's relational algebra [9] and [26] as a kind of a predicate calculus whose interpretations are tied to the database.

Corollary 11 (extensional FOL semantics [15]). *Let us define the extensional relational algebra for the FOL by*

$$\mathscr{A}_{\mathfrak{R}} = \left(\mathfrak{R}, R_=, \{\langle\,\rangle\}, \{\bowtie_S\}_{S \in \mathscr{P}(\mathbb{N}^2)}, \sim, \{\pi_{-n}\}_{n \in \mathbb{N}}\right), \qquad (10)$$

where $\{\langle\rangle\} \in \mathfrak{R}$ *is the algebraic value correspondent to the logic truth and* $R_=$ *is the binary relation for extensionally equal elements. We will use "=" for the extensional identity for relations in* $\mathfrak{R}$.

Then, for any Tarski's interpretation I_T *its unique extension to all formulae* $I_T^* : \mathscr{L} \rightarrow \mathfrak{R}$ *is also the homomorphism* $I_T^* : \mathscr{A}_{FOL} \rightarrow \mathscr{A}_{\mathfrak{R}}$ *from the free syntax FOL algebra into this extensional relational algebra.*

Proof. Directly from definition of the semantics of the operators in $\mathscr{A}_{\mathfrak{R}}$ defined in precedence, let us take the case of conjunction of logic formulae of the definition above where $\varphi(x_i, x_j, x_k, x_l, x_m, y_i, y_j)$ (its tuple of variables is obtained by the method defined in the FOL introduction) is the virtual predicate of the logic formula $\phi(x_i, x_j, x_k, x_l, x_m) \wedge \psi(x_l, y_i, x_j, y_j)$: $I_T^*(\phi \wedge \psi) = I_T^*(\varphi) = \{(g(x_i), g(x_j), g(x_k), g(x_l), g(x_m), g(y_i), g(y_j)) \mid I_T^*(\varphi/g) = t\} = \{(g(x_i), g(x_j), g(x_k), g(x_l), g(x_m), g(y_i), g(y_j)) \mid I_T^*(\phi/g \wedge \psi/g) = t\} = \{(g(x_i), g(x_j), g(x_k), g(x_l), g(x_m), g(y_i), g(y_j)) \mid I_T^*(\phi/g) = t$ and $I_T^*(\phi/g) = t\} = \{(g(x_i), g(x_j), g(x_k), g(x_l), g(x_m), g(y_i), g(y_j)) \mid (g(x_i), g(x_j), g(x_k), g(x_l), g(x_m)) \in I_T^*(\phi)$ and $(g(x_l), g(y_i), g(x_j), g(y_j)) \in I_T^*(\phi)\} = I_T^*(\phi) \bowtie_{\{(4,1),(2,3)\}} I_T^*(\psi)$.

Thus, it is enough to show that $I_T^*(\top) = \{\langle\rangle\}$ is also valid, and $I_T^*(\neg\top) = \emptyset$. The first property comes from the fact that $\top$ is a tautology, thus satisfied by every assignment g, that is, it is true, that is, $I_T^*(\top) = t$ (and t is equal to the empty tuple $\{\langle\rangle\}$). The second property comes from the fact that $I_T^*(\neg\top) = \sim (I_T^*(\top)) = \sim (\{\langle\rangle\}) = \mathscr{D}^0 \setminus \{\langle\rangle\} = \{\langle\rangle\} \setminus \{\langle\rangle\} = \emptyset$. That is, the tautology and the contradiction have the true and false logic value, respectively, in $\mathfrak{R}$.

We have also that $I_T^*(\dot= (x, y)) = I_T(\dot=) = R_=$ for every interpretation I_T because $\dot=$ is the built-in binary predicate, that is, with the same extension in every Tarski's interpretation.

Consequently, the mapping $I_T^* : (\mathscr{L}, \dot=, \top, \wedge, \neg, \exists) \rightarrow \mathscr{A}_{\mathfrak{R}}$ is a homomorphism that represents the extensional Tarskian semantics of the FOL. $\square$

Consequently, we obtain the following Intensional/extensional FOL semantics [15].

For any Tarski's interpretation I_T of the FOL, the following diagram of homomorphisms commutes.

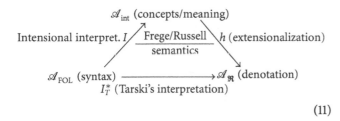

$$\tag{11}$$

where $h = is(w)$ and $w = I_T \in \mathscr{W}$ is the explicit possible world (extensional Tarski's interpretation).

This homomorphic diagram formally expresses the fusion of Frege's and Russell's semantics [27–29] of meaning and denotation of the FOL language and renders mathematically correct the definition of what we call an "intuitive notion of

intensionality," in terms of which a language is intensional if denotation is distinguished from sense: that is, if both denotation and sense are ascribed to its expressions. This notion is simply adopted from Frege's contribution (without its infinite sense-hierarchy, avoided by Russell's approach where there is only one meaning relation, one fundamental relation between words and things, here represented by one fixed intensional interpretation I), where the sense contains mode of presentation (here described algebraically as an algebra of concepts (intensions) $\mathscr{A}_{int}$), and where sense determines denotation for any given extensionalization function h (correspondent to a given Traski's interpretation I_T). More about the relationships between Frege's and Russell's theories of meaning may be found in the Chapter 7, "Extensionality and Meaning", in [18].

As noted by Gottlob Frege and Rudolf Carnap (he uses terms Intension/extension in the place of Frege's terms sense/denotation [30]), the two logic formulae with the same denotation (i.e., the same extension for a given Tarski's interpretation I_T) need not have the same sense (intension), thus such codenotational expressions are not *substitutable* in general.

In fact there is exactly *one* sense (meaning) of a given logic formula in $\mathscr{L}$, defined by the uniquely fixed intensional interpretation I, and *a set* of possible denotations (extensions) each determined by a given Tarski's interpretation of the FOL as follows from Definition 4:

$$\mathscr{L} \xrightarrow{I} \mathscr{D} \Longrightarrow_{h=is(I_T)\&I_T\in\mathscr{W}=\mathfrak{I}_T(\Gamma)} \mathfrak{R}. \tag{12}$$

Often "intension" has been used exclusively in connection with possible worlds semantics; however, here we use (as many others; as Bealer for example) "intension" in a more wide sense, that is, as an *algebraic expression* in the intensional algebra of meanings (concepts) $\mathscr{A}_{int}$, which represents the structural composition of more complex concepts (meanings) from the given set of atomic meanings. Consequently, not only the denotation (extension) is compositional, but also the meaning (intension) is compositional.

4. Conclusion

Semantics is a theory concerning the fundamental relations between words and things. In Tarskian semantics of the FOL, one defines what it takes for a sentence in a language to be truely relative to a model. This puts one in a position to define what it takes for a sentence in a language to be valid. Tarskian semantics often proves quite useful in logic. Despite this, Tarskian semantics neglects meaning, as if truth in language were autonomous. Because of that the Tarskian theory of truth becomes inessential to the semantics for more expressive logics, or more "natural" languages.

Both Montague's and Bealer's approaches were useful for this investigation of the intensional FOL with intensional abstraction operator, but the first is not adequate and explains why we adopted two-step intensional semantics (intensional interpretation with the set of extensionalization functions).

At the end of this work, we defined an extensional algebra for the FOL (different from standard cylindric algebras) and the commutative homomorphic diagram that expresses the generalization of the Tarskian theory of truth for the FOL into the Frege/Russell's theory of meaning.

References

[1] J. Pustejovsky and B. Boguraev, "Lexical knowledge representation and natural language processing," *Artificial Intelligence*, vol. 63, no. 1-2, pp. 193–223, 1993.

[2] M. Fitting, "First-order intensional logic," *Annals of Pure and Applied Logic*, vol. 127, no. 1-3, pp. 171–193, 2004.

[3] T. Braüner, "Adding intensional machinery to hybrid logic," *Journal of Logic and Computation*, vol. 18, no. 4, pp. 631–648, 2008.

[4] T. Braüner and S. Ghilardi, "First-order modal logic," in *Handbook of Modal Logic*, pp. 549–620, Elsevier, 2007.

[5] S. Bond and M. Denecker, "I-logic: an intensional logic of informations," in *Proceedings of the 19th Belgian-Dutch Conference on Artificial Intelligence*, pp. 49–56, Utrecht, The Netherlands, November 2007.

[6] M. A. Orgun and W. W. Wadge, "Towards a unified theory of intensional logic programming," *The Journal of Logic Programming*, vol. 13, no. 4, pp. 413–440, 1992.

[7] G. Bealer, "Universals," *The Journal of Philosophy*, vol. 90, no. 1, pp. 5–32, 1993.

[8] G. Bealer, "Theories of properties, relations, and propositions," *The Journal of Philosophy*, vol. 76, no. 11, pp. 634–648, 1979.

[9] E. F. Codd, "Relational completeness of data base sublanguages," in *Data Base Systems: Courant Computer Science Symposia Series 6*, Prentice Hall, Englewood Cliffs, NJ, USA, 1972.

[10] D. K. Lewis, *On the Plurality of Worlds*, Blackwell, Oxford, UK, 1986.

[11] R. Stalnaker, *Inquiry*, The MIT Press, Cambridge, Mass, USA, 1984.

[12] R. Montague, "Universal grammar," *Theoria*, vol. 36, no. 3, pp. 373–398, 1970.

[13] R. Montague, "The proper treatment of quantification in ordinary English," in *Approaches to Natural Language*, J. Hintikka, P. Suppes, J. M. E. Moravcsik et al., Eds., pp. 221–242, Reidel, Dordrecht, The Netherlands, 1973.

[14] R. Montague, *Formal Philosophy. Selected Papers of Richard Montague*, Yale University Press, London, UK, 1974.

[15] Z. Majkić, "First-order logic: modality andintensionality," http://arxiv.org/abs/1103.0680v1.

[16] Z. Majkić, "Intensional first-order logic for P2P database systems," in *Journal on Data Semantics 12*, vol. 5480 of *Lecture Notes in Computer Science*, pp. 131–152, Springer, Berlin, Germany, 2009.

[17] Z. Majkić, "Intensional semantics for RDF data structures," in *Proceedings of the 12th International Symposium on Database Engineering & Applications Systems (IDEAS '08)*, pp. 69–77, Coimbra, Portugal, September, 2008.

[18] G. Bealer, *Quality and Concept*, Oxford University Press, New York, NY, USA, 1982.

[19] Z. Majkić, "Weakly-coupled ontology integration of P2P database systems," in *Proceedings of the 1st International Workshop on Peer-to-Peer Knowledge Management (P2PKM '04)*, Boston, Mass, USA, August 2004.

[20] Z. Majkić, "Intensional P2P mapping between RDF ontologies," in *Proceedings of the 6th International Conference on Web Information Systems (WISE '05)*, M. Kitsuregawa, Ed., vol. 3806 of *Lecture Notes in Computer Science*, pp. 592–594, New York, NY, USA, November 2005.

[21] Z. Majkić, "Intensional semantics for P2P data integration," in *Journal on Data Semantics 6*, vol. 4090 of *Lecture Notes in Computer Science*, Special Issue on 'Emergent Semantics', pp. 47–66, 2006.

[22] Z. Majkić, "Non omniscient intensional contextual reasoning for query-agents in P2P systems," in *Proceedings of the 3rd Indian International Conference on Artificial Intelligence (IICAI '07)*, Pune, India, December 2007.

[23] Z. Majkić, "Coalgebraic specification of query computation in intensional P2P database systems," in *Proceedings of the International Conference on Theoretical and Mathematical Foundations of Computer Science (TMFCS '08)*, pp. 14–23, Orlando, Fla, USA, July 2008.

[24] Z. Majkić, "RDF view-based interoperability in intensional FOL for Peer-to-Peer database systems," in *Proceedings of the International Conference on Enterprise Information Systems and Web Technologies (EISWT '08)*, pp. 88–96, Orlando, Fla, USA, July 2008.

[25] L. Henkin, J. D. Monk, and A. Tarski, *Cylindic Algebras I*, North-Holland, Amsterdam, The Netherlands, 1971.

[26] A. Pirotte, "A precise definition of basic relational notions and of the relational algebra," *ACM SIGMOD Record*, vol. 13, no. 1, pp. 30–45, 1982.

[27] G. Frege, "Über Sinn und Bedeutung," *Zeitschrift für Philosophie und philosophische Kritik*, vol. 100, pp. 22–50, 1892.

[28] B. Russell, "On Denoting," in *Logic and Knowledge*, vol. 14 of *Mind*, Reprinted in Russell, pp. 479–493, 1905.

[29] A. N. Whitehead and B. Russell, *Principia Mathematica*, vol. 1, Cambridge, Mass, USA, 1910.

[30] R. Carnap, *Meaning and Necessity*, Chicago, Ill, USA, 1947.

9

Reinforcement Learning in an Environment Synthetically Augmented with Digital Pheromones

Salvador E. Barbosa and Mikel D. Petty

University of Alabama in Huntsville, 301 Sparkman Drive, Huntsville, AL 35899, USA

Correspondence should be addressed to Salvador E. Barbosa; seb0005@uah.edu

Academic Editor: Ozlem Uzuner

Reinforcement learning requires information about states, actions, and outcomes as the basis for learning. For many applications, it can be difficult to construct a representative model of the environment, either due to lack of required information or because of that the model's state space may become too large to allow a solution in a reasonable amount of time, using the experience of prior actions. An environment consisting solely of the occurrence or nonoccurrence of specific events attributable to a human actor may appear to lack the necessary structure for the positioning of responding agents in time and space using reinforcement learning. Digital pheromones can be used to synthetically augment such an environment with event sequence information to create a more persistent and measurable imprint on the environment that supports reinforcement learning. We implemented this method and combined it with the ability of agents to learn from actions not taken, a concept known as fictive learning. This approach was tested against the historical sequence of Somali maritime pirate attacks from 2005 to mid-2012, enabling a set of autonomous agents representing naval vessels to successfully respond to an average of 333 of the 899 pirate attacks, outperforming the historical record of 139 successes.

1. Introduction

Sequences of events resulting from the actions of human adversarial actors such as military forces or criminal organizations may appear to have random dynamics in time and space. Finding patterns in such sequences and using those patterns in order to anticipate and respond to the events can be quite challenging. Often, the number of potentially causal factors for such events is very large, making it infeasible to obtain and analyze all relevant information prior to the occurrence of the next event. These difficulties can hinder the planning of responses using conventional computational methods such as multiagent models and machine learning, which typically exploit information available in or about the environment.

A real-world example of such a problem is Somali maritime piracy. Beginning in 2005, the number of attacks attributed to Somali pirates steadily increased. The attacks were carried out on a nearly daily basis during some periods of the year and often took place despite the presence of naval patrol vessels in the area [1]. They were often launched with

little warning and at unexpected locations. We would like to use the attributes of past attacks to anticipate and respond to future attacks. However, the set of attack attributes potentially relevant to doing so is quite large; it includes the relative position of patrolling naval forces, the rules of engagement of those patrols, the type of boats and armaments pirates use, the experience level of the pirates, the speed of the targeted ships, and the skill of their captains and crews, the counter-piracy rules of the shipping companies operating the targeted ships, the inclination of those companies to pay ransoms for hijacked ships, the weather and sea state, and many others. Moreover, because the number of ships vulnerable to these attacks are in the tens of thousands annually, the patrolling navies of many countries are not under a unified command but operate independently of one another, the shipping companies are reluctant to reveal the amount of any ransoms paid, and pirate networks are notoriously opaque as to their operations, much information that could be useful to a model of pirate attacks is unavailable. Finally, even if all the information relevant to the pirate attacks was known, the large number of combinations resulting from an even modest number of options for each of the applicable attributes would likely make it infeasible to exhaustively evaluate all possibilities in a timely manner or to draw inferences from such a large state space in light of a comparatively small sequence of events.

The difficulty of this real-world problem is illustrated by the fact that patrolling navies in the area, equipped with highly sophisticated surveillance systems and staffed with expert military intelligence personnel only managed a timely and successful response to one in six pirate attacks over the period in question [1]. An alternate and appropriate question then is whether there are hidden patterns in the data, such as the frequency and number of attacks in a given area, the timing, and location of an attack relative to those that preceded it, or the penchant of pirates for returning to the general location of a previous attack, that may be detected and exploited using model-free methods to aid in positioning naval assets to defend against future attacks.

Definitions of computational agents differ in detail, but they generally agree that agents are computational entities that perceive and react to their environment with varying levels of autonomy [2, 3]. However, for an agent-based solution to be effective, the environment must provide enough information for the agent to perform its task. There are many levels of agents including deductive, reactive, and hybrid agents [3]. Of these, reactive agents are most reliant on information, as they generally operate solely by reacting to their (usually local) environment. These agents are typically simple and have only a few behaviors, but they may exhibit emergent behaviors, which are behaviors that are not explicitly programmed into individual agents but rather result from the interactions of the agents with each other or with the environment [4].

Along with supervised learning [5] and unsupervised learning [6], reinforcement learning is one of the primary branches of machine learning. Computational agents using reinforcement learning may be found in both model-based and model-free contexts [7]. In this paradigm, an agent interacts with its environment without necessarily having any prior training in it or knowledge of its dynamics. In any given state, the agent chooses an available action and upon executing that action is rewarded based on the effectiveness of the action. From the reward, the agent learns about taking that action in that particular state and possibly in similar states. Any time the agent encounters a previously unseen state, exploration of the environment is taking place. As state-action pairs are encountered, the agent builds a memory of optimal behaviors for future use [7]. Such value iteration agents are deemed by the authors to be in the continuum of reactive agents.

Biologically inspired, multiagent methods have been applied to a range of difficult optimization problems [8]. This approach, often known as swarm intelligence, is modeled on the simple behaviors of individual members (agents) of groups found in nature, such as ants (e.g., ant colony optimization by Dorigo and Stützle [9]) or birds and fish (e.g., particle swarm optimization by Kennedy and Eberhart [10]), which collectively result in emergent properties and features that lead to good solutions. While these techniques do not guarantee convergence to the problem's optimum solution, they have been applied successfully in many areas [8, 11]. Most agents in these approaches fit the definition of reactive agents [3].

The Somali piracy problem may seem a poor fit for a model-based approach, as attempts to implement the model may be hampered by a lack in the required information (pirate tactics or skill of transiting ship captains, for instance). When viewed from a model-free perspective, we would like to learn from the event sequence for this and similar problems, including crime, military operations, and other sequences that, either by nature or intent, may appear unpredictable. However, it could be difficult for an environment with only two states (event and no event) to provide sufficient, distinct, and consistently recurring patterns for the learning algorithm to exploit. We purport that the use of model-free reinforcement learning with reactive agents can be a useful approach to this class of problems, if sufficiently informative states can be constructed from the sequence of the events to position agents in anticipation of upcoming events.

To that end, we introduce a method to generate informative states from an event sequence and to control a set of reactive agents using model-free reinforcement learning, with the goal of positioning agents in proximity of impending events (in essence predicting the next event in time and space). We do this by synthetically augmenting the environment with digital pheromones to indicate both the location of events and areas occupied by agents. These and other information augmenters derived or calculated from the pheromones are used to create discrete signatures in the environment (states) that agents assess and react to (actions). We propagate these markers to a spatiotemporal neighborhood around the event. Regularities in the timing and location of events result in the same state signatures and may be exploited using reinforcement learning by relating them to the signatures of augmenters encountered at the site of past events.

To extend this augmentation concept and improve agent learning speed, we artificially increase the number of learning opportunities by giving agents the ability to learn from fictive or counterfactual actions. This is accomplished by assigning to each agent a "ghost" fictive agent who is colocated with the agent but selects (possibly different) actions using an alternate policy. Actions by the fictive agent that would have resulted in a success, had they been executed by the real agent, are used to update the real agent's learning table, thereby affecting its future action selections.

The overall method intentionally includes both domain-specific and domain-independent elements. The augmenters to be used for the Somali piracy problem are largely specific to the domain (e.g., an augmenter for Shipping lanes will be defined). The piracy augmenters will likely have to be adapted or replaced for other applications, such as criminal acts in an urban area. However, the other elements of the method, including the reinforcement learning algorithm, the use of fictive learning, and the method's central idea of applying reinforcement learning to a synthetically augmented environment are independent of the domain and could be used for other applications once the augmenters for that application have been developed.

This research is intended to address some fundamental questions regarding the feasibility of environment augmentation supporting reinforcement learning agents, the viability of the proposed fictive learning method, and the overall effectiveness of the approach in solving real-world problems. Specifically, we aim to address the following questions.

(1) Can an environment consisting of a sequence of events be synthetically augmented to allow the use of model-free reinforcement learning methods and algorithms in controlling agents?

　(1.1) Do the results of applying different types of information augmenters differ significantly from one another, and if so, which augmenters are most effective?

　(1.2) How does the proposed fictive learning method compare to the standard reinforcement learning approach?

　(1.3) How do different action selection policies compare to one another?

(2) Does the outcome of the proposed methodology compare favorably to the historical record of success or to current means of responding to the real-world events of interest?

This paper is organized as follows. Section 2 briefly introduces the Somali piracy problem and surveys relevant aspects and research in reinforcement learning, multiagent reinforcement learning, fictive learning, and pheromone-inspired computing, the key concepts utilized in this work. Section 3 motivates the need for this novel method and explains the information-augmentation approach by defining the environment of interest and specifying a set of digital pheromones intended to augment that environment so as to enable use of a reinforcement-learning algorithm. Section 4 describes the scenario, formulates the reinforcement learning problem, presents agent behavior and attributes, including the fictive learning ability, and introduces the research platform. Section 5 reports and analyzes the results of applying the proposed approach to positioning naval vessels to defend against Somali pirate attacks, in light of the research questions. Finally, Section 6 states the conclusions, briefly discusses the limitations of the research, and identifies possible avenues for future work.

2. Background and Related Work

In this section brief background introductions are given of the Somali piracy problem, reinforcement learning, multiagent reinforcement learning, fictive learning, and pheromone-inspired computing, and selected relevant research literature is referenced. Research related to maritime piracy is also summarized.

2.1. Somali Piracy. Data compiled and reported by the International Maritime Bureau over a seven and a half year period (2005 through mid-2012) detail nearly one thousand

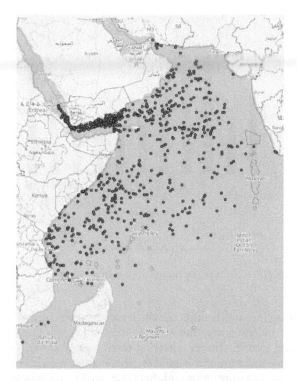

Figure 1: Attacks attributed to Somali pirates (January 2005 through June 2012).

incidents of ships of all types having been fired at, chased, boarded, or hijacked by pirates [12–19]. The attacks generally occurred in the northwest portion of the Indian Ocean and were concentrated in the Gulf of Aden (Figure 1).

Vessels hijacked by pirates are often ransomed by their owners and insurers for as much as tens of millions of dollars, a value that is usually a small percentage of the value of the vessel and its cargo. As a result, Somali piracy is a very profitable business with the pirates as the most visible aspect of a network that involves rich and powerful people at the top, an entire cast of middle men and enablers, and many others who profit from supplying the pirates, feeding or guarding hostages, or acting as lookouts [1, 20].

In light of the increasing multimillion dollar ransoms, insurance and shipping companies are willing to pay to get ships and crews back [21], the demand for ransom payouts likely continues to be high in the foreseeable future.

Since the hijacking of the Ukrainian ship MV *Faina* in September 2008, which was carrying a shipment of lethal military equipment to southern Sudan [22], three naval task forces purposely established to deal with the piracy problem have been patrolling the waters around Somalia and the Gulf of Aden, aided by vessels from other navies outside of their command and control structure [23]. The approximately 25 to 40 naval vessels available at any point in time [1] face the daunting task of stopping attacks in an area of over 6.5 million square kilometers (2.5 million square miles) [24]. The bulk of naval counter piracy efforts are centered on the Gulf of Aden.

In the early years of Somali piracy, a group of four to eight pirates trolled the waters in small boats known as skiffs,

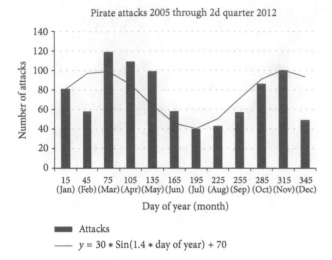

FIGURE 2: Pirate attacks by month appear to show a cyclical pattern.

looking for victim ships. As their success grew, pirates used commandeered medium-sized vessels to tow multiple skiffs farther into the ocean, allowing them to stay at sea longer and to conduct multiple attacks. These larger vessels became known as mother ships and their increased use is believed to be a significant enabler in the higher number of attacks seen in recent years [22]. While accurate counts of the number of ships transiting the entire area vulnerable to piracy are not available, more than 20,000 vessels are estimated to have passed through the Gulf of Aden in 2009 [20, 25].

The concentration in geography of pirate attacks is likely due to both the availability of victim shipping vessels, as well as the relatively narrow gulf waterway (when compared to the wide open ocean). However, an analysis of the number of attacks also revealed a pattern of approximately 8.5 months in duration as shown in Figure 2.

2.2. Reinforcement Learning. Reinforcement learning is a powerful computational paradigm employing well-understood algorithms [26] that may be used in a model-free context. Its applicability has been stretched to a vast class of problems and to multiple agents, through various modifications or restrictions. In its basic form, reinforcement learning involves a single agent, with all other actions (including those of an adversary) emanating from a stationary environment. A working definition of a stationary environment is that the true value of actions does not change over time [7].

As mentioned earlier, reinforcement learning is reward-based. At any time t, the agent seeks to maximize the total reward it will receive through some future time T. When T is finite, the task being performed is said to be *episodic*, with T denoting the end of an episode. When T is infinite, the task is said to be *continuing* [7].

Thus, the projected total reward at time t, denoted R_t, is defined as

$$R_t = r_{t+1} + \gamma r_{t+2} + \gamma^2 r_{t+3} + \cdots = \sum_{k=0}^{T} \gamma^k r_{t+k+1}, \quad (1)$$

where all r_i are the rewards received in successive time steps. The discount rate γ, with $0 \leq \gamma \leq 1$, serves to keep the result finite when T is infinite and to enable the calculation of the present value of future rewards.

To obtain a reward, the agent assesses its state and selects an action available in that state. The agent is then atomically rewarded (that term also applying to no reward or to negative rewards, which are understood as punishments) and transitioned to the next state. The selection of an action in any given state may be deterministic or probability based. This mapping from states to actions is known as the agent's policy and is normally denoted π. The goal of reinforcement learning is the determination of an action policy to maximize total reward.

A central focus of reinforcement learning algorithms is the estimation of value functions. The value function is a measure of the worth of being in a particular state or of taking an action while in a given state, while observing a specific policy. The two primary value functions used are $V^\pi(s)$, the state-value function, and $Q^\pi(s, a)$, the action value function [7]. These functions are defined as follows, where s is the state, a is the action, and $E_\pi\{\}$ is the expected value while following policy π:

$$V^\pi(s) = E_\pi\{R_t \mid s_t = s\} = E_\pi\left\{\sum_{k=0}^{\infty} \gamma^k r_{t+k+1} \mid s_t = s\right\}$$

$$Q^\pi(s, a) = E_\pi\{R_t \mid s_t = s, a_t = a\} \quad (2)$$

$$= E_\pi\left\{\sum_{k=0}^{\infty} \gamma^k r_{t+k+1} \mid s_t = s, a_t = a\right\}.$$

Temporal differences are the driving force that propel and enable online learning. Whereas Monte Carlo methods used in reinforcement learning are predicated on averaging all returns seen over an episode or trial, temporal difference learning updates knowledge at each time step, as experience is gained during an episode or trial [7]. The simplest form of temporal difference methods, TD(0), may be used in model-free contexts and is defined for the state-value function and action-value function, respectively, as

$$V(s_t) \longleftarrow V(s_t) + \alpha\left[r_{t+1} + \gamma V(s_{t+1}) - V(s_t)\right],$$

$$Q(s_t, a_t) \longleftarrow Q(s_t, a_t) \quad (3)$$

$$+ \alpha\left[r_{t+1} + \gamma Q(s_{t+1}, a_{t+1}) - Q(s_t, a_t)\right].$$

In both cases, the value estimate for time t is updated by being summed with a scaling of the reward received upon transition to time $t + 1$ (as a result of the state and action at time t) plus the difference between the discounted value estimate for the state and action at time $t + 1$ and the original estimate for the value at time t. The scaling parameter α is known as the learning rate and determines how much of the difference should be applied at any given time step.

In this research we used the temporal difference algorithm using state values shown in Algorithm 1 with the ε-greedy policy (detailed in a later section). Note that the Q-Learning algorithm [27] is a temporal difference method that

initialize all $V(s)$ arbitrarily

for all episodes
   initialize s
   repeat
         choose the next state s' using policy
         observe r
         $V(s) \leftarrow V(s) + \alpha\left[r + \gamma V(s') - V(s)\right]$
         $s \leftarrow s'$
   until s is terminal state

where $V(s)$ is the value of being in state s and $V(s')$ is the value estimate
of the resultant state s', γ is the discount rate, and α is the learning rate.

ALGORITHM 1: Temporal difference learning algorithm (adapted from [7]).

learns the value of state-action pairs (each possible action in every state has a value and leads to an end state). Thus, when the agent makes a choice for its next move, it is guided by the value stored for the state-action pair. As an example, an agent on a *diving board* (the state) may have 3 actions available to it: (1) *jump into the pool*, (2) *jump onto the ground*, or (3) *climb down the ladder onto the ground*. The action is selected based on the value stored for each of the state-action pairs. Thus, while the latter two actions both result in a transition to the state *ground*, the climbing down option may have greater value than jumping down. In this research the state-value is used, meaning we are concerned with the utility, or worth, of being in a particular state and not the means by which we reach that state. Thus, parallel to the previously provided example, the agent is faced with two reachable end states *pool* and *ground* and selects its end state from the best of the two values (there are no explicit actions, only reachability). Therefore, references to the term "action" throughout this paper should be construed as the selection of a state transition available to the agent at any point in time, and not in the state-action pair sense.

In this work, two issues with conventional reinforcement learning must be acknowledged. First, reinforcement learning algorithms ordinarily assume that the environment is stationary (as defined earlier); if it is not, the agent must potentially keep relearning states and actions [28]. Research on the nonstationarity problem has shown that reinforcement learning can still be an effective tool even in such cases [7, 28, 29]. Second, reinforcement learning can be compromised in a multiagent environment. When multiple agents operate within the same environment, they exacerbate the nonstationarity problem as their actions affect other agents directly or indirectly via the environment, and they are in turn affected by the actions of others.

2.3. Multiagent Reinforcement Learning.

In [3], an *agent* is defined as a computer system located in some environment and capable of autonomous action toward an objective. Agents have also been described as perceiving their environment through sensors and acting upon it [2]. A multiagent system is one where multiple agents act in response to their environment.

Because reinforcement learning is predicated on a single agent's interactions with the environment, having multiple agents presents three difficulties to its straightforward use: (1) it aggravates the lack of stationarity, as the actions of other agents alter the environment in an uncontrollable way, when viewed from the perspective of any single agent; (2) it raises the problem of how to distribute rewards, and (3) it introduces a possible requirement for some level of coordination and communication among the agents. Prior work overcomes some difficulties of multiagent reinforcement learning [30–32].

The agents in this work are simple, loosely coupled, homogeneous, and independent (in that there is no direct cooperation required in tasks) and utilize minimal coordination, which is achieved indirectly through digital pheromones. While they are multiple agents within the same environment and their behaviors impact those of other agents (sharing of rewards, for instance), agents have no awareness of one another. Given the agent simplicity and independence, the single agent approach to reinforcement learning is employed in this research.

2.4. Fictive Learning.

Reinforcement learning enables learning through rewarding particular actions chosen by an agent in a given state. In general, the agent only learns from the actions it chooses and does not have the ability to learn from "what might have been" if it had selected a different action. However, some reinforcement learning research has focused on fictive learning (also referred to as counterfactual learning or learning through actions not taken). This concept is closely related to the notion of regret when making decisions under uncertainty. Fictive learning is usually adopted to speed up the learning process by either allowing the agent to learn from alternate actions it could have taken or from the actions of others [33]. We review some work on this alternate form of learning in this section.

A neuroscience imaging study of the human brain during decision making explored choice making in games with rewards [34]. The work reviews human behavior as subjects are presented with various situations to identify areas of the brain associated with reward expectation. The model employed used standard Q-Learning [27] expanded by two factors: a component representing the outcomes of actions of others in comparable states and a factor indicating what should have been the best possible action in the situation.

Another Magnetic Resonance Imaging study was conducted on subjects making financial investment decisions [35]. In that study, subjects invested a sum of money and were then presented with the market results (gain or loss of the investment made). The fictive learning signal output was the difference between the best outcome that could have been possible and the actual outcome. The task was repeated multiple times to image areas of the brain as the subjects' decision making were affected by the gains and losses.

Another form of fictive learning is referred to as difference rewards and is intended for use in multiagent environments. The difference reward is defined as a system level reward that evaluates the performance of all agents collectively and subtracts from that the performance attained with all agents except one. This difference, calculated separately for each agent by excluding that agent's performance, in effect assesses the contribution of each agent to the overall team performance. Two application studies utilizing this method are an aviation traffic flow manager [36] and a variation of the El Farol bar congestion problem [37].

2.5. Digital Pheromones. Digital pheromones are a computational artifact patterned after the chemical substances deposited in the environment for communication by many social insects, such as ants [38]. Since the introduction of the ant colony optimization heuristic [9], the concept of digital pheromones has found a number of uses beyond its originally intended use for finding shortest paths. Those applications are quite diverse, including job scheduling [39], weapon-target assignment [40], and assembly line balancing [41]. In this section, some of that work that closely parallels our approach is reviewed.

In [42], pheromones are used in a multiplanar cooperative search application. The area of interest is subdivided for search by multiple unmanned vehicles in different media (air, sea, and land) and the goal is to search the entire area at the same rate. Since the vehicles have different speeds and sensor apertures, and the search area of a large sensor may overlap those of several smaller sensors, pheromones are used to mark locations as searching takes place. Agents are then able to calculate where their search services can best contribute to the global goal. Their technique relies on more than stigmergic signals for coordination in that visited grid cells and timestamps are transmitted to neighboring agents.

A patrolling problem of minimizing the duration between successive visits to subareas within a larger area requiring coverage is posed in [43]. In that work, the *Pants* algorithm (for probabilistic ants) is developed to use pheromones dropped by prior patrolling entities to calculate the best area to be visited by a given agent. The pheromone content is used to compute potential fields that "pull" agents toward areas of low pheromone concentrations. They use local neighborhoods to restrict both the state information flowing to agents and the decision making.

The problem differs slightly in [44], where the goal of minimal delay between patrol visits is applied to an area that may not be fully known. Their approach uses the dispersion of pheromone to neighboring, but possibly not previously visited grid cells. Agents descend to areas of lower pheromone and are restricted to moving to neighboring grid cells. Their technique enforces the single agent per grid cell policy to improve coverage.

Another use of pheromones, reported by Sauter et al. [45], is geared toward patrolling by unmanned vehicles. They use four types of pheromones, including one that identifies areas needing to be visited at a given frequency and one to mark areas that have been visited recently. The *Lawn* pheromone is emitted from sites requiring revisit at specified rates. These pheromones are considered to have been "cut" when the required visit is made by an agent and they begin "growing" again after some time. The *Visited* pheromone is dropped by agent and has the effect of repelling other agents, while its level is above a set value in order to avoid duplication of effort.

Monekosso and Remagnino use synthetic pheromones for multiagent reinforcement learning in their *Phe-Q* Learning algorithm [46]. Their basic premise relies on agent communication through the dispersal and diffusion of pheromones as many other approaches do. In that work, a belief factor is added to reflect the trust an agent has in pheromones deposited by other agents. This factor is controlled by the number of tasks that the agents successfully complete (rewards).

In a crime simulation reported by Furtado et al. [47], pheromones are used by agents representing criminals. That study exploits the preferential attachment mechanism associated with the predilection criminals have for committing crimes in places with which they are familiar. The pheromones placed in the environment by criminal agents are followed by other agents within their networks, based on communications patterns and criminals' experience level. That model also restricts agent sensing and decision making to a limited neighborhood.

2.6. Maritime Piracy Studies. A multiagent model of Somali piracy is documented in a sequence of studies [48–50]. That model focuses primarily on the Gulf of Aden, the geographic area within which most pirate attacks have taken place, and does not attempt to model the entire region where attacks have been experienced. The investigation is centered on game-theoretic routing of shipping vessels, pirates, and patrolling navies. Synthetic shipping traffic is generated and routes automatically planned for the cargo vessels. Risk maps, based on historical attack sites, are used to position defensive vessels to respond to pirate attacks. The pirate model is described as using "simple reinforcement learning" to avoid the defensive vessels, but details are not provided.

The Piracy Attack Risk Surface model is the subject of a thesis from the US Naval Postgraduate School [51]. The model predicts likely piracy attacks in the coming 72-hour period. It is implemented as a Monte Carlo simulation that factors in weather and sea state, prior attacks, and military intelligence factors to determine the locations at most risk.

In a maritime counter-piracy study [52], an agent based model is used to explore defense against pirate attacks and vulnerabilities of vessels during attack. The simulation is a tactical one that pits a single large commercial ship against a fast pirate attack boat. The analysis employs the MANA agent model from the New Zealand Defense Technology Agency.

Another tactical simulation of an attack on a high-value commercial ship was done by Walton et al. [53]. That work models an attack by a small suicide boat against the larger vessel, which is protected by armed sea marshals.

3. Information-Augmentation for Reinforcement Learning

This section motivates and explains the technical approach used in this work by defining the environments of applicability and by specifying a set of digital pheromones intended to augment that environment so as to support a reinforcement-learning algorithm.

The class of problems of interest consists of a sequence of events, caused or generated by a human actor, which happen in relative proximity of one another in both time and space, and for which a model-based approach may be practically intractable (with respect to timeliness) or incomplete (due to information requirements). A team of agents has an interest in being favorably positioned within a specified proximity of the events in order to respond to them.

Our approach is to create artificial patterns in the environment, directly related to the events in question, which may be exploited through use of reinforcement-learning algorithms. We employ reactive agents that use reinforcement learning to evaluate the state of the augmented environment and to select actions that would place them within a given proximity of an event. An envisioned application of this research is a real-time online controller or recommender system for positioning a set of agents tasked with being in proximity of the events of interest, using learning from prior events.

3.1. Motivation. Reinforcement learning is founded upon the concept of a Markovian state, which is to say that the state contains sufficient information and history to enable selection of the best action. Thus, reinforcement learning problems are often defined as Markov Decision Processes [7]. However, for most interesting and real-world problems, the Markovian property does not hold and there is insufficient information to select the best action. An additional complication is that the true value of actions tends to change over time, making the environment nonstationary.

When the Markovian state signal is not available, the environment is deemed to be only partially observable. This problem is then said to be a Partially Observable Markov Decision Process (POMDP). In a POMDP, the signals perceived from the environment are interpreted as observations that are mapped to true (but not fully observable) states via a probability distribution. There are many techniques used to solve POMDPs, including heuristic-based techniques, value iteration approaches, and approximation methods [54]. However, nearly all of these methods are model-based techniques that require *a priori* knowledge of the observations to state mapping functions, the state transition functions, and the rewards functions. Since these models are generally not available for real-world problems, an alternate option for obtaining them is to attempt to recover or to derive an approximation of them from observations. These methods have been deemed prohibitive in literature, due to time and difficulty [54].

Another approach available for handling a POMDP in a model-free manner is to treat observations as states, and to map those directly to actions [54]. It is that method we employ in this research, with the understanding that doing so does not directly address partial observability or nonstationarity.

3.2. Information Augmenters. Three categories of augmenters are defined for the augmentation process. A primary augmenter is a scalar quantity with maximum value at the time and location of an event and declining value over time and distance from the event. A map probability augmenter is also used and describes additional domain information pertaining to the geography of events. In this research, this augmenter does not change over time, although nothing precludes it from having a dynamic value to support multiple epochs. Finally, a set of secondary augmenters, which are derived from computations using one or more of the primary and map probability augmenters, are also used.

This research experimented with a total of seven information augmenters. The three primary augmenters are based on digital pheromones, the map probability augmenter represents geographically related information, and three secondary augmenters are calculated from one or more of the primary augmenters and/or the map probability. At this stage of the research only one of the augmenters, selected *a priori*, is used during a single simulation execution and no dynamic augmenter selection mechanism is in place. However, the *Weighted* augmenter described below enables a combination of multiple augmenters into a single measure that considers multiple facets at once. The details of the augmenters follow.

The primary augmenters are as follows.

(1) The *Event* pheromone is deposited at the occurrence of each event and is spread over a parameter-controlled radius of grid cells around the event's location. Its effect evaporates/decays at a medium rate over time, as optimized for the application domain. In the context of Somali piracy, an event is a pirate attack on a vessel. The rationale for this augmenter is to identify areas of previous events of interest, as both a region amenable to such events and one that potentially appeals to aspects of human psychology, such as the penchant of criminals to return to locations where they have successfully committed crimes [55]. The evaporation rate (herein both "evaporation" and "decay" are used interchangeably refering to the reduction of a pheromone's value over time) is set to

a medium level because it may be some time before a revisit to the vicinity of a previous event takes place.

(2) The *Cyclical* pheromone is released over a given radius of grid cells around the site of each event to capture any known cyclical aspects or frequency of the events' occurrence over time. The parallel to nature's pheromones are suspended with respect to this augmenter to allow both its decay and intensification over time. This repeating phenomenon is modeled using a sinusoidal wave with a given period in days and a linearly decreasing amplitude over time. Complete evaporation of this pheromone may be delayed for quite some time, in which case it serves as a long term memory of the events in an area. In the context of the Somali piracy application, this pheromone represents the seasonal pattern described earlier.

(3) The *Occupied* pheromone is deposited by the agents in the grid cells in which they are positioned and is dispersed to the nearby vicinity. This pheromone is designed to dissuade an agent from moving to a grid it has recently occupied. It has the added effect of improving map coverage by reducing "bunching up" near likely event areas, even though agents are unaware that there are other agents in the environment who also deposit this repelling pheromone. It is set to a high evaporation rate and is a computational aid for agent positioning that does not have a direct historical parallel in the Somali piracy domain.

The *Map Probability* augmenter is used to communicate domain information regarding the likelihood of the events of interest taking place at the various locations in the environment. It takes on a value between 0 and 1 for each grid cell represented. In the Somali piracy application, this value represents the shipping traffic levels in the region of interest, and reflects the fact that attacks are more probable in areas where more potential targets are present.

The secondary augmenters are as follows.

(1) The *Event Count* augmenter is a count of past events in a grid cell. It is linked to the *Cyclical* pheromone (which is deposited along with every *Event* pheromone but has a slower rate of decay) and is simply a count of the instances of that pheromone affecting previously attacked grid cells at any given time.

(2) The *Ratio* augmenter is the ratio of the value of the *Event* pheromone to that of the *Occupied* pheromone. This augmenter serves to indicate when a given grid cell may need to be visited, if it is high, or whether a visit may be postponed, if its value is low.

(3) The *Weighted Combination* augmenter is a weighted sum of any of the other augmenters, with weights summing to 1. This allows the agent to react to a single quantity that represents multiple facets of the environment.

3.3. Resultant Augmented Environment. The augmentation or transformation creates a synthetic "memory" in the environment, associated with each event, which persists over some time and distance. The values of the augmenters over time are sensed by an agent as the state and enable action selection using reinforcement learning. A contrast, with respect to time, between a nonaugmented environment and one that has been augmented is shown in Figure 3. The upper time line depicts an environment characterized solely by event occurrences, with little persistent and measurable information between events. The augmented environment "fills in" the gaps between events with changing levels of the pheromones and other augmenters, thereby providing dynamic and measurable quantities that persist over time and space and serve as synthetic states to which agents respond.

The spatial impact of an augmented environment is shown in Figure 4. Three events are shown (row, column coordinates) in grid cells (3, 7), (5, 3), and (7, 7) with the latter having taken place in an earlier time step. The nonaugmented environment presents a static snapshot in time and provides little information to help position agents. By contrast, the augmented environment presents a number of facts not discernible in the first case: dynamics that may be compared to those of prior events to exploit patterns, the fact that grid cells (3, 5) and (4, 5) have pheromone content that are equal to those at attack sites and thus may become candidates for future moves, and an indication that the highest pheromone content is cell (5, 5), at the intersection of the five cell by five cell pheromone fields of the three events.

4. Reinforcement Learning Problem Formulation

The information augmentation process was carried out for the Somali piracy historical sequence of attacks to demonstrate an application of the proposed method. We note here that the Somali piracy domain is challenging in several ways: the true values of state and actions do change over time, the proposed approach utilizes a limited sensor range and does not provide complete information, and states may be aliased because pheromone levels at a particular point are the same for an attack at a specific range but from varying directions or may be composed of deposits stretching across time and space that happen to combine to a specific value. As mentioned earlier, observations are treated as states in this application and agents react directly to them.

The experiments were conducted on a custom research platform with a discretized grid representation of the pirate attack area, the historical sequence of pirate attacks over a seven and one half year period, and a set of agents representing naval vessels. The simulation proceeds in a time-stepped mode, with each time step corresponding to one actual day in the historical account. No time steps are skipped because agents act at each time increment whether or not an attack occurs. The reinforcement learning problem formulation follows.

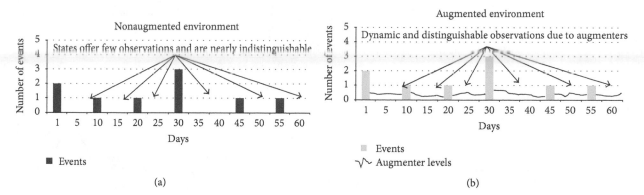

(a)   (b)

FIGURE 3: Contrast between nonaugmented and augmented environments (temporal).

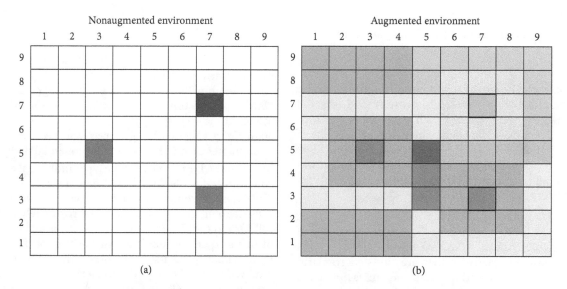

(a)   (b)

FIGURE 4: Contrast between nonaugmented and augmented environments (spatial).

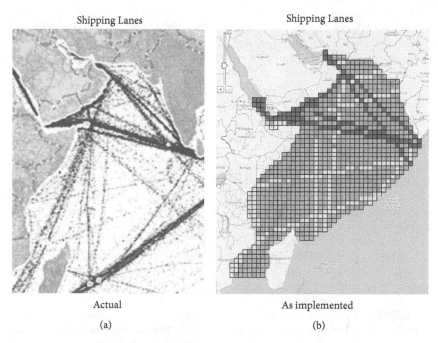

FIGURE 5: Shipping lanes in the piracy region (adapted from [56]).

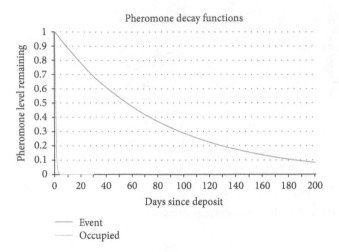

FIGURE 6: Pheromone exponential decay functions.

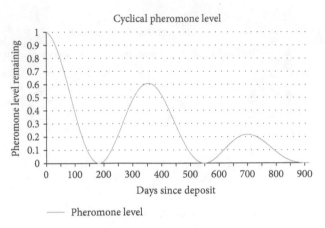

FIGURE 7: Decay function for the *Cyclical* pheromone.

4.1. Environment. The area of attacks was discretized into one degree of latitude by one degree of longitude grid cells and is represented by one thousand such grids, each of which has a preset *Map Probability* augmenter to represent one of four shipping traffic levels in the region: low, medium, high, and very high traffic (see Figure 5). The grid resolution was chosen to roughly correspond to the action radius of agents (described later).

4.2. Events. The pirate attacks in the region are the events of interest. The International Maritime Bureau (IMB) reports contain a mixture of statistics that are updated regularly, along with regional subsections that contain facts on the date, time, location, and victim vessel information for each attack, as well as a descriptive narrative that recounts how the attack unfolded and includes other details such as whether the military successfully intervened. Attacks are classified into four categories: *Hijacked, Boarded, Fired Upon,* or *Attempted.* Because the naval vessel agents' goal is to deter all attacks, we make no distinction between attack categories and consider attacks from any category to be an event of equal interest.

The research dataset was assembled from IMB annual reports for 2005 through 2011 and quarterly reports for the first six months of 2012 [12–19]. Table 1 shows an excerpt of an attack from an IMB report and its format in the research database. The IMB reports for the period January 2005 through June 2012 inclusive list 943 attacks under the sections for Somalia and Gulf of Aden. A number of these records are missing information, such as the attack's latitude and longitude or its time of day. In order to retain the highest possible number of historical events for this research, all of the attacks in the IMB reports were used except the 44 records missing the geographical coordinates of the attack. The data deemed relevant for the analysis was extracted, and the narrative portion was keyword searched to glean additional data regarding military intervention and use of pirate mother ships. This process resulted in a dataset of 899 attacks (events) over the 2,738-day period (1 January 2005 through 30 June 2012).

4.3. States. The information augmenters are each represented by a floating point value in each grid cell, along with globally applicable functions that determine changes in their value with respect to time and distance. The levels are calculated at each time step by applying the functions to the list of augmenters affecting the grid cell. The *Event* and *Occupied* pheromones each use a standard exponential decay function (e^{-kt} where k is each pheromone type's individual evaporation constant, and t is the number of time steps since its deposit). The *Event* pheromone is applied over a radius of four grid cells surrounding the attack site (approximately 240 nautical miles), and the *Occupied* pheromone is posted over a radius of one grid cell around the last position of the each agent (approximately 60 nautical miles). These pheromones are removed from affected grid cells once their value drops below a given threshold (0.1 in the research configuration). Figure 6 shows the pheromone decay functions.

The level of the *Cyclical* pheromone is computed using a sinusoidal wave with a gradually decreasing amplitude. The daily level calculation uses an annual cycle period and MAXD days to complete evaporation. The level is calculated as

$$0.5 \times \left[1 - \frac{t}{\text{MAXD}} \times \cos\left(t \times \text{YEARS PER DAY} \times 2\pi\right) \right.$$
$$\left. +1 - \frac{t}{\text{MAXD}} \right], \tag{4}$$

where t is the number of days elapsed since the pheromone was deposited, and YEARS PER DAY is 1/365 (a base period other than annual may be chosen and the parameters adjusted accordingly). Coincident with the *Event* pheromone, the *Cyclical* pheromone is spread over a radius of four grid cells surrounding the attack site. This pheromone yields a memory of MAXD = 913 days (two and one half years). The resulting sinusoidal wave is shown in Figure 7.

A single distance-effect function is used for all pheromone types to establish the pheromone's level in grid cells. It is a Gaussian function with a parameterized width that is centered at the location of the event. The result of the distance function is combined with that of the time decay functions previously described to determine

TABLE 1: Data conversion from IMB report to research database format.

Date Time	Name of ship/type /flag/Grt/IMO #	Position	Narration
02.02.2011 0830 UTC Steaming Fired upon	Duqm Tanker Panama 160160 9410387	20:16N—063:36E (around 225 NM ESE of Ras al Hadd, Oman), off Somalia	About eight pirates in two skiffs armed with RPG and automatic weapons chased and fired upon the tanker underway. The tanker raised alarm, increased speed, and contacted warship for assistance. The two skiffs kept firing with automatic weapons. Warship arrived at location and the skiffs stopped chasing and moved away. A helicopter from the warship arrived at location and circled the tanker. The helicopter contacted the pirates by VHF radio and ordered them to surrender their weapons. Pirates replied that they would kill the Iraqi and Pakistani hostages held onboard the mother ship if the warships attacked the skiffs.

Excerpt from IMB report [18]

Days since[1]	Lat D	Lat M	H[2]	Lon D	Lon M	H[2]	Mother ship[3]	Military aid[3]
2224	20	16	N	63	36	E	Y	Y

Resultant database entry

Notes:

Most columns are self-explanatory.

[1]This field was created for the simulation and indicates the number of days since December 31, 2004 (thus, simulation day 1 is January 1, 2005).

[2]These fields show the attack's north-south and east-west hemispheres, respectively.

[3]These fields represent whether a mother ship or a military intervention played a role in the attack; this information was gleaned from the free text narrative describing the attack (Y: yes and N: no).

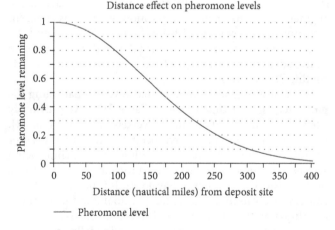

FIGURE 8: Effect of distance on pheromone levels.

the pheromone level at each affected grid cell. Figure 8 depicts the distance-effect function utilized in the research platform. The values of the evaporation constant k, chosen for the pheromones after some experimentation, yield a persistence of 180 days and 2 days for the *Event* and *Occupied* pheromones, respectively, at the deposit site (and fewer days in surrounding grid cells due to the distance decay).

The state of each grid cell in the simulated world is computed at each time step from the values of the augmenter chosen *a priori* for action selection during simulation

execution, which we term the operational augmenter, and represents the following:

(1) The augmenter level discretized to one of four absolute levels.

(2) Whether the augmenter value has increased or decreased since the previous time step.

(3) Whether the augmenter value is the maximum or minimum within the agent's neighborhood.

The agents perceive and react to these states. Using the above descriptions, there are nine possible combinations for each of the four discretized augmenter levels, for a total of the 36 augmenter state signatures, as shown in Table 2.

4.4. Agents, Fictive Agents, and Actions. Agents are mobile entities that perceive the state of the operational augmenter of individual grids in a restricted local area referred to as its neighborhood, react to those states, and learn individually as they receive rewards. An agent is unable to sense outside its neighborhood and exploits the environment based solely on local information. At each time step, the agent selects as its action a transition to a grid cell containing the state signature with the highest state value, from the signatures present in the grid cells of its neighborhood of radius r. As such, it may choose an action that places it in any of up to $(2r + 1)^2$ grid cells in its neighborhood (a radius of 2 was used in

TABLE 2: Grid cell state signatures.

Operational augmenter characteristics
Level X, not minimum or maximum, not increasing or decreasing
Level X, not minimum or maximum, decreasing
Level X, minimum, not increasing or decreasing
Level X, minimum, decreasing
Level X, maximum, not increasing or decreasing
Level X, maximum, decreasing
Level X, not minimum or maximum, increasing
Level X, minimum, increasing
Level X, maximum, increasing

this research, representing a naval vessel's approximate range when traveling at 20 knots for eight to ten hours during a 24-hour period and resulting in a neighborhood size of up to 25 grid cells). The geographical layout of the environment may at times lead to neighborhoods of size less than $(2r + 1)^2$, such as when an agent is located adjacent to non-navigable grid cells (representing land in the Somali piracy case). If no distinct maximum state value exists, the agent applies a heuristic that biases its action to the highest operational augmenter level present in the neighborhood. We refer to this heuristic as the *Level-bias*.

Regardless of the operational augmenter used, when multiple cells in the neighborhood have the chosen signature, the grid with the highest concentration of the *Event* pheromone is preferred as the destination. This technique is termed the *Event-Bias* and is a key attribute of agent behavior, as it has the effect of keeping agents in, or drawing them to, areas with high event concentration. If all *Event* pheromone values are equal across the neighborhood, a grid is randomly chosen.

The action set used in our approach (a move to a desired end state, which is to say, a grid cell with a particular operational augmenter signature) is a domain-independent abstraction with no direct equivalent in the realm represented, since domains are unlikely to have actions like "Move to a grid cell where the operational augmenter is a Level 2, Not Minimum or Maximum, Decreasing." When reinforcement learning is combined with this method, the end result is selection of grid cells that have similar augmenter state signatures to those that have received the highest accumulated rewards, thereby exploiting patterns, if they exist.

In order to prevent multiple agents from clustering in the same grid cell, an auction system based on the state value of each agent's selected action decides the order in which agents choose their destination grid cell, the agent with the highest state value having first choice. Once a grid cell is selected by an agent, it is not available as a destination option to other agents, and agents vying for that cell must reenter the auction. This restriction is enforced to improve agent coverage of the geographical area and is removed only when, after repeated auctions, an agent has only one possible destination remaining, in which case a move to that grid cell is permitted regardless of whether the cell is occupied. The behavior of these simple, reactive agents may be summarized by the commented algorithm shown in Algorithm 2.

To enable fictive learning, each of the real agents is paired with a fictive agent. The role of the fictive agent is to increase the experience of the real agent, by helping to populate the learning table more quickly. This fictive agent "ghost" begins each time step at the same location as its parent agent but chooses its action based on a separate policy. In this research, the alternate policy applied was the *Level-bias* technique, which biases the action to the highest operational augmenter level found in the neighborhood. Additionally, unlike the real agent, the fictive agent destination grid cells are not restricted to those that are not occupied. Finally, the fictive agent used in our methodology is a nonlearning agent that, in each time step, simply executes the best action available per the *Level-bias* heuristic. The fictive learning approach used in this research is novel and unlike others encountered in the literature. The behavior algorithm for fictive agents is shown in Algorithm 3.

The agents represent naval vessels seeking to be in position to deter, thwart, or mitigate the effects of an attack by responding within 30 minutes of a hijack in progress call. The 30-minute response is a stated goal of coalition naval forces [25–57]. The calculation of the effective ranges stems from parameters stated in those references, such as helicopter launch times and speeds, and is set at 36 nautical miles (67 kilometers) in the simulation. Each vessel agent has an action radius of two grid cells in any direction. This action range is the domain equivalent of 8 to 10 hours of a vessel moving at 20 knots during a 24-hour patrol period.

The individual agents do not correspond to specific actual naval vessels in the historic account, as the daily position of those vessels is not available. The agents are placed in random locations initially and move over time as they react to the augmented environment. The position of agents is coherent over time and is computed from the prior location and the size of the neighborhood. The aim of this study was to develop a methodology that might be of use in positioning such assets continually over time.

Data on the exact number of naval vessels patrolling the piracy region over time is not available. We have previously cited the estimate of 25 to 40 vessels mentioned in [1]. However, this may only have been the case in the latter period represented by the data, with additional ships being assigned to the area as the piracy problem grew. Because a precise historical number of naval vessels is not available, we conservatively used the lower number found in the literature (25 ships) as the agent count. Three different schemes for reaching that agent count were employed as follows.

(1) Initialize with 25 agents and maintain at 25 agents over the simulation.

(2) Initialize with 5 agents and increase to 25 agents linearly over time, with 1 agent added every 130 days in a random geographical location. This method results in a fleet that averages 15.03 agents over the simulation.

(3) Initialize with 5 agents and increase to 25 agents linearly over the number of attacks (events), with 1 agent added every 42 attacks in a random geographical

```
Algorithm: agentAct
Input: agent location, loc
Returns: destination grid cell, g

S ← get States In Neighborhood(loc)   // set of augmenter states in agent's neighborhood
s ← max(S)                            // augmenter signature with highest learned value
if s == null                          // no distinct maximum state value exists
    s = Level-Bias(S)                 // augmenter signature with highest augmenter level

G ← get Grid Cells(s)                 // set of all neighborhood grid cells having state s
g ← Event-Bias(G)                     // grid cell g from G with highest Event pheromone level
if g == null                          // all Event pheromone levels are equal
    g ← randomGrid(G)                 // choose g at random from G

ok ← auction(value(s), g)             // enter auction with state s value and destination grid g
                                      // auction returns true if the grid cell is unclaimed or if the
                                      // grid cell g is the last destination option for the agent

if not(ok) agent Act(loc)
return (g)
```

ALGORITHM 2: Agent action selection algorithm.

```
Algorithm: fictiveAgentAct
Input: agent location, loc
Returns: destination grid cell, g

S ← get States In Neighborhood(loc)   // set of augmenter states in agent's neighborhood
s = Level-Bias(S)                     // augmenter signature with highest augmenter level

G ← get Grid Cells(s)                 // set of all neighborhood grid cells having state s
g ← Event-Bias(G)                     // grid cell g from G with highest Event pheromone level
if g == null                          // all Event pheromone levels are equal
    g ← randomGrid(G)                 // choose g at random from G

return (g)
```

ALGORITHM 3: Fictive agent action selection algorithm.

location. This method results in a fleet that averages 11.68 agents over the simulation.

Note. Vessels are unable to remain at sea indefinitely and are routinely replaced. To simplify the model, the assumption was made that relieving vessels proceed to the location of the vessel being replaced and continue operations from that position, using its predecessor's amassed knowledge.

4.5. Rewards. Agents receive rewards according to their success against events. The determination of success is based on proximity, and requires that an agent be within a specified distance radius of an event at the time that event takes place. A reward of 1 is given for every success. In the event that more than one agent is successful against the same event, the reward is divided equally among those agents. All unsuccessful agents receive a reward of 0. This reward structure also applies to fictive agents as well, with two exceptions: successful fictive agents do not share rewards, and the update for fictive agent rewards is always made to the

value table of its counterpart real agent, and only when the fictive agent is successful.

4.6. Policy. The selection policy used to choose agent actions is the ε-greedy technique [58]. From the available actions, the action selection mechanism previously described is employed with probability $1 - \varepsilon$. Alternatively, a random action from all possible actions is taken with probability ε. The research platform supports both a fixed ε and one that varies over the course of the simulation. Both methods were explored and the fixed ε results reported in this paper were marginally better.

4.7. Learning. During initialization, the simulation reads the scenario configuration values, including the number of time steps to simulate. The simulation then proceeds iteratively, repeating the same basic sequence. At each time step the agents mark their positions with the *Occupied* pheromone, assess their state, and select and execute an action. Events for that time step are then posted to the environment and the relevant event augmenters are applied. In time steps where there are one or more events, all agents receive a reward per the method described earlier and update their reinforcement learning table accordingly. The process continues until the simulation ends at the last time step.

After some experimentation, the following values for reinforcement learning parameters were set for the reasons indicated as follows.

(1) Learning rate (α) = 0.1—the learning rate parameter is often varied from a high to a low value in reinforcement learning applications. However, in nonstationary environments, a fixed learning rate is recommended [7] as it gives greater weight to more recent rewards compared to those in the distant past. A low value was chosen to reduce variability in agent behavior by accepting only a fraction of the measured temporal difference.

(2) Discount rate (γ) = 0.75—this discount rate was chosen through experimentation and provided a good compromise between emphasis on immediate versus future rewards.

Learning is accomplished via the temporal difference learning algorithm previously described. Given the small size of the state space, tabular storage is used. The research platform provides the ability to evaluate joint learning, where agents update a common value table, as well as individual learning where agents have separate tables. Experimentation was carried out with both modes but the approach reported in this research employed individual learning.

Agents make continual use of state values to determine their action at every time step. However, learning takes place only in time steps in which one or more events take place, which is to say when the agent has an event to succeed against. In these time steps, the agent receives a reward greater than zero if successful or zero if unsuccessful, and the table is updated accordingly. In time steps without any events, agents continue to select actions based on the learning attained to date but no learning updates take place, as there is no possibility of success. As previously mentioned, the fictive learning mechanism is designed to help speed-up agent learning, and as such only successes (rewards greater than zero) are updated in the agent's table. The learning algorithm used by agents is depicted in Algorithm 4. The first statement is always executed and the conditional statement is executed when fictive learning is used.

4.8. Example Neighborhoods, States, and Transitions. An example of states, neighborhoods, actions, and rewards is provided here to illustrate those concepts in the context of a simulation time step. A state is a 6-bit integer value that indexes the agent learning table. It is defined as follows (the most significant bit is first): discrete augmenter level, 2 bits, values 0–3; increased since last time step, 1 bit, 0 = no 1 = yes; decreased since last time step, 1 bit, 0 = no 1 = yes; maximum in neighborhood, 1 bit, 0 = no 1 = yes; minimum in neighborhood, 1 bit, 0 = no 1 = yes.

TABLE 3: States by time step.

(a) Neighborhood states at time t

	1	2	3
3	Aug (Raw): 0.5	Aug (Raw): 0.3	Aug (Raw): 0.1
	Aug (Level): 0	Aug (Level): 0	Aug (Level): 0
	Increase?: N	Increase?: N	Increase?: N
	Decrease?: Y	Decrease?: Y	Decrease?: Y
	Nbhd Max?: N	Nbhd Max?: N	Nbhd Max?: N
	Nbhd Min?: N	Nbhd Min?: N	Nbhd Min?: Y
	State: 4	State: 4	State: 5
2	Aug (Raw): 1.7	Aug (Raw): 1.1	Aug (Raw): 0.7
	Aug (Level): 1	Aug (Level): 1	Aug (Level): 0
	Increase?: N	Increase?: N	Increase?: N
	Decrease?: Y	Decrease?: Y	Decrease?: Y
	Nbhd Max?: N	Nbhd Max?: N	Nbhd Max?: N
	Nbhd Min?: N	Nbhd Min?: N	Nbhd Min?: N
	State: 20	State: 20	State: 4
1	Aug (Raw): 2.1	Aug (Raw): 1.9	Aug (Raw): 1.3
	Aug (Level): 2	Aug (Level): 1	Aug (Level): 1
	Increase?: N	Increase?: N	Increase?: N
	Decrease?: Y	Decrease?: Y	Decrease?: Y
	Nbhd Max?: Y	Nbhd Max?: N	Nbhd Max?: N
	Nbhd Min?: N	Nbhd Min?: N	Nbhd Min?: N
	State: 38	State: 20	State: 20

(b) Neighborhood states at time $t + 1$

	1	2	3
3	Aug (Raw): 0.9	Aug (Raw): 0.6	Aug (Raw): 0.5
	Aug (Level): 0	Aug (Level): 0	Aug (Level): 0
	Increase?: Y	Increase?: Y	Increase?: Y
	Decrease?: N	Decrease?: N	Decrease?: N
	Nbhd Max?: N	Nbhd Max?: N	Nbhd Max?: N
	Nbhd Min?: N	Nbhd Min?: N	Nbhd Min?: Y
	State: 8	State: 8	State: 9
2	Aug (Raw): 1.7	Aug (Raw): 1.8	Aug (Raw): 1.4
	Aug (Level): 1	Aug (Level): 1	Aug (Level): 1
	Increase?: N	Increase?: Y	Increase?: Y
	Decrease?: N	Decrease?: N	Decrease?: N
	Nbhd Max?: N	Nbhd Max?: N	Nbhd Max?: N
	Nbhd Min?: N	Nbhd Min?: N	Nbhd Min?: N
	State: 16	State: 24	State: 24
1	Aug (Raw): 2.5	Aug (Raw): 2.6	Aug (Raw): 2.2
	Aug (Level): 2	Aug (Level): 2	Aug (Level): 2
	Increase?: Y	Increase?: Y	Increase?: Y
	Decrease?: N	Decrease?: N	Decrease?: N
	Nbhd Max?: N	Nbhd Max?: Y	Nbhd Max?: N
	Nbhd Min?: N	Nbhd Min?: N	Nbhd Min?: N
	State: 48	State: 56	State: 48

For simplification, we present a neighborhood of radius 1 across two time steps. Table 3(a) shows the states of the grid composing the neighborhood at time t. The *Event* pheromone

---

Algorithm: **agentLearn**
Input: Agent selected state s, agent next state s', agent reward r,
     fictive agent selected state fs, fictive agent next state fs', fictive agent reward fr
$V(s) \leftarrow V(s) + \alpha[r + \gamma V(s') - V(s)]$
if $(s \mathrel{!=} s'$ and $fr > 0)$
    $V(fs) \leftarrow V(fs) + \alpha[fr + \gamma V(fs') - V(fs)]$

ALGORITHM 4: Agent learning algorithm (with fictive learning).

is the augmenter shown, and its levels are discretized as follows:

if raw augmenter < 1, Level = 0,

if 1 <= raw augmenter < 2, Level = 1,

if 2 <= raw augmenter < 3, Level = 2,

if raw augmenter >= 3, Level 3.

The neighborhood coordinates are given in row, column form. The agent is positioned in the center grid (2, 2) and can reach any of the other grids in the neighborhood. In this example, the agent's learning table (not depicted) may indicate that state 20 has the highest value, and thus grids (1, 2), (1, 3), (2, 1), and (2, 2) would be candidates for the agent's move. We note that the agent would prefer grid (1, 2) due to the *Level*-bias. However, it may end up in any of the candidate grids, based on its standing in the auction.

In time step $t + 1$ an event is posted to grid (1, 3) and the dispersal of the event's pheromones result in the new states in Table 3(b). Any agent moving to grid (1, 3) at time t shares the reward of 1 and updates its learning table for state 20, as it is the state the agent moved to immediately preceding the event (and can thus be considered an indicator of impending events). Agents who are not successful update their table for the state chosen at time t with a reward of 0.

4.9. Research Platform Description and Screenshots. The research platform, shown in Figure 9, uses the JMapViewer tool for visualization and OpenStreetMap maps (both open source products). The application window is subdivided into a control panel, a map display, and an output panel summarizing simulation results.

In the map overlay, the *Occupied* pheromone is depicted via the Blue component of the RGB color definition, with the brightness of the color expressing its value. The remaining augmenters are conveyed through the Red and Green channels either as the sole augmenter or as a composite value (*Weighted* augmenter) and are rendered with green indicating low levels and red high levels. Figure 10 illustrates the dispersion of pheromones following an event (shown as the small circle), and those left in grid cells previously visited by an agent (depicted as the diamond).

5. Experiments, Results, and Analysis

In this section, we describe the experiments conducted in a stepwise manner, and in light of the research questions posed

earlier. We conclude by presenting and analyzing the results obtained from applying the information augmentation and learning approach to the Somali piracy domain.

5.1. Research Questions and Approach. Two related but distinct research questions were of interest in this work. We take up the first research question, which we subdivided into three subquestions, the first of which concerned the comparative effectiveness of different information augmenters. This subquestion was addressed in three steps as follows.

(1) *Evaluate individual augmenters.* Each of the augmenters (excluding the *Occupied* pheromone) was tested individually as the operational augmenter. Multiple trials were conducted for each and the averaged results analyzed.

(2) *Evaluate combinations of the Weighted augmenter.* To avoid overfitting, a few predetermined combinations and weightings of various augmenters as the composite *Weighted* augmenter were tested. From among the combinations evaluated, the best weightings were selected and defined as the standard for this augmenter. The composition reported here is made up of weightings of 0.5 *Ratio* augmenter and 0.5 *Shipping Lane* (map probability) augmenter.

(3) *Select the best performing augmenter.* The total number of successes using the individual augmenters were statistically assessed and the best one chosen for further evaluation.

The second subquestion addressed the relative effectiveness of the proposed fictive learning method over standard reinforcement learning. We expanded this evaluation by adding a third nonlearning mode, in order to complete a more thorough analysis. For each operational augmenter we evaluated the following.

(1) The *Level*-bias heuristic in nonlearning mode.

(2) Standard reinforcement learning (using the temporal difference approach).

(3) The proposed fictive learning method.

The final subquestion was addressed by evaluating four policies for the best performing augmenter, using a complement of 25 agents. The first two techniques are nonlearning and the last two utilize fictive learning as follows.

(1) *Random Moves.* The absolute minimum expected number of successes was established by conducting

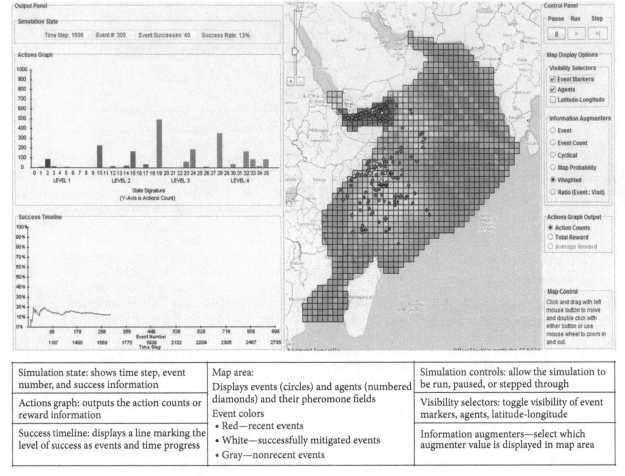

Simulation state: shows time step, event number, and success information	Map area:	Simulation controls: allow the simulation to be run, paused, or stepped through
Actions graph: outputs the action counts or reward information	Displays events (circles) and agents (numbered diamonds) and their pheromone fields	Visibility selectors: toggle visibility of event markers, agents, latitude-longitude
Success timeline: displays a line marking the level of success as events and time progress	Event colors • Red—recent events • White—successfully mitigated events • Gray—nonrecent events	Information augmenters—select which augmenter value is displayed in map area

FIGURE 9: Research platform screenshot.

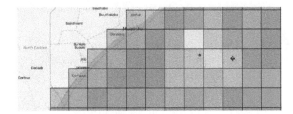

FIGURE 10: Pheromones dispersed by an event (circle) and agent (numbered diamond).

simulation runs where at each time step each agent simply moved randomly to any grid cell within its local neighborhood. These trials were conducted without the use of any information augmenters or reinforcement learning methods.

(2) *Random Actions.* This set of simulation trials was conducted using $\varepsilon = 1.0$, which is in effect a non-learning method. The approach amounted to agents randomly choosing any action possible from the operational augmenter signatures in grid cells within its neighborhood. This differed from the *Random Moves* case in that while the agents did not get to select

the signature of the operational augmenter through a value table, the *Event-bias* was still used to determine the destination grid cell from the set returned by the randomly chosen end-state. In this case, it was expected that performance would improve since the *Event-bias* ensured that agents remained in, or were drawn to, areas affected by events. It was determined *a priori* that the proposed learning methods would have to outperform the number of successes obtained through this approach, in order to be considered viable.

(3) *Random Actions if State Values are Equal.* The method applied in this set of trials utilized $\varepsilon = 0.05$ and in it agents selected either the best (highest state value) action from prior learning (using fictive learning) or a random action with probability ε or when state values for the operational augmenter states within the neighborhood were all equal. The *Event-bias* was then applied to select the destination grid cell. Since this was approach which made use of learned values, the expectation was that it would outperform the simple *Random Actions* case.

(4) *Level-Bias if State Values are Equal.* Finally, we tested the viability of our proposed augmentation with

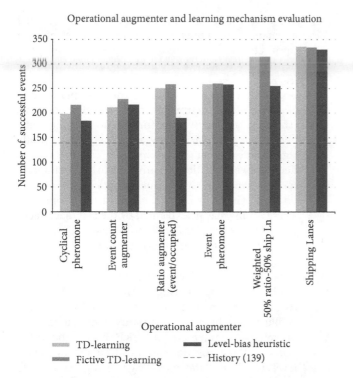

FIGURE 11: Summary of simulation results by augmenters and learning mechanisms.

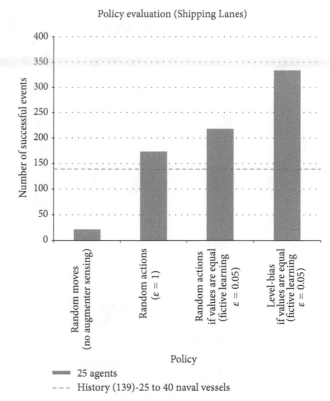

FIGURE 12: Summary of policy evaluation for the *Shipping Lanes* augmenter.

fictive learning and the *Level-bias*. The test scenario was executed multiple times, with agents selecting actions based on the best (highest state value) action from prior learning or by applying the *Level-bias* when no distinct best action existed. A random action was chosen with probability ε (0.05). The *Event-bias* was used to select the destination grid cell. Given the demonstrated effectiveness of the *Level-bias* heuristic, it was expected that this policy would outperform the *Random Actions if State Values Equal* policy.

The final research question concerned the effectiveness of the information augmentation and fictive learning approach, when applied to real-world problems. We addressed this in two steps as follows.

(1) *Execute simulations for different agent counts*. For the test application, the number of agents available at any particular time is only approximately stated in the available data. To account for this uncertainty, three different approaches to setting the agent population, all conservative with respect to the available data, were tested through multiple simulation trials for each of the augmenters, using the proposed fictive learning technique.

(2) *Compare historical and simulation outcomes*. The number of successes observed in simulation results was compared to the historical record of actual successes in defending against pirate attacks, using each of the different augmenters and agent counts tested. A comparison was considered favorable if a

95% confidence interval for the mean number of successes in simulation trials included or was greater than the number of historical successes.

5.2. Results. A set of 30 simulation trials were conducted for each of configurations described above. In each trial agents started without any knowledge and executed the appropriate policy and reinforcement learning algorithm with the described augmenters. Events in which one or more agents were positioned within the specified proximity were considered a success and the appropriate statistics calculated. The simulation results are presented here and analyzed in the next section. Figure 11 illustrates the output for combinations of learning mechanisms and individual augmenters.

Figure 12 depicts the outcome of action selection policies evaluation for the *Shipping Lanes* map probability augmenter, which was the operational augmenter with the best performance.

Figure 13 portrays the results of employing the proposed fictive learning method with the *Level-bias if State Values Equal* policy for combinations of augmenters and agent count schemes.

Table 4 summarizes the results shown in Figure 12 along with statistical details. The "Agents" column in Table 3 indicates how many agents were present during the simulation. In that column, "25" means that 25 agents were present during the entire simulation, "5 → 25 by time" means that the simulation started with 5 agents and ended with 25, with

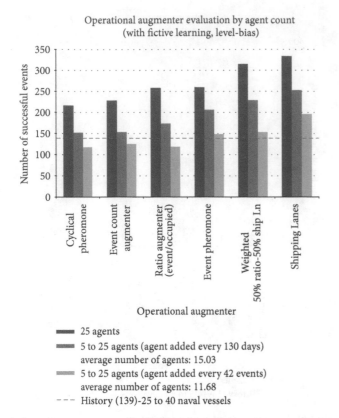

Operational augmenter evaluation by agent count
(with fictive learning, level-bias)

Operational augmenter

 ■ 25 agents
 ■ 5 to 25 agents (agent added every 130 days)
   average number of agents: 15.03
 ■ 5 to 25 agents (agent added every 42 events)
   average number of agents: 11.68
 --- History (139)-25 to 40 naval vessels

FIGURE 13: Summary of operational augmenter by agent count schemes.

one agent being added every 130 time steps, and "5 → 25 by event" means that the simulation started with 5 agents and ended with 25, with one agent being added every 42 events. For each of the combinations, 30 executions of the simulation were performed. The "Min", "Max", "Q1", and "Q3" show the minimum, maximum, first quartile, and third quartile values for the number of successes during the 30 executions. Similarly, the "Median", "Mean", and "Std Dev" columns report those statistics for successes during the 30 trials. Finally, the "Confidence interval" column reports a confidence interval for the mean number of successes during the 30 trials, calculated using the Student's t-distribution with $\alpha = 0.05$, confidence level $c = (1 - \alpha) = 0.95$, and critical value $t_c = 2.05$. When examining the table, recall that the historical record had 139 successes with 25 to 40 naval vessels.

5.3. Analysis. We now analyze each set of results beginning with learning methods evaluation. The statistical significance reported here was established through conducting an analysis of variance (ANOVA) and applying Tukey's Test to establish differences (the less conservative Fisher test only changed one outcome from those reported here).

(1) *Level-Bias Heuristic.* As mentioned, this heuristic is a nonlearning approach that simply selects the highest level of the operational augmenter found in the neighborhood, to which the *Event-bias* is then applied. Given that description, the heuristic is likely

to perform well when the distribution of operational augmenter signatures at the time of an event tend toward the higher discretized levels. Results using the heuristic were statistically indistinguishable from the learning methods when using the *Event* pheromone operational augmenter. Using the best performing *Shipping Lanes* augmenter, both learning methods (standard and fictive reinforcement learning) outperformed the heuristic by a small, but statistically significant, margin. When applying Tukey's test, the heuristic was statistically equivalent to both reinforcement learning methods, but Fisher's test showed a difference in favor of the fictive learning approach. These results may be explained by the fact that attacks tended to occur in area previously attacked (especially the case in the Gulf of Aden) and in places with very heavy shipping traffic (nearly half of all pirate attacks took place at the highest discretized *Shipping Lanes* level). Thus, simply biasing to those higher levels led to good performance. The drawback to this heuristic is illustrated by its performance when used with operational augmenters for which the distribution of states at attack time does not favor higher augmenter levels (*Cyclical*, *Ratio*, and *Weighted* augmenters). It's worth noting that the choosing of parameters for the proposed augmenters is more art than science, and a resultant state distribution not amenable to application of this heuristic is very likely. In spite of its performance, the greatest limitation of the heuristic is that it is a non-learning rule and is thus not adaptable to changes in the behavior of the human actors behind the events. In summary, the proposed fictive learning method statistically outperformed the heuristic for four or five of the six augmenters, depending on the statistical test used.

(2) *Standard Reinforcement Learning.* Use of nonfictive reinforcement learning was statistically superior or equivalent to the performance of the *Level-bias* in all augmenter cases.

(3) *Fictive Reinforcement Learning.* The analysis of the comparative performance of the *Level-bias* heuristic and the proposed fictive learning approach has been presented in the section analyzing the former. Here, we compare fictive learning to standard (nonfictive) reinforcement learning. Our proposed learning approach was statistically superior to using standard reinforcement learning for two of the operational augmenters. The statistically significant improvements however were modest (approximately 8% in both cases). Fictive learning was statistically equivalent to standard reinforcement learning in the other cases. Given these results, the fictive reinforcement learning approach was chosen as the learning method for further experimentation.

The comparative analysis of the action selection policies follows. In all cases, except for the *Random Moves* case which does not sense augmenters, the *Shipping Lanes* augmenter was used.

TABLE 4: Statistical results for the Somali piracy application.

	Method	Agents	Min.	Max.	Q1	Q3	Median	Mean	Std Dev	Confidence Interval
Policies	*Random moves (no augmenter)*	25	11	33	19.00	24.00	20.50	21.33	4.54	[19.64, 23.03]
	Random actions (shipping lanes)	25	146	194	164.25	181.75	175.50	173.10	11.39	[168.85, 177.35]
	Random actions if state values equal (shipping lanes)	25	169	261	206.75	229.25	218.50	217.87	19.99	[210.40, 225.33]
Operational augmenters (Fictive learn + level-bias)	Cyclical	25	179	259	203.75	222.75	216.00	216.30	18.76	[209.29, 223.31]
		5 → 25 by time	100	184	137.25	168.50	151.00	151.73	20.29	[144.16, 159.31]
		5 → 25 by event	76	153	106.75	130.50	118.50	117.23	20.36	[109.63, 124.84]
	Event Count	25	177	264	213.25	247.50	226.50	228.23	21.57	[220.18, 236.29]
		5 → 25 by time	94	204	127.75	173.75	158.50	153.33	31.76	[141.48, 165.19]
		5 → 25 by event	88	163	110.00	138.25	137.50	125.30	18.70	[118.32, 132.28]
	Ratio	25	221	285	248.25	270.25	258.00	258.37	16.73	[252.12, 264.61]
		5 → 25 by time	146	207	161.25	189.00	170.50	173.83	18.01	[167.11, 180.56]
		5 → 25 by event	55	170	104.00	131.00	118.50	118.97	25.75	[109.35, 128.58]
	Event	25	232	278	255.25	266.75	261.50	260.07	10.15	[256.28, 263.86]
		5 → 25 by time	181	232	200.00	213.25	205.00	206.40	13.31	[201.43, 211.37]
		5 → 25 by event	107	173	142.25	158.25	151.50	148.27	15.49	[142.48, 154.05]
	Weighted	25	295	333	305.50	323.00	316.00	314.73	10.73	[310.72, 318.74]
		5 → 25 by time	196	272	214.25	243.75	226.00	228.63	20.44	[221.00, 236.26]
		5 → 25 by event	83	187	141.25	169.00	154.50	153.43	21.75	[145.31, 161.55]
	Shipping Lanes	25	321	348	329.00	338.00	333.50	333.43	6.86	[330.87, 336.00]
		5 → 25 by time	220	273	250.00	259.00	254.00	252.73	11.81	[248.33, 257.14]
		5 → 25 by event	169	216	191.75	203.00	197.50	196.30	11.15	[192.14, 200.46]

(1) *Random Moves.* Given the lack of the *Event-bias* mechanism to keep agents in the areas experiencing attacks, the *Random Moves* policy resulted in a very low success rate, with a mean of only 21.33 successes.

(2) *Random Actions.* The *Random Actions* policy fared significantly better as the *Event-bias* mechanism ensures that agents remain in or are attracted to areas affected by events. This case illustrates the importance of that aspect of agent behavior, with a mean outcome of 173.10 successes, an over eight-fold increase over the *Random Moves* policy.

(3) *Random Actions if State Values are Equal.* In this case, actions learned using fictive learning were executed whenever a clear best action (highest value) was indicated in the learning table, and a random action was chosen otherwise. This policy resulted in a 25% increase in the number of successes, when compared to the *Random Actions* case (217.87 versus 173.10).

(4) *Level-Bias Heuristic with Fictive Learning.* Finally, the policy utilizing both the *Level-bias* heuristic and fictive learning was used. The mean of 333.43

successes demonstrated the significance of supplementing action selection with the *Level-bias* heuristic whenever a clear best action was not indicated by entries in the learning table. The number of successes posted an increase of 53% over the *Random Actions if State Values Equal* case.

The analysis of results for the operational augmenters versus fleet size, are now presented. As might be expected, the simulation results showed that for any given action selection basis, the fixed size fleet (25 agents throughout the simulation) performed best, followed by the time-based variable fleet (which averaged 15.03 agents over the simulation) and ending with the event-based variable fleet (which averaged 11.68 agents over the simulation). The latter two fleet count schemes are extremely conservative in light documented history.

For all fleet configurations, when using the best performing Shipping Lanes augmenter, the environment augmentation and fictive learning methods produced more successful responses to pirate attacks than the historical number of successful responses by the actual naval vessels (139). The patrol and search procedures and doctrine used by the naval vessels have not been made public, so a definitive explanation of the difference in results is not possible. We conjecture that the commanders of the naval vessels were following doctrine that was either static or imposed by external superiors or both, and thus they could not benefit from learning the signatures of likely pirate attacks in the way that the algorithm did. Of the 18 combinations of augmenters and fleet configurations investigated, the 95% confidence interval for simulation results either exceeded or included the historical number of successes in all but three cases (Event Count, Cyclical, and Ratio augmenters with the event-based fleet size case). The time-based variable fleet and the fixed fleet exceeded the historical number of successes with all augmenter combinations.

Detailed analysis for the 25 agent fixed fleet using the different augmenters is shown here in order of increasing effectiveness.

(1) The *Cyclical* augmenter yielded the lowest number of successes (216.30), besting the historical record by almost 56%. The likely cause of this performance is that given time period it considers (two and one half years) this augmenter may increase agent actions to grid cells that may have experienced a lot of attacks in the past but are no longer favored by pirates.

(2) The *Event Count* augmenter's performance was close to that of the *Cyclical* augmenter as it also operates on information that may be two and one half years old. A possible explanation for the increase (228.23 versus 216.30) is that the *Cyclical* augmenter is more diffuse as it is applied over a radius around an attack site, whereas the *Event Count* augmenter applies only to attacked grids.

(3) The *Ratio* augmenter's results averaged 258.37 successes, an 86% outperformance of history. Given the composition of this augmenter, ratio of *Event* pheromone to *Occupied* pheromone, these results closely parallel those obtained with the former.

(4) The *Event* augmenter yielded a mean of 260.07 successes, an 87% improvement over the historical record. Since this method uses both the *Level-bias* and the *Event-bias*, this is the greedy case (choose the grid with the highest concentration of *Event* pheromone from those containing the highest discretized levels of that augmenter).

(5) The *Weighted* augmenter used in this case was composed of 0.5 *Ratio* and 0.5 *Shipping Lanes* weighting. It posted a mean of 314.73 successes, more than 226% of the historical record. We believe that the inclusion of the *Shipping Lanes* component is the driver for this performance.

(6) The *Shipping Lanes* augmenter yielded the best outcome, with a mean of 333.43 successes (240% of history). The likely cause for this performance is that the pirate attacks were more heavily skewed toward areas of very high maritime traffic. That, combined with the *Level-bias* in effect reduced the action space to areas of high levels of the augmenter containing high concentrations of the *Event* pheromone.

6. Conclusions, Limitations, and Future Work

With a mean of over 333 successes, our learning method with the *Shipping Lanes* augmenter enabled a successful response to over 37% of the historical sequence of 899 attacks. The success rate at various time points during simulation execution exceeded 50%. This performance substantially surpassed the actual historical record of 139 successful responses by naval vessels documented in the International Maritime Bureau reports, and was accomplished with a number of agents possibly smaller than the historical 25–40 vessel fleet reported in [1]. Use of the historic record of events, consisting only of dates and locations, combined with the performance attained lends credence to the viability and usefulness of our information augmentation and fictive learning approaches.

We acknowledge some limitations of this work as follows:

(1) Our focus in this research was to evaluate the use of model-free reinforcement learning methods in the maritime piracy domain. We therefore avoided the model-based and POMDP approaches. However, we conjecture that employing a mechanism robust to nonstationarity could result in improved performance.

(2) The number of events in the relatively confined Gulf of Aden likely contributed to the performance attained, since agents responding there were able to continually react to nearby attacks. Of course, our method did enable this geography to be exploited.

(3) This is not a two-sided game-theoretic model, and as such treats the sequence of events as deterministic; the pirates do not explicitly respond to defensive successes, for instance. However, the historical attack sequence already factors in at least some of the deterrent effect of thwarts due to historical interventions and thwarts. Many of the historical attacks took place despite successes by forces against piracy in the area in the recent past, that is, naval successes did not always dissuade the pirates. Adaptability by the pirates to naval tactics would likely take the form of a planned attack either not taking place at all, or being moved in time and/or space. Our methodology is robust to this adaptive behavior since only attacks that actually take place are marked with augmenters and factored into the reinforcement learning process. Thus, we always respond to the actual event sequence, without regard to whether the time and place of those events is a result of adaptive behavior.

(4) No limits were placed on where agents could move; that is, no ocean grid cells were considered to be off limits or impassable. This may not always reflect reality, for example, transient considerations such

as weather may prevent sea or air operations in particular areas. However, it is worth noting that any weather impacting naval vessels are likely to have a similar or greater impact on the smaller pirate skiff and mother ships. Nevertheless, this can be remedied by restricting the world at each time step to a subset of the grid cells.

(5) The agents are homogeneous and act on local information only. This often led to agents congregating at events in their neighborhoods, while other events remain unattended to. This shortfall may be addressed by specializing agents in order to enable a search function, or by subdividing areas of responsibility.

(6) The determination of weights for the *Weighted* augmenter was done *a priori*. An automated process to establish such weights and allow them to vary over time would be beneficial.

(7) Choosing a single operational augmenter *a priori* may limit the success of our approach. A method to vary the operational augmenter during execution, without exploding the state space could provide increased performance.

The research may be extended in a number of ways. The limitations listed earlier implicitly suggested opportunities for future work. Some additional areas for consideration include the following.

(1) Develop and apply a learning method better able to deal with non-stationarity.

(2) Convert agents from local to global behavior; Jones and Matarić provide an example process for this [59].

(3) Create distinct agent roles, such as patrollers and responders, with differing capabilities.

(4) Dynamically allocate agent roles during simulation execution.

(5) Optimize the number of agents for a given scenario.

(6) Further develop this approach towards its actual use as a decision support system for tasking naval forces.

(7) Define and test additional information augmenters, alone and in combination.

In spite of of these limitations, the obtained results justify further investigation into the use of model-free, fictive reinforcement learning with simple reactive agents, which through information augmentation are able to respond to patterns in a spatiotemporal environment.

Conflict of Interests

The authors declare that there is no conflict of interests regarding the publication of this paper.

Acknowledgments

The authors thank the anonymous reviewer of an earlier version of this paper, whose comments led to substantial improvements in the paper.

References

[1] J. Bahadur, *The Pirates of Somalia: Inside Their Hidden World*, Pantheon Books, New York, NY, USA, 2011.

[2] S. J. Russell and P. Norvig, *Artificial Intelligence: A Modern Approach*, Prentice Hall, Upper Saddle River, NJ, USA, 2nd edition, 2003.

[3] M. J. Wooldridge, *An Introduction to Multiagent Systems*, Wiley & Sons, West Sussex, UK, 2nd edition, 2009.

[4] G. P. Williams, *Chaos Theory Tamed*, Joseph Henry Press, Washington, DC, USA, 1997.

[5] P. Tan, M. Steinbach, and V. Kumar, *Introduction to Data Mining*, Addison Wesley, New York, NY, USA, 2006.

[6] H. Witten, E. Frank, and M. A. Hall, *Data Mining: Practical Machine Learning Tools and Techniques*, Morgan Kaufmann, New York, NY, USA, 3rd edition, 2011.

[7] R. S. Sutton and A. G. Barto, *Reinforcement Learning: An Introduction*, MIT Press, Cambridge, Mass, USA, 1998.

[8] D. Floreano and C. Mattiussi, *Bio-Inspired Artificial Intelligence: Theories, Methods, and Technologies*, MIT Press, Cambridge, Mass, USA, 2008.

[9] M. Dorigo and T. Stützle, *Ant Colony Optimization*, MIT Press, Cambridge, Mass, USA, 2004.

[10] J. Kennedy and R. Eberhart, *Swarm Intelligence*, Morgan Kaufmann, San Francisco, Calif, USA, 2001.

[11] Z. Michalewicz and D. B. Fogel, *How to Solve it: Modern Heuristics, 2nd Revised and Extended Edition*, Springer, New York, NY, USA, 2004.

[12] International Maritime Bureau, *Piracy and Armed Robbery Against Ships Annual Report 1 January-31 December 2005*, International Maritime Bureau, London, UK, 2006.

[13] International Maritime Bureau, *Piracy and Armed Robbery Against Ships Annual Report 1 January-31 December 2006*, International Maritime Bureau, London, UK, 2007.

[14] International Maritime Bureau, *Piracy and Armed Robbery Against Ships Annual Report 1 January-31 December 2007*, International Maritime Bureau, London, UK, 2008.

[15] International Maritime Bureau, *Piracy and Armed Robbery Against Ships Annual Report 1 January-31 December 2008*, International Maritime Bureau, London, UK, 2009.

[16] International Maritime Bureau, *Piracy and Armed Robbery Against Ships Annual Report 1 January-31 December 2009*, International Maritime Bureau, London, UK, 2010.

[17] International Maritime Bureau, *Piracy and Armed Robbery Against Ships Annual Report 1 January-31 December 2010*, International Maritime Bureau, London, UK, 2010.

[18] International Maritime Bureau, *Piracy and Armed Robbery Against Ships Report for the Period 1 January-31 December 2011*, International Maritime Bureau, London, UK, 2012.

[19] International Maritime Bureau, *Piracy and Armed Robbery Against Ships Report for the Period 1 January-30 June 2012*, International Maritime Bureau, London, UK, 2012.

[20] R. I. Rotberg, "Combating maritime piracy: a policy brief with recommendations for action," Policy Brief #11, World Peace Foundation, Medford Somerville, Mass, USA, 2010.

[21] Oceans Beyond Piracy, "The Economic Cost of Somali Piracy 2011," 2011, http://oceansbeyondpiracy.org/sites/default/files/economic_cost_of_piracy_2011.pdf.

[22] P. Eichstaedt, *Pirate State: Inside Somalia's Terrorism at Sea*, Chicago Review Press, Chicago, Ill, USA, 2010.

[23] A. Shortland and M. Vothknecht, "Combating maritime terrorism off the Coast of Somalia," Working Paper 47, European Security Economics, Vienna, Austria, 2011.

[24] Combined Maritime Forces, 2012, http://www.cusnc.navy.mil/cmf/cmf_command.html.

[25] R. Mirshak, "Ship Response Capability Models for Counter-Piracy Patrols in the Gulf of Aden," Technical Memorandum DRDC CORA TM, 2011-139, Maritime Operations Research Team, Defence R&D Canada, Ottawa, Canada, 2011, http://cradpdf.drdc-rddc.gc.ca/inbasket/DRP_CORA.111027_0949.TM2011-139_A1b.pdf.

[26] S. Marsland, *Machine Learning: An Algorithmic Perspective*, Chapman & Hall/CRC, New York, NY, USA, 2009.

[27] C. H. Watkins and P. Dayan, "Q-learning," *Machine Learning*, vol. 8, no. 3-4, pp. 279–292, 1992.

[28] B. C. da Silva, E. W. Basso, A. L. C. Bazzan, and P. M. Engel, "Dealing with non-stationary environments using context detection," in *Proceedings of the 23rd International Conference on Machine Learning (ICML '06)*, pp. 217–224, June 2006.

[29] V. Bulitko, N. Sturtevant, and M. Kazakevich, "Speeding up learning in reel-time search via automatic state abstraction," in *Proceedings of the 20th National Conference on Artificial Intelligence and the 17th Innovative Applications of Artificial Intelligence Conference (AAAI '05)*, pp. 1349–1354, July 2005.

[30] L. Panait and S. Luke, "Cooperative multi-agent learning: the state of the art," *Autonomous Agents and Multi-Agent Systems*, vol. 11, no. 3, pp. 387–434, 2005.

[31] L. Buşoniu, R. Babuška, and B. De Schutter, "A comprehensive survey of multiagent reinforcement learning," *IEEE Transactions on Systems, Man and Cybernetics C*, vol. 38, no. 2, pp. 156–172, 2008.

[32] L. Jing and N. Cerone, "Thoughts on multiagent learning: from a reinforcement learning perspective," Technical Report CSE-2010-07, Department of Computer Science and Engineering, York University, Ontario, Canda, 2010.

[33] L. Oliwenstein, "From dendrites to decisions," *Engineering and Science*, vol. 74, no. 3, pp. 14–21, 2011.

[34] P. R. Montague, B. King-Casas, and J. D. Cohen, "Imaging valuation models in human choice," *Annual Review of Neuroscience*, vol. 29, pp. 417–448, 2006.

[35] T. Lohrenz, K. McCabe, C. F. Camerer, and P. R. Montague, "Neural signature of fictive learning signals in a sequential investment task," *Proceedings of the National Academy of Sciences of the United States of America*, vol. 104, no. 22, pp. 9493–9498, 2007.

[36] A. Agogino and K. Tumer, "Regulating air traffic flow with coupled agents," in *Proceedings of the 7th International Joint Conference on Autonomous Agents and Multiagent Systems*, vol. 2, pp. 535–542, 2008.

[37] K. Tumer and N. Khani, "Learning from actions not taken in multiagent systems," *Advances in Complex Systems*, vol. 12, no. 4-5, pp. 455–473, 2009.

[38] D. M. Gordon, *Ants at Work: How An Insect Society Is Organized*, The Free Press, New York, NY, USA, 1999.

[39] K. L. Huang and C. J. Liao, "Ant colony optimization combined with taboo search for the job shop scheduling problem," *Computers and Operations Research*, vol. 35, no. 4, pp. 1030–1046, 2008.

[40] Z. J. Lee, C. Y. Lee, and S. F. Su, "An immunity-based ant colony optimization algorithm for solving weapon-target assignment problem," *Applied Soft Computing Journal*, vol. 2, no. 1, pp. 39–47, 2002.

[41] J. Bautista and J. Pereira, "Ant algorithms for a time and space constrained assembly line balancing problem," *European Journal of Operational Research*, vol. 177, no. 3, pp. 2016–2032, 2007.

[42] M. Gosnell, S. O'Hara, and M. Simon, "Spatially decomposed searching by heterogeneous unmanned systems," in *Proceedings of the International Conference on Integration of Knowledge Intensive Multi-Agent Systems (KIMAS '07)*, pp. 52–57, May 2007.

[43] J. G. M. Fu and M. H. Ang, "Probabilistic ants (PAnts) in multi-agent patrolling," in *Proceedings of the International Conference on Advanced Intelligent Mechatronics*, pp. 1371–1376, 2009.

[44] H. Chu, A. Glad, O. Simonin, F. Sempé, A. Drogoul, and F. Charpillet, "Swarm approaches for the patrolling problem, information propagation vs. pheromone evaporation," in *Proceedings of the 19th IEEE International Conference on Tools with Artificial Intelligence (ICTAI '07)*, pp. 442–449, October 2007.

[45] J. A. Sauter, R. Matthews, H. Van Dyke Parunak, and S. A. Brueckner, "Performance of digital pheromones for swarming vehicle control," in *Proceedings of the 4th International Conference on Autonomous Agents and Multi agent Systems (AAMAS '05)*, pp. 1037–1044, July 2005.

[46] N. Monekosso and P. Remagnino, "An analysis of the pheromone Q-learning algorithm," in *Proceedings of the 8th Ibero-American Conference on Artificial Intelligence*, pp. 224–232, 2002.

[47] V. Furtado, A. Melo, A. L. V. Coelho, R. Menezes, and R. Perrone, "A bio-inspired crime simulation model," *Decision Support Systems*, vol. 48, no. 1, pp. 282–292, 2009.

[48] O. Vaněk, B. Bošanský, M. Jakob, and M. Pěchouček, "Transiting areas patrolled by a mobile adversary," in *Proceedings of the IEEE Conference on Computational Intelligence and Games (CIG '10)*, pp. 9–16, August 2010.

[49] M. Jakob, O. Vanek, S. Urban, P. Benda, and M. Pechoucek, "Agent C: agent-based testbed for adversarial modeling and reasoning in the maritime domain," in *Proceedings of the International Conference on Autonomous and Multiagent Systems*, pp. 1641–1642, 2010.

[50] M. Jakob, O. Vaněk, and M. Pěchouček, "Using agents to improve international maritime transport security," *IEEE Intelligent Systems*, vol. 26, no. 1, pp. 90–95, 2011.

[51] L. A. Slootmaker, *Countering piracy with the next-generation piracy performance surface model [M.S. thesis]*, Naval Postgraduate School, Monterey, Calif, USA, 2011.

[52] J. Decraene, M. Anderson, and M. Low, "Maritime counter-piracy study using agent-based simulations," in *Proceedings of the Spring Simulation Multiconference (SpringSim '10)*, pp. 82–89, April 2010.

[53] D. Walton, E. Paulo, C. J. McCarthy, and R. Vaidyanathan, "Modeling force response to small boat attack against high value commercial ships," in *Proceedings of the 2005 Winter Simulation Conference*, pp. 988–991, December 2005.

[54] M. T. J. Spaan, "Partially observable markov decision processes," in *Reinforcement Learning State-of-the-Art*, M. Wiering and M. van Otterlo, Eds., Springer, Berlin, Germany, 2012.

[55] B. Weitjens, *Geopredict: Geographical crime forecasting for varying situations [M.S. thesis]*, Vrije Universiteit, Amsterdam, The Netherlands, 2010.

[56] P. Kaluza, A. Kölzsch, M. T. Gastner, and B. Blasius, "The complex network of global cargo ship movements," 2010, http://arxiv.org/abs/1001.2172/.

[57] M. West, "Asset allocation to cover a region of piracy," Report DSTO-TN-1030, Maritime Operations Division, Defence Science and Technology Organisation, Australian Government Department of Defense, Canberra, Australia, 2011.

[58] E. Alpaydin, *Introduction to Machine Learning*, MIT Press, Cambridge, Mass, USA, 2nd edition, 2010.

[59] C. Jones and M. J. Matarić, "From local to global behavior in intelligent self-assembly," in *Proceedings of the IEEE International Conference on Robotics and Automation*, pp. 721–726, September 2003.

10

Simulation of Land-Use Development, Using a Risk-Regarding Agent-Based Model

F. Hosseinali,[1] A. A. Alesheikh,[1] and F. Nourian[2]

[1] Faculty of Geodesy and Geomatics Engineering, K.N. Toosi University of Technology, ValiAsr Street, Mirdamad Cross, Tehran 19967-15433, Iran
[2] School of Urban Planning, University of Tehran, Enghelab Avenue, Tehran 14155-6135, Iran

Correspondence should be addressed to F. Hosseinali, frdhal@gmail.com

Academic Editor: Joanna Józefowska

The aim of this paper is to study the spatial consequences of applying different Attitude Utility Functions (AUFs), which reflect peoples' simplified psychological frames, to investment plans in land-use decision making. For this purpose, we considered and implemented an agent-based model with new methods for searching landscapes, for selecting parcels to develop, and for allowing competitions among agents. Besides this, GIS (Geographic Information Systems) as a versatile and powerful medium of analyzing and representing spatial data is used. Our model is implemented on an artificial landscape in which land is being developed by agents. The agents are assumed to be mobile developers that are equipped with several land-related objectives. In this paper, agents mimic various risk-bearing attitudes and sometimes compete for developing the same parcel. The results reveal that patterns of land-use development are different in the two cases of regarding and disregarding AUFs. Therefore, it is considered here that using the attitudes of people towards risk helps the model to better simulate the decision making of land-use developers. The different attitudes toward risk used in this study can be attributed to different categories of developers based on sets of characteristics such as income, age, or education.

1. Introduction

Land-Use/Cover Change (LUCC) is one of the most profound human-induced alterations of the earth's system [1–3]. LUCC is a complex process caused by the interaction between natural and social systems at different spatial scales [4, 5]. The heterogeneity and contiguity of space creates many difficulties in spatial models of residential land-use development. Therefore, there is no simple, uniform way to analyze and explain the dynamics of land-use changes [6]. A group of models have recently emerged and gained popularity in the LUCC scientific community. These models are commonly referred to as agent-based models (ABMs) [7]. These models use the real actors of land-use changes (individuals or institutions) as objects of analysis and simulation and pay explicit attention to the interactions of the "agents" of change [7]. Numerous attempts have been made to define the concept of agents [8, 9]. In

this paper, we adopted the definition of Maes [10]: "An agent is a system that tries to fulfill a set of goals in a complex, dynamic environment. An agent is situated in the environment: it can sense the environment through its sensors and act upon the environment using its actuators." Agents can represent individuals, groups of individuals, and, if appropriate, inanimate objects such as houses or cars [11]. ABMs rely on interactions between many distributed agents to form emergent larger-scale patterns [12]. All agents structurally deal with an environment and with each other by a set of rules. Essentially, each agent behaves autonomously [13]. By simulating the individual actions of many diverse but interrelated actors and by measuring the resulting system outcomes over time (e.g., the changes in patterns of land-use in suburbs), ABMs can provide useful tools for assessing residential development [14]. In this paper, we developed and implemented an agent-based model equipped with new methods for searching landscapes, for selecting parcels to develop, and for allowing competitions among agents. Also, this paper links a Geographic Information System (GIS) with a simulation/modeling system purposely built.

Many ABMs have been proposed [15–20]. Therefore, several classifications of ABMs have been presented [15, 21]. Most models, however, are based on riskless axioms of rational choice. Risk is described as knowledge of the possibilities of undesirable results [22]. Comprehensive models that delineate the impact of attitudes towards risk on land-use development are rare. This paper aims to build a conceptual framework for including risk-explicit attitudes in the modelling of land-use development. Evaluating the patterns of land-use development in two cases of regarding and disregarding risk into account will elucidate the impact of attitudes of people toward risk on land-used development. Therefore, we defined and implemented two scenarios of regarding and disregarding risk. Also, since the attitudes of actual people towards risk in land-use development are difficult to detect, at least when the number of people gets large, this paper also attempts to suggest some criteria that categorize risky behaviors of people in land-use development.

In this study, an artificial raster landscape was prepared using GIS. The agents represent land-use developers that traverse the landscape seeking for land parcels to develop. The search is exercised in two scenarios, either regarding or disregarding risk. Ligmann-Zielinska (2009) studied the impact of risk-taking attitudes on a land-use pattern with ABM [23]. In her model the agents do not move in the landscape and they are randomly seeded. Moreover, there are only one to three agents who act in the landscape. In our model, the agents are not seeded randomly. They move explicitly in the landscape. Furthermore, number of agents is not limited and can be defined as appropriate to the conditions of study area. We also developed a new method for competition among agents.

In this study, the agents are categorized into five groups based on their desires and properties. Categorizing the developers helps the model to perform a better simulation of real situations. For instance, Loibl and Toetzer (2003) developed an ABM for urban sprawl in Vienna, Austria, with agents that were classified into six categories based on their characteristics [24]. However, here the classification is implemented by two methods: one method is through the different weights that they assign to the criteria maps and the other method is through considering different AUFs for them which reflects the attitudes of the developer agents toward risk. Tian et al. (2011) also reflected heterogeneity of agents by using different sets of weights according to the criteria maps [25]. On the other hand, Ligtenberg et al. (2008) developed a spatial planning model combining a multiagent simulation approach with cellular automata to simulate the urban development in the mideast of the Netherlands [8]. In that model, two types of actors were defined: the reconnaissance actors who had voting power during a planning process and the planning actors who had the authority to change the spatial organization. In that study, two scenarios have been defined and compared, although no validation method has been presented. Besides

this, Bakker and van Doorn (2009) considered farmers as agents who change the land-use [26]. They defined four types for farmers and demonstrated that each farmer type shows a different relationship between landscape factors and land use changes.

In the rest of the paper, first Attitude Utility Functions are described. Then, the proposed methodology is explained using Overview, Design concepts, and Details (ODD) protocol. Next, implementation of pilot application is expressed. Afterward results and discussions will appear and the last section will be the conclusions and recommendations.

2. Utility Functions to Define Risk-Taking Agents

As highlighted in the introduction, two scenarios of regarding and disregarding risk are defined in this paper. Regarding risk is performed by considering an Attitude Utility Function (AUF) which reflected the attitudes of people toward risk. Therefore, AUF is briefly expressed here.

Considering the different attitudes of individuals, the consequences of particular decisions may be felt by some as gains and by others as losses [27]. In their most general form, attitudes are defined as relatively stable psychological tendencies that are expressed by evaluating specific entities with some degree of favor or disfavor [28]. Ligmann-Zielinska (2009) defined five-attitude templates, namely, Unbiased (risk-impartial), Reckless (risk seeking), Cautious (risk averse), Poor (risk avoiding), and Rich (risk bearing) that are mathematically presented in the following equations [23]:

$$y = x,$$

$$y = \frac{(e^{ax} - 1)}{a},$$

$$y = \frac{\ln(ax + 1)}{a}, \tag{1}$$

$$y = ax^a,$$

$$y = \left(\frac{x}{a}\right)^{(1/a)},$$

where a is a curving coefficient driving the shape of an AUF, equaling 3 in the above approximation, x is the original value of criterion c for option p, and y is the recalculated value of criterion c for option p based on the attitude. These AUFs are used in our paper.

3. Proposed Model and Its Main Features

In this study two methods of risk-regarding and risk-disregarding agents are considered. Heterogeneity of agents is articulated through diverse perceptions of decision criteria, which are embedded in AUFs. The model is explained in the following ODD protocol [29, 30].

```
Searching step                              Developing Step
  Start                                       Start
    For all agents                              While there is any unsatisfied agent
      For the number of allowed districts to search   Select an agent randomly
        For the number of allowed regions to search   Select the first choice settlement
          Select a parcel                             If there is any request for this cell
          Repeat                                        Go to the competition
            Assess and save the state of ...           Register the cell as developed
            the neighborhood of the cell               Change the probability
            Go to the best neighbor around the cell  Else
          Until allowed movement                       Register the cell as developed
      End For                                          Change the probability
    End For                                          End If
  End For                                          End While
```

FIGURE 1: Pseudocode that shows the simplified algorithm of the model.

3.1. Overview

3.1.1. Purpose.
The purpose of this paper is to establish an agent-based model of urban land-use development considering explicit risk attitudes in residential settlements using GIS environment.

3.1.2. Entities, State Variables, and Scales.
The classification of agents follows the described categorization in Section 2. The landscape is a 500*600 grid of cells and is divided into eight districts. Besides their type, each agent has a location in a cell of a landscape, a limited movement, a minimum required location change in a district, a number of districts to search, and a number of parcels to develop each session. Furthermore, the weights of criteria maps (Figure 3) may vary for different agent types, and every agent also has a Frustration (see Section 3.3.3(3)). Each run of the model is divided into four sessions and corresponds to one year. The model is run for five years.

3.1.3. Process Overview and Scheduling.
There are two main steps in the model: the searching step and the development step.

Searching Step. In searching step the agents explore the landscape. At the beginning, the required number of agents is created and they are distributed in the districts. The selection of districts is based on the primary probability of selection, which is assigned to the districts. Neighborhoods of initially developed area are often exposed to further developments. Hence, when agents go to the districts, at first they move randomly to the neighborhoods of initially developed areas. Wherever the agent starts its activities, it assesses and records the state of its current parcel (standing parcel) and also its eight adjacent parcels. Next, the agent moves to its best neighbor parcel, or if more than one parcel achieves the same score, it chooses one of them randomly. If the agent movement is finished or it is not able to move to a neighbor parcel, the agent changes the search region in the district and jumps to another position in the same district. Moreover,

the agents can search a specific number of districts in the same way. Thus, at the end of each searching step, each agent records the situation of several visited parcels and sorts them in descending order. This list may be known as investment list. The cells in the investment list of each agent are called searched cells for that agent.

Developing Step. When all agents finish the search, the Developing step starts, and agents choose the top scoring parcels in their sorted investment list to develop. In the conflict cases, the winner and the loser(s) are determined through the competition. The cells that are developed by the agents are assumed as developed cells hereafter. The pseudocode of the model algorithm is shown in Figure 1.

A searching step and a developing step are performed in each session. Properties of a session are like a year. Nevertheless, at the end of a year, the desired parcels of agents are developed so they are assumed to be initially developed in the next years. However this is not the case in the sessions. At the end of a session the agents have chosen their desired parcels but they have not developed them. Hence, those selected (reserved) cells are still undeveloped and the agents may traverse them in searching steps of next sessions. However, in developing step the reserved parcels cannot be chosen to develop. Therefore, the agents are forced to the less suitable parcels.

3.2. Design Concepts

3.2.1. Emergence.
All of the resultant spatial land-use data from a completed simulation are emergent phenomena and include elements such as the pattern of development and the probability of districts to be selected.

3.2.2. Adaptation.
After each session of runs, the probability of selecting districts for each type of agent is modified. This probability varies based on the settlements of the agents. Moreover, probable new clusters of developed cells in the previous year are now considered as initially developed area where attract the agents for further searches.

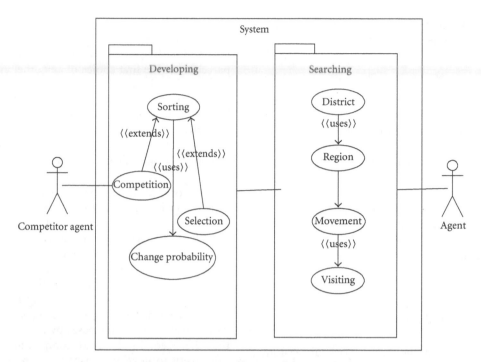

FIGURE 2: Use case diagram of the model.

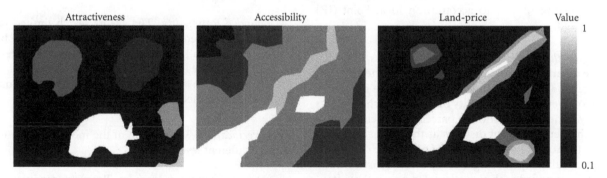

FIGURE 3: Three criteria maps, the lighter color means the higher suitability in the corresponding criteria map.

3.2.3. Objectives. The objectives of the agents are to find the most appropriate parcels (in the agent's judgment) for development and then to develop their predefined number of parcels, taking the most desired parcels from their search.

3.2.4. Sensing. The agents are free to surf the landscape. They know the districts, their borders, and their developed areas. The agents perceive the state of standing parcel and its neighbors. The state of adjacent parcels guides the agents to move to the best neighbor of its standing parcel. In developing steps, the agents may compete with some other agents to develop parcels.

3.2.5. Interaction. Each agent collects and saves the state of visited parcels. The high-score visited parcels are used to revise the probabilities of the districts. The changes in the probabilities of districts are indirect interactions among the

agents. Competition is the direct interaction among agents who compete to develop a parcel.

3.2.6. Stochasticity. Choosing the districts is probabilistic. In the district, selecting the region of search is random, as well. Thus, there is a little variation in the several runs of the model. Hence, to ensure the stability of the results, the model is executed ten times.

3.2.7. Collectiveness. The agents are divided into five types with different aims and utilities.

3.2.8. Observation. For analyzing the results, the new developments simulated by the model can be assessed in some aspects. For each developed parcel, year of development, the type of the agent that has developed it, and number of requests for that parcel can be observed. Also, the total number of conflicts during the development which cause the competitions in each year is observable.

3.3. Details

3.3.1. Initialization. At the beginning, three criteria maps and the map of initially developed area are uploaded into the model. A predefined number of agents are created and moved onto the landscape. In this step, the probabilities of selecting districts are the same for all types of agents (Figure 2(a)).

3.3.2. Input Data. Using the GIS extension of NetLogo, input maps (Figure 3) are read from the files and then are converted to the initial software-specific format. The input maps are three criteria maps, the map of initially developed area, and the map of districts.

3.3.3. Submodels. There are some detailed aspects of models that can be briefly explained here.

(1) Ranking the Parcels. In the case of risk disregarding, the desirability of each parcel is obtained by a weighted summation of the value of that parcel in each layer. Otherwise, taking AUFs into account, an Ideal Point (IP) method is used.

(2) Changing the Probability of Selecting Districts. The districts have an arbitrary probability of being selected by each type of agents, which is assumed to be the same on initialization. However, the functionality of the agents changes this probability. When the selection of parcels for development is finished, the percentages of districts at the top half and top quarter of the sorted investment list of agents are calculated. Next, the calculated percentages from a top quarter with a weight of 2 are added with the calculated percentages from the top half with a weight of 1. After that, the result is compared with the previous probabilities and the difference for each district is calculated. The differences (which can be positive or negative for each district) are multiplied by a coefficient named the "coefficient of communication" and then are multiplied by a coefficient equal to (number of searched districts/number of whole districts). Finally, the results are added to the previous probabilities. Coefficient of communication is a parameter which regulates the impact of agents on changing the probabilities of districts.

(3) Competition. The competition among agents in cases of conflict is considered based on empirical observations. There are some heuristics in the competition of people for land. (1) All people do not compete for a parcel at the same time; they may find parcels at different times. (2) The power of people in competition is not equal. (3) People who lost some parcels in competition have more interest and pressure to win the next competition.

Based on these assumptions, the competition was implemented as follows: when the search in districts finished, the selection of parcels for development starts. The agents are selected one by one randomly until all of the agents develop their desired number of parcels. The top scoring parcel of each agent is considered for development. If that parcel is not the first choice of any other agent, the parcel is developed by the agent. Otherwise, the winner is determined via a competition. In a contest, the agent who achieves the highest score wins. The score is calculated with the following formula:

$$\text{Score} = W_{\text{Type}} \times \text{Score}_{\text{Type}} + W_{\text{Frustration}} \times \text{Frustration}, \quad (2)$$

where $\text{Score}_{\text{Type}}$ is the score assigned to each type of agent, Frustration is a digit that shows how many times an agent has lost a parcel, and W_{Type} and $W_{\text{Frustration}}$ are the weights considered for $\text{Score}_{\text{Type}}$ and Frustration, respectively. The score and the weight of score for each type of agents should be evaluated, but, for the sake of simplicity, it is assumed equal for all types of agents in this paper. The value of Frustration is equal to zero for all agents at the beginning. However, whenever an agent loses a parcel in a competition, its Frustration value increases by one. This increase means that the agent in the next competition will have higher propensity to develop a parcel. Figure 2 shows a use case diagram of the model.

(4) Bounded Rationality. The agents search limited parcels of landscape. Moreover, the parcels are traversed one by one and cannot be totally random. Furthermore, the perceptions of agents of the searched parcels are not the same because the AUF is taken into account. These are the bounded rationalities assumed for the agents in this study.

3.3.4. Verification. Verification of the model was performed at three different levels.

(1) *Unit Testing of Modules.* Program modules (code) were tested individually. For example, the method that moves an agent across the landscape was tested to make sure that an agent correctly moves towards districts, correctly moves in districts, and correctly jumps to different regions.

(2) *Testing of Basic Model Behaviors.* Interactions of agents can involve different program modules and thus are outside of the testing described above. Examples tested include competition for development. The model was executed with different numbers of agents and different types of agents, and conflicts were assessed. It was expected that conflicts would increase by increasing the number of agents of the same type.

(3) *Detailed Test.* The overall test could fail to detect some logical errors. Therefore, some aspects must be checked more precisely. For instance, the investment list of agents and their desirability, the suitability of parcels before and after using AUFs, the Frustration of agents when losing a parcel, and the nonexistent of repeated parcels in the investment lists of the agents were checked.

4. Implementation

Three artificial criteria maps (layers), namely, land price, attractiveness, and accessibility, were used (Figures 3 and 4) in this study. Because we wanted to emulate real-world conditions, we attempted to produce maps similar to a real land use.

The artificial landscape is composed of 300,000 raster cells with 600 rows and 500 columns. The parameters of the model are shown in Table 1.

The weights of three criteria maps are set to 0.1 but the weight of adjacency is tested in two cases equal to 0.5 and 1. Therefore, eight configurations of the model are constructed, and, for each configuration, five outputs that correspond to the five-year intervals are estimated. Because the maps are artificial, they may not match the real situation. For example, in the reality suburbs of the cities often have high accessibility and land price. Thus, the suburbs of the cities are exposed to development. However, this may not be the case in our artificial maps. In consequence, we assumed adjacency to the initially developed area. To implement the adjacency, number of adjacent initially developed cells is counted. Then, that number is multiplied by the weight of adjacency and is treated like a criteria map. This method directs the agents to the suburbs of initially developed area.

It should be mentioned that the artificial maps were created and prepared using AutoCAD Map 2009. NetLogo 4.1 and its GIS extension were used for agents-based modeling and ArcGIS 9.3 was used for preparing maps and statistical analysis.

4.1. Regarding and Disregarding Risk. Two major cases (scenarios) of regarding and disregarding risk are considered in this study. In the risk-regarding case, AUFs are used (1); thus the decisions of the agents are affected by their attitudes toward risk. On the other hand, in risk-disregarding case, decisions of the agents are based on weighted summation method and thus no attitude toward risk is considered.

In this situation where assessing and comparing the behavior of agents regarding and disregarding risk is desired, the parameters are set the same for both scenarios. After several executions of the model, the parameters tabulated in Table 1 were selected. The proportion of development was estimated after preliminary experimentations.

5. Results and Discussions

Figure 5 shows the developed area after a one- and five-year interval. A precise look at the development after one year reveals that, in the risk-regarding case, the development is scattered around the initially developed area where the three criteria maps (accessibility, attractiveness, and land price) are suitable. In the risk-disregarding case, however, almost all developments happened adjacent to the initially developed area. While, in the disregarding-risk case, all agents have randomly developed the landscape; in the risk-regarding case only two classes of agents, those of "poor" and "reckless," were seen in the surrounding area. When the weights of the three maps are the same and when the weight

of adjacency to the initially developed area was considered higher than the others, the disregarding-risk agents are absorbed in the landscape adjacent to the initially developed area. However, this situation does not occur when dealing with a risky case. Based on the three criteria maps, the scattered developing regions have high attractiveness, low land prices and include good accessibility. However, they are not adjacent to the initially developed landscapes. If a high weight is assigned to adjacency to a developed area, the agents move toward the neighborhood of the initially developed area. Nevertheless, this movement is not the case for poor and reckless developers. For these classes of agents, the importance of wining perception is greater. Thus, their developed areas gain relative superiority, making them become scattered all over the region. Unbiased agents (not affected by risk) are proper for comparing agent behaviors. All unbiased agents were settled in the neighborhood of the initially developed area. This settlement confirmed that such an area is the best choice. Rich and cautious agents perceive the relative superiority of the area not adjacent to the initially developed area as less than their actual values. Therefore, these agents tend to settle into the neighborhood of the initially developed area. To clarify the results, Figure 6 shows the statistical conditions of development by diagrams. Here, the developing cells that are not adjacent to the initially developed area are counted by their class of developers.

According to Figure 6, after the first year, the cells developed by poor and reckless agents are now initially developed. Gradually, when the neighborhood of initially developed cells is occupied, some rich, cautious, or unbiased agents choose free cells (cells not directly in the neighborhood of initially developed cells) for development. However, the poor and reckless classes of developers still have the largest number of agents that select cells not adjacent to the initially developed area. Expressing the differences between the behavior of poor and reckless agents is still complex and requires further study. Exploring the details of developing cells in the map also reveals that a number of remote sites were chosen only by reckless agents and that developing areas chosen by poor agents are limited.

The difference between the two cases, those of regarding and disregarding risk, is clearly presented in Figure 6. When AUFs are neglected, all agents would be of the same type, and their behavior would be similar. This fact is revealed in Figure 6, Figures 6(a) and 6(b). However, in considering risk, each class of agent behaves differently. This trend is noticeable in Figures 6(c), 6(d), 6(e), and 6(f). Also, unbiased agents should have the same behavior in the two cases, which is also noticeable in Figure 6. Any changes in the behavior of unbiased agents are justifiable because the conditions of the agents in the two scenarios are different. In the risk-regarding case, unbiased agents must compete with other types of agents. Another parameter that can be set is the number of districts each agent visits. When this number is increased, the rationality of the agent increases and the agents are able to make better choices for development.

Some important observations are made during the execution of the model.

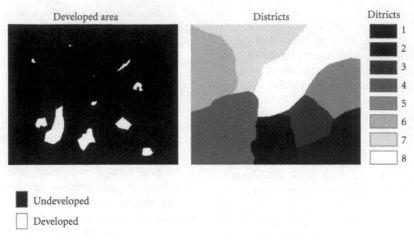

Undeveloped
Developed

FIGURE 4: Maps of developed area and districts.

TABLE 1: The parameters of the model.

Number of agents	Number of executions (years)	Number of sessions per year	Agent movement (parcel)	Number of jumps in each region	Number of districts to search	Number of developments per session
50 (10 agents of each type)	5	4	21	2	5 and 6	3 and 5

(i) In the risk-disregarding case, agents may choose free cells to develop. If two or more agents search the same area adjacent to a initially developed area, then at least one of the agents may lose its desirable choices in competition; thus, it is possible to choose free cells for development. Moreover, the increase in session executions intensifies this behavior. At the end of each session, the parcels that have been chosen by agents are reserved. These parcels are not assumed to be developed. Therefore, in the next sessions, agents may search the reserved parcels but they are unable to select them for development. So, they may refer to the other searched parcels. Actually, the reserved parcels in sessions exclude some neighboring parcels of initially developed areas from selection by agents.

(ii) In the risk-disregarding case, when free cells are developed in a year, in the next year they are assumed to be initially developed and so will be the destination of search by agents. However, the area and perimeter of these newly developed parcels are less than the others. Consequently, the probability of losing their neighborhood in competition among agents increases. Therefore, some agents are pushed into another area.

(iii) In the risk-regarding case, the number of free cells is decreased. This reduction is mostly due to a decrease in the tendency of poor and reckless agents to free cells. The free cells are primarily chosen by poor and reckless agents. This choice means that those selected free cells are preferred in comparison to the neighborhood of initially developed areas. In the next years, the neighborhood of newly developed areas that have almost the same situation may also be chosen by agents, but they are not assumed to be free cells anymore because they are now in the neighborhood of the developed era.

(iv) In the risk-regarding case, the number of free cells selected by rich, cautious, and unbiased agents is decreased. The reason is similar to the reasons given for the first case.

One other item that is able to show the effect of AUFs is the trend of changes in the probability of districts to be selected. Figure 7 shows these probabilities besides the primary assigned probabilities for each district. The primary probability for each district to be selected for districts 1 through 8 are 20, 7, 13, 30, 5, 4, 6, and 15 percent, respectively, for all types of agents.

If AUFs are omitted, the behaviours of agents, such as the changes in the probability of districts, must be similar. Figure 7 substantiates this matter. The maximum difference in the probability of a district is less than 1.5 percent, whereas this maximum is about 4 percent when using AUFs. Figure 7 shows that the selection probabilities of districts 2 and 5 increase, although this issue was not observed for reckless agents. Moreover, unbiased agents show similar probabilities in both scenarios for regarding or disregarding AUFs. This fact verifies the unbiased operations. Nevertheless, it is important to notice that no superiority has been regarded for various types of agents in competition. Also, the coefficient of communication among agents has been set to 0.5. It is obvious that distinguishing different superiorities for different types of agents and increasing the coefficient of communication will increase differences in the probabilities of districts to be chosen by different types of agents.

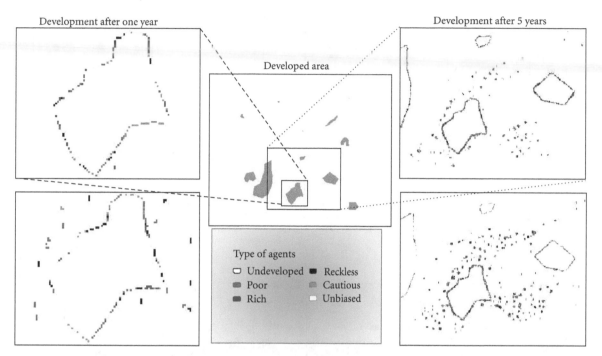

FIGURE 5: Developed area after one- and five- year intervals, top: without risk, and bottom: with risk. The parameters of the model are: weight of Adjacency to Developed area (WAD) = 1, Number of Districts to Search (NDS) =5, Development Per Session (DPS) = 3.

Proof of different behaviors of agents when taking risk into account will be helpful if the real land-use developers can be categorized according to their AUFs. The more precise the categories of land-use developers is, the more precise the simulation of their behaviors is in the landscape. Because a psychological categorization of land-use developers is almost impossible, an external reflection of their operations is helpful. Thus, this study attempts to propose a classification for land-use developers based on their AUFs. Referring to the paper of Loibl and Toetzer (2003) [24], five types of agents can be defined from economical and educational points of view. Such a classification is appropriate for describing the preferences of agents and for evaluating the importance of various development criteria. In this regard, cautious agents are suggested to be considered as lower income developers who seek low land prices. Poor agents are suggested to be treated as moderate income, highly educated younger developers, and unbiased agents are suggested to be defined as moderate to high income developers. Rich agents are also suggested to be defined as high income, highly educated developers, and last, reckless agents are suggested to be regarded as weekend-home seekers and enterprise founders. However, more studies are necessary to define such assignments.

6. Conclusions and Recommendations

This paper presented the concepts and specifications of an agent-based model for the simulation of urban land-use sprawl in a Geospatial Information Systems (GIS) environment. The multiagent system of residential development implemented in this paper demonstrated the critical impact of attitudes to risk on land-use patterns. Moreover, disregarding the attitude to risk in agents not only means assuming a more extended rationality for the agents but also puts all developers in the same category, which is not the case in real societies. This study demonstrated that the proposed method of risk-aware agents has a better compatibility with modeling patterns of land-use development compared to the model of neglecting risk. Also, it is imperative to note that competition among agents plays an important role in the pattern of settlement. Furthermore, the results affirmed that linking GIS with ABM can enhance the capabilities of a simulation/modeling system for spatial problem purposes.

Agent-based models allow accounting for agent-specific behaviour, that is, acknowledging that not all agents are optimizers and that they may have personal views on how to reach a particular goal. This information could contribute to land-use change understanding and eventually to better land-use change predictions. While the application of simulations to study human-landscape interactions is burgeoning, developing a comprehensive and empirically based framework for linking the social and geographic disciplines across space and time remains for further paper. A newly developed method for searching landscapes, selecting parcels, and having competitions among agents, in addition to taking into account AUFs, brings us better ways to simulate the behavior of land-use developers. This paper proposed that the different agents, corresponding to different attitudes to risk, may have external equivalents in a real society. However, a better model for heterogeneous agents requires defining and setting other parameters, such as heterogeneous weights for layers, considering dominance of agents during competition, different searching abilities,

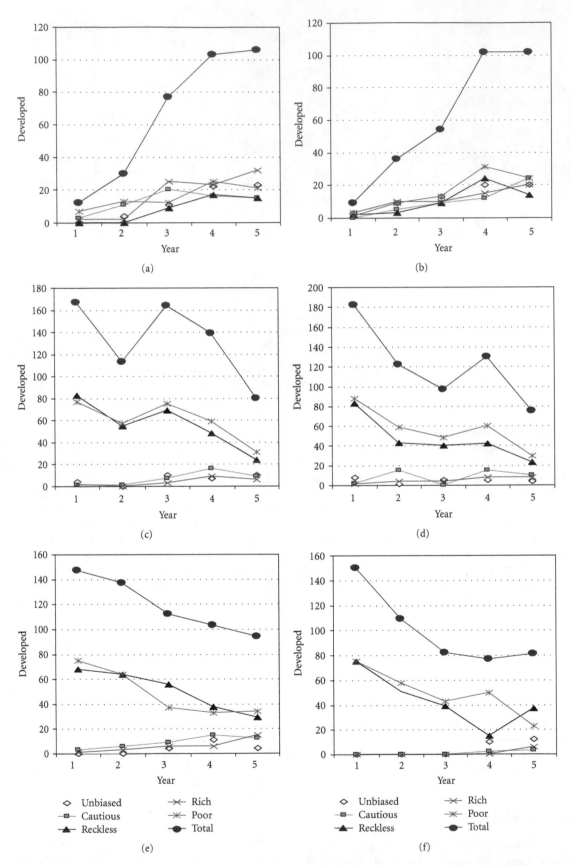

FIGURE 6: The cells—developed by agents—are not adjacent to a primarily developed area. (a) Disregarding risk, WAD = 1, NDS = 5, DPS = 3. (b) Disregarding risk, WAD = 1, NDS = 6, DPS = 3. (c) Regarding risk, WAD = 0.5, NDS = 5, DPS = 3. (d) Regarding risk, WAD = 0.5, NDS = 6, DPS = 3. (e) Regarding Risk, WAD = 1, NDS = 5, DPS = 3. (f) Regarding risk, WAD = 1, NDS = 6, DPS = 3.

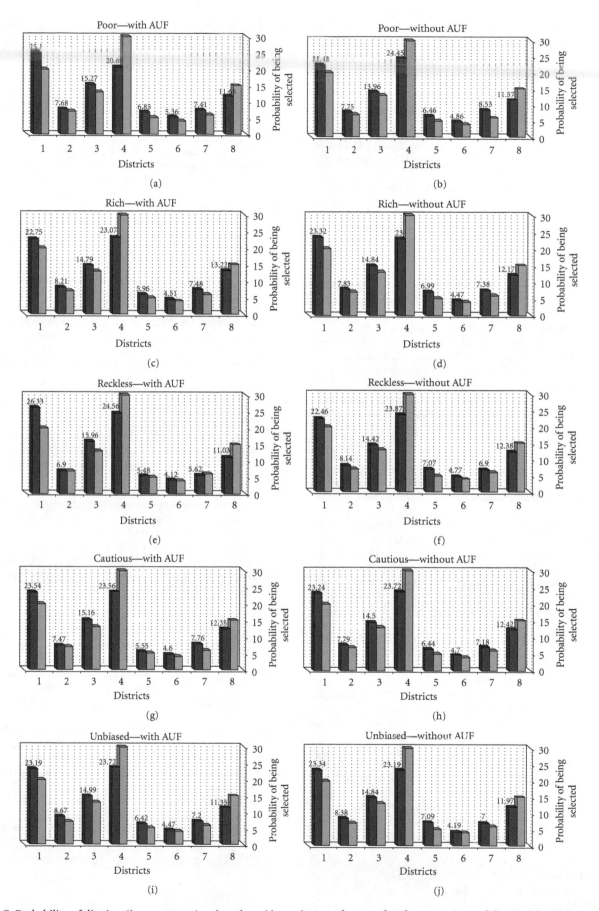

FIGURE 7: Probability of districts (in percentage) to be selected by each type of agent after five executions of the model. (Light purple) for primary probabilities which are the same for all of the agents when the model is initialized, (dark purple) for newly achieved probabilities.

varying probabilities of selecting districts, and various compatibilities for land-use development. Further paper will be needed to define and set these parameters and to implement the proposed model with real data.

References

[1] P. M. Vitousek, H. A. Mooney, J. Lubchenco, and J. M. Melillo, "Human domination of Earth's ecosystems," *Science*, vol. 277, no. 5325, pp. 494–499, 1997.

[2] Q. B. Le, S. J. Park, P. L. G. Vlek, and A. B. Cremers, "Land-Use Dynamic Simulator (LUDAS): a multi-agent system model for simulating spatio-temporal dynamics of coupled human-landscape system. I. Structure and theoretical specification," *Ecological Informatics*, vol. 3, no. 2, pp. 135–153, 2008.

[3] R. V. Sheeja, S. Joseph, D. S. Jaya, and R. S. Baiju, "Land use and land cover changes over a century (1914–2007) in the Neyyar River Basin, Kerala: a remote sensing and GIS approach," *International Journal of Digital Earth*, vol. 4, no. 3, pp. 258–270, 2011.

[4] R. R. Rindfuss, S. J. Walsh, B. L. Turner, J. Fox, and V. Mishra, "Developing a science of land change: challenges and methodological issues," *Proceedings of the National Academy of Sciences of the United States of America*, vol. 101, no. 39, pp. 13976–13981, 2004.

[5] D. Valbuena, P. H. Verburg, and A. K. Bregt, "A method to define a typology for agent-based analysis in regional land-use research," *Agriculture, Ecosystems and Environment*, vol. 128, no. 1-2, pp. 27–36, 2008.

[6] B. C. Pijanowsld, A. Tayyebi, M. R. Delavar, and M. J. Yazdanpanah, "Urban expansion simulation using geospatial information system and artificial neural networks," *International Journal of Environmental Research*, vol. 3, no. 4, pp. 495–502, 2009.

[7] J. C. Castella and P. H. Verburg, "Combination of process-oriented and pattern-oriented models of land-use change in a mountain area of Vietnam," *Ecological Modelling*, vol. 202, no. 3-4, pp. 410–420, 2007.

[8] A. Ligtenberg, A. K. Bregt, and R. Van Lammeren, "Multi-actor-based land use modelling: spatial planning using agents," *Landscape and Urban Planning*, vol. 56, no. 1-2, pp. 21–33, 2001.

[9] M. Wooldridge, *An Introduction to Multi-Agent Systems*, John Wiley and Sons, Chichester, UK, 2002.

[10] P. Maes, "Modeling adaptive autonomous agents," *Artificial Life*, vol. 1, no. 1-2, pp. 135–162, 1993.

[11] N. Malleson, A. Heppenstall, and L. See, "Crime reduction through simulation: an agent-based model of burglary," *Computers, Environment and Urban Systems*, vol. 34, no. 3, pp. 236–250, 2010.

[12] A. Crooks, C. Castle, and M. Batty, "Key challenges in agent-based modelling for geo-spatial simulation," *Computers, Environment and Urban Systems*, vol. 32, no. 6, pp. 417–430, 2008.

[13] D. G. Brown, R. Riolo, D. T. Robinson, M. North, and W. Rand, "Spatial process and data models: toward integration of agent-based models and GIS," *Journal of Geographical Systems*, vol. 7, no. 1, pp. 25–47, 2005.

[14] R. B. Matthews, N. G. Gilbert, A. Roach, J. G. Polhill, and N. M. Gotts, "Agent-based land-use models: a review of applications," *Landscape Ecology*, vol. 22, no. 10, pp. 1447–1459, 2007.

[15] D. C. Parker, S. M. Manson, M. A. Janssen, M. J. Hoffmann, and P. Deadman, "Multi-agent systems for the simulation of land-use and land-cover change: a review," *Annals of the Association of American Geographers*, vol. 93, no. 2, pp. 314–337, 2003.

[16] I. Benenson and P. M. Torrens, *Geosimulation: Automata-Based Modeling of Urban Phenomena*, John Wiley & Sons, 2004.

[17] J. C. Castella, S. Boissau, T. N. Trung, and D. D. Quang, "Agrarian transition and lowland-upland interactions in mountain areas in northern Vietnam: application of a multi-agent simulation model," *Agricultural Systems*, vol. 86, no. 3, pp. 312–332, 2005.

[18] R. B. Matthews, N. G. Gilbert, A. Roach, J. G. Polhill, and N. M. Gotts, "Agent-based land-use models: a review of applications," *Landscape Ecology*, vol. 22, no. 10, pp. 1447–1459, 2007.

[19] D. Valbuena, P. H. Verburg, A. K. Bregt, and A. Ligtenberg, "An agent-based approach to model land-use change at a regional scale," *Landscape Ecology*, vol. 25, no. 2, pp. 185–199, 2010.

[20] A. Ligtenberg, R. J. A. van Lammeren, A. K. Bregt, and A. J. M. Beulens, "Validation of an agent-based model for spatial planning: a role-playing approach," *Computers, Environment and Urban Systems*, vol. 34, no. 5, pp. 424–434, 2010.

[21] G. Weiss, *Multiagent Systems: A Modern Approach to Distributed Artificial Intelligence*, Intelligent Robotics and Autonomous Agents, MIT Press, 1999.

[22] T. Spradlin, *A Lexicon of Decision Making*, Decision Support Systems Resources, 2004.

[23] A. Ligmann-Zielinska, "The impact of risk-taking attitudes on a land use pattern: an agent-based model of residential development," *Journal of Land Use Science*, vol. 4, no. 4, pp. 215–232, 2009.

[24] W. Loibl and T. Toetzer, "Modeling growth and densification processes in suburban regions—simulation of landscape transition with spatial agents," *Environmental Modelling and Software*, vol. 18, no. 6, pp. 553–563, 2003.

[25] G. Tian, Y. Ouyang, Q. Quan, and J. Wu, "Simulating spatiotemporal dynamics of urbanization with multi-agent systems—a case study of the Phoenix metropolitan region, USA," *Ecological Modelling*, vol. 222, no. 5, pp. 1129–1138, 2011.

[26] M. M. Bakker and A. M. van Doorn, "Farmer-specific relationships between land use change and landscape factors: introducing agents in empirical land use modelling," *Land Use Policy*, vol. 26, no. 3, pp. 809–817, 2009.

[27] L. A. Kuznar and W. G. Frederick, "Environmental constraints and sigmoid utility: implications for value, risk sensitivity, and social status," *Ecological Economics*, vol. 46, no. 2, pp. 293–306, 2003.

[28] A. H. Eagly and S. Chaiken, *The Psychology of Attitudes*, Harcourt Brace Jovanovich College Publishers, Fort Worth, Tex, USA, 1993.

[29] V. Grimm, U. Berger, F. Bastiansen et al., "A standard protocol for describing individual-based and agent-based models," *Ecological Modelling*, vol. 198, no. 1-2, pp. 115–126, 2006.

[30] V. Grimm, U. Berger, D. L. DeAngelis, J. G. Polhill, J. Giske, and S. F. Railsback, "The ODD protocol: a review and first update," *Ecological Modelling*, vol. 221, no. 23, pp. 2760–2768, 2010.

11

Power Transformer Differential Protection Based on Neural Network Principal Component Analysis, Harmonic Restraint and Park's Plots

Manoj Tripathy

Department of Electrical Engineering, Indian Institute of Technology Roorkee, Roorkee 247 667, India

Correspondence should be addressed to Manoj Tripathy, manoj_tripathy1@rediffmail.com

Academic Editor: Deacha Puangdownreong

This paper describes a new approach for power transformer differential protection which is based on the wave-shape recognition technique. An algorithm based on neural network principal component analysis (NNPCA) with back-propagation learning is proposed for digital differential protection of power transformer. The principal component analysis is used to preprocess the data from power system in order to eliminate redundant information and enhance hidden pattern of differential current to discriminate between internal faults from inrush and overexcitation conditions. This algorithm has been developed by considering optimal number of neurons in hidden layer and optimal number of neurons at output layer. The proposed algorithm makes use of ratio of voltage to frequency and amplitude of differential current for transformer operating condition detection. This paper presents a comparative study of power transformer differential protection algorithms based on harmonic restraint method, NNPCA, feed forward back propagation neural network (FFBPNN), space vector analysis of the differential signal, and their time characteristic shapes in Park's plane. The algorithms are compared as to their speed of response, computational burden, and the capability to distinguish between a magnetizing inrush and power transformer internal fault. The mathematical basis for each algorithm is briefly described. All the algorithms are evaluated using simulation performed with PSCAD/EMTDC and MATLAB.

1. Introduction

Power transformer is one of the most important components in power system, for which various types of protective and monitoring schemes have been developed for many years. Differential protection is one of the most widely used methods for protecting power transformer against internal faults. The technique is based on the measurement and comparison of currents at both side of transformer: primary and secondary lines. The differential relay trips whenever the difference of the currents in both sides exceeds a predetermined threshold. This technique is accurate in most of the cases of transformer internal faults however mal-operation of differential relay is possible due to inrush currents, which result from transients in transformer magnetic flux. The transients in transformer magnetic flux may occur due to energization of transformer, voltage recovery after fault clearance or connection of parallel transformers.

The existence of such current disturbances has made the protection of power transformers a challenging problem for protection engineers. Therefore, accurate classification of currents in a power transformer is need of this challenging problem, in preventing maloperation of the differential relay under different nonfault conditions including magnetizing inrush, over-excitation, external fault, and saturation of current transformers [1].

Since last 1960s, researchers have considerable interest in the area of digital protection of power apparatus [1]. The main features which have attracted researchers to investigate the feasibility of designing digital relays for power system protection are its speed of operation, dependability, stability, economy, flexibility, and possibility of integrating a digital relay into the hierarchical computer system within the substation and with the grid. Further the digital relay not only provides protection, but also is used for status monitoring of power apparatus. Moreover, with the application

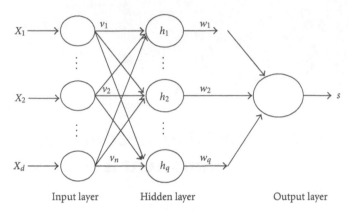

FIGURE 1: Typical neural network principal component analysis architecture.

of artificial intelligence in protective devices, the decision-making capability of the relays is enhanced.

Early methods were based on desensitizing or delaying the relay to overcome the transients [2]. These methods are unsatisfactory nevertheless, since the transformer were exposed to long unprotected times. Improved security and dependability then was appreciated when the second harmonic content with respect to the fundamental one was introduced as an identification criterion, known as harmonic restraint differential protection [3]. However, some researchers reported the existence of a significant amount of the second harmonic in some winding faults [4, 5]. In addition, the new generations of power transformers use low-loss amorphous material in their core, which can produce inrush currents with lower harmonics contents and higher magnitudes [5]. In such cases, some authors have modified the ratio of second harmonic to fundamental restraining criterion by using other ratios defined at a higher frequency [6]. While other researchers proposed hidden Markov's model [7], fuzzy-logic-based techniques [4, 8], wave shaped recognition technique [1, 9], and also artificial neural networks- (ANNs-) [10, 11] based learning pattern approach to get better classification accuracy, low computational burden, and fast response of the relay. However, these techniques depend on fixed threshold index (either in time domain or in frequency domain) and these may require large computational burden. Moreover, the performance of an ANN very much depends on its generalization capability, which in turn is dependent upon the data representation. One important characteristic of data representation is uncorrelated. In other words, a set of data presented to an ANN ought not to consist of correlated information. This is because correlated data reduce the distinctiveness of data representation and thus introduce confusion to the ANN model during learning process and hence, producing one that has low generalization capability to resolve unseen data. This suggests a need for eliminating correlation in the sample data before they are being presented to an ANN. This can be achieved by applying the principal Component Analysis (PCA) technique [12] onto input data sets prior to the ANN training as well as testing process and hence the neural network model becomes

neural network principal component Analysis (NNPCA) model.

In this paper, a simple decision-making method based on the NNPCA is proposed for discriminating internal faults from inrush currents. The algorithm has been developed by considering different behaviors of the differential currents under internal fault and inrush condition. The NNPCA method extracts the relevant features from the differential current and reduces a training dataset to a lower dimension. The algorithm uses a data window of 12 samples per cycle. The algorithm also considers CT saturation and distinct scenarios such as changes in transformer load, source impedance, and remanent flux. All the mentioned conditions are simulated in PSCAD/EMTDC.

The accuracy in classification, speed of response, and computational burden of the harmonic restraint method, NNPCA, feed-forward back-propagation neural network (FFBPNN), and symmetrical component based method are compared in the presented work.

2. Neural Network Principal Component Analysis

Neural network principal component analysis (NNPCA) is basically an adaptive nonparametric method of extracting relevant information from confusing datasets [13]. It expresses data set in such a way as to highlight their similarities and differences. In 1982, Oja found a simple linear neuron model with a constrained Hebbian learning rule [13, 14]. For this work Hebbian learning is used. Generally, NNPCA is used for data reduction in statistical pattern recognition, signal processing, and image compression [13].

A typical architecture of NNPCA is shown in Figure 1. This network architecture has multilayer structure that is one input layer, one hidden layer, and one output layer. In back-propagation method a bounded and differentiable activation function is required. The sigmoid type activation function has all these properties making it popular in this training. In the present work due to these reasons, the hidden unit and output units use sigmoid-type of activation function. The architecture is defined by corresponding weights and connection scheme.

For a d-dimensional input data vectors $z_1, z_2, \ldots z_d$ to m, output of neural network $s_1, s_2, \ldots, s_m$ is given by (1) as

$$s_i = \Phi \sum_{i=1}^{m} w_i z_i, \tag{1}$$

where

w = Connecting weight, $w_i = [w_{i1}, w_{i2}, \ldots, w_{im}]^T$,

Φ = Nonlinear sigmoid activation function.

The weight adapting (2) for neurons i is as following:

$$\Delta w_{ij} = \eta \left[s_i z_i - s_i \sum_{k=1}^{j} w_{kj} s_k \right], \tag{2}$$

where

η = learning rate,

$j = 1, 2, \ldots, d$ and $i = 1, 2, \ldots, m$.

3. Simulation and Training Cases

Power transformer operating conditions may be classified as

   (i) normal condition,

   (ii) magnetizing inrush/sympathetic inrush condition,

   (iii) over-excitation condition,

   (iv) internal fault condition,

   (v) external fault condition.

In the normal condition, rated or less current flows through the transformer. In this condition normalized differential current is almost zero (only no load component of current). Whenever there is large and sudden change in the input terminal voltage of transformer, either due to switching-in or due to recovery from external fault getting, a large current is drawn by the transformer from the supply. As a result, the core of transformer gets saturated. This phenomenon is known as magnetizing inrush, or in other words, inrush can be described by a condition of large differential current occurring when either the transformer is just switched on or the system recovers from an external fault. Similar condition occurs when transformer is energized in parallel with another transformer that is already in service; it is known as "*sympathetic inrush*" condition. Among the various faults in transformer, phase-to-ground fault occurs most frequently. On the basis of fault current, phase-to-ground fault, for protective device operation view point, may be further classified as

   (i) heavy faults,

   (ii) medium level fault and,

   (iii) low level fault.

In all the cases, the abnormality nature is almost same but the magnitudes of currents resulting due to that are quite different. If the level of fault can be detected and accordingly

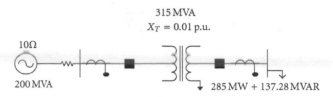

FIGURE 2: Typical three-phase power system.

protective action is taken, then the major damage to the protected element can be prevented.

A simulation software PSCAD/EMTDC is used to generate the training and testing signals under different operating conditions of transformer that are normal, overexcitation, magnetizing inrush, sympathetic inrush, and fault (phase-to-phase, phase-to-ground, and external fault) conditions. While simulating different operating conditions of transformer, energization angle, remanent flux in the core and load condition are considered as the magnitude and the wave-shape of differential current depends on these factors. Energization angle is varied from 0 to 360 degrees in interval of 30 degrees and remanent flux varying from 0% to 80% of the peak flux linkages generated at rated voltage with no-load and full-load conditions to generate training signals while, in case of testing signals energization angle is varied in interval of 15 degrees. The desired remanence can be set in unenergized transformer with controlled DC current sources in PSCAD/EMTDC model [15]. As transformers are not expected to be subjected to more than 15% overvoltage hence, overexcitation condition is simulated by applying 115% of the rated voltage at full load.

Three-phase transformers of 315 MVA at 400/220 kV, 200 MVA at 220/110 kV and 160 MVA at 132/220 kV, are modeled by using PSCAD/EMTDC. For the simulation of these transformers through PSCAD/EMTDC, the realistic data obtained from the M P State Electricity Board, Jabalpur India, is used. Typical connection of a 3-phase transformer of 315 MVA, 400/220 kV, 50 Hz, delta-star grounded connection is shown in Figure 2. In the high side, there is a source 200 MVA, 400 kV, and 10ω as internal impedance; in low side, there is a three-phase load of 285 MW and 137.28 MVAR. In case of internal fault condition, training and testing relaying signal is obtained by simulating fault varying from 1% to 99% of the power transformer winding turns, whereas in case of phase-to-ground fault condition, the fault is simulated at different location as 5%, 15%, 25%, 40%, 50%, and 100% (i.e., terminal fault) of the winding. Figure 3 shows a typical PSCAD/EMTDC transformer model required to simulate internal faults (turn to turn, phase to ground, and phase to phase) at different location of transformer winding from the neutral end of the windings. In this model MVA rating, voltage rating, base frequency, leakage reactance, magnetizing current, fault location (in %), and so forth can be defined.

In [16] (3) is proposed to avoid saturation in CT and reduce the impact over the protective relays. However, in this work a reduced CT ratio as 600 : 5 and 1200 : 5 is selected to

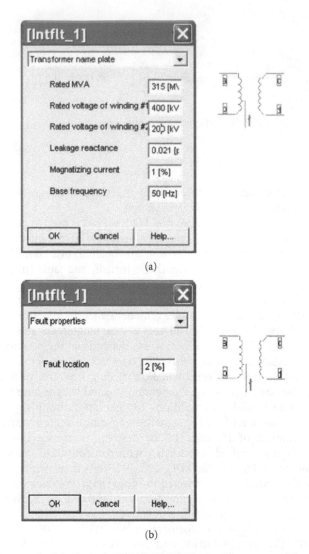

(a)

(b)

FIGURE 3: (a) Typical PSCAD/EMTDC transformer model to simulate internal fault (b) Typical PSCAD/EMTDC transformer model to simulate internal faults at different locations.

allow distortion in the waveform of the differential current as part of the stable state operation.

Consider

$$\left| \frac{X}{R} + 1 \right| \cdot I_F \cdot Z_B \leq 20, \qquad (3)$$

where I_F, is maximum fault current per unit of CT rating, Z_B is CT burden per unit of standard burden, and X/R is the reactance/resistance ratio of power system, respectively.

The test signals (typical magnetizing inrush and internal fault conditions) obtained by simulation of transformer are shown in Figures 4 to 5. The simulation was done at the rate of 12 samples per cycle of 50 Hz AC supply in view of reported experience on different digital relay deigns [17]. The developed fault detection algorithm was implemented in MATLAB on Intel P-IV processor-based desktop with front-side bus (FSB) speed of 400 MHz.

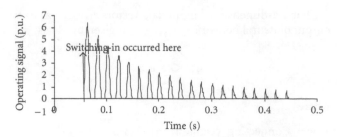

FIGURE 4: Typical magnetizing inrush current waveform.

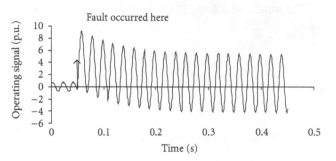

FIGURE 5: Typical phase-to-ground fault current waveform.

4. Implementation of NNPCA-Based Algorithm, Results and Analysis

The differential current is typically represented in discrete form as a set of 12 uniformly distributed samples obtained over a data window of one cycle of fundamental frequency signal, that is, the sampling rate is 12 samples per cycle. These 12 samples are called a "*pattern*." The sliding data window, consisting, one most recent and other of previous windows is used to generate patterns under above-mentioned power transformer operating conditions.

Each row of the input training matrix represents one pattern while corresponding row of target matrix represents desired output. Suppose that the inrush condition signal is characterized by the following sequence:

$$i = [i_1, i_2, \ldots, i_k]. \qquad (4)$$

The first row of inrush matrix takes 12 samples of i (i.e., i_1 to i_{12}), and then second row elements are from i_2 to i_{13} and so on until all the elements of i are completed. In a similar fashion, the internal fault condition matrix elements are also arranged for training and testing. The complete training matrix contains both inrush and fault patterns.

Two types of principal component analysis (PCA) data processors had been used for the purpose. The first one is called the preprocessor PCA, which is responsible for pre-processing input training data, to eliminate correlation in training patterns. The second is called postprocessor PCA, used to transform the validation and test datasets according to their principal components. The implementation was carried out with aid of built-in function supported by MATLAB Neural Network Toolbox.

In proposed NNPCA architecture three-layered structure is used. The input layer has 12 neurons. The hidden layer

Power Transformer Differential Protection Based on Neural Network Principal Component Analysis, Harmonic
Restraint and Park's Plots

117

consists of 11 neurons, as the number of neurons in hidden layer increases, the error decreases but after certain number of neurons it increases again, and in this case the minimum error is obtained for 11 neurons in the hidden layer. Therefore, the number of neurons in the hidden layer is optimal for this application. As only single output (trip or not) is required, the output layer consists of just one neuron. After much experimentation on various neural network architectures, the presented model is proposed which has lesser neurons in all three layers.

To differentiate between the fault and inrush conditions, the inrush condition is indicated by "0" and "1" indicates the fault condition. Out of 925 sets of data (patterns), 777 pattern sets are used to train the proposed NNPCA model. Out of these 777 pattern sets, 444 pattern sets are for the inrush (including sympathetic inrush patterns) and 333 are for the internal fault. The remaining 148 sets (which are not made part of training sets) are used to test the network's generalization ability. These 148 test exemplar pattern sets contain internal fault and inrush condition only as these two conditions are very difficult to discriminate as compared to other operating conditions such as external fault, overexcitation, and normal condition. Out of 148 test patterns, 74 test sets were inrush patterns and remaining 74 test sets were internal fault patterns. The inrush test patterns consist of sympathetic inrush patterns and magnetizing inrush patterns at different switching-in angles, while internal fault test patterns are made up of phase-to-ground fault and phase-to-phase fault at different locations.

After the NNPCA model had been trained, their generalization performances were calculated based on the mean absolute error (MAE) given by

$$\text{MAE} = \sum_{i=1}^{P} |T_i - S_i|, \qquad (5)$$

where P is the total number of test patterns, T_i is the actual output, and S_i is the NNPCA's estimated output for the ith test pattern.

Flow chart of the proposed algorithm (Figure 6) clearly indicates the steps for discriminating different operating conditions of power transformer. The external fault and normal operating condition are ruled out based on amplitude of two consecutive peaks of the operating signal. The overexcitation condition is determined by comparing voltage-to-frequency ratio with the rated voltage-to-frequency ratio. If this condition does not exist, then inrush and internal fault conditions are checked by NNPCA model. It gives tripping signal only if internal fault condition is detected.

For different conditions of the test set, fault current magnitude, load condition, remanent flux, and switching angle are changed to investigate the effects of these factors on the performance of the proposed algorithm. Since the wave-shape of inrush current changes with variation of switching-in instant of transformer, hence it is varied between 0 to 360 degrees. Similarly, due to the presence of the remanence flux, magnitude of inrush current may be as high as 2 to 6 times of inrush current without that, although the wave-shape remains same. It is found that the NNPCA

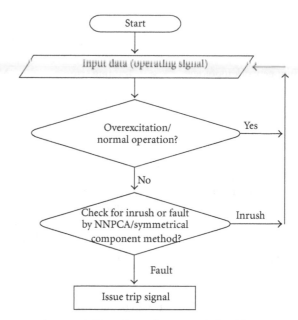

FIGURE 6: Flow chart of presented algorithm.

classifier-based relay is stable even with such high magnitude of inrush current caused by remanence flux whereas, the conventional harmonic-based relay may maloperate due to such high magnitude of inrush current [4, 18]. A rigorous experimentation has been made to evaluate performance of the NNPCA model. The proposed NNPCA model is successfully tested using relaying signals obtained by modeling the transformer on PSCAD/EMTDC and simulating various operating conditions as mentioned in the previous section. The results of proposed algorithm are shown in Table 1 (Tables 1(a) and 1(b)). All the test patterns were accurately classified by the NNPCA model (i.e., 100% accuracy in classification). This detection is without any false positive or negative (as given in (6)); thus NNPCA has good generalization capability to distinguish between magnetizing inrush and internal fault condition of transformer. From Table 1, it is clear that the accuracy in classification of NNPCA is better than the FFBPNN based classifier in spite of using the same topology, same tuning parameter, and training algorithm as used in case of NNPCA method.

We halve the following:

Classification Error (in %)

$$= \frac{\text{No. of False Positive} + \text{No. of False Negative}}{\text{Total Number of Test Cases}} \times 100,$$

Classification Accuracy (in %)

$$= 100 - \text{Classification Error (in \%)}.$$

$$(6)$$

Table 2 presents the number of postdisturbance samples required for decision making by the proposed NNPCA-based transformer differential protection algorithm. In internal fault cases, it requires 6 samples (and 9 samples for light internal fault case) after the fault occurrence that means

TABLE 1:

(a) Performance of NNPCA and FFBPNN having topology of 12-11-1

Neural network topology	Training error	Max. epoch	Inrush		Fault	
			P	A	P	A
NNPCA	0.0001	1000	−1.0	0.0	0.96	1.0
FFBPNN	0.0001	1000	−1.0	0.0	0.96	1.0

P: predicted, A: actual.

(b) Accuracy in classification (%)

Trained transformer ratings	Tested transformer ratings					
	315 MVA		200 MVA		160 MVA	
	FFBPNN	NNPCA	FFBPNN	NNPCA	FFBPNN	NNPCA
315 MVA	99.32	100	94.59	100	98.64	100
200 MVA	94.59	100	99.32	100	98.64	100
160 MVA	94.59	100	96.32	100	100	100

TABLE 2: Number of postdisturbance samples required for decision by NNPCA-based relay.

Cases	Number of samples required (actual)	Maximum samples required (Logical)
Magnetizing inrush (0°)	8	12
Internal fault (5% to 98%)	6	12
Internal fault (light phase-to-ground fault at 2%)	9	12

about 10–15 ms are required for the fault detection while in case of inrush condition only 8 samples are required, that is, 13.33 ms. However, it is observed that the relay operation is independent from the harmonic present in the operating signal, and therefore no filtering is required in this method. In addition to that it does not require any threshold index to discriminate between the inrush and internal fault condition of transformer.

The same power transformers are tested with symmetrical component method and harmonic restraint (HR) method based on discrete fourier transform (DFT) (see the section Appendix).

Park's vector $\bar{I}_p$ is a function of positive-, negative-sequence currents and independent of zero-sequence currents. When plotting vectors in Park's space, α is represented in the horizontal axis, while β component is plotted in the vertical axis. The secondary winding currents are not affected by the fault or inrush if the vector $\bar{I}_p$ is plotted in Park's space. Internal faults and inrush currents may be characterized by particular plot shape of $\bar{I}_p$. When Park's vector is plotted in Park's space, transformer internal fault and inrush currents are clearly distinguished from their plot shape as shown in Figures 7 and 8. From Figures 7 and 8, it is observed that the plots are symmetrical for internal fault condition and asymmetrical for inrush condition. The shape characterizations in two groups are not dependent on the type of differential signal (fault or inrush). The use of Park's vectors reduces appreciably the computation requirements, since their values are directly calculated from a scalar matrix product.

Discrete fourier-transform- (DFT-) based harmonic restraint method is implemented, to compare performance of the proposed optimal NNPCA-based algorithm in power transformer differential protection. Figure 9 shows the ratio of second harmonic to fundamental of the differential current under typical magnetizing inrush and internal fault conditions, respectively. During one cycle under internal fault condition, the ratio of the second harmonic is quite high and in the same range as in case of magnetizing inrush condition. Therefore, it is difficult to discriminate between internal fault and inrush conditions merely setting a preset threshold. From Figure 9, it is also clear that the ratio values are fluctuating, which create problem to decide a preset threshold. Moreover, due to the presence of second harmonic during internal fault condition, digital relay will take longer time to make trip decision (one cycle or more than one cycle). In contrast, the optimal NNPCA based method is able to detect such a fault in 6 ms (half cycle or with in half cycle) and in light internal fault cases, it requires 9 samples after the fault occurrence that means about 15 ms are required for the fault detection while in case of inrush condition only 8 samples are required, that is, 13.33 ms. However, it is observed that the relay operation is independent from the harmonic present in the operating signal, and therefore no filtering is required in this method.

However, the harmonic restraint method and symmetrical component method are capable to discriminate between these two conditions but do not seem to be intelligent to take decision in case of fluctuating ratio of second harmonic to fundamental of the differential current due to different

Power Transformer Differential Protection Based on Neural Network Principal Component Analysis, Harmonic Restraint and Park's Plots

119

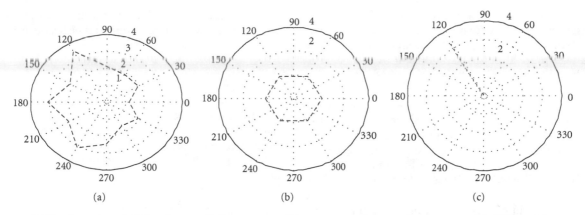

FIGURE 7: Plot for an inrush ((a), primary winding currents, (b) centre secondary winding currents, (c) differential current).

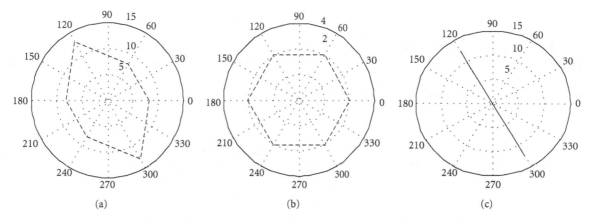

FIGURE 8: Plot for internal fault condition ((a), primary winding currents, (b) centre secondary winding currents, (c) differential current).

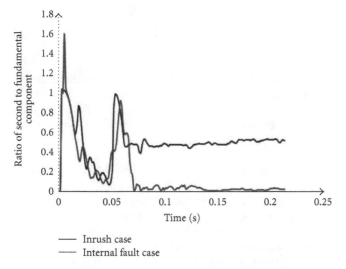

— Inrush case
— Internal fault case

FIGURE 9: Ratio of second harmonic to fundamental of the differential current under typical inrush and internal fault condition.

loading conditions, severity of internal faults, switching-in angles, and so forth, and hence maloperation of relay will occur. In case of symmetrical component method, Park's space plot is to be analyzed for its symmetry than only relay

can take decision. Moreover, these methods take more time to take decision as compared to NNPCA-based transformer differential method and depend on the harmonic contain present in the relaying signal.

5. Conclusion

This paper presents a novel intelligent approach based on neural network principal component analysis (NNPCA) model to solve the problem of distinguishing between transformer internal fault and magnetizing inrush condition. The performance of NNPCA-based method is compared with feed-forward back-propagation neural network (FFBPNN), harmonic restraint method, and Park's plot method.

The proposed NNPCA algorithm is based on waveform identification technique which is more accurate than traditional harmonic-restraint-based technique, especially in case of modern power transformers which use high-permeability low-coercion core materials. The conventional harmonic restraint technique may fail because high second harmonic components may be generated during internal faults and low second harmonic components during magnetizing inrush with such core materials.

However, the harmonic restraint method and symmetrical component method are capable to discriminate between these two conditions but do not seem to be intelligent to take decision in case of fluctuating ratio of second harmonic to fundamental of the differential current. Moreover, these methods take more time to take decision as compared to NNPCA-based transformer differential method.

The proposed optimised NNPCA technique is simple in architecture, fast in operation, and robust. The present neural network model issues tripping signal in the event of internal fault within 6–15 ms of fault occurrence. The method is also immune from the DC offset in relaying signals due to saturation of CT core in the event of internal or external fault. Moreover, the NNPCA-based algorithm has 100% accuracy in classification which is not possible to achieve by using FFBPNN in the application of power transformer differential application.

Appendix

A. Discrete Fourier Transform (DFT) Algorithm

Any continuous waveform $f(t)$, having a finite energy in the interval $(0.T)$, can be represented in the interval as a Fourier series:

$$f(t) = \frac{a_0}{2} + \sum_{n=1}^{\infty}(a_n \sin(n\omega t) + b_n \cos(n\omega t)), \qquad \text{(A.1)}$$

with coefficients

$$a_0 = \frac{2}{T}\int_0^T f(t)dt,$$

$$a_n = \frac{2}{T}\int_0^T f(t)\sin(n\omega t)dt, \qquad \text{(A.2)}$$

$$b_n = \frac{2}{T}\int_0^T f(t)\cos(n\omega t)dt,$$

where a_0 is the dc component (average value) and a_n and b_n are the sine and cosine components of the Fourier coefficients, respectively. If the waveform is sampled at time t_i, space δt apart, so that there are $N = T/\delta t$ samples, then for samples 1 to N, the coefficients a_n and b_n in (A.2) can be rewritten as

$$a_n = \frac{2}{N}\sum_{i=0}^{n}X(t_i)\sin\left(\frac{2\pi ni}{N}\right),$$

$$\qquad \text{(A.3)}$$

$$b_n = \frac{2}{N}\sum_{i=0}^{n}X(t_i)\cos\left(\frac{2\pi ni}{N}\right),$$

where $X(t_i)$ are the discrete sampled current signals and $i = 1, 2, 3, \ldots, N$.

Hence, for 12 samples per data window, 12 Fourier coefficients will have an array size of 12×1. Both sine and cosine terms will have an array size of 12×12. The

differential current is analyzed in terms of its Fourier series, and amplitude of each harmonic can be found as follows:

$$F_n^2 = a_n^2 + b_n^2, \qquad \text{(A.4)}$$

where F_n = Fourier coefficients and $n = 1, 2, 3, \ldots, N$.

For power transformers protection, F_1, F_2, and F_5 represent the Fourier coefficients of the fundamental, the second harmonic, and the fifth harmonic component, respectively, of current waveform. For a three-phase transformer, the combined harmonic components of the differential currents are

$$F_{n\text{Combined}}^2 = a_{na}^2 + b_{na}^2 + a_{nb}^2 + b_{nb}^2 + a_{nc}^2 + b_{nc}^2, \qquad \text{(A.5)}$$

where $n = 1, 2,$ and 5.

B. Symmetrical Component Approach [6]

A function of instantaneous line currents (i_{r1}, i_{y1}, i_{b1}), the current Park's vector components are obtained as follows:

$$\begin{bmatrix} i_{\alpha 1} \\ i_{\beta 1} \\ i_{01} \end{bmatrix} = [c]\begin{bmatrix} i_{r1} \\ i_{y1} \\ i_{b1} \end{bmatrix}, \qquad \text{(B.1)}$$

where the transformation matrix $[c]$ is defined as

$$[c] = \frac{2}{3}\begin{bmatrix} 1 & -\frac{1}{2} & -\frac{1}{2} \\ 0 & \frac{\sqrt{3}}{2} & -\frac{\sqrt{3}}{3} \\ \frac{1}{2} & \frac{1}{2} & \frac{1}{2} \end{bmatrix}, \qquad \text{(B.2)}$$

$$\begin{bmatrix} i_{\alpha 2} \\ i_{\beta 2} \\ i_{02} \end{bmatrix} = [c]\begin{bmatrix} i_{r2} \\ i_{y2} \\ i_{b2} \end{bmatrix}. \qquad \text{(B.3)}$$

Park's vector $\bar{I}_p$ is defined as the vector difference between Park's vectors obtained by means of (B.1) and (B.3) is used. And it is analytically demonstrated that the park's vector $\bar{I}_p$ is related to the time-dependent symmetrical components as follows:

$$\bar{I}_p = n\Sigma\left[I_1^{(n)}e^{j(\phi_{r1}^{(n)}+n\omega t)} + I_2^{(n)}e^{-j(\phi_{r2}^{(n)}+n\omega t)}\right], \qquad \text{(B.4)}$$

where I_1 is the instantaneous rms value (i.e., since the rms of the current I_1 changes over the time during transients and this values is considered to be recalculated for every instant) of the positive sequence current for the differential current, I_2 is the instantaneous rms value of the negative sequence current for the differential current, ϕ_{r1} is the phase angle of the positive sequence current in line r, ϕ_{r2} is the phase angle of the negative sequence current in line r, t the time, ω is the supply fundamental frequency, n is the order of the considered harmonic, and superscript (n) refers to the nth order harmonic value.

Park's vectors are obtained from the instantaneous line currents by means of the $[C]$ matrix of (B.2). Thus,

Power Transformer Differential Protection Based on Neural Network Principal Component Analysis, Harmonic Restraint and Park's Plots

121

the transformation of nth-order harmonic time-dependent symmetrical components into Park's vector components is achieved as follows:

$$
\begin{bmatrix} i_\alpha^{(h)} \\ i_\beta^{(h)} \\ i_0^{(h)} \end{bmatrix} = [c][s]^{-1} \frac{\sqrt{2}}{2} \times \begin{bmatrix} I_1^{(h)} e^{j(\phi_{r1}^{(h)}+h\omega t)} + I_2^{(h)} e^{-j(\phi_{r2}^{(h)}+h\omega t)} \\ I_2^{(h)} e^{j(\phi_{r2}^{(h)}+h\omega t)} + I_1^{(h)} e^{-j(\phi_{r1}^{(h)}+h\omega t)} \\ I_0^{(h)} \left[e^{j(\phi_0^{(h)}+h\omega t)} + e^{-j(\phi_0^{(h)}+h\omega t)} \right] \end{bmatrix}.
$$
(B.5)

The plot in Park's plane of the α and β components accounting for all the harmonics is then

$$
\sum_n \left(i_\alpha^{(n)} + j i_\beta^{(n)} \right) = \sum_n \left[I_1^{(n)} e^{j(\phi_{r1}^{(n)}+n\omega t)} + I_2^{(n)} e^{-j(\phi_{r2}^{(n)}+n\omega t)} \right].
$$
(B.6)

In Park's space, α is represented in the horizontal axis, while β component is plotted in the vertical axis.

References

[1] M. Tripathy, R. P. Maheshwari, and H. K. Verma, "Advances in transformer protection: a review," *Electric Power Components and Systems*, vol. 33, no. 11, pp. 1203–1209, 2005.

[2] P. Arboleya, G. Díaz, J. Gómez-Aleixandre, and C. González-Morán, "A solution to the dilemma inrush/fault in transformer differential relaying using MRA and wavelets," *Electric Power Components and Systems*, vol. 34, no. 3, pp. 285–301, 2006.

[3] H. K. Verma and G. C. Kakoti, "Algorithm for harmonic restraint differential relaying based on the discrete Hartley transform," *Electric Power Systems Research*, vol. 18, no. 2, pp. 125–129, 1990.

[4] M. C. Shin, C. W. Park, and J. H. Kim, "Fuzzy logic-based relaying for large power transformer protection," *IEEE Transactions on Power Delivery*, vol. 18, no. 3, pp. 718–724, 2003.

[5] S. A. Saleh and M. A. Rahman, "Modeling and protection of a three-phase power transformer using wavelet packet transform," *IEEE Transactions on Power Delivery*, vol. 20, no. 2, pp. 1273–1282, 2005.

[6] S. Ala, M. Tripathy, and A. K. Singh, "Identification of internal faults in power transformer using symmetrical components and Park's plots," in *Proceedings of IEEE International Conference on Power Systems*, IIT, Kharagpur, India, December 2009.

[7] X. Ma and J. Shi, "New method for discrimination between fault and magnetizing inrush current using HMM," *Electric Power Systems Research*, vol. 56, no. 1, pp. 43–49, 2000.

[8] D. Barbosa, U. C. Netto, D. V. Coury, and M. Oleskovicz, "Power transformer differential protection based on Clarke's transform and fuzzy systems," *IEEE Transactions on Power Delivery*, vol. 26, no. 2, pp. 1212–1220, 2011.

[9] J. Ma, Z. Wang, Q. Yang, and Y. Liu, "Identifying transformer inrush current based on normalized grille curve," *IEEE Transactions on Power Delivery*, vol. 26, no. 2, pp. 588–595, 2011.

[10] L. G. Perez, A. J. Flechsig, J. L. Meador, and Z. Obradovic, "Training an artificial neural network to discriminate between magnetizing inrush and internal faults," *IEEE Transactions on Power Delivery*, vol. 9, no. 1, pp. 434–441, 1994.

[11] P. Bastard, M. Meunier, and H. Regal, "Neural network-based algorithm for power transformer differential relays," *IEE Proceedings*, vol. 142, no. 4, pp. 386–392, 1995.

[12] J. E. Jackson, *A User's Guide to Principal components*, Wiley, Hoboken, NJ, USA, 2003.

[13] S. Haykin, *Neural Network: A Comprehensive Foundation*, Pearson Education, New Delhi, India, 2008.

[14] C. M. Bishop, *Neural Networks for Pattern Recognition*, Oxford University Press, New York, NY, USA, 1995.

[15] D. Woodford, *Introduction To PSCAD V3*, Manitoba HVDC Research Centre, Manitoba, Canada, 2001.

[16] S. E. Zocholl, *Analyzing and Applying Current Transformers*, Schweitzer Engineering Laboratories, Pullman, Wash, USA, 2004.

[17] M. S. Sachdev, "Microprocessor relays and protection systems," IEEE Tutorial Course Text 88EH0269-1-PWR, 1988.

[18] M. R. Zaman and M. A. Rahman, "Experimental testing of the artificial neural network based protection of power transformers," *IEEE Transactions on Power Delivery*, vol. 13, no. 2, pp. 510–515, 1998.

12

Selection for Reinforcement-Free Learning Ability as an Organizing Factor in the Evolution of Cognition

Solvi Arnold, Reiji Suzuki, and Takaya Arita

Graduate School of Information Science, Nagoya University, Furo-cho, Chikusa-ku, Nagoya 464-8601, Japan

Correspondence should be addressed to Solvi Arnold; solvi@alife.cs.is.nagoya-u.ac.jp

Academic Editor: Bikramjit Banerjee

This research explores the relation between environmental structure and neurocognitive structure. We hypothesize that selection pressure on abilities for efficient learning (especially in settings with limited or no reward information) translates into selection pressure on correspondence relations between neurocognitive and environmental structure, since such correspondence allows for simple changes in the environment to be handled with simple learning updates in neurocognitive structure. We present a model in which a simple form of reinforcement-free learning is evolved in neural networks using neuromodulation and analyze the effect this selection for learning ability has on the virtual species' neural organization. We find a higher degree of organization than in a control population evolved without learning ability and discuss the relation between the observed neural structure and the environmental structure. We discuss our findings in the context of the environmental complexity thesis, the Baldwin effect, and other interactions between adaptation processes.

1. Introduction

This paper explores the relation between the structure of an environment and the structure of cognitions evolved in that environment. Intuitively, one would expect a strong relation between the two. In the past, some have taken this intuition very far. Spencer [1] viewed the evolution of life and mind as a process of internalization of progressively more intricate and abstract features of the environment. He traced the acquisition of such "correspondence" between the internal and external from basic life processes (e.g., the shape of an enzyme molecule has a direct and physical relation to the shape of the molecule whose reactions it evolved to catalyze), all the way up to cognitive processes (such as acquisition of complex causal relations between entities removed in space and time). That a certain correspondence should exist between the shapes of enzyme and substrate will be uncontroversial, but how far can this concept of correspondence take us when cognition is concerned?

Certainly, when we hand-code an AI to function within a given environment, we can typically recognize much of the environmental organization in the structure of our AIs'

cognitions. However, as the history of connectionism demonstrates, fit behaviour does not necessarily involve intelligible neural structure. More often than not, the neural organization of evolved artificial neural networks (ANNs) allows little if any interpretation in terms of environmental structure. If we demand that models of the mind in some sense "reflect" their environment, then the lack of Spencerian correspondence in evolved ANNs poses a conundrum. One possible response is to abandon our "correspondence intuition" altogether [2]. Another response is to declare such ANNs unfit as models of cognition (see, e.g., [3–5]). We believe that both of these responses in fact mask a deeper issue: we do not actually have a clear understanding of how cognitive evolution arrives at the sort of clearly structured solutions that we find in ourselves (and observe in numerous other species).

For exploring this issue, ANNs should be an excellent tool, since they allow for large variation in what we might call their "degree of organization". By evolving networks that initially lack organization in various environments and under various constraints, we can study the processes that give them shape and structure and identify the environmental features that drive those processes. This type of approach is found in work on the evolution of modularity, for example [6–8]. Here we apply this sort of approach to studying the effect of learning on emergence of neurocognitive organization.

Let us first have a closer look at the intuitions that our messy ANNs seem to violate. Our own cognition seems quite organized: we have a high degree of functional differentiation, with distinct innate cognitive faculties specializing on distinct aspects of the environment. In a sense, the environment we evolved is reflected in our innate cognitive and neural architecture. On a shorter timescale, our thoughts and mental representations refer to and individuate the contents of the world around us. Advanced cognition does not *just work somehow* (as is often said of ANNs); it works by actively establishing (both on evolutionary and lifetime timescales) highly specific correspondence relations with the environment.

In stark contrast, connectionism forcefully reminds us of the unintuitive fact that any mapping that can be implemented can be implemented in infinitely many ways. Implementations composed of building blocks mapping one to one to the building blocks of the environment are but one option, and there is a whole spectrum of viable candidates seemingly reaching from one to one across many to many all the way to all to all. Why should evolution prefer implementations that allow interpretation in terms of Spencerian one to one correspondence? Connectionism shows us that, *in general, it doesn't*. Evolution is a behaviourist. If your behaviour is fit, then you are fit, regardless of the details of your cognitive architecture. But we can ask a better question: under what circumstances *does* evolution favour correspondence? Building on our previous work [9], we present a hypothesis on how the evolution of learning ability leads evolution to correspondence, and we provide a proof of principle in the form of a simple artificial life model in which we simulate the evolution of a simple form of reinforcement-free learning. Section 2 explains the theory, Section 3 explains the choice for reinforcement-free learning, Section 4 describes our computational model, and results are analyzed in Section 5, followed by discussion and conclusions in Sections 6 and 7.

2. Learning and Neurocognitive Organization

That the evolution of learning should somehow lead to correspondence may seem like an odd suggestion: the history of connectionism has made it quite clear that regardless of whether we train them (using learning algorithms like e.g. error back-propagation) or evolve them (using genetic algorithms), artificial neural network structures usually do not admit much interpretation in terms of the environments they were trained or evolved in. Why would a combination of learning and evolution do any better? The answer lies in how these two adaptation processes interact (Figure 1).

We define *behaviour* as a mapping from stimuli to responses:

$$B : S \longrightarrow R. \tag{1}$$

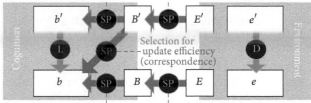

FIGURE 1: Selection for correspondence. SP: selection pressures/evolutionary adaptation processes. L: learning/lifetime adaptation processes (implementation of learning ability updates implementation of behaviour). D: environmental dynamics. Selection for learning implies selection for update efficiency in the implementation of behaviour, that is, alignment of the dynamics of B with the dynamics of E. This alignment depends on correspondence between the structure of the behaviour implementation and the structure of the environment, leading to selection on correspondence (diagonal arrow).

We define learning as a mapping from stimulus-behaviour pairs to behaviours, that is, "stimulus-caused updates of behaviour":

$$B' : (S, B) \longrightarrow B =$$
$$B' : (S, S \longrightarrow R) \longrightarrow (S \longrightarrow R). \tag{2}$$

Learning updates behaviour on a within-lifetime timescale and both behaviour and learning are products of evolution. We also define the environment as a mapping, one from responses to stimuli. An agent acts, and this (potentially) affects the subsequent stimulus it receives:

$$E : R \longrightarrow S. \tag{3}$$

Note that an environment is much like an inverse behaviour (mapping responses to stimuli instead of stimuli to responses). Just as behaviour may change, so may the environment, either as the result of the agent's responses or spontaneously. We denote change in E as E' without specifying it further.

We have defined behaviour, learning, and environment as mappings, but organisms and environments are physical objects, not mathematical objects. In order for these mappings to exist in the physical world they must have implementations. For each of the mappings defined above, we let its lowercase partner denote its implementation: b, b', e, e'. Here e and e' should be understood as the actual physical reality of the environment. In reality, e and e' are generally not clearly distinguishable. Physically speaking, learning occurs via modification of b by b'.

Selection for a given behaviour (B) is selection for implementation of that behaviour (b), but as noted before, any given behaviour can be implemented in infinitely many ways. We may expect evolution to favour implementations that execute efficiently (in terms of time or energy consumption of whatever is precious in a given setting), but as connectionist history shows, selection for execution efficiency should not be expected to produce correspondence.

If the environment is dynamic in a sufficiently organized and predictable way as to make learning possible, then there is selection pressure on evolution of B' and hence b'. Analogously to B and b above, execution efficiency in b' may be selected for but this should not be expected to produce correspondence. But something interesting happens between b' and b. Given that b' must update b, different b call for different b'. For example in the highly unnatural case that b would take the form of a table defining an output for each possible input independently, then b' would operate by rewriting entries of this table. So whether and how feasible evolution of B' is strongly depends on the architecture of b. If there is selection pressure on B', then mutations in b that are beneficial to B' are beneficial mutations (even if they have no effect whatsoever on B). As an extreme scenario, we could imagine B remaining stable while b evolves to facilitate B'. This possibility shows that there is a fundamental difference between selection for a specific mapping and selection for a specific implementation of that mapping.

So while evolution working on B alone does not care much about the structure of b, "coevolution" (if we may abuse the term a little) of B' and b *does* care about the structure of b. Along the long horizontal arrows in Figure 1, evolution treats its objects as black boxes (selecting on input-output relations alone, i.e., B and B'), but indirectly, via selection pressure on learning, it peeks inside b and selects for implementation structure (diagonal arrow).

B' constrains b, but we have not said anything yet about what sort of b is favoured by B'. We will claim that B' benefits most from b that employs correspondence with the environment. The basic idea is as follows: if the environment and (consequently) the optimal behaviour are static, then difference in the structure of their implementations poses no problem. But if the environment and (consequently) the optimal behaviour may change (by means of E' and B', respectively), then the more the structure of b and e differ, the harder it is for B' to update B in sync with E'. The implementations (e) of environments that cognition evolves in are composed of distinct aspects (food sources, temperatures, other agents, spatial layouts, etc.) that act and interact to give rise to E. Let us call a change in one such aspect a *simple* change. Simple changes in e often lead to *complex* changes in E: multiple input-output pairs change. Consequently a complex update of B is required. If b contains an aspect corresponding to the changed aspect of e, in a functionally similar position, then the required complex change in B can be realized by a simple change in b. This makes B' quite feasible. If no such corresponding aspect exists, a complex implementation update is required. In this case no straightforward relation exists between the environmental change and the appropriate behaviour change, making B''s work difficult or infeasible.

So the organization that evolves in b to facilitate B' should in one form or another capture the variable aspects of the environment along with their functional roles therein. This is what we mean by correspondence, and also what we take Spencer to mean by correspondence. Note that we do neither claim that B' is strictly impossible without correspondence between e and b nor that such correspondence cannot occur

in absence of B'. What we claim is that selection pressure on B' translates into selection pressure on correspondence between e and b, and that this "selection pressure conversion" is an organizing factor in the evolution of cognition.

Note that, in general, not all of b receives this organizing influence. Innate behaviour that is impervious to modification by learning should not be affected. As such the hypothesis here recuperates neither our intuitions nor Spencer's correspondence-based theory of the evolution of mind in full. However, the parts of b that *are* modifiable by learning seem quite central to advanced cognition, and the hypothesis provides a candidate explanation of why these parts should be as organized as they are. One especially notable aspect of cognition that (in our present conceptualization) falls outside the scope of this organizing influence is learning ability itself (as it is not affected by learning). Learning ability could be placed under similar organizing influence by introducing a second-order learning process updating the first (see discussion), but we do not further consider this possibility here.

Our concept of correspondence here is intentionally broad, as there may be a lot of variation in how correspondence might be realized. However, reasoning from the purpose served by correspondence, we can make some more easily objectively verifiable predictions. If our reasoning is correct, then behaviour implementations evolved under selection for learning should distinguish themselves from implementations under no such pressure by (1) functional differentiation and (2) compactness.

(1) Functional differentiation: if distinct aspects of the environment are in some sense replicated in the implementation of behaviour, then we should expect to find functionally distinct substructures in that implementation.

(2) Compactness: if no updating of behaviour is required, then nothing keeps the implementation from spreading out over the available implementation substance. If updating is required, then correspondence helps to minimize the amount of physical change that needs to be made to realize the required updates. This should constrain distribution and promote a more focused implementation in which large, controlled behaviour updates can be made with minimal physical change.

In assessing our results we will consider these measures in addition to our assessment of correspondence.

Before we move on to the next section, let us briefly address a complicating factor in establishing correspondence. We discussed how, given correspondence between b and e, simple change in e could be met with simple change in b. It could be objected that, more often than not, changes in e are not simple. Consider the changing of the seasons. Although triggered by a simple change in a distal aspect of e (the angle at which the earth faces the sun), the effect on the local environment is a complex change (many aspects of e change), which reveals itself to cognitions in that environment as a complex change in E. Given their common cause, the simple changes comprising the complex change in e will cooccur, and we may find it being handled with a simple change in some aspect of b. Can this aspect of b now be said to correspond? If so, what to? To all the aspects of e that changed or to the aspect that triggered all those other changes (the angle at which the earth faces the sun)? In the former case we would have a one to many correspondence, which strays from our original concept somewhat, and in the latter case we would have a correspondence with something so distal that calling it a correspondence seems odd. We will not attempt to answer this or other questions arising from causal relations between environmental changes here. Regardless of whether and what to this aspect of b would correspond, we can see that having it would be advantageous precisely in environments with changing seasons, so organization is still selected for by environmental dynamics.

3. Reinforcement-Free Learning

If we hypothesize internalization of environmental regularities to be of importance for efficient learning, then the question arises why traditional machine learning algorithms (supervised learning and reinforcement learning) seem to do fine without. We think the answer is that such algorithms model only some very limited subclasses of the learning abilities found in nature. While undemanding in terms of internalization of environmental regularities, they require explicit examples or rewards to drive the learning process. When examples or rewards are explicitly provided, then all that is needed to make learning possible is an ability to recognize examples/rewards as such (and this ability is tacitly assumed in such learning algorithms). (This is enough to make learning *possible*, but in most cases such learning could be made more efficient by exploitation of environmental regularities, as was shown in [9].) We will not discuss example-driven learning here, as its limitations are evident. However when we look at reward-based learning, there is a relevant parallel between the fields of machine learning and psychology.

Reward-based learning algorithms are designed to be applicable without prior knowledge of the environment. Behaviourism tried to capture all learning in terms of universally applicable conditioning rules. In this sense traditional machine learning and behaviourism are alike: they deal in universal, reinforcement-driven learning rules. In both cases, one could say that it is the aim for universality that prevents them from reaching an accurate understanding of learning as it occurs in nature, as most if not all of the learning ability found in nature is nonuniversal and based on more or other information than a simple reward signal (the clearest example being language acquisition). Such nonuniversal learning, sensitive to and capable of using the information its specific environment provides, is where dependence on environmental structure, and hence selection for correspondence, can be expected to be most prominent.

So how can we computationally approach nonuniversal learning ability as it occurs in nature? We believe that the most sensible approach is to evolve learning ability from scratch, starting with a mechanism for *arbitrary behaviour change*, and letting it evolve into forms of learning ability that will use not just reward information but whatever available information it can find a use for. Examples of learning evolved

from mechanisms for behaviour change are found in [10–15]. Performance wise, such systems do not yet compare favourably to conventional machine learning approaches. However, if the aim is to study evolution of cognition as it occurs in nature, we believe this approach to be the correct one.

In the present paper, we intentionally omit a reward-signal altogether, forcing evolution of *reinforcement-free* learning ability. The motivation for this choice is twofold: it eliminates the risk of dependence on reward muddying our results and shows how evolved learning can solve a task that would leave standard reinforcement learning algorithms stuck at zero. The next section explains our computational approach.

4. Evolving Reinforcement-Free Learning

If, as argued in the previous section, selection pressure on learning ability translates into selection pressure on alignment of cognitive and environmental organization, then it should be possible to make such alignment evolve by evolving learning ability. We start with a description of our baseline model, in which behaviour is shaped by evolution alone. In this model, no learning occurs (in the terminology of Section 2, we evolve b in absence of selection pressure on B'). Then we extend this baseline model (introducing selection for learning and a mechanism for neural plasticity) to create our main model in which the same behaviour as in the baseline model is acquired via a combination of evolution and learning instead. We compare the networks evolved in these two models to see whether they show any differences that pertain to our hypothesis.

4.1. Baseline Model. A population of simple feed-forward neural networks was evolved to "catch" prey in a simple toroidal 20×20 binary grid world. The agent's body occupies one cell. Prey are represented by 2 adjacent 1-cells. To avoid ambiguity, two prey objects never occupy adjacent cells (e.g., a 2×2 block of 1-cells could equally well represent two vertically oriented prey or two horizontally oriented prey, so we prevent such ambiguous configurations from occurring). The environment always contains 40 prey. Interaction with prey is illustrated in Figure 2. Prey is "caught" by stepping on it from a suitable angle, yielding one fitness point. Stepping on it from a bad angle instead costs one fitness point. In either case, the prey disappears and respawns outside the net's field of view. Prey are otherwise stationary. The species has a repertoire of 4 movement actions: step forward, jump forward, turn right, and turn left. Turns are always 90 degrees. The jump action moves the organism forward by two cells instead of one, without touching the cell in between (so this action can be used to jump over prey when the step action would cause incorrect approach, and it is also generally the faster mode of movement). Each individual has its own private environment, so no interaction between individuals occurs.

The neural networks take as input the organism's field of view (turquoise area in Figure 2), taking the cell values (0 or 1) as activation values for the input neurons. The input

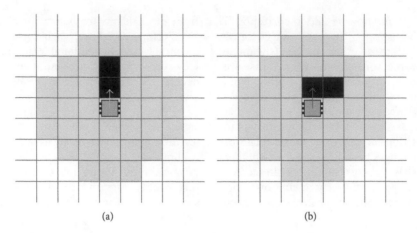

(a)   (b)

FIGURE 2: Catching prey. Up is forward. The turquoise area indicates the field of view. (a) If the prey is stepped or jumped on longitudinally, the organism gains one fitness point (the prey is caught and eaten). (b) If the prey is stepped or jumped on laterally, the organism loses one fitness points (the prey injures the organism and flees).

layer additionally contains a bias neuron with its activation always set to 1.0, and a noise neuron with its activation set to a random value in $[0, 1]$ at every time step (included to provide a source of randomness to drive exploratory behaviour, if such behaviour were to be selected for), making for a total of 39 input neurons. There is a hidden layer of 16 neurons, using the hyperbolic tangent activation function (activation range $[-1, +1]$). There are 4 output neurons, one for each action. At each time step, the action of the output neuron with the highest activation value is performed.

Connection weights are evolved using a simple Genetic Algorithm. 10 independent trials of the baseline model were performed (i.e., 10 independent populations of networks were evolved), using the following settings: lifetime: 400 time steps, population size: 90, parent pool size: 40, elite group size: 10 (parent pool and elite group are nonexclusive). Individuals in the elite group are copied unaltered to the next generation; individuals in the parent group produce two offspring each, to which mutation is applied. Mutation is single point. Selection is rank based. To get a good spread of heavily and subtly mutated individuals, a genome to be mutated first gets a random mutation sensitivity value in the range $[0.0, 0.0075]$. This sensitivity value is then used as the mutation probability for every connection weight in the network. Mutation of a connection has a 0.75 probability of adding a random value from $[-0.5, +0.5]$ to the connection weight and a 0.25 probability of resetting the connection to 0. Weights are clipped to the $[-2, +2]$ range, and connection weights of the first generation are also randomly picked from this range.

Unsurprisingly, the population quickly evolved the ability to approach prey correctly and scored high fitness ever after (Figure 3). In the next section we use these scores as a baseline for assessing the efficacy of learning ability evolved in the main model.

4.2. Main Model. For the main model, we introduce an element of unpredictability in order to create selection pressure on learning ability, and we introduce a mechanism

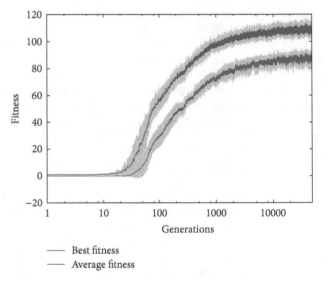

FIGURE 3: Evolution process of baseline model. Averages over 10 runs. Gray areas indicate standard deviation over the runs. Note the log scale on the x-axis.

for behaviour change (*not* a learning algorithm) that can be *evolved into* the necessary learning ability.

The unpredictability we use is randomization of the assignment of actions to output neurons. In the baseline model, this assignment is invariant over the population (e.g., for any individual, output neuron #1 was assigned the "step" action, etc.). In the main model, the assignment is randomized for every new individual. Consequently, every individual first has to learn how to control itself before it can competently catch prey. In our terminology of Section 2, this variation in output-action assignment is the environmental dynamic E' that necessitates evolution of B', which should lead to incorporation of structural features of e into b.

This learning process could be driven by reward (the organism could experiment with various actions in various states and reinforce whatever yields reward), but as our aim is to evolve reinforcement-free learning ability, we explicitly block this possibility as follows: we introduce a "learning phase" that takes place in a "learning environment", in which there is sensory input but no reward. Individuals first spend 800 time steps in this learning environment and are then placed in the regular environment where their performance is assessed as in the baseline model. Learning is disabled during this performance phase, to guarantee that all learning takes place in the learning environment.

In the learning environment there are no prey objects, but "toy" objects, which consist of a single 1-cell (to avoid ambiguity, toy objects never occupy adjacent cells). The learning environment is otherwise identical to the performance environment. Toy objects have no effect on fitness, but they provide sensory feedback when an organism performs an action. For example, when an organism takes a step forward, the positions of all objects within the field of view will be shifted down by one cell. Each action is associated with such a characteristic transformation of the content of the field of view, so the environment provides the information necessary to overcome the randomization of the action-output assignment, but without offering any reinforcement to drive a reward-based learning process.

Note that there is no target behaviour for the learning phase (since no fitness is awarded, any behaviour is as good as any other). Moreover, the states that will provide opportunities to score rewards never occur during the learning phase (as there are no prey objects in the learning environment).

Here we evolve this unusual type of learning ability, using a modification of the neuromodulation concept of Soltoggio et al. [14, 15]. The idea is to include special "modulatory" neurons in the network, that can dynamically alter the plasticity of the connections of the neurons they project to. These modulatory neurons mostly behave like regular neurons (they take input from regular neurons and apply their activation function like regular neurons), but instead of an activation signal they send out a modulation signal. Regular neurons sum the modulation signals they receive, apply their activation function, and then use the resulting value as their plasticity value for the present time step. This dynamic plasticity is then used as learning rate in an otherwise Hebbian weight update. This update rule captures the core concept of heterosynaptic plasticity as is known to underpin much learning ability in biological brains, albeit in highly simplified and abstracted form (biological neuromodulation comprises a collection of complex chemical processes modifying the way neural activation affects synapse strength).

For the main model we added 6 of these modulatory neurons in the hidden layer of the network species used in the baseline model (Figure 4). These too use the hyperbolic tangent activation function. Since individuals must learn by observing how their actions transform the content of their field of view, some form of memory of the previous time step is necessary. We provide this memory by adding "echo neurons" to the input layer. These trivially copy the pattern of the regular input neurons, but with one time step of lag. To keep comparison with the baseline model fair, the echo neurons are only connected to the modulatory neurons (so they only serve learning and do not directly influence

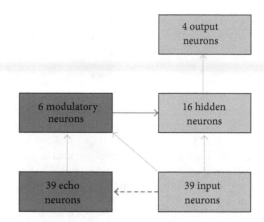

FIGURE 4: Network topology used in main model. Light-blue arrows are regular activatory connections (full connectivity). The purple arrow indicates modulatory connections (full connectivity). The dashed arrow indicates a copying operation with one step of lag (one to one connectivity, see text). The input, hidden and output neurons occur in both models; the echo and modulatory neurons are unique to the main model.

action selection). Since weight updates only occur during the learning phase, neither the modulatory neurons nor the echo neurons have any influence whatsoever during the performance phase. In the terminology of Section 2, the input, hidden, and output neurons comprise b, while the echo and modulatory neurons comprise b'. The update rule for connection weights is as follows:

$$\Delta W_{ij} = 0.01 \cdot m_i \cdot a_i \cdot a_j, \qquad (4)$$

where W_{ij} is the weight of the connection from neuron i to neuron j, m_i is the modulation at neuron i, and a_i is the activation of neuron i. Weights are again clipped to the range $[-2, +2]$. The update rule contains a multiplication by 0.01 to avoid excessively large sudden weight changes. Our experiments suggest that a wide range of values can be used here. No attempts were made to optimize this value. Weights are updated after observation of the state resulting from the chosen action. Note that since only the hidden neurons receive modulation, only the top layer connections are updated during the lifetime.

We provide the learning process information on which action was performed using what can be thought of as mutual inhibition between output neurons: the activation of the output neuron whose action is performed is set to 1, and the activation of the other output neurons is set to 0 (mutual inhibition was also applied in the baseline model but serves no function there).

We found that for connections exposed to learning, very small innate weights work best. These are hard to evolve with the mutation settings of the baseline model, so for these connections mutation strength and clipping range are divided by 200. All other connections use the same parameters as in the baseline model.

The baseline model provides an upper limit for what the main model might achieve. The performance of the main model should approach that of the baseline model to the extent that the learning ability evolved in the main model can overcome the randomization of the action-output assignment. (The comparison we make might seem odd, since we varied two aspects (task and network type) instead of one. However, varying just one of these makes little sense: evolving nets without learning ability in an environment that requires it is not informative (average fitness remains stuck at around 5), and evolving nets with learning ability in an environment that does not require it is unlikely to produce interesting learning ability. The aspect we aim to vary is how behaviour is realized: by evolution alone or by evolution and learning together. Varying this aspect requires varying both task and network type.) Figure 5 shows performance of the main model. Evolution in the main model is slower than in the baseline model, as is to be expected given the increased complexity of the task and the larger genotype. Once stabilized, generation best and generation average fitness values do not quite match those of the baseline model, but they get fairly close (±109 versus ±100 and ±87 versus ±65, resp.). The difference in genotype size accounts for part of the difference in average performance (both models use the same range of per-connection mutation probabilities, and the networks in the main model have substantially more connections, so we should expect to find a larger proportion of dysfunctional mutants in the population). For comparison, evolving populations without learning ability under the randomization condition of the main model produces average fitness values of about 5 (results not shown). Considering that the main model's nets have just an 800-time-step learning phase to wire up a solution from experience while the baseline model's nets benefit from 50000 generation of connection weight refinement, we can conclude that the evolved learning ability copes with the output-action assignment randomization fairly well.

5. Network Structure Analysis

The results discussed so far show that it is quite possible to evolve reinforcement-free learning ability using a neuromodulation approach. Next we discuss the effect of the need for learning on the neural organization of the networks, assessing whether or not evolution of learning ability leads to increased organization, and whether their organization expresses any aspects of the environment.

Figures 7 and 8 show the connection patterns of the hidden neurons of the best individual of the last generation of each run for baseline and main model, respectively. The plot format is explained in Figure 6. Looking at Figures 7 and 8 we can note two differences. (1) In the main model, we see that many hidden neurons end up with uniform upward connections (visible in that the four columns showing upward connections of such neurons all take on the same colour). Given that actions are selected by picking the output neuron with the highest activation, we can conclude that these neurons are not functionally involved in action selection. (Since this observation could possibly be explainable as an effect of the relatively small number of modulatory neurons, we performed a small number of runs with 12 instead of 6 modulatory neurons (results not shown). These did not reveal

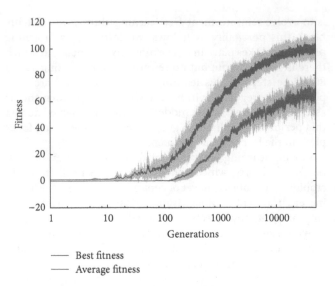

Figure 5: Evolution process of main model. Averages over 10 runs. Gray areas indicate standard deviation over the runs. Note the log scale on the x-axis.

a higher number of functionally involved neurons, suggesting that a small number of functionally involved neurons (i.e., a compact solution) is somehow advantageous.) Neurons like these are rare or absent in the baseline model. (2) In the main model, we see a small number of connection patterns occur time and time again over multiple runs. While not absent in the baseline model, this tendency is notably stronger in the main model.

Figure 9 shows the result of CT clustering [16] (modified to handle sign symmetry; see Figure 6(b)) applied to the hidden neurons' connection patterns. We see that CT clustering identified a conspicuous trio of clusters of seven neurons each. This trio of clusters reflects a single solution that evolved in 7 out of the 10 runs of the main model. (2 runs evolved another 3-neuron solution. The remaining run was not stable at the time of termination and had traits of both solutions.) Although similar connections patterns do occur in the baseline model (most notably connection pattern #4 of the main model is common in the baseline model as well), the variability in connection patterns is larger there (resulting in a larger number of clusters), and the tendency to evolve characteristic sets of neurons is weaker. Figure 10 gives an idealization and explanation of the solution highlighted in Figure 9. We can easily see how this triplet produces the behaviour the environment demands.

How do these findings relate to our theory? We said that a species that needs to learn will tend to evolve solutions that are (1) more compact, (2) show increased functional differentiation, and (3) exploit environmental regularities. That the solutions evolved in the main model are more compact than those of the baseline model is visible in the larger number of neurons that is not functionally involved in action selection. As for functional differentiation, we might have expected to see neurons specializing on a single specific action or situation, but the results here are clearly different. We see that functionally involved neurons in the main model specialize

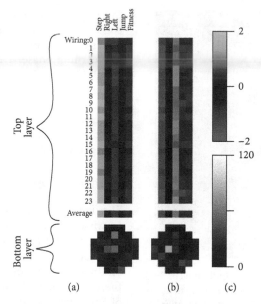

FIGURE 6: Explanation of neural connectivity plots used in Figures 7 and 8. (a) This plot shows the weights of all incoming and outgoing connections of a single hidden neuron. The bottom part shows weights of incoming connections (from input neurons), arranged after the positions in the field of view that the input neuron gets its input from (e.g., we see that this example neuron has a negative connection to the input neuron that perceives the state of the cell directly to the left of the organism and a positive connection to the input neuron that perceives the state of the cell two steps ahead of the organism). These weights are innately fixed in both models. In the main model, the outgoing connections (to output neurons, top part of plot) are subjected to learning. To plot these, we ran the individual with every possible output-action assignment (24 assignments in total), repeating each assignment 25 times. The connection weights shown (numbered rows) are averages over the 25 lifetimes per assignment, and a global average over all assignments. For convenience, we arrange the weights of the outgoing connections not by output but by action of the output neuron the connection projects to (e.g., the first column shows strength of connection to the output neuron assigned to the "step" action, regardless of which output neuron that is under a given output-action assignment). In the baseline model the weights of all connections are constant over the lifetime and only a single output-action assignment exists, so in plots of baseline model networks there is only a genetic weight to show for each outgoing connection. The rightmost column of the top part shows the fitness of the individual containing the neuron. In case of the main model, fitness is shown as average per assignment and as global average, like the connection weights. For the baseline model, we show a global average over the same number of lifetime runs used for the global averages of the main model, that is, $24 \times 25 = 600$. Note that fitness columns are identical for all neurons from a single individual. (b) Flipping the sign on all incoming and outgoing connections yields a functionally identical connection pattern. This symmetry was taken into account in further analysis. (c) Colour scales for connection weight and fitness value.

not on single actions but on making specific distinctions required for correct action choice (caption Figure 10). This sharp role division between neurons, each handling a specific distinction, constitutes clear functional differentiation. The reason for specialization on distinctions becomes clear when we search for exploitation of environmental regularities.

The question whether the evolved neural networks exploit environmental regularities is more difficult to answer, but we believe the answer to be yes. Consider what happens during the learning process when an upward connection is established. When the L neuron of Figure 10 is negatively connected to the left-turn output neuron, then observation of horizontal prey to the left comes to promote leftward turns. Additionally, as a side effect, vertically oriented prey straight ahead will come to *inhibit* leftward turns. These two effects are not a priori related. That turning left is a bad idea when there is a prey straight ahead might seem trivial when phrased like this, but bear in mind that the spatial coherence of the environment is never explicitly given and that the output-action wiring is randomized. That this feature of the learning

system is remarkable will be clearer when we phrase it from the nets' point of view:

> *That action **a** will favourably transform input vector **P** implies that action **a** will NOT favourably transform input vector **Q**.*

This relation evidently does not hold in general. There are plenty of different input vector configurations that are all advantageously transformed by the same action. Of course in a spatially coherent environment, there will be many pairs of input vectors for which the above relation *does* hold (if **P** is an input vector representing horizontally oriented prey to the left and **Q** is an input vector representing prey straight ahead, the above relation holds for **a** = "turn left"), but we cannot a priori identify them *without reference to that environment's spatial coherence*. Similar arguments can be made for the R and SJ neurons.

Similar arguments seem also applicable for the alternative solution that evolved in 2 runs. Given this solution's low number of occurrences we cannot extract as clear an

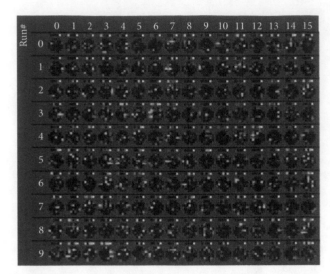

FIGURE 7: Connectivity of hidden neurons in best individual of final generation for 10 runs of the baseline model. Each row of 16 neurons represents one such individual (see Figure 6(a) for explanation of plot).

image from the data, and the instances we have seem more diffuse than the instances of the more common solution, but Figure 11 attempts to illustrate the basic mechanism. We see that control is similarly carved up into a small number of choices, but the choices implemented by two of the neurons (TF and LR in Figure 11) differ from the more common solution.

By combining recognition of multiple situations into single neurons, the control systems evolved in the main model allow the networks to exploit structural aspects of the environment. Hence we see that when the species is forced to evolve learning ability, these aspects find their way into the implementation of behaviour. It is clear how exploitation of such relations benefit learning. It is also clear that a system without learning ability has little use for such relations. Thus their internalization depends on the need for learning ability and is markedly more prominent in the main model than in the baseline model. This in turn can also explain why functionality becomes highly focused in a small number of neurons: in order to weigh two action choices, the perceptual information pertaining to those choices must be brought together. These observations support the hypothesis put forth in Section 2.

Although it is not in the scope of this research to explore the intricacies of the learning process itself (as mentioned above, the implementation of the learning process is not under the organizing selection hypothesized in Section 2), the connection patterns shown in Figures 10 and 11 suggest the interesting possibility that the nets may be employing perception biases to make useful learning material out of fitness-wise meaningless situations. Assume that there is a 1-cell positioned two steps ahead. During the performance phase a 1-cell in this position could equally well be part of a laterally or longitudinally approached prey, so the situation of a toy object two steps ahead during the learning phase is quite ambiguous. Yet the response of the SJ neuron resembles

the response it gives to a laterally approached prey (and comes to trigger the same behavioural response). Similar biases exist for many of the other states encountered during the learning phase. We will not pursue this line of inquiry here, but it would be interesting to explore if and how such biases relate to the role of imagination in play behaviour. In play behaviour too, fitness-irrelevant situations are often perceived and responded to as fitness-relevant situations, especially where the actual fitness-relevant situations are too scarce or dangerous to drive the learning process.

6. Discussion

The hypothesis presented in Section 2 is closely related to what Godfrey-Smith calls the *environmental complexity thesis*, the idea that environmental complexity is the driving force behind the evolution of cognition [17–19]. Godfrey-Smith identifies Spencer as the first to hold a version of the environmental complexity thesis [18], and we see some of Spencer's continuity between life and mind in Godfrey-Smith's own version of the thesis: "[Cognitive] capacities vary across different types of organism and are not sharply distinguished from other biological capacities, some of which have a "proto-cognitive" character." [19]. However, in his own version of the thesis, Godfrey-Smith steers clear from claims of correspondence between cognitive and environmental organization, opting to defend a weaker version than Spencer. Our results suggest that there is a tenable intermediate position, weaker than Spencer's but stronger than Godfrey-Smith's. This position states that those parts of cognition that evolved under selection pressure for learning ability will tend to express correspondence with the environment.

The organizing effect shown here may also seem related to the Baldwin effect [20], so it seems appropriate to shortly discuss how the effects differ. The interpretation of the Baldwin effect commonly studied in artificial life [21] is that learning ability can accelerate evolution or even allow evolution to find solutions that are extremely hard to find without learning, by "smoothening" the fitness landscape [22, 23]. Learning plays a supportive role, facilitating evolution of traits that by themselves improve fitness. The effect demonstrated in the present paper is different, in that the trait being evolved is learning ability itself. The organization that emerges as a side effect of the evolution of learning is only adaptive in context of the learning ability that it supports. In other words, instead of letting learning ability facilitate evolution of some fit trait, we evolved learning ability to trigger emergence of a trait that facilitates learning. Although closely related (traits supporting learning seem quite susceptible to Baldwinian evolution [9]), these effects do not trivially translate into one another.

Let us also note the described mechanism's relation to the concept of *evolution of evolvability* from the field of bioinformatics. The simplest case of evolution of evolvability can be observed by switching the evolutionary target (the optimal phenotype) back and forth between two options every so many generations. Under these conditions, direct fitness of an individual depends on its phenotype alone, but the fitness of its descendents will additionally depend on how

FIGURE 8: Connectivity of hidden neurons in best individual of final generation for 10 runs of the main model. Each row of 16 neurons represents one such individual (see Figure 6(a) for explanation of plot).

readily the individual's genotype can evolve to a genotype that expresses as the noncurrent target phenotype. Hence lineages that can flick back and forth between the two targets most "efficiently" (e.g., requiring only a small number of common mutations) have an evolutionary advantage. Thus a lineage-level evolution process comes to optimize the genotype's *evolvability* with respect to the environmental dynamic, such that the "regular" evolution process accelerates over time, taking less and less time to move the population from one target to the other. This two-target scenario is explored by Crombach and Hogeweg [24] using gene regulatory networks. The resulting genotypes' propensity to mutate back and forth

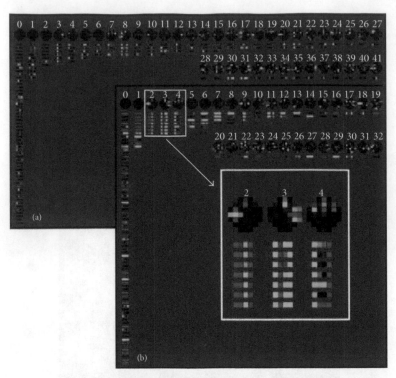

FIGURE 9: We pooled all neurons shown in Figure 8 and pooled all neurons shown in Figure 9, then applied CT clustering [16] to each pool in order to detect evolutionary trends over the different runs of the models. Clustering was performed on basis on the incoming connections only (as these are set by evolution only in both models). Each column shows one cluster of neurons. The pattern at the top of each column is an average over the downward connections of all neurons in the cluster. Below it are the upward connection patterns for each member neuron (for the main model, these are averages as shown in Figure 7(a)). Connection patterns were sign-flipped whenever this led to smaller distance to cluster center, to account for sign symmetry (see Figure 7(b)). (a) Result for baseline model. (b) Result for main model. The inset shows the triplet of neurons identified as the common solution evolved in 7 of the 10 runs of the main model. This triplet alone suffices for adequate behaviour.

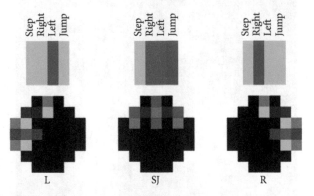

FIGURE 10: Idealization of the solution evolved in runs 0, 1, 2, 3, 5, 7, and 8 of the main model. These patterns were named L (for left turn), R (for right turn) and SJ (for step or Jump). Signs of the L pattern are flipped with respect to Figure 9. L and R detect horizontally oriented prey to the left and right, respectively, and promote the corresponding turn action when appropriate (by increasing activation on the output neuron assigned the "turn left" action and lowering activation on all other output neurons). When moving neither right nor left, SJ assesses whether it is better to step or jump (by increasing activation on the output neuron assigned the preferred action, and lowering activation on the other). Connections coloured blue varied over different occurrences of the SJ neuron (they do not affect behaviour).

between the targets with minimal "mutational effort" is a lineage level adaptation to the environment's target switching dynamic and might in a broad sense be said to correspond to it. Kashtan and Alon [25] evolve neural networks and electronic circuits in a more complex task-switching scenario and find modularization and motif formation in the evolved architectures. The mechanism explored in the present paper is essentially the same mechanism, except occurring between a different pair of adaptation processes (evolution and learning instead of lineage evolution and evolution). Depending on the

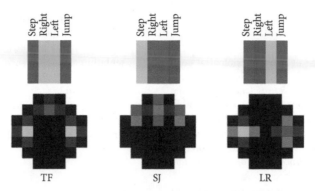

FIGURE 11: Attempted idealization of the solution evolved in runs 4 and 9 of the main model. These patterns were named TF (for turn or Forward), LR (for left or Right) and SJ (for step or Jump). TF promotes the step and jump actions when there is vertically oriented prey straight ahead and both turn actions when there is horizontally oriented prey to a side. SJ works as in Figure 10, assessing whether it is better to step or jump, such that the correct forward action is picked in case TF selects forward movement. LR promotes leftward turns and inhibits right turns when there is horizontally oriented prey to the left and not to the right and vice versa, such that the correct turn direction is picked in case TF selects to make a turn. Blue connections may vary.

adaptation processes involved, the mechanism may pertain to different ranges of biological phenomena, with cases where learning is involved being particularly pertinent to advanced cognition.

In the field of AI, there is a tendency to view learning and evolution as interchangeable: adaptation is adaptation, be it via advantageous mutations being picked out from the detrimental ones by natural selection or via advantageous behaviours being picked out the from detrimental ones by reinforcement. Evolutionary algorithms are often even classed as a type of learning algorithms. The results presented here suggest that this tendency is detrimental and should be selected against. To understand the evolution of cognition, we should pay close attention to the interactions between learning and evolution, and this requires that we clearly distinguish the various levels of adaptation at work. For a given type of interaction to occur, the nature of the adaptation processes involved may well be immaterial, but even so the same interaction will never occur between a single adaptation process. Furthermore, as stated above, the same type of interaction occurring between different pairs of adaptation processes will pertain to different natural phenomena, making the distinctions between these processes quite important. Let us shortly add another candidate instance of the interaction type we have focused on here.

In this paper we discussed innate correspondence, emerging over the course of the evolution. Advanced cognition makes use of correspondence at a different level as well as hinted at in the introduction: mental representation can be thought of as a form of correspondence that individuals dynamically acquire as they interact with an environment, that is, correspondence acquired via learning instead of evolution. When the adaptation processes involved are evolution and learning, the interaction discussed here does not cover such correspondence. However, the mechanism may be able to account for acquired correspondence if we shift our focus to yet another pair of adaptation processes: learning and second-order learning. We report on our attempts at such extension elsewhere [26, 27].

7. Conclusions

In this paper we discussed a novel theory on the effect of selection for learning on the structure of cognition. We hypothesized that the evolution of learning causes assimilation of environmental structure into neurocognitive structure. Using a simple form of neuromodulation, we built a model in which a form of reinforcement-free learning is made to evolve in neural networks. We found evidence for the hypothesized effect in our evolved networks and considered this evidence in the context of the environmental complexity thesis. We believe that a position in between Spencer's and Godfrey-Smith's is tenable, and that this position provides a useful angle for the computational study of the evolution of neurocognitive organization. We also discussed how the interaction effect demonstrated here can be viewed as an instance of a general pattern of interaction between adaptation processes.

Acknowledgments

The first author thanks Gerard Vreeswijk, Thomas Müller, and Janneke van Lith for many helpful comments.

References

[1] H. Spencer, *The Principles of Psychology*, Appleton, New York, NY, USA, 3rd edition, 1885.

[2] R. A. Brooks, "Intelligence without representation," *Artificial Intelligence*, vol. 47, no. 1–3, pp. 139–159, 1991.

[3] J. A. Fodor and Z. W. Pylyshyn, "Connectionism and cognitive architecture: a critical analysis," *Cognition*, vol. 28, no. 1-2, pp. 3–71, 1988.

[4] J. Fodor and B. P. McLaughlin, "Connectionism and the problem of systematicity: why Smolensky's solution doesn't work," *Cognition*, vol. 35, no. 2, pp. 183–204, 1990.

[5] B. P. McLaughlin, "Systematicity redux," *Synthese*, vol. 170, no. 2, pp. 251–274, 2009.

[6] R. A. Jacobs, "Computational studies of the development of functionally specialized neural modules," *Trends in Cognitive Sciences*, vol. 3, no. 1, pp. 31–38, 1999.

[7] J. A. Bullinaria, "Understanding the emergence of modularity in neural systems," *Cognitive Science*, vol. 31, no. 4, pp. 673–695, 2007.

[8] J. A. Bullinaria, "The importance of neurophysiological constraints for modelling the emergence of modularity," in *Computational Modelling in Behavioural Neuroscience: Closing the Gap Between Neurophysiology and Behaviour*, D. Heinke and E. Mavritsaki, Eds., pp. 187–208, Psychology Press, 2009.

[9] S. F. Arnold, R. Suzuki, and T. Arita, "Evolving learning ability in cyclically dynamic environments: the structuring force of environmental heterogeneity," in *Proceedings of Artificial Life XII*, pp. 435–436, MIT press, 2010.

[10] P. M. Todd and G. F. Miller, "Exploring adaptive agency II: simulating the evolution of associative learning," in *Proceedings of the 1st International Conference on Simulation of Adaptive Behavior*, pp. 306–315, 1991.

[11] S. Nolfi, J. L. Elman, and D. Parisi, "Learning and evolution in neural networks," *Adaptive Behavior*, vol. 3, no. 1, pp. 5–28, 1994.

[12] S. Nolfi and D. Parisi, "Learning to adapt to changing environments in evolving neural networks," *Adaptive Behavior*, vol. 5, no. 1, pp. 75–98, 1996.

[13] E. Robinson and J. A. Bullinaria, "Neuroevolution of auto-teaching architectures," in *Connectionist Models of Behavior and Cognition II*, J. Mayor, N. Ruh, and K. Plunkett, Eds., pp. 361–372, World Scientific, Singapore, 2009.

[14] A. Soltoggio, P. Dürr, C. Mattiussi, and D. Floreano, "Evolving neuromodulatory topologies for reinforcement learning-like problems," in *Proceedings of the IEEE Congress on Evolutionary Computation (CEC '07)*, pp. 2471–2478, September 2007.

[15] A. Soltoggio, J. A. Bullinaria, C. Mattiussi, P. Dürr, and D. Floreano, "Evolutionary advantages of neuromodulated plasticity in dynamic, reward-based scenarios," in *Proceedings of Artificial Life XI*, pp. 569–576, MIT Press, 2008.

[16] L. J. Heyer, S. Kruglyak, and S. Yooseph, "Exploring expression data identification and analysis of coexpressed genes," *Genome Research*, vol. 9, no. 11, pp. 1106–1115, 1999.

[17] P. Godfrey-Smith, "Spencer and Dewey on Life and Mind," in *Proceedings of the Artificial Life 4*, R. Brooks and P. Maes, Eds., pp. 80–89, MIT Press, 1994.

[18] P. Godfrey-Smith, *Complexity and the Function of Mind in Nature*, Cambridge University Press, 1996.

[19] P. Godfrey-Smith, "Environmental complexity and the evolution of cognition," in *The Evolution of Intelligence*, R. Sternberg and J. Kaufman, Eds., pp. 233–249, Lawrence Erlbaum, Mahwah, NJ, USA, 2002.

[20] J. M. Baldwin, "A new factor in evolution," *American Naturalist*, vol. 30, pp. 441–451, 1896.

[21] P. Turney, D. Whitley, and R. W. Anderson, "Evolution, learning, and instinct: 100 years of the baldwin effect," *Evolutionary Computation*, vol. 4, no. 3, pp. 4–8, 1996.

[22] G. E. Hinton and S. J. Nowlan, "How learning can guide evolution," *Complex Systems*, vol. 1, pp. 495–502, 1987.

[23] R. Suzuki and T. Arita, "Repeated occurrences of the baldwin effect can guide evolution on rugged fitness Landscapes," in *Proceedings of the 1st IEEE Symposium on Artificial Life (IEEE-ALife'07)*, pp. 8–14, April 2007.

[24] A. Crombach and P. Hogeweg, "Evolution of evolvability in gene regulatory networks," *PLoS Computational Biology*, vol. 4, no. 7, article e1000112, 2008.

[25] N. Kashtan and U. Alon, "Spontaneous evolution of modularity and network motifs," *Proceedings of the National Academy of Sciences of the United States of America*, vol. 102, no. 39, pp. 13773–13778, 2005.

[26] S. F. Arnold, R. Suzuki, and T. Arita, "Modelling mental representation as evolved second order learning," *Proceedings of the 17th International Symposium on Artificial Life and Robotics*, pp. 674–677, 2012.

[27] S. F. Arnold, R. Suzuki, and T. Arita, "Second order learning and the evolution of mental representation," in *Proceedings of Artificial life XIII*, pp. 301–308, MIT press, 2012.

13

Contribution to Semantic Analysis of Arabic Language

Anis Zouaghi,[1] Mounir Zrigui,[2] Georges Antoniadis,[3] and Laroussi Merhbene[2]

[1] *LATICE, ISSAT, University of Sousse, Cité Ibn Khaldoun, Taffala, 4003 Sousse, Tunisia*
[2] *LATICE, FSM, University of Monastir, Avenue de l'Environnement, 5000 Monastir, Tunisia*
[3] *LIDILEM, University of Stendhal, BP 25, 38040 Grenoble Cedex 9, France*

Correspondence should be addressed to Anis Zouaghi, anis.zouaghi@gmail.com

Academic Editor: Srinivas Bangalore

We propose a new approach for determining the adequate sense of Arabic words. For that, we propose an algorithm based on information retrieval measures to identify the context of use that is the closest to the sentence containing the word to be disambiguated. The contexts of use represent a set of sentences that indicates a particular sense of the ambiguous word. These contexts are generated using the words that define the senses of the ambiguous words, the exact string-matching algorithm, and the corpus. We use the measures employed in the domain of information retrieval, Harman, Croft, and Okapi combined to the Lesk algorithm, to assign the correct sense of those proposed.

1. Introduction

Human language is ambiguous; many words can have more than one sense: this sense is dependent on the context of use. The word sense disambiguation (WSD) allows us to find the most appropriate sense of an ambiguous word. This work is a contribution in a general frame-work which aims at understanding the Arabic speech [1, 2]. In this paper, we are interested in determining the meaning of Arabic ambiguous words which we can meet in the messages transcribed by the module of speech recognition.

We propose some steps [3] to build a system for Arabic word sense disambiguation. First, we use a predefined list of stopwords (which do not affect the meaning of the ambiguous words) to eliminate them from the original sentence containing the ambiguous word. After that, we apply the routing [4] for the words contained in the glosses of the ambiguous word. Then we use the exact string-matching algorithm [5] to be able to extract the contexts of uses from the corpus used. Finally, we apply the measures of Harman [6], Croft [7], and Okapi [8] that compares the original sentence with the generated contexts of use and returns a score that corresponds to the closest context of use [9]. The Lesk algorithm [10] will be used to choose the exact sense from the different senses given by these measures.

This paper is structured as follows. We describe in Section 2 the main used approaches for WSD. After that, in Section 3, we present the proposed algorithm for lexical disambiguation of Arabic language. Finally, in Section 4, we present the obtained results.

2. Main Used Approaches

Most of the works related to the word sense disambiguation were applied to the English. They achieve a disambiguation rate of around 90%. There are many approaches which are classified using the source of knowledge adapted for the differentiation of the senses.

2.1. Knowledge-Based Methods. They were introduced in 1970, based on the dictionary, thesaurus, and lexicon. Using these resources they extract the information necessary to disambiguate words. Some of them [10] tested the adequate definitions given by the electronic dictionary Collins English Dictionary (CED) and the Dictionary of Contemporary English (LDOCE) for the automatic treatment of the disambiguation. Some others try to provide a basis for determining closeness in meaning among pairs of words described by the thesaurus like Roget International Thesaurus or by the semantic lexicon like Wordnet [11].

2.2. Corpus-Based Methods. Since the evolution of the statistic methods based on large text corpus, two principal orientations appear.

(i) Unsupervised methods: these methods are based on training sets and use a non-annotated corpus. They are divided into type-based discrimination [12] and token-based discrimination [13]: the first one used algorithms to measure the similarities after the representation of the contexts. The contexts are represented by high-dimensional spaces defined by word co-occurrences. The second one clusters the contexts that contain a specified target word such that the resulting clusters will be made up of contexts that use the target word in the same sense.

(ii) Supervised and semi-supervised methods: they use an annotated training corpus inducing the appropriate classification models [14]. For the supervised systems we can cite: the probabilistic methods; the majority of them use the naïve bayes algorithm and the maximum entropy approach. Methods are based on the similarity of the examples that use a similarity metric to compare the set of learned vector prototypes (for each word sense). The methods based on discriminating rules use selective rules associated with each word sense. The methods based on rule combine heterogeneous learning modules.

3. Proposed Method

As we have mentioned before, the majority of the works related to the WSD were applied to the English. However, there are some works applied to Arabic. We can state the unsupervised approach of Bootstrapping Arabic Sense Tagging [15], the naïve Bayes classifier for AWSD [16], the Arabic WSD by using the variants of Lesk algorithm [17], the WSD-AL system [18, 19], and so forth. Here, we define an unsupervised method named. Figure 1 below describes the principle of this method. We use the dictionary of "Al-Mu'jam Al-Wasit" to construct a database that contains the words and there definitions (an electronic version of this dictionary).

Subsequently we eliminate stopwords from the original sentence, using the list of stop words defined in our database (see Section 4.1.3). Using the glosses of the word to be disambiguated, we generate the contexts of use for each sense from the corpus. The idea consists of combining the algorithm of stemming (see Section 3.1.1) [4] to extract the roots and the algorithm of approximate string matching (see Section 3.1.2) to find occurrences of the stems. Stems and their occurrences are saved in the knowledge base. The sentences containing these occurrences with the ambiguous word represent the contexts of use.

The second step of the proposed method is to measure the similarity between the different contexts of use generated from the glosses and the current context. The context that obtains the highest score of similarity with the current context will represent the most probable sense of the ambiguous word. The Algorithm 1 below describes the proposed

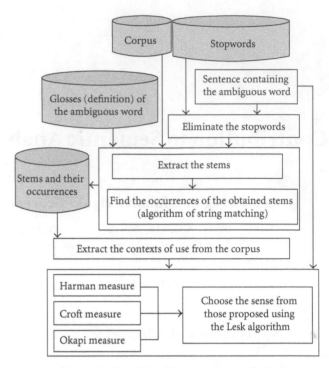

FIGURE 1: Principle of the proposed method.

algorithm of Arabic WSD and the score measure. In what follows we describe with more details each step cited above.

3.1. Construction of the Context of Use: Motivation and Implementation. To maximize the probability of finding the context for each gloss, we proposed as a solution to generate the occurrences of the most significant words. To extract the most significant words, we eliminate the non-informative words (stop words in English) using a predefined list (this list contains 20000 words). Given that the Arabic word has flexional morphology, we used an algorithm to extract the word roots and then an algorithm for matching words to find occurrences of this root. Obtaining instances of a root consists of adding a suffix to the beginning of a word or a prefix in the end.

3.1.1. Routing. To extract the stems of the Arabic words we use the Al-Shalabi-Kanaan algorithm [4]. Its advantage is that it does not use any resources. This algorithm extracts word roots by assigning weights to word's letters (the weights are real numbers predefined between 0 and 5) multiplied by the rank which depends on the letter's position. The roots are composed of three to five consonant letters and 85% of Arabic roots are trilateral. For that reason we use this algorithm which returns only three consonants.

The weights affiliated to letters were determined through experiments on Arabic texts, for example, we assign the most highest weight "5" to the letters "ا, ة" "a, t" because the words in the Arabic language begin and finish by these letters. The rank of letters in a word depends on the length of the word, and if the word contains an even or odd number of letters. The three letters with the lowest weights are selected.

S: Sentence contained the word to be disambiguated;
CU: Context of use generated;
C: Corpus; R_4: root;
G: Glosses from the dictionary generated in Section 3;
AW: ambiguous word;
w, y: word;
(1)   For each $w \in S$ {
(2)   Assign weight p = the position on the left or on the right of the ambiguous word;
        }
(3)   For each $w \in$ Glosses of AW {
(4)   Lemmatizing (w); // Generate the root
(5)   For each $y \in C$ {
(6)   Approximate String-Matching (char w, int m, char y, int n); // Generate a list of occurrences $L(R_4)$;
    }
(7)   For each $w_1 \in L(R_4)$ {
(8)   Load all the sentences that contains these occurrences to generate the context of use CU;
    }}
Context-Matching (S, CU) {
(9)   For each $w \in S$ {
(10)   For each CU containing AW {
(11) $C(w) = -\log(n(w)/N) \times [0.5 + (1 - 0.5) \times (n_{cu}(w)/\text{Max}_{x \in uc}\, n_{cu}/(w))]$;
(12) $O(w) = \log[(N - n(w) + 0.5)/n(w) + 0.5] \times [n_c(w)/(n_{cu}(w) + (T(cu)/T_n(B)))]$;
(13) $H(w) = -\log(n(w)/N) \times [\log(n_{cu}/(w) + 1)/\log(T(cu))]$;
(14)   If the result given by each measure are different then
(15)   Apply the leak algorithm between the proposed glosses proposed;
        Else
(16)   Affiliate the sense proposed by the different similarity measures;
    }}

ALGORITHM 1: WSD-AL algorithm.

TABLE 1: Execution of the stemming algorithm to extract the root of the word "الحساب" "alhissab".

word	الحساب					
Letters	ب	ا	س	ح	ل	ا
Wheights	0	5	1	0	1	5
Rank	1.5	2.5	3.5	4	5	6
Multiplication	0	15	3.5	0	5	30
Root	حسب					

In Table 1, we give a sample of the execution of the algorithm for the word "الحساب" "alhissab".

This algorithm achieves accuracy in the average of 90% [10]. The output of this step is a list of the root of the words contained in the gloss of the ambiguous word $R(g_i) = \{R_1, R_2, \ldots, R_n\}$, where g_i is the ith gloss and R_n is the ith obtained stem.

3.1.2. Approximate String Matching.
Unlike English, Arabic has a rich derivational system and it is one of the characteristics that makes it ambiguous. The Arabic words are based on roots, generally trilateral. We use the algorithm of approximate string matching [5] to find the possible occurrences of a stem obtained using the last step. This

algorithm will be applied only for the roots that we do not find in our database.

It is based on two steps [20]. The first step (see Algorithm 2) consists of filling the matrix of the two words to be compared to x and t. Let $|x| < |t|$ and δ = substitution.

After that we use the step of back-tracking (see Algorithm 3), to find the shortest common subsequence. Let be γ the operation of insertion and $\sigma_{i,j}$ the operation of suppression. The words containing this common subsequence (stem obtained previously) will be considered as the occurrences of the stem. A list $L(\text{Ri})$ of the occurrences will be generated.

We use the corpus described in the experimental results, to extract the sentences containing the words of the glosses and their occurrences. These texts represent the contexts of use. This algorithm takes so much time during its execution; to facilitate that, we generated a table in our knowledge base in which are recorded occurrences of each root are recorded. Until now this table has a list of 7,349 roots with an average of seven occurrences for each root.

3.2. Score Measure: Motivation and Implementation.
We propose some measure that determines the degree of similarity between a sentence (containing an ambiguous word) and a document (that represents the contexts of use for a given sense of the ambiguous word). Let CC = $m_1, m_2, \ldots, m_k$ the context where the ambiguous word m appear. Suppose that

```
Begin
(i) (i.a) Construct the matrix M with size (|x| + 1) * (|t| + 1);   //
Filling the matrix
        (i.b) For i := 1 à |x| do M[i, 0] := i * δ end;
              For j := 0 à |t| do M[0, j] := 0 end;
(ii)          For i := 1 à |x| do
                  For j := 1 à |t| do
                      M[i, j] := min{M[i − 1, j − 1] + 1,
                                     M[i, j − 1] + 1,
                                     M[i − 1, j] + δ}
              End
End
```

ALGORITHM 2: First step "filling the matrix" for the approximate string matching algorithm.

```
(iii) (iii.a) Select q, 1 ≤ q ≤ |t|
telle que M[|x|, q] = min_{1≤j≤|t|}{M[|x|, j]}; // Back-Tracking
              i := |x|; j := q;
        (iii.b) whiel (i ≠ 0 & j ≠ 0) do
If M[i, j] = M[i, j − 1] + γ than j := j − 1
else
                          if M[i, j] = M[i − 1, j − 1] + σ_{i,j} than
                              j := j − 1; i := i − 1
                  else i := i − 1
                      end if
              end if
        end do;
        (iv) p := j + 1;
              x′ := t_{p,q}
end
```

ALGORITHM 3: Second step "back-tracking" of the approximate string matching algorithm.

$S_1, S_2, \ldots, S_k$ are the possible senses of m out of context. And $CU_1, CU_2, \ldots, CU_K$ are the possible contexts of use of m for which the meanings of m are, respectively: $S_1, S_2, \ldots, S_k$.

To determine the appropriate sense of m in the current context CC we used the information retrieval methods (Okapi, Harman, and Croft), which allow the system to calculate the proximity between the current context (context of the ambiguous word), and the different use contexts of each possible sense of this word. The results of each comparison are a score indicating the degree of semantic similarity between the CC and given CU. This allows our system to infer the exact meaning of the ambiguous word. The following (1) describes the method used to calculate the score of similarity between two contexts:

$$S_t(CC, CU) = \frac{(\Sigma_{i \in RC} E(m_i) + \Sigma_{i \in LC} E(m_i))}{(\Sigma_{i \in RC} FE(m_i) + \Sigma_{i \in LC} FE(m_i))}, \quad (1)$$

where $\Sigma_{i \in RC} E(m_i)$ and $\Sigma_{i \in LC} E(m_i)$ are, respectively, the sums of weights of all words belonging at the same time, the current context CC and the context of use (CU). $FE(m_i)$ corresponds to the first member of $E(m_i)$, and $E(m_i)$ can be replaced by one of the information retrieval methods: Croft, Harman, or Okapi, whose equations are, respectively, as follows.

3.2.1. Harman Measure. Consider

$$H(m) = W_H(m, CU(t)) = -\log\left(\frac{n(m)}{N}\right)$$
$$\times \left[\frac{\log(n_{cu}(m) + 1)}{\log(T(cu))}\right], \quad (2)$$

where $W_H(m, CU(t))$ is the weight attributed to m in the use contexts CU of the ambiguous word t by the Harman measure; $n(m)$ is the number of the use contexts of t containing the word m; N is the total number of the use contexts of t; $n_{cu}(m)$ is the occurrence number of m in the use context CU; $T(cu)$ is the total number of words belonging to CU.

3.2.2. Croft Measure $C(m)$. Consider

$$C(m) = W_C(m, CU(t)) = -\log\left(\frac{n(m)}{N}\right)$$
$$\times \left[k + (1 - k) \times \left(\frac{n_{cu}(m)}{Max_{x \in uc} n_{cu}(x)}\right)\right], \quad (3)$$

where $W_C(m, CU(t))$ is the weight attributed to m in the context of use (CU) of t by the Croft measure; k is a constant

```
Begin
    Score ← 0
    Sens ← 1        // Choose the sense
    C ← context (t)        //Context of the word t
    For all I ∈ [1, N]
        D ← description (si)
    Sup ← 0
    For all w ∈ C do
        w ← description (w)
        sup ← sup + score (D, w)
    if sup > score then
        Score ← sup
        Sens ← i
End.
```

ALGORITHM 4: Simplified Lesk algorithm.

that determines the importance of the second member of $C(m)$ ($k = 0{,}5$); $\text{Max}_{x \in \text{uc}} n_{\text{cu}}(x)$ is the maximal number of occurrences of word m in CU.

3.2.3. Okapi Measure. Consider

$$O(m) = W_O(m, \text{CU}(t)) = \log\left[\frac{(N - n(m) + 0{,}5)}{n(m) + 0.5}\right] \\ \times \left[\frac{n_c(m)}{(n_{\text{cu}}(m) + (T(\text{cu})/T_m(B)))}\right], \quad (4)$$

where $W_O(m, \text{CU}(t))$ is the weight attributed to m in CU of t by the Okapi measure; $T_m(B)$ is the average of the collected use contexts lengths. This will enable us to increase the probability of finding the nearest context to the original sentence containing the ambiguous word.

3.2.4. The Simplified Lesk Algorithm.
The Lesk algorithm, introduced in 1986, was derived and used in several studies of Pedersen and Bruce [21] and Sidorov and Gelbukh [22], and so forth. We can also cite the work of Vasilescu et al. [23] that evaluates variants of the Lesk approach for disambiguating words on the Senseval-2 English all words. This evaluation measures a 58% precision, using the simplified Lesk algorithm [24], and only a 42% under the original algorithm. The algorithm of Lesk is used to find the gloss that matches more with the candidate glosses of the words contained in the same sentence including the word to be disambiguated. This algorithm presented some limits (cited in paragraph 4.3) to generate the correct sense. Since that, we test a modified version of the Lesk algorithm using five measures of similarities. These measures will be applied to find the similarity between each sense of the ambiguous word proposed in AWN and the senses of the other words contained in the same sentence.

We adapted simplified Lesk algorithm [24] that adapts the Lesk algorithm [10] to calculate the number of words that appear in the current context of ambiguous word and the different contexts of use, which was considered as semantically closer to the results of methods used previously.

The input of the algorithm is the word t and $S = (s_1, \ldots, s_N)$ are the candidate senses corresponding to the different contexts of use achieved by applying methods of information retrieval. The output is the index of s in the sense candidates. Algorithm 4 below details the simplified Lesk algotithm.

The choice of the description and context varies for each word tested by this algorithm.

The function context (t) is obtained by the application of the input context. The function description (si) finds all the candidate senses obtained by the information retrieval methods. The function score returns the index of the candidate sense: score (D, w) = Score (description (s), w).

The application of this algorithm allowed us to obtain a rate of disambiguation up to 76%.

4. Experimental Results

To check the validity of the algorithm presented in the previous section, tests were conducted using some free tools. The English works were evaluated using Senseval-1 or Senseval-2. However in our work we have to make our experimental data using a totally different set of resources. To measure the rate of disambiguation, we use the most common evaluation techniques, which select a small sample of words and compare the results of the system with a human judge. We use the metric of the precision P (see (5)), recall R (see (6)), and finally the balanced F-score which determines the weighted harmonic mean of precision and recall (see (7)):

$$P = \frac{\text{correct answers provided}}{\text{answers provided}}, \quad (5)$$

$$R = \frac{\text{correct answers provided}}{\text{total answers provided}}, \quad (6)$$

$$F\text{-score} = \frac{2(P \times R)}{(P + R)}. \quad (7)$$

After that, as an upper bound, we use the context of use that corresponds to the most frequent sense (MFS).

TABLE 2: Description of the used dictionary.

Number of letters	Number of pages	Average number of glosses per word
29	1407	12 glosses/words

TABLE 3: Characteristics of the collected corpus.

Measure	Value
Total size of the corpus	1500 texts
Number of ambiguous words	50 words
Average number of synonyms of each ambiguous word	4
Average number of the possible senses	12
Average size of each context of use	970 words, 130 sentences
Average size of the text	500 words

4.1. Used Tools and Experimental Data

4.1.1. Dictionary. We use the dictionary of "Al-Mu'jam Al-Wasit" that contains the Arabic lexicography. Therefore, we construct a database that contains the words of an electronic version of this dictionary and their glosses. Table 2 below describes the characteristics of the dictionary.

We give in what follows a sample of glosses for the word "عين" "ayn" given by the dictionary Al-Wasit.

First gloss

عضو الإبصار للإنسان وغيره من الحيوان

Transcription

Organ vision of man and other animals.

Second gloss

يَنْبُوعُ الماء يَنْبُعُ من الأرض ويجري

Transcription

Fountain water flows from the land being.

In this work we choose to work on fine-grained senses. This choice makes our work more difficult and complex because it increases the number of the considered senses.

4.1.2. Corpus. We chose to work on texts dealing with multiple domains (sport, politics, religion, science, etc.). These texts are extracted from newspaper articles, which were recorded in the corpus of Al-Sulaiti and Atwell [25]. Table 3 below describes the characteristics of the collected corpus.

These documents have the advantage of possessing an explicit structure that facilitates their presentation and their exploitation in different contexts to find relevant words more efficiently.

4.1.3. Stopwords. We have compiled a list of stop words which have no influence on the meaning of the sentence. This list contains 20000 empty words or stop words. To build this list, we collected from the net pronouns, noun, names, letters, noun-verb, and some words considered insignificant by humans.

TABLE 4: Results obtained by different measures after and before pretreatment.

Method	Without rooting	Without string-matching	Final rate	MFS
P	0.52	0.61	0.78	0.86
R	0.39	0.52	0.65	0.74
F-score	0.44	0.56	0.71	0.84

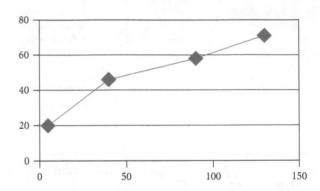

FIGURE 2: The *F*-Score obtained by varying the size of the context of use.

4.1.4. Experimental Data. Fifty words have been chosen. For each one of these ambiguous words, we evaluate 20 examples per sense. This number may be judged as not enough due to the problems encountered during the experimentation cited in what follows.

(i) The important number of glosses given by a dictionary for the ambiguous word.

(ii) The problem of the sentence segmentation due to the ambiguity of the Arabic language [1].

(iii) Finding the samples for the tests that can be judged as well as not so different for the process of disambiguation.

4.2. Obtained Results

4.2.1. Influence of the Stemming and String-Matching. We measure the performance of our system using the metrics presented above, with and without the respective use of the stemming algorithm and the string-matching algorithm (see Table 4).

Table 4 shows that the combination of the stemming algorithm with the string-matching algorithm gives the best results.

4.2.2. Influence of the Size of the Use Contexts. To determine the size of the collected context of use for each sense, we evaluate the results given by our system varying the size of that context of use (50 words, 100 words, and 150 words).

Figure 2 shows how the performance varies across the size of the context of use. We conclude that the lowest rate of disambiguation is mainly due to the insufficient number of contexts of use, which results in the failure to meet all

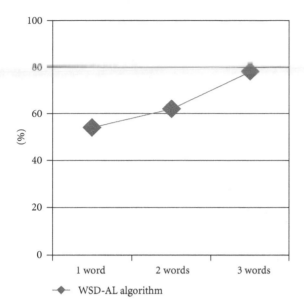

FIGURE 3: Results obtained for different window sizes.

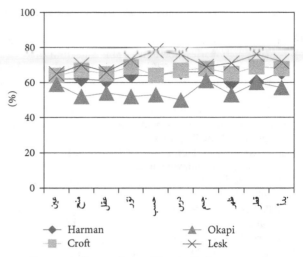

FIGURE 4: Comparison of the similarity measures.

possible events. For that we try to collect as many texts as we can, to extend the size of the knowledge database.

4.2.3. Influence of the Window Size. In the work of Yarowsky [26], a study of the influence of the window size on WSD shows that the most useful keywords for the WSD are included in a micro-context from six to eight words. However, we have to point out that in a so large context, it is difficult to discern the key elements for determining the meaning of a word. It seems obvious that a fixed size of the context window is not adapted for all the words. In order to solve this problem, we suggest determining the optimal size of the appropriate context for each test. We use a window size of 3 words (three words on the left and three words on the right of the ambiguous word), 2 words and one word. Figure 3 below shows as a final result of the experience the fact that the best rate of precision (P) and recall (R) is obtained for the word عين (ayn), especially by using a window size of three words.

The best similarity measure is obtained using a window size of three words. The Croft measure was the best one between those proposed.

4.2.4. Comparison of the Similarity Measures. Figure 4 presents a comparison between the results given by the Lesk algorithm and those given by the Croft, Harman, and Okapi measures. These results are shown for ten of the fifty words evaluated. This figure shows that the Lesk algorithm ameliorates the rate of disambiguation.

5. Conclusion

This paper has presented an unsupervised method to perform word sense disambiguation in Arabic. This algorithm is based on segmentation elimination of stop words, stemming

and applying the approximate string matching algorithm for the words of the glosses. We measure the similarity between the contexts of use corresponding to the glosses of the word to be disambiguated and the original sentence. This algorithm will affiliate a score for the most relevant sense of the ambiguous word. For a sample of fifty ambiguous Arabic words that are chosen by their number of senses out of context (the most ambiguous words), the proposed algorithm achieved a precision of 78% and recall of 65%.

We propose that in future works, we ameliorate the correspondence between words and their glosses to build a system based on rules to disambiguate Arabic words.

References

[1] A. Zouaghi, M. Zrigui, and G. Antoniadis, "Automatic understanding of Spontaneous arabic speech—a numerical model," *TAL*, vol. 49, no. 1, pp. 141–166, 2008.

[2] M. Belgacem, A. Zouaghi, M. Zrigui, and G. Antoniadis, *Amelioration of the Performance of a Semantic Analyzer for the Comprehension of the Spontaneous Arabic Speech*, Applied Imagery Pattern Recognition, Washington, DC, USA, 2009.

[3] A. Zouaghi, L. Merhbene, and M. Zrigui, "A hybrid approach for arabic word sense disambiguation," *IJCPOL*. In press.

[4] H. Al-Serhan, G. Kanaan, and R. Al-Shalabi, "New approach for extracting Arabic roots," in *Proceedings of the Arab conference on Information Technology (ACIT'2003)*, pp. 42–59, Alexandria, Egypt, 2003.

[5] T. H. Cormen, C. E. Leiserson, and R. L. Rivest, *Introduction to Algorithms*, chapter 34, MIT Press, Cambridge, Mass, USA, 1990.

[6] D. Harman, "An experimental study of factors important in document ranking," in *Proceedings of the 9th Annual International ACM SIGIR Conference on Research and Development in Information Retrieval*, pp. 186–193, 1986.

[7] W. Croft, "Experiments with representation in a document retrieval system," *Research and Develpment*, vol. 2, no. 1, pp. 1–21, 1983.

[8] S. Robertson, M. Walker, and M. Gatford, Okapi at TREC-3, TREC-3, NIST Special Publication, 1994.

[9] A. Zouaghi, L. Merhbene, and M. Zrigui, "Combination of information retrievalmethods with LESK algorithm for arabic

nse   disambiguation," *Artificial Intelligence Review*, vol. 38, no. 4, pp. 257–269, 2012.

[10] M. Lesk, "Automatic sense disambiguation using machine readable dictionaries: how to tell a pine cone from an ice cream cone," in *Proceedings of the 5th Annual International Conference on Systems Documentation (SIGDOC'86)*, pp. 24–26, 1986.

[11] S. Banerjee and T. Pedersen, *Adapting the lesk algorithm for word sense disambiguation to WordNet [M.S. thesis]*, Partial Fulfillment of the Requirements, 2002.

[12] S. Derwester, S. T. Dumais, G. W. Furnas, T. K. Landauer, and R. Harshmann, "Indexing by latent semantic analysis," *Journal of the American Society for Informartion Science*, vol. 41, pp. 391–407, 1990.

[13] T. Pedersen and R. Bruce, "Distinguishing word senses in untagged text," in *Proceedings of the 2nd Conference on Empirical Methods in Natural Language Processing*, 1997.

[14] E. Agirre and P. Edmond, *Word Sense Disambiguation: Algorithms and Applications*, Springer, New York, NY, USA, 2006.

[15] M. Diab and P. Resnik, "An unsupervised method for word sense tagging using parallel corpora," in *Proceedings of the 40th Annual Meeting on Association for Computational Linguistics (ACL'02)*, pp. 255–262, Association for Computational Linguistics, Philadelphia, Pa, USA, 2002.

[16] S. Elmougy, H. Taher, and H. Noaman, "Naïve bayes classifier for arabic word sense disambiguation," in *Proceedings of the Neuro-Linguistic Programming (NLP)*, 2008.

[17] A. Zouaghi, L. Merhbene, and M. Zrigui, "Word sense disambiguation for arabic language using the variants of the lesk algorithm," in *Proceedings of the International Conference on Artificial Intelligence (ICAI'11)*, vol. 2, pp. 561–567, 2011.

[18] L. Merhbene, A. Zouaghi, and M. Zrigui, "Ambiguous Arabic words disambiguation," in *Proceedings of the 11th ACIS International Conference on Software Engineering, Artificial Intelligence, Networking and Parallel/Distributed Computing (SNPD'10)*, pp. 157–164, London, UK, June 2010.

[19] L. Merhbene, A. Zouaghi, and M. Zrigui, "Arabic word sense disambiguation," in *Proceedings of the 2nd International Conference on Agents and Artificial Intelligence (ICAART'10)*, pp. 652–655, January 2010.

[20] M. Elloumi, "Comparison of strings belonging to the same family," *Information Sciences*, vol. 111, no. 1–4, pp. 49–63, 1998.

[21] T. Pedersen and R. Bruce, "Distinguishing word senses in untagged text," in *Proceedings of the 2nd Conference on Empirical Methods in Natural Language Processing*, 1997.

[22] G. Sidorov and A. Gelbukh, "Word sense disambiguation in a spanish explanatory dictionary," in *Proceedings of the Tratamiento Automático de Lengauje Natural (TALN'01)*, pp. 398–402, Tours, France, 2001.

[23] F. Vasilescu, P. Langlais, and J. Lapalme, "Evaluating variants of the lesk approach for disambiguating words," in *Proceedings of the Language Resources and Evaluation*, pp. 633–636, Lisbon, Portugal, 2004.

[24] F. Vasilescu, *Monolingual corpus disambiguation by the approaches of lesk [M.S. thesis]*, University of Montreal, Faculty of Arts and Sciences, Faculty of Graduate Studies, 2003.

[25] L. Al-Sulaiti and E. Atwell, "The design of a corpus of contemporary arabic," *International Journal of Corpus Linguistics*, vol. 11, no. 2, pp. 135–171, 2006.

[26] D. Yarowsky, "One sense per collocation," in *Proceedings of the ARPA Workshop on Human Language Technology*, pp. 266–267, Princeton, NJ, USA, 1993.

14

Soccer Ball Detection by Comparing Different Feature Extraction Methodologies

Pier Luigi Mazzeo, Marco Leo, Paolo Spagnolo, and Massimiliano Nitti

Istituto di Studi sui Sistemi Intelligenti per l'Automazione, CNR, Via G. Amendola 122/D, 70126 Bari, Italy

Correspondence should be addressed to Pier Luigi Mazzeo, mazzeo@ba.issia.cnr.it

Academic Editor: Djamel Bouchaffra

This paper presents a comparison of different feature extraction methods for automatically recognizing soccer ball patterns through a probabilistic analysis. It contributes to investigate different well-known feature extraction approaches applied in a soccer environment, in order to measure robustness accuracy and detection performances. This work, evaluating different methodologies, permits to select the one which achieves best performances in terms of detection rate and CPU processing time. The effectiveness of the different methodologies is demonstrated by a huge number of experiments on real ball examples under challenging conditions.

1. Introduction

Automatic sport video analysis has become one of the most attractive research fields in the areas of computer vision and multimedia technologies [1]. This has led to opportunities to develop applications dealing with the analysis of different sports such as tennis, golf, American football, baseball, basketball, and hockey. However, due to its worldwide viewership and tremendous commercial value, there has been an explosive growth in the research area of soccer video analysis [2, 3] and a wide spectrum of possible applications have been considered [4–6]. Some applications (automatic highlight identification, video annotation and browsing, content-based video compression, automatic summarization of play, customized advertisement insertion) require only the extraction of low-level visual features (dominant color, camera motion, image texture, playing field line orientation, change of camera view, text recognition) and for this reason they have reached some maturity [7, 8]. In other applications (such as verification of referee decision, tactics analysis, and player and team statistic evaluations), instead, more complex evaluations and high-level domain analysis are required. Unfortunately, the currently available methods have not yet reached a satisfactory accuracy level and then new solutions have to be investigated [9].

In particular, the detection and localization of the ball in each frame is an issue that still requires more investigation. The ball is invariably the focus of attention during the game, but, unfortunately, its automatic detection and localization in images is challenging as a great number of problems have to be managed: occlusions, shadowing, presence of very similar objects near the field lines and regions of player's bodies, appearance modifications (e.g., when the ball is inside the goal, it is faded by the net and it also experiences a significant amount of deformation during collisions), and unpredictable motion (e.g., when the ball is shot by players).

In the last decade, different approaches have been proposed to face the ball detection problem in soccer images. The most successful approaches in literature consist of two separate processing phases: the first one aims at selecting, in each image, the regions which most probably contain the ball (*ball candidates extraction*). These candidates regions are then deeply analyzed in order to recognize which of them really contains the ball (*ball candidate validation*).

Candidate ball extraction can be performed using global information as size, color, and shape or a combination of them. In particular, the circular Hough transform (CHT) and several modified versions have long been recognized as robust techniques for curve detection and have been largely applied by the scientific community for candidate ball detection purposes [10].

The choice of the best methodology for the validation of ball candidates is more controversial. In [11], a candidate verification procedure based on Kalman filter is presented. In [12], size, color, velocity, and longevity features are used to discriminate the ball from other objects. These approaches experience difficulties in ball candidate validation when many moving entities are simultaneously in the scene (the ball is not isolated) or when the ball abruptly changes its trajectory (e.g., in the case of rebounds or shots). To overcome this drawback, other approaches focus on ball pattern extraction and recognition: for example, in [13], the wavelet coefficients are proposed to discriminate between ball candidates and nonball candidates. More recently, the possibility to use scale-invariant feature transform (SIFT) to encode local information of the ball and to match it between ball instances has been also explored [14].

This paper presents a comparison of different feature extraction approaches in order to recognize soccer ball patterns. This kind of detecting problem is related to the flat object recognition problem from 2D intensity images that has been largely studied by the scientific community. The comparison is carried out by using a framework in which candidate ball regions are extracted by a directional circular Hough transform (CHT), then the image patterns are preprocessed by one of the comparing approaches and finally a probabilistic classifier is used to label each pattern as ball or no-ball. In particular, wavelet transform (WT), principal component analysis (PCA), scale-invariant feature transform (SIFT), and Histogram have been applied to the patterns in order to get a more suitable representation, possibly making use of a reduced number of coefficients. These techniques have been compared in order to choose the best one for our application domain. The technique producing the highest detection rate combined with the lowest CPU processing time has been then used in the final ball detection system.

The considered approaches were tested on a huge number of real ball images acquired in presence of translation, scaling, rotation, illumination changes, local geometric distortion, clutter, and partial and heavy occlusion.

In the rest of the paper, Section 2 gives system overview whereas Sections 3 and 4 detail its fundamental steps. Section 5 presents the setup used for the experiments, while in Section 6, the experimental results, a comparison with implemented approaches, and an extensive discussion are presented. Finally, in Section 7, conclusions are drawn.

2. Ball Detection System Overview

As introduced in Section 1 we have implemented a vision system which automatically detects the ball in an acquired soccer video sequence. The proposed system is composed of three main blocks: in the first one, a background subtraction technique is combined with a circle detection approach to extract ball candidate regions. Then a feature extraction scheme is used to represent image patterns, and finally data classification is performed by using a supervised learning scheme. Figure 1 schematizes the proposed approach,

whereas, in the following sections, a detailed description of the involved algorithmic procedures is given.

3. Candidate Ball Regions Detection

Ball candidates are identified in two phases: at first, all the moving regions are detected making use of a background subtraction algorithm.

The procedure consists of a number of steps. At the beginning of the image acquisition, a background model has to be generated and later continuously updated to include lighting variations in the model. Then, a background subtraction algorithm distinguishes moving points from static ones. Finally, a connected components analysis detects the blobs in the image.

The implemented algorithm uses the mean and standard deviation to give a statistical model of the background. Formally, for each frame, the algorithm evaluates

$$\overline{\mu^t(x,y)} = \alpha\mu^t(x,y) + (1-\alpha)\overline{\mu^{t-1}(x,y)}, \qquad (1)$$

$$\overline{\sigma^t(x,y)} = \alpha\left|\mu^t(x,y) - \overline{\mu^t(x,y)}\right| + (1-\alpha)\overline{\sigma^{t-1}(x,y)}. \qquad (2)$$

It should be noted that (2) is not the correct statistical evaluation of standard deviation, but it represents a good approximation of it, allowing a simpler and faster incremental algorithm which works in real time. The background model described above is the starting point of the motion detection step. The current image is compared to the reference model, and points that differ from the model by at least two times the correspondent standard deviation are marked. Formally, the resulting motion image can be described as

$$M(x,y) = \begin{cases} 1 & \text{if } \left|I(x,y) - \overline{\mu^t(x,y)}\right| > 2 \cdot \overline{\sigma^t(x,y)} \\ 0 & \text{otherwise,} \end{cases} \qquad (3)$$

where $M(x,y)$ is the binary output of the subtraction procedure. An updating procedure is necessary to have a consistent reference image at each frame a requirement of all motion detection approaches based on background. The particular context of application imposed some constraints. First of all, it is necessary to quickly adapt the model to the variations of light conditions, which can rapidly and significantly modify the reference image, especially in cases of natural illumination. In addition, it is necessary to avoid including in the background model players who remain in the same position for a certain period of time (goalkeepers are a particular problem for goal detection as they can remain relatively still when play is elsewhere on the pitch). To obtain these two opposite requirements, we have chosen to use two different values for α in the updating equations (1) and (2). The binary mask $M(x,y)$ allows us to switch between these two values and permits us to quickly update static points ($M(x,y) = 0$) and to slowly update moving ones ($M(x,y) = 1$). Let α_S and α_D be the two updating values for static and dynamic points, respectively,

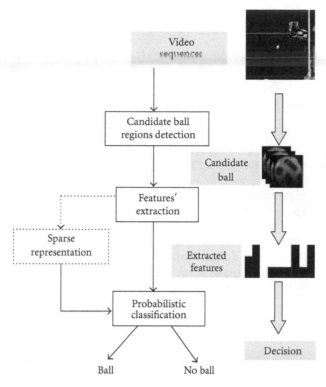

FIGURE 1: Graphical overview of the proposed approach.

$$\alpha(x, y) = \begin{cases} \alpha_S & \text{if} \quad M(x, y) = 1 \\ \alpha_D & \text{otherwise.} \end{cases} \quad (4)$$

In our experiments, we used $\alpha_S = 0.02$ and $\alpha_D = 0.5$. The choice of a small value for α_S is owed to the consideration that very sudden changes in light conditions can produce artifacts in the binary mask: in such cases, these artifacts will be slowly absorbed into the background, while they would remain permanent if we had used $\alpha_S = 0$.

The binary image of moving points, the output of the background subtraction phase, is the input of the following circle detection algorithm.

3.1. Circle Detection. The circle hough transform (CHT) aims to find circular patterns of a given radius R within an image. Each edge point contributes a circle of radius R to an output accumulator space. The peak in the output accumulator space is detected where these contributed circles overlap at the center of the original circle. In order to reduce the computational burden and the number of false positives typical of the CHT, a number of modifications have been widely implemented in the last decade. The use of edge orientation information limits the possible positions of the center for each edge point. In this way, only an arc perpendicular to the edge orientation at a distance R from the edge point needs to be plotted. The CHT and also its modifications can be formulated as convolutions applied to an edge magnitude image (after a suitable edge detection) [13]. We have defined a circle detection operator that is applied over all the image pixels and produces a maximal

value when a circle is detected with a radius in the range $[R_{\min}, R_{\max}]$:

$$u(x, y) = \frac{\iint_{D(x,y)} \vec{e}(\alpha, \beta) \cdot \vec{O}(\alpha - x, \beta - y) \, d\alpha \, d\beta}{2\pi(R_{\max} - R_{\min})}, \quad (5)$$

where the domain $D(x,y)$ is defined as

$$D(x, y) = \left\{ (\alpha, \beta) \in \mathfrak{R}^2 \mid R_{\min}^2 \leq (\alpha - x)^2 + (\beta - y)^2 \leq R_{\max}^2 \right\}, \quad (6)$$

$\vec{e}$ is the normalized gradient vector:

$$\vec{e}(x, y) = \left[\frac{E_x(x, y)}{|E|}, \frac{E_y(x, y)}{|E|} \right]^T, \quad (7)$$

and $\vec{O}$ is the kernel vector

$$\vec{O}(x, y) = \left[\frac{\cos(\tan^{-1}(y/x))}{\sqrt{x^2 + y^2}}, \frac{\sin(\tan^{-1}(y/x))}{\sqrt{x^2 + y^2}} \right]^T. \quad (8)$$

The use of the normalized gradient vector in (9) is necessary in order to have an operator whose results are independent from the intensity of the gradient in each point: we want to be sure that the circle detected in the image is the most complete in terms of contours and not the most contrasted in the image. Indeed it could be possible that a circle that is not well contrasted in the image gives a convolution result lower than another object that is not exactly circular but has a greater gradient. The kernel vector contains a normalization factor (the division by the distance of each point from the center of the kernel) which is fundamental for ensuring we have the same values in the accumulation space when circles with different radii in the admissible range are found. Moreover, the normalization ensures that the peak in the convolution result is obtained for the most complete circle and not for the greatest in the annulus. As a last consideration, in (5), the division by $(2\Pi \cdot (R_{\max} - R_{\min}))$ guarantees the final result of our operator in the range $[-1, 1]$ regardless of the radius value considered in the procedure. The masks implementing the kernel vector have a dimension of $(2 \cdot R_{\max} + 1) \times (2 \cdot R_{\max} + 1)$, and they represent in each point the direction of the radial vector scaled by the distance from the center. The convolution between the gradient versor images and these masks evaluates how many points in the image have the gradient direction concordant with the gradient direction of a range of circles. Then, the peak in the accumulator array gives the candidate center of the circle in the image.

4. Feature Extraction Methodologies

In this step, the selected subimages are processed by different feature extraction methodologies in order to represent them only by coefficients containing the most discriminant information. A secondary aim is also to characterize the images with a small number of features in order to gain in computational time. Object recognition by using a learning-from-examples technique is in fact related to computational issues. In order to achieve real-time performances, the computational time to classify patterns should be small. The main parameter connected to high computational complexity is certainly the input space dimension. A reduction of the input size is the first step to successfully speed up the classification process. This requirement can be satisfied by using a feature extraction algorithm able to store all the important information about input patterns in a small set of coefficients.

Wavelet transform (WT), principal component analysis (PCA), scale-invariant feature transform (SIFT), and histogram representation (HR) are different approaches allowing to reduce the dimension of the input space, because they capture the significant variations of input patterns in a smaller number of coefficients. In the following four subsections, we briefly review WT, PCA, SIFT, and HR approaches.

4.1. Wavelet Transform. The WT is an extension of the Fourier transform that contains both frequency and spatial information [15]. The WT operator $F : L^2(\mathfrak{R}) \rightarrow L^2(\mathfrak{R})$ can be defined as follows:

$$F(f(s)) = \hat{f}(s) = \int_{-\infty}^{+\infty} f(u)\Psi_{s,t}(u)du \qquad (9)$$

with

$$\Psi_{s,t}(u) = \frac{1}{|s|^p}\Psi\left(\frac{u-t}{s}\right), \qquad (10)$$

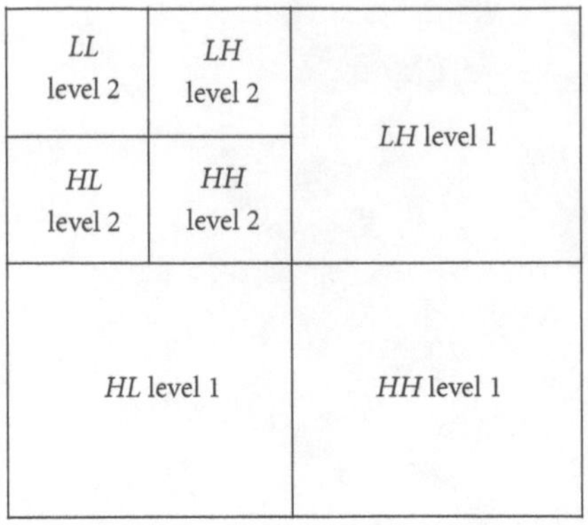

LL level 2	LH level 2	LH level 1
HL level 2	HH level 2	
HL level 1		HH level 1

FIGURE 2: The decomposition of the image with a 2-level wavelet transform.

when s changes, the frequencies which the function Ψ operates are changed, and when t changes, the function Ψ is moved on all the support of the function f. In this paper, we have used a discrete wavelet transform supplying a hierarchical representation of the image implemented with the iterative application of two filters: a low-pass filter (approximation filter) and its complementary one in frequency (detail filter). A bidimensional WT breaks an image down into four subsampled or decimated images. In Figure 2, the final result of a 2-level WT is shown. In each subimage, the capital letters refer to the filters applied on the image of the previous level: H stands for a high-pass filter, and L stands for a low-pass filter. The first letter is the filter that has been applied in the horizontal direction, while the second letter is the filter that has been applied in the vertical direction. The bands LL is a coarser approximation of the original image. The band LH and HL record the changes of the image along horizontal and vertical directions. The band HH shows the high-frequency components of the image. Decomposition is iterated on the LL subband that contains the low-frequency information of the previous stage. For example, after applying a 2-level WT, an image is subdivided into subbands of different frequency components (Figure 3). Numerous filters can be used to implement WT: we have chosen Haar and Daubechies filters for their simplicity and orthogonality.

4.2. Principal Component Analysis (PCA). Principal component analysis (PCA) provides an efficient method to reduce the number of features to work with [16]. It transforms the original set of (possibly) correlated features into a small set of uncorrelated ones. In particular, PCA determines an orthogonal basis for a set of images involving an eigenanalysis of their covariance matrix. Such a basis is given by the eigenvectors (principal components) of that matrix. They are obtained by solving the following eigenvalue problem:

$$Su = \lambda u, \qquad (11)$$

where S is the covariance matrix of the original set of images, u is the vector of eigenvectors, and λ is the vector of eigenvalues. We have used the SVD technique to

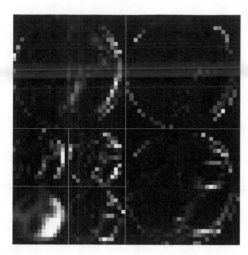

FIGURE 3: The 2-level wavelet transform on a subimage containing the soccer ball.

solve eigenstructure decomposition problem. The covariance matrix has been evaluated on the entire set of training images. The new set of uncorrelated features is obtained projecting the images (old features) into that basis both in the training and in the testing phases. Many algorithms for PCA return u and λ ranked from highest to lowest. The first eigenvectors capture the largest variability of images, and each succeeding one accounts for the remaining variability. Therefore, the new set of uncorrelated features is obtained as a linear combination of the old ones considering that the first eigenvectors contain the highest information level. The significant variations in images are captured by few vectors (less dimensionality) with respect to the input space.

4.3. Scale-Invariant Feature Transform (SIFT). The scale-invariant feature transform is a method for extracting distinctive invariant features from the images that can be used to perform reliable matching between different views of an object or a scene [17]. The features are invariant to image scale and rotation, and they provide robust matching across a substantial range of affine distortion, change in 3D viewpoint, addition of noise, and change in illumination. The features are highly distinctive, in the sense that a single feature can be correctly matched with high probability against a large database of features from many different images. The algorithm consists of four main steps:

(1) scale-space extrema detection;

(2) keypoints localization;

(3) orientation assignment;

(4) keypoint description.

The first stage identifies locations and scales that can be assigned under differing views of the same object. Detecting locations that are invariant to scale change of the image can be accomplished by searching for stable features across all possible scales, using a continuous function of scale known as a scale space. Under a variety of reasonable assumptions,

the only possible scale-space kernel is the Gaussian function. Therefore, the scale space of an image is defined as a function $L(x, y, \sigma)$, that is produced from the convolution of a variable-scale Gaussian, $G(x, y, \sigma)$, with an input image, $I(x, y)$, that is,

$$L(x, y, \sigma) = G(x, y, \sigma) * I(x, y), \qquad (12)$$

where $*$ is the convolution operator and $G(x, y, \sigma)$ is defined as

$$G(x, y, \sigma) = \frac{1}{2\pi\sigma^2} e^{-(x^2+y^2)/2\sigma^2}. \qquad (13)$$

The keypoints are detected using scale-space extrema in the difference of Gaussian (DoG) function D convolved with the image $I(x, y)$:

$$\begin{aligned} D(x, y, \sigma) &= [G(x, y, k\sigma) - G(x, y, \sigma)] * I(x, y) \\ &= L(x, y, k\sigma) - L(x, y, \sigma), \end{aligned} \qquad (14)$$

where k is the multiplicative constant factor which separates two nearby scales. In order to detect the local maxima and minima of $D(x, y, \sigma)$, each sample point is compared to its eight neighbors in the current image and to its nine neighbors in the scale above and below. It is selected only if it is larger than all of these neighbors or smaller than all of them. Once a keypoint candidate has been found by comparing a pixel to its neighbors, the next step is to perform a detailed fit to the nearby data for location, scale, and ratio of principal curvatures. This information allows points to be rejected if they have low contrast (and are therefore sensitive to noise) or are poorly localized along an edge. A 3D quadratic function is fitted to the local sample points. The approach starts with the Taylor expansion (up to the quadratic terms) with sample point as the origin

$$D(X) = D + \frac{\partial D^T}{\partial X} X + \frac{1}{2} X^T \frac{\partial^2 D}{\partial X^2} X, \qquad (15)$$

where D and its derivatives are evaluated a the sample point $X = (x, y, \sigma)^T$. The location of the extremum is obtained taking the derivative with respect to X and setting it to 0, giving

$$\hat{X} = -\frac{\partial^2 D^{-1}}{\partial X^2} \frac{\partial D}{\partial X}, \qquad (16)$$

that is, a 3×3 linear system easily solvable. The function value a the extremum

$$D(\hat{X}) = D + \frac{1}{2} \frac{\partial D^T}{\partial X} \hat{X} \qquad (17)$$

is useful for rejecting unstable extrema with low contrast. A this point, the algorithm rejects also keypoints with poorly defined peaks, that is, those points having, in the difference of Gaussian function, a large principal curvature across the edge but a small one in the perpendicular direction. By assigning a consistent orientation, based on local image properties, the keypoint descriptor can be represented relative to this orientation and therefore achieve invariance to image rotation.

After the localization of the interest points in the candidate ball images, the region around each of them has to be accurately described in order to encode local information in a representation that can assure robustness for matching purposes. A consistent orientation is firstly assigned to each detected point: in this way, further information representation can be done relative to this orientation achieving invariance to image rotation that is fundamental to getting an effective representation especially when ball images are handled.

Instead of directly using pixel differences, the orientation is associated to each point after computing a corresponding edge map in the surrounding circular area with radii R. The edge map E is computed as suggested in [18]. Then, for each edge point $E(x, y)$, corresponding magnitude and theta values are computed:

$$G_x(x, y) = \sum_{i=-1}^{1} I(x + i, y + 1)$$
$$- \sum_{i=-1}^{1} I(x + i, y - 1) + I(x, y + 1) - I(x, y - 1),$$
$$G_y(x, y) = \sum_{i=-1}^{1} I(x + 1, y + i)$$
$$- \sum_{i=-1}^{1} I(x - 1, y - i) + I(x + 1, y) - I(x - 1, y),$$
$$\theta(x, y) = \tan^{-1}\left(\frac{G_y(x, y)}{G_x(x, y)}\right).$$

$$(18)$$

A 36-bin orientation histogram is then formed from the gradient orientation of sample points within a region of radii R around the interest point.

Peaks in the orientation histogram correspond to dominant directions of the local gradient. The highest peak in the histogram and any other local peak that is within 80% of the highest peak are then detected.

The previous operations have assigned an image location, scale, and orientation to each interest point. These parameters impose a repeatable local 2D coordinate system to describe the local image region and therefore provide invariance to these parameters. The next step is to compute a descriptor for the local image region that is highly distinctive and is as invariant as possible to remaining variations.

To do that, the first step is to smooth the image I to the appropriate level considering the associated radii R of the interest point.

Then, a descriptor is created by first computing the gradient magnitude and orientation at each image sample point in a region around the interest point location. These samples are then accumulated into orientation histograms summarizing the contents over 4×4 subregions. This results in a feature vector containing 128 elements.

Unfortunately the number of interest points can differ from a candidate ball image to another: this makes it very complex to compare two different images until an intermediate processing level is introduced.

Figure 4 shows some keypoints localized on two different ball images, and Figure 5 illustrates how two keypoints match among two ball images.

In this paper, the fixed-length feature vectors are obtained in this way: the descriptors of the regions around the detected interest points in a set of manually labeled ball images are, at first, quantized into visual words with the k-means algorithm. A candidate ball image is then represented by the frequency histogram of visual words obtained by assigning each descriptor of the image to the closest visual word. In Figure 6 is an example of how this processing pipeline works: starting from the ball image (Figure 6(a)), each region around any of the detected interest point is described by a descriptor having 128 elements, (Figure 6(b)). Then, the descriptor is associated to a cluster between the N clusters (code-book elements) built by vector quantization based on k-means algorithm. Finally, all the clusters associate to the descriptors in the same image are counted and a fixed-length feature vector V is associated to the resulting histogram representation, Figure 6(c).

4.4. Image Histogram. The distributions of colors or gray levels of images are commonly used in the image analysis and classification. The gray level distribution can be presented as a gray level histogram:

$$H(G) = \frac{n_G}{n} \quad G = 0, 1, \ldots, NG - 1, \quad (19)$$

where n_G is the number of pixels having gray level G, n is the total number of pixels, and NG is the total number of gray levels.

4.5. Probabilistic Classification. The following step in the proposed framework aims at introducing an automatic method to distinguish between ball and no-ball instances on the basis of the feature vector extracted by one of the previously mentioned preprocessing strategies. To accomplish this task, a probabilistic approach has been used. Probabilistic methods for pattern classification are very common in literature as reported by [19]. The so-called naive Bayesian classification is the optimal method of supervised learning if the values of the attributes of an example are independent given the class of the example. Although this assumption is almost always violated in practice, recent works have shown that naive Bayesian learning is remarkably effective in practice and difficult to improve upon systematically. On many real-world example datasets naive Bayesian learning gives better test set accuracy than any other known method [20]. In general, a Naïve Bayes classifier is also preferable for its computational efficiency.

Probabilistic approaches to classification typically involve modelling the conditional probability distribution $P(C \mid D)$, where C ranges over classes and D over descriptions, in some language, of objects to be classified. Given a description d

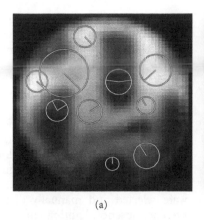
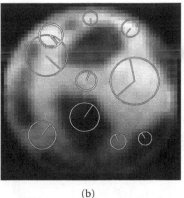

(a)   (b)

FIGURE 4: The keypoints localized on two different ball images.

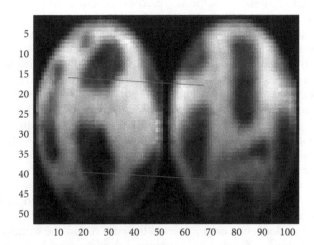

FIGURE 5: Two keypoints matching among two ball images.

of a particular object, the class $\text{argmax}_c\, P(C = c \mid D = d)$ is assigned. A Bayesian approach splits this posterior distribution into a prior distribution $P(C)$ and a likelihood $P(D \mid C)$:

$$\text{argmax}_c\, P(C = c \mid D = d)$$
$$= \text{argmax}_c\, \frac{(P(D = d \mid C = c)P(C = c))}{P(D = d)}. \tag{20}$$

The key term in (21) is $P(D = d \mid C = c)$, the likelihood of the given description given the class (often abbreviated to $P(d \mid c)$). A Bayesian classifier estimates these likelihoods from training data. If the assumption that all attributes are independent given the class:

$$P(A_1 = a_1, \ldots, A_n = a_n \mid C = c) = \prod_{i=1}^{n} P(A_i = a_i \mid C = c), \tag{21}$$

then a naive Bayesian classifier (often abbreviated to *naive Bayes*) is introduced. This means that a naive Bayes classifier ignores interactions between attributes within individuals of the same class.

Further details and discussions about the practical consequences of this assumption can be found in [21].

5. Experimental Setup

Experiments were carried out on image sequences acquired in a real soccer stadium by a Mikroton EOSens MC1362 CCD camera, equipped with a 135 mm focal length. The camera has the area around the goal in its field of view. Using this experimental setup, the whole image size was 1280x1024 pixels whereas the ball corresponded to a circular region with radii in the range ($R_{\text{MIN}} = 24, R_{\text{MAX}} = 28$) depending on the distance of the ball with respect to the optical center of the camera. The camera frame rate was 200 fps with an exposure time of 1 msec in order to avoid blurring effect in the case of high ball speed. A Nike T90 Strike Hi-Vis Soccer Ball (FIFA approved) was used during the experiments.

Images were continuously acquired in a sunny day from 1 PM (when the sun shined and the ball was bright) to 7 PM (just before sunset when the acquired images have become dark and a part of the ball was almost not visible in the scene): in this way, a wide range of different ball appearances was collected providing the possibility to verify the effectiveness of the proposed approach in very different lighting conditions.

During the data acquisition session, a number of shots on goal were performed: the shots differed in ball velocity and direction with respect to the goalmouth. In this way, differently scaled (depending on the distance between the ball and the camera), occluded (by the goal posts), and faded (by the net) ball appearances were experienced. Moreover, some shots hit a rigid wall placed on purpose inside the goal in order to acquire some instances of deformed ball and then to check the sensitiveness of the ball recognition system in the case of ball deformation.

During the acquisition session, about 4,5 million images were collected. Each image was processed to detect candidate ball regions by finding circular arrangement in the edge magnitude map: edge point contributes a circle to an output accumulator space, and the peak in the output accumulator

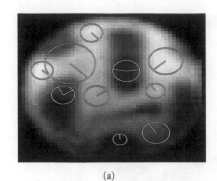

(a)

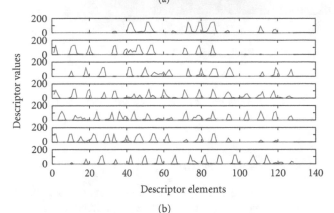

(b)

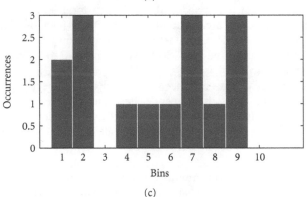

(c)

FIGURE 6: (a) Ball image and the detected interest points, (b) relative descriptors (128 elements in each) of the surrounding regions, and (c) the 10-bin histogram representing the ball image using a fixed-length vector.

space is detected where these contributed circles overlap at the center of the original circle.

The main benefits of this method are the low computational cost and the high detection rate when the ball is visible in the image. The main drawback lies in the impossibility of detecting occlusions and ball absence in the image. The circle detection algorithm determines in every situation the highest peaks in the accumulator space. Then, it is difficult to differentiate between images containing and not containing the ball.

In Figure 7(a), one image containing the ball is shown, whereas Figure 7(b) displays the corresponding Hough space (highest values are white, lowest ones are black). Figure 7(c) shows instead two candidate ball regions extracted in

correspondence with two peaks in the Hough accumulation space: the region on the left is relative to a ball, whereas the region on the right contains a nonball object.

For each image, a candidate ball region (of size $(2 * R\_MAX+1)x(2 * R\_MAX+1)$, i.e., 52×52) was then extracted around the position corresponding to the highest value in the accumulator space.

After that for each candidate ball region, all pixels outside the circular area with radii R_MAX were set to 0 in order to discard information certainly belonging to the background and not to the ball region (see Figure 7(c)).

After this preliminary step, 2574 candidate ball regions were selected and manually divided on the basis of ball presence/absence, lighting conditions, and ball appearance: these sets of images formed the experimental ground truth. The ground truth dataset contained ball acquired in both good lighting conditions (patches acquired from 1 pm to 5 pm) (see Figure 8(a)) and poor lighting conditions (patches acquired during the last 2 hours of acquisition) (see Figure 8(b)). The ground truth data contained a subset (**O**) of examples in which the ball was partially and heavily occluded. In particular, the ball was considered partially occluded if at least half of the ball surface is visible (see Figure 8(d)), otherwise it is heavily occluded (see Figure 8(e)) (contained in the subset (**O**)). In the acquired images, partially or heavily occluded balls occurred either while the ball crosses the goal mouth appearing behind the goal posts or when a person interposes himself/herself between the ball and the camera.

Other special cases in the dataset were the faded ball occurrences, that is, patches relative to balls positioned inside the goal when a net is inserted between it and the camera. Two kinds of faded balls occurred: undeformed ball (see Figure 8(c)) and deformed ball acquired while hitting the rigid wall placed inside the goal (see Figure 8(f)). Figure 8 shows some examples of the ball appearances observed during the experimental phase depending on their different aspects.

6. Experimental Results

The experimental section aims at evaluating the ball candidate validation performance in presence of different preprocessing techniques.

For the SIFT methodology, the codebook of visual words was built by quantizing (using k-means algorithm [22]) the 128 long feature vectors relative to the detected points of interest in 50 patches containing fully visible balls under good light conditions.

For all the preprocessing methodologies, the naive Bayes classifier was built by considering the 50 above-considered patches and 50 new patches (extracted at the beginning of the acquisition session then with good lighting conditions) which did not contain the ball.

The 100 resulting feature vector elements were finally fed into the naive Bayes classifier that estimated the conditional probability distribution to have a ball instance given a feature configuration. The experimental tests were then carried out

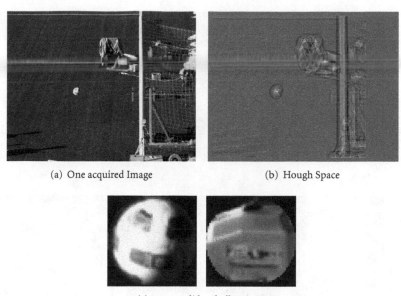

(a) One acquired Image   (b) Hough Space

(c) two candidate ball regions

FIGURE 7: (a) One acquired image, (b) the corresponding Hough space, and two candidate ball regions. The region on the left has been properly centered on the ball, whereas the one on the right is relative to a nonball object in the scene corresponding to a high value in the Hough accumulation space.

considering all the patches that were not used in the learning phase. These patches representations were supplied as input to the learned naive Bayes classifier that associates to each representation the probabilities $P(\text{Ball} \mid V)$ and $P(\text{NoBall} \mid V)$, that is the probabilities that the corresponding patch contained a ball or not. Finally, the patches in input were then classified on the basis of the $\operatorname{argmax}[P(\text{Ball} \mid V), P(\text{NoBall} \mid V)]$.

In Table 1, ball classification detection rates using SIFT and different number of clusters in the k-means algorithm, are shown.

Table 2 summarizes the ball recognition results obtained by comparing different feature extraction algorithms on the whole dataset. In the first column of Table 2 are itemized the used feature extraction algorithms, and in the second one are shown the number of coefficients extracted from the relative technique that are input of the probabilistic classifier. From the third to sixth columns are presented, respectively, the values of correct detection of the ball (TP: true positive), the values of the errors in the ball detection (FN: false negative), the values of correct detection of no ball (TN: true negative), and finally the values of errors in detection of ball in the candidate regions in which it does not exist (FP: false positive). In the last column of Table 2 the overall detection performance of each methodology is shown. For all of the compared feature extraction methodologies, we have used the same training set composed of 50 examples of fully visible balls and 50 examples which did not contain the ball. All the training patches are extracted at the beginning of the acquisition session, with good lighting conditions. Except for the SIFT algorithm that is detailed in the first part of this section, we have directly supplied, as input, the extracted coefficient,

in the learned probabilistic classifier. Table 2 gives very encouraging results: even if all training examples consisted only of patches extracted from images acquired under good light conditions, the tests demonstrated a good capability of quite all proposed approaches to rightly recognize the ball instance also under very different and challenging conditions (poor light condition, ball occluded or deformed). At the same time, no-ball patches were well classified, avoiding a huge number of false ball validations. Six patches extracted from the test set are reported in Figure 9: in the first row, three patches extracted in correspondence with no-ball objects in the scene (a bench, the net of the goal, and the head of a person); in the second row, three patches having similar appearance but containing the ball.

However, if Table 2 is deeply observed, it should be noted that the best performance, in terms of ball detection rate, is obtained by using wavelet decomposition (in particular Daubechies family slightly better than Haar family). The used approximation coefficients are obtained applying low-pass filter in both directions (vertical and horizontal) till the third level of decomposition. The worst method, in this application context, is the SIFT combined with the bag-of-words (BoW) representation.

However, SIFT-based approach outperforms the others in the classification of partially/heavy occluded ball instances or in case of very bad lighting conditions.

This is proved in Table 3 where the different preprocessing methodologies are compared on a test subset consisting of 116 examples (only partially/heavy occluded or poor lighted balls).

In this case, SIFT representation allowed the probabilistic classifier to obtain the best result in terms of detection rate.

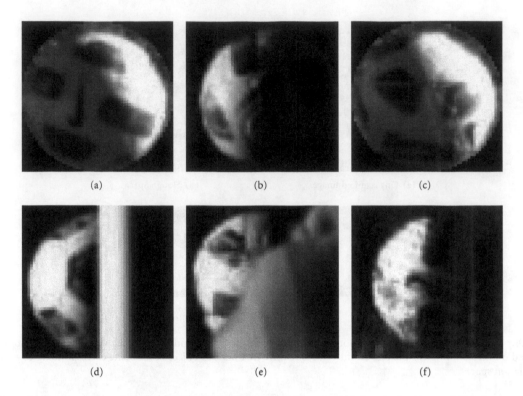

FIGURE 8: Different ball appearances observed during the experimental phase: (a) ball acquired with good lighting conditions; (b) ball acquired with poor lighting conditions; (c) ball faded by the net; (d) ball partially occluded by the goal post subset; (e) ball heavy occluded by a person in the scene; (f) ball deformed during impact.

TABLE 1: Ball classification performance using SIFT and different number of clusters in the k-means algorithm on whole dataset.

SIFT descriptors length	TP	FN	TN	FP	Detection rate (%)
10	579	658	988	249	63.33%
20	621	616	1059	178	67.90%
30	558	579	1056	181	65.23%
40	519	718	1091	146	65.07%

TABLE 2: Ball recognition results using different features on the whole dataset.

Ball features	Number of input	TP	FN	TN	FP	Detection rate (%)
Wavelet HAAR	64 (8 × 8)	1179	58	1028	209	89.20%
Wavelet DB3	121 (11 × 11)	1166	71	1060	177	89.97%
Histogram	256	1174	63	958	279	86.17%
SIFT (BoW)	20	621	616	1059	178	67.90%
PCA	30	999	238	890	347	76.35%

Also histogram representation gave satisfying results, whereas wavelet and PCA representation leaded to very inadequate classification rate.

This leads to a consideration: in a soccer match, the ball, in addition to be often occluded or faded, could be under different lighting conditions depending on the weather conditions or the position into the playing field and then it is better to choose a preprocessing technique that keeps the classifier under acceptable classification rate also when the testing patches differ from those used in the learning phase.

Moreover, computation aspects should be considered in choosing the appropriate preprocessing methodology: from this point of view, wavelet and SIFT methodologies take much more time than histogram calculation and PCA.

Summing up, the histogram extraction methodology is the most suited for the considered issue.

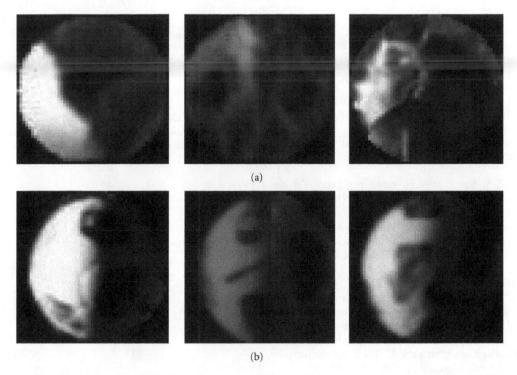

FIGURE 9: Some examples of ball (a) and no-ball (b) patches: many objects in the scene can appear, in particular conditions, very similar to the ball.

TABLE 3: Ball recognition results using different Features on the dataset (III) containing partially and heavily occluded balls.

Ball features	TP	FN	Detection rate (%)
Wavelet HAAR	66	50	66/116 (56.89%)
Wavelet DB3	52	64	52/116 (44.82%)
Histogram	76	40	76/116 (65.51%)
SIFT (BoW)	86	30	86/116 (74.13%)
PCA	40	76	40/116 (34.48%)

It allows the system to recognize the ball instances in real time with a good classification rate even under challenging conditions (occlusions, poor lighting conditions, etc.).

6.1. Computational Remarks. The proposed algorithm was run on personal computer with an Intel i3 CPU 3.20 GHz and 4 GB RAM, the available Microsoft Visual C++ 2005 implementation; it takes about 2 msec to detect the ball in each high-resolution input image (i.e., max 500 frames can be processed in each second). This is a very desirable result considering that visual technologies aimed at assisting the referee team in deciding if the ball really has crossed the goal line (the algorithm described in this work is part of that system) require the analysis of up to 500 frames per second, in order to cope with the high ball speed (that could reach 130 km/h).

7. Conclusions

This paper presented different approaches to recognize soccer ball patterns through a probabilistic analysis. It investigated the different feature extraction methodologies applied in ball soccer detection.

Experimental results on real ball examples under challenging conditions and a comparison with some of the more popular feature extraction algorithms from the literature demonstrated the suitability of the classical histogram approach in this application context in which real-time performances are a constraint.

Future works are addressed to study new algorithms which cope with occluded balls, taking into account overall ball detection performances and computational time constraints.

Moreover, even if some images have been acquired in rainy days, more intensive tests concerning effects of inclement weather (rain, snow, fog) on the algorithms will be performed.

Acknowledgments

The authors thank Liborio Capozzo and Arturo Argentieri for technical support in the setup of the devices used for data acquisition.

References

[1] M. H. Hung, C. H. Hsieh, C. M. Kuo, and J. S. Pan, "Generalized playfield segmentation of sport videos using color features," *Pattern Recognition Letters*, vol. 32, no. 7, pp. 987–1000, 2011.

[2] K. Choi and Y. Seo, "Automatic initialization for 3D soccer player tracking," *Pattern Recognition Letters*, vol. 32, no. 9, pp. 1274–1282, 2011.

[3] X. Gao, Z. Niu, D. Tao, and X. Li, "Non-goal scene analysis for soccer video," *Neurocomputing*, vol. 74, no. 4, pp. 540–548, 2011.

[4] A. Watve and S. Sural, "Soccer video processing for the detection of advertisement billboards," *Pattern Recognition Letters*, vol. 29, no. 7, pp. 994–1006, 2008.

[5] J. Liu, X. Tong, W. Li, T. Wang, Y. Zhang, and H. Wang, "Automatic player detection, labeling and tracking in broadcast soccer video," *Pattern Recognition Letters*, vol. 30, no. 2, pp. 103–113, 2009.

[6] M. Leo, N. Mosca, P. Spagnolo, P. L. Mazzeo, T. D'Orazio, and A. Distante, "A visual framework for interaction detection in soccer matches," *International Journal of Pattern Recognition and Artificial Intelligence*, vol. 24, no. 4, pp. 499–530, 2010.

[7] A. Ekin, A. M. Tekalp, and R. Mehrotra, "Automatic soccer video analysis and summarization," *IEEE Transactions on Image Processing*, vol. 12, no. 7, pp. 796–807, 2003.

[8] Z. Theodosiou, A. Kounoudes, N. Tsapatsoulis, and M. Milis, "MuLVAT: a video annotation tool based on XML-dictionaries and shot clustering," *Lecture Notes in Computer Science (ICANN)*, vol. 5769, no. 2, pp. 913–922, 2009.

[9] T. D'Orazio and M. Leo, "A review of vision-based systems for soccer video analysis," *Pattern Recognition*, vol. 43, no. 8, pp. 2911–2926, 2010.

[10] V. Pallavi, J. Mukherjee, A. K. Majumdar, and S. Sural, "Ball detection from broadcast soccer videos using static and dynamic features," *Journal of Visual Communication and Image Representation*, vol. 19, no. 7, pp. 426–436, 2008.

[11] X. Yu, H. W. Leong, C. Xu, and Q. Tian, "Trajectory-based ball detection and tracking in broadcast soccer video," *IEEE Transactions on Multimedia*, vol. 8, no. 6, pp. 1164–1178, 2006.

[12] J. Ren, J. Orwell, G. A. Jones, and M. Xu, "Tracking the soccer ball using multiple fixed cameras," *Computer Vision and Image Understanding*, vol. 113, no. 5, pp. 633–642, 2009.

[13] T. D'Orazio, C. Guaragnella, M. Leo, and A. Distante, "A new algorithm for ball recognition using circle Hough transform and neural classifier," *Pattern Recognition*, vol. 37, no. 3, pp. 393–408, 2004.

[14] M. Leo, T. D'Orazio, P. Spagnolo, P. L. Mazzeo, and A. Distante, "Sift based ball recognition in soccer images," in *Proceedings of the 3rd international conference on Image and Signal Processing (ICISP '08)*, pp. 263–272, 2008.

[15] S. Mallat, *A Wavelet Tour of Signal Processing*, AP Professional, London, UK, 1997.

[16] I. T. Jolliffe, *Principal Component Analysis*, Springer, New York, NY, USA, 2002.

[17] D. G. Lowe, "Distinctive image features from scale-invariant keypoints," *International Journal of Computer Vision*, vol. 60, no. 2, pp. 91–110, 2004.

[18] J. Canny, "A computational approach to edge detection," *IEEE Transactions on Pattern Analysis and Machine Intelligence*, vol. 8, no. 6, pp. 679–698, 1986.

[19] I. Tošić and P. Frossard, "Dictionary learning," *IEEE Signal Processing Magazine*, vol. 28, no. 2, pp. 27–38, 2011.

[20] F. Colas and P. Brazdil, "Comparison of SVM and some older classification algorithms in text classification tasks," *IFIP International Federation for Information Processing*, vol. 217, pp. 169–178, 2006.

[21] P. A. Flach and N. Lachiche, "Naive Bayesian classification of structured data," *Machine Learning*, vol. 57, no. 3, pp. 233–269, 2004.

[22] J. B. MacQueen, "Some methods for classification and analysis of multivariate observations," in *Proceedings of the 5th Berkeley Symposium on Mathematical Statistics and Probability*, vol. 1, pp. 281–297, 1967.

15

Predicting Asthma Outcome Using Partial Least Square Regression and Artificial Neural Networks

E. Chatzimichail,[1] **E. Paraskakis,**[2] **and A. Rigas**[1]

[1] *Department of Electrical and Computer Engineering, Democritus University of Thrace, 67100 Xanthi, Greece*
[2] *Department of Pediatrics, Democritus University of Thrace, 68100 Alexandroupolis, Greece*

Correspondence should be addressed to E. Chatzimichail; echatzim@ee.duth.gr

Academic Editor: Elpida Keravnou

The long-term solution to the asthma epidemic is believed to be prevention and not treatment of the established disease. Most cases of asthma begin during the first years of life; thus the early determination of which young children will have asthma later in their life counts as an important priority. Artificial neural networks (ANN) have been already utilized in medicine in order to improve the performance of the clinical decision-making tools. In this study, a new computational intelligence technique for the prediction of persistent asthma in children is presented. By employing partial least square regression, 9 out of 48 prognostic factors correlated to the persistent asthma have been chosen. Multilayer perceptron and probabilistic neural networks topologies have been investigated in order to obtain the best prediction accuracy. Based on the results, it is shown that the proposed system is able to predict the asthma outcome with a success of 96.77%. The ANN, with which these high rates of reliability were obtained, will help the doctors to identify which of the young patients are at a high risk of asthma disease progression. Moreover, this may lead to better treatment opportunities and hopefully better disease outcomes in adulthood.

1. Introduction

Artificial neural networks (ANNs) are one of the main constituents of the artificial intelligence (AI) techniques. Besides the different applications in many other areas, neural networks are also used in health and medicine areas, such as biomedical signal processing, diagnosis of diseases, and medical decision [1, 2].

ANNs have an excellent capability of learning the relationship between the input-output mapping from a given dataset without any prior knowledge or assumptions about the statistical distribution of the data [3]. This capability of learning from a certain dataset without any a priori knowledge makes the neural networks suitable for classification and prediction tasks in practical situations. Furthermore, neural networks are inherently nonlinear which makes them more practicable for accurate modeling of complex data patterns, in contrast to many traditional methods based on linear techniques. Due to their performance, they can be applied in a wide range of medical fields such as cardiology,

gastroenterology, pulmonology, oncology, neurology, and pediatrics [1].

Several studies have proposed ANN models for the prediction of various diseases. The authors of [4] developed an ANN to determine whether patients had breast cancer or not. If they had, its type could be determined by using ANN and BI-RADS evaluation, based on the age of the patient, mass shape, mass border, and mass density. In another study, an ANN model combined with six tumor markers in auxiliary diagnosis of lung cancer was investigated in order to differentiate lung cancer from lung benign disease, normal control, and gastrointestinal cancers [5].

The most commonly used neural network for disease prognosis systems is the multilayer perceptron (MLP) due to its clear architecture and comparably simple algorithm. The backpropagation algorithm is widely recognized as a powerful tool for training of the MLP structures. Even though MLPs have been successfully used in selected medical applications, they are still faced with skepticism by many scientists in the medical community, due to the "black box" nature of the ANN procedure. Specht and Shapiro [6] have developed an alternative neural network, the probabilistic neural network (PNN), which uses Bayesian strategies for pattern classification, a process familiar to medical decision makers. PNNs are exceptionally fast, since their training phase only requires one pass through the training patterns. Due to the fact that PNN provides a general solution to pattern classification problems, it is suitable for disease diagnosis systems.

Asthma is a chronic inflammatory disorder of the airways characterized by an obstruction of airflow, which may be completely or partially reversed with or without specific therapy [7]. Airway inflammation is the result of interactions between various cells, cellular elements, and cytokines. In susceptible individuals, airway inflammation may cause recurrent or persistent bronchospasm, with symptoms like wheezing, breathlessness, chest tightness, and cough, particularly at night or after exercise. Most of the children who suffer from asthma develop their first symptoms before the 5th year of age. However, asthma diagnosis in children younger than five years old remains a challenge for the clinical doctors [8–10].

Most of the times, it is difficult to discriminate asthma from other wheezing disorders of the childhood because they might have similar symptoms. Thus, children with asthma may often be misdiagnosed as a common cold, bronchiolitis, or pneumonia. For the diagnosis of asthma a detailed medical history and physical examination along with a lung function test are usually required. On the other hand, lung function test is difficult to be performed in children younger than six years old. Hence, the diagnosis in the preschoolers is mainly based on clinical signs and symptoms and remains a challenge for the clinician. Finally, the main question deals with the possibility if a patient with asthma symptoms before the 5th year will either continue to have such symptoms or not. Asthma is a disease with polymorphic phenotype affected by several genetic environmental and genetic factors which play a key role in the development and persistence of the disease [11–14]. These factors include family history of asthma, presence of atopic dermatitis or allergic rhinitis, bronchiolitis episodes during childhood, maternal smoking during pregnancy, lower respiratory tract infections, patient's diet, and several perinatal factors other than maternal smoking. Early identification of patients at risk for asthma disease progression may lead to better treatment opportunities and hopefully better disease outcomes in adulthood [15, 16].

In preventive medicine, the value of a test lies in its ability to identify those individuals who are at high risk of an illness and who therefore require intervention, while excluding those who do not require such intervention. The accuracy of the risk classification is of particular relevance in the case of asthma disease. Due to the high prevalence of this condition, inaccurate risk prediction will lead to overtreatment of a large number of people and undertreatment of many other. In recent years, several large-scale studies have shown that in people at high risk of asthma the prevalence of asthma can be reduced if some common asthma triggers are avoided during the first years of life [17].

Several studies in order to answer the question of which young children with recurrent wheezing will have asthma at school age have utilized the Asthma Predictive Index (API). The API was developed 12 years ago by using data from 1246 children in the Tucson Children's Respiratory study [18]. The positive API score includes frequent wheezing episodes during the first 3 years of life and either one of two major risk factors (parental history of asthma or eczema) or two of three minor risk factors (eosinophilia, wheezing without colds, and allergic rhinitis). A loose index requires any wheezing episodes during the first 3 years of life as well as the same risk factors with the positive API. A positive stringent API score by the age of 3 years was associated with a 77% chance of active asthma from the ages of 6 to 13 years while over 95% of children with a negative API score never had active asthma during their school years. After API, some other scoring systems were also developed in order to identify which of the young children will have asthma later in their life [19]. To the knowledge of the authors, this is the first study where ANNs are used in the prediction of persistent asthma.

The paper is organized as follows: in Section 2 the experimental material, which has been used, is presented; Section 3 shows the feature selection method and the prognosis model, while the results and the final conclusions are described in Sections 4 and 5, respectively.

2. Description of the Asthma Database

Data from 148 patients from the Pediatric Department of the University Hospital of Alexandroupolis, Greece, were collected and recorded during the period 2008–2010. A group of 148 patients who received a diagnosis of asthma were studied prospectively from the 7th to 14th year of age. All patients with missing data were excluded, leaving a total of 112 patients. A case history, including data on asthma, allergic diseases, and lifestyle factors, was obtained by questionnaire. All participants, parents and their children, filled out a questionnaire about asthmatic and allergic symptoms, wheezing episodes until the 5th year, pet keeping, family members, parental history, and some other useful information. The prognostic factors that were used in the questionnaire have been described by previous studies [11–15].

All the 48 prognostic factors are summarized in Table 1. A kind of encoding is necessary for a few of these factors in order to be efficiently utilized. Their encoding is presented in Table 2.

3. Methodology

3.1. The Proposed Algorithm. The prediction algorithm which has been employed in this study consists of two stages: the feature reduction through partial least square regression and the classification stage by MLP and PNN classifiers. The flowchart diagram of the used system is shown in Figure 1.

3.2. Partial Least Square Regression. The selection of input features plays a very important role in the successful implementation of prediction problems [20]. It is, therefore,

TABLE 1: Prognostic factors.

Category	Prognostic factors
Demographic	Age, sex, ethnicity[#], height, weight, waist's perimeter, residence[#]
Wheezing episodes	Until 3rd year, between 3rd–5th year, until 5th year
Symptoms	Wheezing[*], cough[*], allergic rhinitis[*], runny nose[*], congestion[*], eczema[*], food allergy[*], pharmaceutical allergy[*], allergic conjunctivitis[*], dyspnea[*], seasonal symptoms[#]
Parental history	Asthma[*]
House conditions	Number of family members, pets[*], type of heating[#]
Pharmaceutical therapy	Bronchodilators, corticosteroids inhaled[*], corticosteroids per os[*], antileukotriene[*], antihistamine[*]
Breathing tests	$FEV_1\%$, $FEF_{25/75}\%$
Tests	IgE U/ML
Allergens	D. pteronyssinus[#], D. farinae[#], olive[#], pellitory[#], graminaceae[#], pine[#], cypress[#], cat[#], dog[#], alternaria[#]
Neonatal period	Pregnancy duration, breastfeeding duration[#], smoking during pregnancy[*]
Asthma	Diagnosis of asthma[*], treatment[*]

[*]The encoding is binary: yes (1) or no (0).
[#]The encoding is shown in Table 2.
All other factors are numerical.

TABLE 2: Encoding of prognostic factors.

Prognostic factor	Coding					
Sex	0 (Male)	1 (Female)				
Residence	0 (Urban)	1 (Semiurban)	2 (Rural)			
Season of the symptoms	0 (None)	1 (Winter)	2 (Autumn)	3 (Spring)	4 (Summer)	5 (>2 Seasons)
Type of heating	0 (Central heating)	1 (Wood stove)	2 (Oil Stove)	3 (Fireplace)	4 (Central heating + Fireplace)	
Pregnancy duration in weeks	0 (<37)	1 (37-38)	2 (>38)			
Allergens	0 (0)	1 (3.5–6 mm)	2 (>6 mm)			

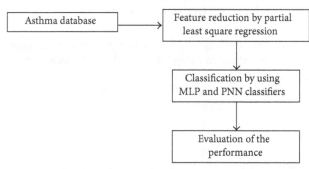

FIGURE 1: Flowchart diagram for the asthma prediction system.

necessary to use the inputs carrying the maximum amount of information to the output. Redundant or uninformative inputs may overshadow the performance of the ANNs. In addition to that, the detection of the essential diagnostic factors might support the utilization of smaller and simpler datasets for ANNs training, as the number of the input features is directly related to the dataset size. The reduction of the dimension of the features space could lead to a quicker and possibly more accurate classifier [21, 22].

A partial least square (PLS) regression is applied for the selection of the most relevant input features among the preselected factors [23]. PLS regression is a technique used with data which contain correlated, predictor variables. This technique constructs new predictor variables, the so-called components, as linear combinations of the original predictor variables. PLS constructs these components while considering the observed response values, leading to a parsimonious model with reliable predictive power.

Let **X** be the matrix where the rows represent the predictor variables, some of which are highly correlated and the columns the number of the patients. Additionally, let **Y** be the matrix where the number of rows is the asthma outcome and the number of columns is the number of the patients. In PLS regression, matrices **X** and **Y** are decomposed into principal components and regression coefficients (loadings):

$$\mathbf{X} = \mathbf{TW}',$$
$$\mathbf{Y} = \mathbf{UQ}', \tag{1}$$

where **T** and **U** are the matrices of scores and **W** and **Q** are the matrices of loadings. PLS regression places two conditions in the decomposition of **X** and **Y** [21]. The first requires orthogonality of **W** and **Q** and the second requires maximal correlation between the columns of **T** and **U**. After decomposition, **U** is regressed on **T** as follows:

$$\mathbf{U} = \mathbf{TB} + \mathbf{E}, \qquad (2)$$

where **B** is the matrix of regression coefficients for **T** and **E** is an error (noise) term.

In order to choose the number of components 10-fold cross-validation was used. Overfitting was avoided by not reusing the same data to fit a model and to estimate the prediction error. Thus, the estimate of prediction error was not optimistically biased downwards. After choosing the number of the components, the PLS weights which are the linear combinations of the original variables that define the PLS components were investigated. The PLS weights were used in order to select only those variables which contribute the most to each component. The best prediction can be performed by only using 9 factors: wheezing episodes until 5th year, wheezing episodes between 3rd and 5th year, wheezing episodes until 3rd year, weight, waist's perimeter, seasonal symptoms, $FEF_{25/75}$, number of family members, and corticosteroids inhaled.

3.3. MLP and PNN Classifiers.

Several factors are crucial in designing a feed forward neural network topology for prediction problems. Such factors are the input, the hidden, and the output layer configuration as well as the used training methodology. The neural network architecture is determined by experimentation in practice. In this paper, the number of input layers is 48 corresponding to the input features in the original dataset. It has been shown by Cybenko [24] and Patuwo et al. [25] that neural networks with one hidden layer are generally sufficient for most problems. Thus, all the networks investigated in this study use one hidden layer. There are many choices for the number of the neurons in the hidden layer. In order to achieve the best neural network configuration, the simulations have been started with a minimal MLP neural network (48-1-1 structure) and step by step more nodes have been added in the hidden layer.

One binary output layer is employed, corresponding to the two classes of either having persistent asthma or not. The target values for each node are either zero (absence of asthma) or one (existence of asthma) depending on the desired output class. The simulation of all the ANNs has been performed using Matlab Neural Network Toolbox due to its user-friendly interface [26].

In order to achieve the best transfer functions for input and hidden layers, the trial and error method was applied. The best result was obtained with a network with tan-sigmoid transfer function in the hidden layer and saturating linear function in the output layer.

Training a neural network involves modifying the weights and biases of the network in order to minimize a cost function [27, 28]. The cost function always includes an error term, which actually indicates how close the network's predictions come to the class labels for the examples in the training set. One of the most widely used error functions is the mean squared error (MSE), while the most commonly used training algorithms are based on the backpropagation algorithm.

In such an algorithm, the synaptic weights and biases are adjusted by backpropagating the error signal through different layers of the network in a chain form. During the learning process, the weights of nodes can be adjusted according to minimizing the overall error:

$$\mathrm{MSE} = \frac{1}{N} \sum_{n=1}^{N} \left[d(n) - y(n) \right]^2, \qquad (3)$$

where N is the number of patterns, $d(n)$ is the predicted output, and $y(n)$ the target. The Levenberg-Marquardt backpropagation learning algorithm was selected for the training of the ANNs due to its faster convergence and better estimated results than other training algorithms.

PNNs, a variant of radial basis function (RBF) neural networks, were also used in order to predict the childhood asthma outcome. Although the PNNs have few applications on medical science, they have had satisfactory performance.

PNN consists of an input layer followed by a radial basis layer (hidden layer) and a competitive layer (output layer). The structure of PNNs has only one hidden layer and the number of neurons for PNN's hidden layer depends on the number of the patterns during PNN's construction. Consequently, the proposed PNN has 112 neurons for the hidden layer as the available data set for PNN implementation, consists of 112 cases. The design of PNN is straightforward and does not depend on the training process. Thus, no learning algorithm was selected during PNN's implementation. The number of neurons in the input layer is 48, equal to the number of the input variables, while the number of neurons in the output layer equals the number of outputs.

The determination of PNN structure for asthma outcome prediction was based on the number of the used input patterns, as well as the spread of radial basis function. The spread was increased from 0.1 to 100, with a step of 0.1.

3.4. Performance Evaluation.

The performance of the neural networks is estimated using false positive (FP), false negative (FN), true positive (TP), and true negative (TN) values. Classification of normal data as abnormal is considered as FP and classification of abnormal data as normal is considered as FN. TP and TN are the cases where the abnormal is classified as abnormal and normal classified as normal, respectively. The accuracy, sensitivity, and specificity are presented in the following equations:

$$\mathrm{Sensitivity} = \frac{N_{\mathrm{TP}}}{N_{\mathrm{TP}} + N_{\mathrm{FN}}} \times 100,$$

$$\mathrm{Specificity} = \frac{N_{\mathrm{TN}}}{N_{\mathrm{TN}} + N_{\mathrm{FP}}} \times 100, \qquad (4)$$

$$\mathrm{Accuracy} = \frac{N_{\mathrm{TP}} + N_{\mathrm{TN}}}{N_{\mathrm{TP}} + N_{\mathrm{TN}} + N_{\mathrm{FP}} + N_{\mathrm{FN}}} \times 100.$$

Sensitivity and specificity are statistical measures of the performance of a binary classification test [29–31]. Sensitivity measures the proportion of positive (asthmatic) people who have been correctly identified to have asthma. Specificity

TABLE 3: Comparison between the original and the optimal MLP classifier.

Feature size of the MLP classifier	MSE		Test success (%)		
	MSE over the training set	MSE over the test set	Sensitivity	Specificity	Accuracy
48	0.2494	0.2190	100	0	83.87
9	1.0553$e-004$	0.0326	96.15	100	96.77

TABLE 4: Comparison between the MLP and PNN classifiers.

Classifier	Feature size	Hidden layer		Output layer		Test success (%)		
		Transfer function	Neurons	Function	Neurons	Sensitivity	Specificity	Accuracy
MLP	48	Tan-sigmoid (tansig)	6	Saturating linear (satlin)	1	100	0	83.87
PNN	48	Radial basis function (RBF) (spread = 100)	112	Competitive (compet)		92.3	60	87.09
MLP	9	Tan-sigmoid (tansig)	6	Saturating linear (satlin)	1	96.15	100	96.77
PNN	9	Radial basis function (RBF) (spread = 25)	112	Competitive (compet)		100	80	96.77

measures the proportion of negative (not asthmatic) people who have been correctly identified not to have asthma. The accuracy is the degree of how close the predicted values are to the actual ones [32].

In this study, a 10-fold cross-validation method was used in order to construct a more flexible model. At first, the 112 patients were divided into 10 almost equal subgroups. One of the 10 subgroups has been used as the evaluation data and the rest as the learning data for the classification. The evaluation data were changed 10 times, so that each group was investigated once as evaluation data. The average value of all obtained accuracies of the evaluation data was considered as the estimation ability of the model.

4. Results

The feature size of the MLP classifier, the MSE over the training and test set, and the training and the test success of the classifier are summarized in Table 3. The correct percentage (overall accuracy) of prediction is 83.87% in the test phase. The neural network statistics for the training set show a sensitivity and specificity of 100% and 0%, respectively. The MSE over the training set and over the test set equals 0.2494 and 0.2190, respectively.

With the 9 highly ranked features, the proposed MLP network is implemented once again. At this time, the structure of the network is 9-6-1. Simulation results show that the new classifier has an average accuracy of 96.77%. Furthermore, the sensitivity and the specificity values are 96.15% and 100%, respectively. The MSE over the training set is decreasing to 1.0553$e-004$ and over the test set to 0.0326. Thus, the new classifier with 9 features performs much more efficiently than the previous one having 48 features.

The best implemented MLP and PNN classifiers, the number of neurons in hidden and output layer, the transfer functions of hidden and output layers for each of the architecture, and the test success of the classifiers are summarized in Table 4.

PNNs have correctly estimated all the normal cases of the test set while the original PNN classifier performs better than the MLP classifier over the negative people. The optimal performance of the reduced MLP and PNN classifiers in terms of asthma outcome prediction is observed from the results.

5. Conclusion and Discussion

The use of ANNs in prognosis problems is well established in the human medical literature, due to their capacity to model complex and nonlinear relationships and their tolerance of missing data and input errors. From the results, it has been shown that the proposed medical decision support system can achieve very high prediction accuracy.

The goal of designing the new classifier is to maximize the classification accuracy and simultaneously minimize the size of the feature set. By selecting a small number of important features, the prediction performance of the constructed classifier has been improved. The improved performance may be attributed to the greater generalization capability of the classifier. After that, a comparison with a PNN classifier was made. It was found, that the PNN networks have had better sensitivity compared to MLP neural networks. The value of specificity has shown that the MLP network classified abnormal data more accurately than PNN network. Based on the obtained values for sensitivity, it is indicated that both the two networks have diagnosed the normal data in a more efficient way than the abnormal data.

Due to the fact that asthma is a serious condition, the various models that have been used to detect it must have high sensitivity so that patients with asthma are not overlooked. An ANN that has been trained to predict 96.77% of patients with asthma may be very useful to physicians.

Moreover, this is the only study that has evaluated the diagnostic accuracy of 48 clinical factors through feature selection and it is concluded that only a set of 9 factors is the most important for the persistent asthma. The present study was also able to show the importance priority of each factor in asthma prediction. The most crucial factor in asthma outcome prediction is wheezing episodes until the 5th year of age. In particular, evidence from a large number of prospective case-control studies shows that wheezing until the 5th year of age of a child is often associated with asthma during subsequent years.

In conclusion, this study will contribute to science by helping doctors to early identify which of the symptomatic young children will continue to develop asthma during their school years and thus to draw a plan in order to change the natural course of the disease.

Acknowledgments

The authors would like to express their gratitude to the personnel of the Pediatric Department of the University Hospital of Alexandroupolis for their comments and collaboration in this work.

References

[1] W. G. Baxt, "Application of artificial neural networks to clinical medicine," *The Lancet*, vol. 346, no. 8983, pp. 1135–1138, 1995.

[2] E. Sourla, S. Sioutas, V. Syrimpeis, A. Tsakalidis, and G. Tzimas, "CardioSmart365: artificial intelligence in the service of cardiologic patients," *Advances in Artificial Intelligence*, vol. 2012, Article ID 585072, 12 pages, 2012.

[3] P. S. Heckerling, B. S. Gerber, T. G. Tape, and R. S. Wigton, "Entering the black box of neural networks: a descriptive study of clinical variables predicting community-acquired pneumonia," *Methods of Information in Medicine*, vol. 42, no. 3, pp. 287–296, 2003.

[4] I. Saritas, "Prediction of breast cancer using artificial neural networks," *Journal of Medical Systems*, vol. 36, no. 5, pp. 2901–2907, 2012.

[5] F. Feng, Y. Wu, Y. Wu, G. Nie, and R. Ni, "The effect of artificial neural network model combined with six tumor markers in auxiliary diagnosis of Lung Cancer," *Journal of Medical Systems*, vol. 36, no. 5, pp. 2973–2980, 2012.

[6] D. F. Specht and P. D. Shapiro, "Generalization accuracy of probabilistic neural networks compared with back-propagation networks," in *Proceedings of the International Joint Conference on Neural Networks (IJCNN '91)*, pp. 887–892, July 1991.

[7] W. Eder, M. J. Ege, and E. Von Mutius, "The asthma epidemic," *New England Journal of Medicine*, vol. 355, no. 21, pp. 2226–2235, 2006.

[8] A. Bush, "Diagnosis of asthma in children under five," *Primary Care Respiratory Journal*, vol. 16, no. 1, pp. 7–15, 2007.

[9] W. J. Morgan, D. A. Stern, D. L. Sherrill et al., "Outcome of asthma and wheezing in the first 6 years of life follow-up through adolescence," *American Journal of Respiratory and Critical Care Medicine*, vol. 172, no. 10, pp. 1253–1258, 2005.

[10] F. D. Martinez, A. L. Wright, L. M. Taussig et al., "Asthma and wheezing in the first six years of life," *New England Journal of Medicine*, vol. 332, no. 3, pp. 133–138, 1995.

[11] M. B. Bracken, K. Belanger, W. O. Cookson, E. Triche, D. C. Christiani, and B. P. Leaderer, "Genetic and perinatal risk factors for asthma onset and severity: a review and theoretical analysis," *Epidemiologic Reviews*, vol. 24, no. 2, pp. 176–189, 2002.

[12] N. E. Lange, S. L. Rifas-Shiman, C. A. Camargo, D. R. Gold, M. W. Gillman, and A. A. Litonjua, "Maternal dietary pattern during pregnancy is not associated with recurrent wheeze in children," *Journal of Allergy and Clinical Immunology*, vol. 126, no. 2, pp. 250–e4, 2010.

[13] G. Nagel, G. Weinmayr, A. Kleiner et al., "Effect of diet on asthma and allergic sensitisation in the international study on allergies and asthma in childhood (ISAAC) phase two," *Thorax*, vol. 65, no. 6, pp. 516–522, 2010.

[14] C. Porsbjerg, M. L. Von Linstow, C. S. Ulrik, S. Nepper-Christensen, and V. Backer, "Risk factors for onset of asthma: a 12-year prospective follow-up study," *Chest*, vol. 129, no. 2, pp. 309–316, 2006.

[15] B. G. Toelle, W. Xuan, J. K. Peat, and G. B. Marks, "Childhood factors that predict asthma in young adulthood," *European Respiratory Journal*, vol. 23, no. 1, pp. 66–70, 2004.

[16] W. Balemansa, C. Van der Enta, A. Schilderb, E. Sandersc, G. Zielhuisd, and M. Roversbef, "Prediction of asthma in young adults using childhood characteristics: development of a prediction rule," *Journal of Clinical Epidemiology*, vol. 59, no. 11, pp. 1207–1212, 2006.

[17] C. Bodner, S. Ross, G. Douglas et al., "The prevalence of adult onset wheeze: longitudinal study," *British Medical Journal*, vol. 314, no. 7083, pp. 792–793, 1997.

[18] J. A. Castro-Rodríguez, C. J. Holberg, A. L. Wright, and F. D. Martinez, "A clinical index to define risk of asthma in young children with recurrent wheezing," *American Journal of Respiratory and Critical Care Medicine*, vol. 162, no. 4, pp. 1403–1406, 2000.

[19] J. A. Castro-Rodriguez, "The asthma predictive index: a very useful tool for predicting asthma in young children," *Journal of Allergy and Clinical Immunology*, vol. 126, no. 2, pp. 212–216, 2010.

[20] J. Yang, A. S. Nugroho, K. Yamauchi et al., "Efficacy of interferon treatment for chronic hepatitis C predicted by feature subset selection and support vector machine," *Journal of Medical Systems*, vol. 31, no. 2, pp. 117–123, 2007.

[21] C. L. Chang and C. H. Chen, "Applying decision tree and neural network to increase quality of dermatologic diagnosis," *Expert Systems with Applications*, vol. 36, no. 2, pp. 4035–4041, 2009.

[22] J. Xia, X. Hu, F. Shi, X. Niu, and S. Zhang, "Prediction of disease-resistant gene by using artificial neural network," in *Proceedings of the International Conference on Research Challenges in Computer Science (ICRCCS '09)*, pp. 81–84, December 2009.

[23] A. Coster and M. P. L. Calus, "Partial least square regression applied to the QTLMAS, 2010 dataset," *BMC Proceedings*, vol. 5, 3, p. S7, 2011.

[24] G. Cybenko, "Approximation by superpositions of a sigmoidal function," *Mathematics of Control, Signals, and Systems*, vol. 2, no. 4, pp. 303–314, 1989.

[25] E. Patuwo, M. Y. Hu, and M. S. Hung, "Two-group classification using neural networks," *Decision Sciences*, vol. 24, no. 4, pp. 825–845, 1993.

[26] D. Howard and B. Mark, *Neural Network Toolbox for Use With Matlab*, The Mathworks, Natick, Mass, USA, 2004.

[27] E. Chatzimichail, A. Rigas, E. Paraskakis, and A. Chatzimichail, "Diagnosis of asthma severity using artificial neural networks," in *Proceedings of the 12th Mediterranean Conference on Medical and Biological Engineering and Computing (MEDICON '10)*, pp. 600–603, Chalkidiki, Greece, May 2010.

[28] J. Dheeba and T. Selvi, "A swarm optimized neural network system for classification of microcalcification in mammograms," *Journal of Medical Systems*, vol. 36, no. 5, pp. 3051–3061, 2012.

[29] I. Kononenko, "Inductive and Bayesian learning in medical diagnosis," *Applied Artificial Intelligence*, vol. 7, no. 4, pp. 317–337, 1993.

[30] W. Wongseree, N. Chaiyaratana, K. Vichittumaros, P. Winichagoon, and S. Fucharoen, "Thalassaemia classification by neural networks and genetic programming," *Information Sciences*, vol. 177, no. 3, pp. 771–786, 2007.

[31] J. Chiu, Y. Wang, Y. Su, L. Wei, and J. Liao, "Artificial neural network to predict skeletal metastasis in patients with prostate cancer," *Journal of Medical Systems*, vol. 33, no. 2, pp. 91–100, 2009.

[32] W. Ji, R. N. G. Naguib, and M. A. Ghoneim, "Neural network-based assessment of prognostic markers and outcome prediction in Bilharziasis-associated bladder cancer," *IEEE Transactions on Information Technology in Biomedicine*, vol. 7, no. 3, pp. 218–224, 2003.

16

CardioSmart365: Artificial Intelligence in the Service of Cardiologic Patients

Efrosini Sourla,[1] Spyros Sioutas,[2] Vasileios Syrimpeis,[3]
Athanasios Tsakalidis,[1] and Giannis Tzimas[4]

[1] Computer Engineering & Informatics Department, University of Patras, 26500 Patras, Greece
[2] Department of Informatics, Ionian University, 49100 Corfu, Greece
[3] General Hospital of Patras "Agios Andreas", 26335 Patras, Greece
[4] Department of Applied Informatics in Management & Economy, Faculty of Management and Economics,
   Technological Educational Institute of Messolonghi, 30200 Messolonghi, Greece

Correspondence should be addressed to Efrosini Sourla, sourla@ceid.upatras.gr

Academic Editor: Panayiotis Vlamos

Artificial intelligence has significantly contributed in the evolution of medical informatics and biomedicine, providing a variety of tools available to be exploited, from rule-based expert systems and fuzzy logic to neural networks and genetic algorithms. Moreover, familiarizing people with smartphones and the constantly growing use of medical-related mobile applications enables complete and systematic monitoring of a series of chronic diseases both by health professionals and patients. In this work, we propose an integrated system for monitoring and early notification for patients suffering from heart diseases. CardioSmart365 consists of web applications, smartphone native applications, decision support systems, and web services that allow interaction and communication among end users: cardiologists, patients, and general doctors. The key features of the proposed solution are (a) recording and management of patients' measurements of vital signs performed at home on regular basis (blood pressure, blood glucose, oxygen saturation, weight, and height), (b) management of patients' EMRs, (c) cardiologic patient modules for the most common heart diseases, (d) decision support systems based on fuzzy logic, (e) integrated message management module for optimal communication between end users and instant notifications, and (f) interconnection to Microsoft HealthVault platform. CardioSmart365 contributes to the effort for optimal patient monitoring at home and early response in cases of emergency.

1. Introduction

Internet has broaden the scope of medical information systems and led to the development of distributed and interoperable information sources and services. In the same time, the need for standards became crucial. Federated medical libraries, biomedical knowledge bases, and global healthcare systems offer a rich information sink and facilitate mobility of patients and practitioners [1].

Medical information systems (MISs) may include medical imaging storage and transmission systems, nursing information systems, laboratory information systems, and pharmacy information systems. To treat patients, medical personnel can use different information systems in accordance with their needs, in order to diagnose and run tests, like blood tests, urine sampling, computed tomography scans,

X-ray [2], and so on. A medical information system produces all kinds of medical information in various formats, including texts, numbers, pictures, and static and dynamic images. This heterogeneous information can then be integrated without the need of medical personnel. According to a patient ID, name, or other basic data, the information can be indexed by, for medical use upon request [3].

Additionally, the spectacular penetration of mobile phones in the technological arena and their transformation into smartphones have introduced a new field of software applications' development. Smartphones have been employed widely in health care practice [4]. The level of their use is expected to increase, especially if they are enriched with doctor suitable functions and software applications. The lack of such applications is noticed even in countries with leadership role in mobile technologies, as it is mentioned in [5]. The impact of mobile-handheld technology on hospital physicians' work practices, and patient care is systematically reviewed in [6], where the authors recommend future research about the impact of the mobility devices on work practices and outcomes.

An example which successfully combines MISs with the advantages and capabilities of Smartphones, in Orthopedics, is the integrated system that was developed for recording, monitoring, and studying patients with open tibia fractures [7]. The authors participated in the development of the system, which is based on web and mobile applications. Primary goal was the creation of a system that contains most of the scientifically validated data elements, reducing in this way omission and improving consistency, by standardizing the reporting language among medical doctors. The system's web and mobile interfaces are designed to require almost no text entry and editing and are based on the traditional medical way of acting, thus making it a doctor friendly system.

Artificial intelligence (AI) has significantly contributed in the evolution of medical informatics and biomedicine since it provides a variety of tools available to be exploited, from rule-based expert systems and fuzzy logic to neural networks and genetic algorithms. The earliest work in medical AI dates back to the early 1970s, when the field of AI was about 15 years old. Since then, there is a growing interest in the application of AI techniques in biomedical engineering and informatics, ranging from knowledge-based reasoning for disease classification to learning and discovering novel biomedical knowledge for disease treatment, indicative of the maturity and influence that have been achieved to date [8]. In [9], the integration of AI techniques in biomedical engineering and informatics is presented, especially in the following core topics: (a) feature selection, (b) visualization, (c) classification, (d) data warehousing and data mining, and (e) analysis of biological networks. In literature, a great number of research projects reflect the integration of AI in medicine, from the use of fuzzy expert systems [10, 11] and design patterns [12], to neural networks [4, 13] and decision support systems (DSSs) [14, 15].

This paper presents an integrated system (CardioSmart365) based on web applications, web services, and smartphone applications for lifelong cardiologic patient monitoring, early detection of emergency, and optimal process management of the emergency incident. Cardiologic patient modules with DSSs based in fuzzy logic are developed for the most common heart diseases. The system allows interaction and communication between cardiologic patients, cardiologists, general practitioners, hospitals, and outHospitals health sectors. Everyday clinical practice, medical doctors, cardiologic patients, research and science, and healthcare systems benefit from the proposed system.

The rest of the paper is organized as follows: related work is presented in Section 2 followed by motivation in Section 3. Section 4 presents literature information about the different types of health records, the existing health record providers, and their evaluation. This section can be omitted for expert users. Section 5 presents a thorough description of the implemented system, including its architecture, functionality, components, and software framework. System's added value is discussed in Section 6. Finally, future steps are proposed in Section 7, and the paper concludes in Section 8.

2. Related Work

2.1. Mobile Health Applications. Most health applications in online markets are native applications, patient oriented or medical doctor (MD) oriented. In most cases, the patient-oriented health applications are exploited only by patients, and the information gathered is not available directly to physicians, through a communication channel. Moreover, the MD-oriented health applications serve specific purposes, mostly for educational and quick access to medical literature reasons. On the other hand, frequently, mobile applications that are part of medical research projects, store information, and send it to collaborative servers for additional processing and disposal to physicians.

The use of individual mobile health applications, developed to serve specific purposes, is widely spread. The need for such applications is apparent in every major online market for mobile applications including Android Market, Apple Store, and Samsung Apps. Applications developed for cardiology record blood pressure and cardiac pulses, applications for diabetes record blood glucose [16], and for obesity, they record calories and diet [17], for dementia they use GPS to monitor the patient [18, 19], and applications for chronic diseases target mobile phones with sensors and detect tachycardia or respiratory infections [20].

2.2. Medical Applications for Cardiology. Many mobile applications for cardiology have been developed in order to enhance medical doctors' and medical students' research experience [21–23] such as (a) applications that present a 3D prototype of a human heart and allow users to observe the heart from any angle, (b) calculators with commonly used formulas in cardiovascular medicine, (c) electrocardiography (ECG) guides with samples of different types of ECG, (d) guideline tools for clinical practice and diagnosis, and (e) decision support tools including several criteria and cases. All the above applications are addressed to medical staff, mainly for educational reasons and quick access to literature data, useful for medical doctors. In addition, they are not suitable for cardiologic patients.

A web environment for monitoring cardiologic patients is Heart360 Cardiovascular Wellness Center [24], sponsored by the American Heart Association and American Stroke Association. Heart360 allows patients to monitor their blood pressure, blood glucose, cholesterol, weight, nutrition, and physical activity, while receiving education and information specific to their condition. Heart360 utilizes Microsoft HealthVault [25]. More specifically, patients are able to (a) collect and record their blood pressure, blood glucose, cholesterol, weight, nutrition, and physical activity habits, (b) set goals and track their progress, (c) view their data in charts and graphs that they can print out and share with others involved in their family health, (d) manage multiple user accounts, and (e) get news and articles of potential interest based on their store of health information. This application is patient oriented and does not offer any substantial help to cardiologists or general practitioners.

2.3. Artificial Intelligence in Cardiology. Recently, AI, out of invasive and noninvasive diagnostic tools, becomes the promising method in the diagnosis of heart diseases. In [4], a comparison is presented of multilayered perceptron neural network (MLPNN) and support vector machine (SVM) on determination of coronary artery disease (CAD) existence upon exercise stress testing (EST) data. In [13] neural networks are used as the most suitable solution to outcome prediction tasks in postoperative cardiac patients. An AI-based Computer Aided Diagnosis system is designed in [26] to assist the clinical decision of nonspecialist staff in the analysis of heart failure patients. The system computes the patient's pathological condition and highlights possible aggravations, using four AI-based techniques: a Neural Network, a support vector machine, a decision tree and a fuzzy expert system whose rules are produced by a Genetic Algorithm. Neural networks achieved the best performance with an accuracy of 86%. Another application domain for AI is nuclear cardiology imaging, since the automatic interpretation of nuclear cardiology studies is a complex and difficult task, and a variety of expert systems, neural networks, and case-based reasoning approaches have been attempted in this area [27].

3. Motivation

Although healthcare systems have strongly benefited from the incorporation of new technologies, there is a serious lack of incorporation in the field of clinical medicine. Clinical medicine is involved with patients and their treatment, where medical doctors (MDs) are responsible for the patients' progress.

The direct implication of humans, in particular patients, presupposes that the new technologies incorporated have to be safe, reliable and to offer proven solutions. In addition, MDs are not familiar with new sophisticated applications that change their traditional way of working, justifying in this way the skepticism that MDs present in the incorporation of new technologies.

CardioSmart365 is motivated from the need to proceed in using the advantages of new technologies in the field of clinical medicine. Cardiology is a first-line emergency medical specialty that apart from the emergency incident has to deal with a variety of chronic diseases. Therefore, if CardioSmart365 is proved to be an effective tool in the hands of Cardiologists, general practitioners (GPs), and cardiology patients (CPs), then the same methodology can be used for the development of respective systems for every other medical specialty.

Moreover, to the best of the authors' knowledge, till now there is no any system available that incorporates the following characteristics: (a) to be both patient and medical doctor oriented, (b) to incorporate AI modules, (c) to provide access to end users through multiple channels (web, mobile), (d) to utilize existing and state-of-the-art medical platforms, such as Microsoft Health Vault, and (e) to be easily expandable and deployable. Thus, the detected deficiencies and the willingness to offer enhanced services to patients and medical doctors motivated us to develop a system that incorporates these characteristics into an integrated functionality.

CardioSmart365 is part of collaboration between the Computer Engineering and Informatics Department and School of Medicine of the University of Patras and the General Hospital of Patras "Ag. Andreas" and is currently in testing phase with the following involved parties: (a) nonhospital and hospital cardiologists, (b) nonhospital and hospital general practitioners and (c) cardiologic patients. CardioSmart365 will soon be publicly available at http://www.biodata.gr/cardiosmart365/.

4. Health Records

4.1. Introduction. A personal health record (PHR) is a health record where health data and information related to the care of a patient is maintained by the patient [28]. This stands in contrast with the more widely used electronic medical record (EMR) and electronic health record (EHR) which are operated by institutions (such as hospitals) and contain data entered by clinicians or billing data to support insurance claims. The NAHIT report defines the following [29].

Electronic Medical Record (EMR). An electronic record of health-related information on an individual that can be created, gathered, managed, and consulted by authorized clinicians and staff within one health care organization.

Electronic Health Record (EHR). An electronic record of health-related information on an individual that conforms to nationally recognized interoperability standards and that can be created, managed, and consulted by authorized clinicians and staff across more than one health care organization.

Personal Health Record (PHR). An electronic record of health-related information on an individual that conforms to nationally recognized interoperability standards and that can be drawn from multiple sources while being managed, shared, and controlled by the individual.

In summary, EMRs and EHRs are tools for providers while PHRs are the means to engage individuals in their health and wellbeing.

An EMR or PHR may contain a fairly-wide range of information related directly or indirectly to the health of the user [28], more specifically:

(i) personal information, that is, name, date of birth, and current address,

(ii) names and phone numbers of relatives or people of the owner's friendly environment that can be contacted in case of emergency,

(iii) names, addresses, and telephone numbers of physicians,

(iv) info related to individual health insurance,

(v) current medication (if any) and respective dosages,

(vi) known allergies to foods, drugs, and other substances,

(vii) important events, dates, and hereditary diseases, involving the family history,

(viii) history of the most important diseases encountered by the user in his past,

(ix) results of medical examinations, important medical tests, dental history as well as vaccination history,

(x) recent medical diagnostics: summary of visits to family physician or another specialist,

(xi) information related to physical activity, exercise program, dietary restrictions, and record of medications that do not require a prescription (over the counter - OTC) and/or alternative therapeutic approaches.

PHRs have many potential benefits to patients, caregivers, and institutions [28]. One of the most important PHR benefits is greater patient access to a wide array of credible health information, data, and knowledge. Patients can leverage that access to improve their health and manage their diseases. A critical benefit of PHRs is that they provide an ongoing connection between patient and physician, which changes encounters from episodic to continuous, thus substantially shortening the time to address problems that may arise.

The PHR can benefit clinicians in many ways. First, patients entering data into their health records can elect to submit the data into their clinicians' EHRs. The PHR may also become a conduit for improved sharing of medical records. Finally, asynchronous, PHR-mediated electronic communication between patients and members of their health care teams can free clinicians from the limitations of telephone and face-to-face communication or improve the efficiency of such personal contacts.

4.2. Health Record Providers and Evaluation. In their work, Sunyaev et al. [30] enumerate the existing PHR providers, based on US-oriented and Internet-based PHRs. The two most popular ones are Google Health and Microsoft HealthVault, which are independent products developed by profit-oriented companies or open scientific projects. In [30], these two PHR systems were chosen to be evaluated, due to the relative similarity of their architecture, target markets, and business models. A list of 25 end-user features was elicited, which are necessary for a successful PHR implementation. These features were classified in three categories: patient information, personal control, and additional services. Another work examined and compared the designs of Google Health API and Microsoft HealthVault API [31]. In the evaluation, seven different categories were used: libraries, documentation, authentication, security, data access, data modification, and data messages. The two platforms have advantages and disadvantages and present similarity in some characteristics while they are different in others. However, since Google decided to retire Google Health in January 1, 2012, we can assume that HealthVault will be dominant.

4.3. Microsoft HealthVault. Microsoft HealthVault [25] is a backend cloud-based platform, based on EMR systems, which provides a privacy- and security-enhanced foundation that can be used to store and transfer information between a variety of e-health care customer's applications (desktop, web, and mobile ones), hospital applications, and healthcare devices. It also offers tools to solution providers, device manufacturers, and developers, in order to build innovative new health and wellness management solutions. HealthVault has three major advantages [32]: (a) it presents a low-cost solution in developing and maintaining, (b) it is designed using advanced technology to achieve sustainability, and (c) it offers an easy customization, facilitating programmers to develop customer applications on top of it.

A great number of web and mobile applications that utilize HealthVault are now available. Moreover, many corporations sell portable medical devices (blood pressure monitors, blood glucose meters, pedometers, and more) that take patients' recordings and send them to their HealthVault records. Applications and devices offer a growing range of ways to get the important health information patients that are tracking into their HealthVault record. Many applications let customers analyze and manage that information to help them achieve their health and fitness goals [33].

HealthVault introduces five application connection models in order to help developers decide how their application will integrate with HealthVault [34]: (a) Native HealthVault (Online apps), (b) Linking (Offline apps), (c) Patient Connect, (d) Drop-off/Pick-up, and (e) Software on Device Authentication (SODA).

All these capabilities render HealthVault to be a valuable tool of import and management of health-related information. A major limitation should be stressed; using HealthVault is available only to residents of the United States of America, due to legal obstacles. It is the company's intention to expand its use in other countries, provided that the relevant legal restrictions will be eliminated.

Unlike using it, development of software which supports or uses HealthVault is possible outside the United States as well. For this purpose Microsoft HealthVault Pre-Production Environment (PPE) is available. The PPE is a web server platform that simulates the HealthVault website except that it does not provide access to real user data. It has been designed specifically to support the development of related applications, so that developers can test and evaluate their software. CardioSmart365 uses such an account, created in PPE.

5. CardioSmart365: System Description and Services

5.1. System Architecture. In this work, an integrated system (CardioSmart365) for monitoring and early notification for patients suffering from heart diseases is presented. The system design and implementation use the well-known-service oriented architecture (SOA) to maximize interoperability and scalability, as well as user interface design techniques for optimal presentation. The system consists of web applications, native mobile applications for Smartphones loosely coupled web services and decision support systems, in order to offer its services to the end users: patients, cardiologists, and general doctors. The four main services the system offers are the following.

(1) Creation and maintenance of the complete electronic medical record (EMR) of patients with heart diseases. EMRs are managed by cardiologists responsible for each patient.

(2) Recording and management of patient's measurements of vital signs performed at home on regular basis, such as blood pressure, blood glucose, oxygen saturation, weight, and height.

(3) Detection of out-of-range measurement values using fuzzy logic and alert firing through a DSS.

(4) Formulation of cardiologic patient profiles based on DSS for the most common heart diseases.

(5) Integrated message management module, for optimal communication between end users and instant notifications. The module also includes automated messages.

The system implements a client-server architecture. Authorised end users have access to the integrated system through client applications, a web application, and a native mobile application for smartphones, with friendly- and easy-to-use interfaces. Great emphasis has been given in the design of user friendly and functional interfaces for both physicians and patients. In particular, the interface of mobile devices is designed in such a way to require the minimum volume of typing data. In order to achieve platform independence, the client applications communicate and exchange data with the database through web services, which allow data interchange through heterogeneous systems. The web services provide functionality with which specific information can be accessed by client applications after authenticated access. CardioSmart365 utilizes the Microsoft HealthVault platform as a backend platform, to store and manage important information of patients' EMRs and measurements, into a uniform format. The system's architecture is shown in Figure 1. Since CardioSmart365 has reached version 1.0 offering the aforementioned services, it will be further developed to incorporate an SMS server component, in order to offer an extra channel of communication between end users, as well as an alternative data transfer method between client and server.

5.2. System Functionality. In this section, we proceed to a thorough analysis of CardioSmart365 functionality and the services it offers to end users (Figure 2). The description of the system's functionality and offered services will be accomplished through the presentation of the following generalized services: (a) vital signs measurement, (b) electronic medical records, (c) cardiologic patient modules, and (d) message management module.

5.2.1. Measurements of Vital Signs. Depending on the severity of patients' health condition, their cardiologists advise them to perform measurements of their vital signs on regular basis. The measurement types may include blood pressure, blood glucose, oxygen saturation, weight, and height, and the frequency of measurements depends, in general, on the patient's health condition. CardioSmart365 offers patients tools to record their measurements through web interfaces and mobile applications (Figure 3) and store them to the system's database. Measurements are performed at home and are imported manually by patients themselves or directly from the medical device (when the device supports connection via Bluetooth or Wi-Fi). Patients can also view measurements of a certain type performed in a specified period of time and create charts. The cardiologist, who is assigned to and responsible for each patient, has access to these measurements for a more comprehensive patient monitoring and decision making. Measurements of vital signs are also stored in Microsoft HealthVault.

An extra control module based on fuzzy sets is developed to check out-of-range measurement values and alert the attending MD. Every attending MD, cardiologist or general practitioner is able to define the fuzzy sets of blood pressure, blood glucose, cholesterol, and weight according to every patient's special needs, achieving in this way a first level of personalization. The fuzzification of blood pressure to *very low, low, normal, little high, medium high,* and *very high* is common to all patients, but the triangular fuzzy sets contain different Universe of Discourses. For example, the universe of discourse for the fuzzy set *little high* can be set from the MD for a patient with a history of a recent heart attack to $(100, 120, 140)$. The same MD can set the same values $(100, 120, 140)$ for the fuzzy set *normal*, in the case of another patient with a different medical history than the previous one, such as a patient with hypertension. A fuzzification and control module is also developed for blood glucose, cholesterol, and weight.

5.2.2. Electronic Medical Record. Through CardioSmart365, cardiologists have access to their patients' medical records. In CardioSmart365, an EMR consists of patient's medical history, medication, laboratory examinations, cardiovascular examinations (physical examinations), periodical measurements of vital signals, and demographics.

The medical history for cardiology (Figure 4) consists of detailed information about coronary artery disease (CAD), intervention for CAD, hypertension, heart failure, valvular heart disease, and heart rhythm disorders. It also includes basic information about cholesterol, diabetes mellitus, tobacco use, family history for heart disease, stroke, peripheral arterial disease, thyroid disease, cancer, lung/liver/kidney/neurological/gastrointestinal/autoimmune/hematologic/endocrine/ophthalmologic/psychiatric disease.

Medication (Figure 5) includes information about patient's current and past medicines, dosage, route, duration, and instructions. Laboratory examinations include information for complete blood count, coagulation times, and biochemical examinations. The cardiovascular examination is a physical examination performed at home or in a clinic, by a general doctor or a cardiologist, and consists of information

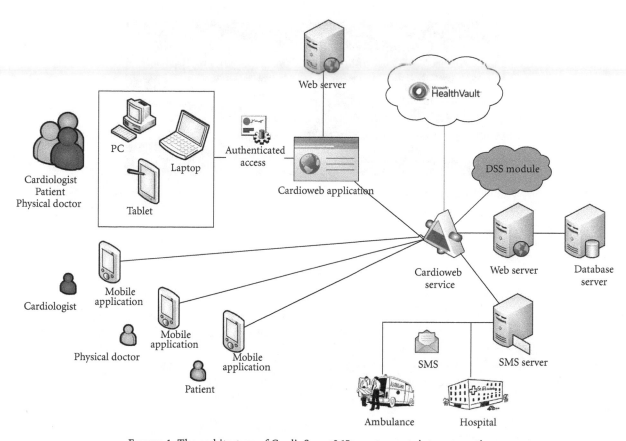

FIGURE 1: The architecture of CardioSmart365: components interconnection.

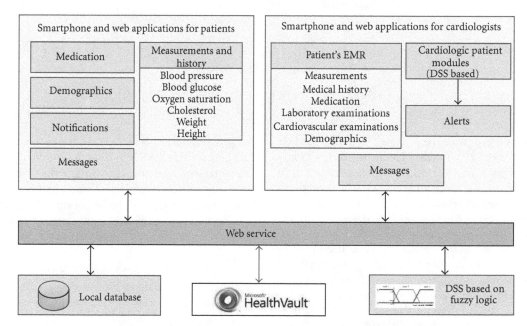

FIGURE 2: The architecture of CardioSmart365: offered services.

about heart pulse (also femoral and foot pulse), jugular venous pulse, cardiac palpation, and auscultation. The system offers an interface for recording information about the examination the same time it is performed (Figure 6). Measurements of vital signs are performed by patients on regular basis and include blood pressure, blood glucose, oxygen saturation, weight, and height measurements. Demographics include general information for a patient such as name, surname, gender, age, insurance details, contact info and emergency contact details.

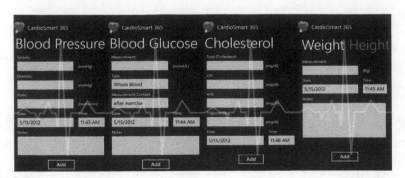

FIGURE 3: CardioSmart365 mobile interfaces for recording vital signs measurements.

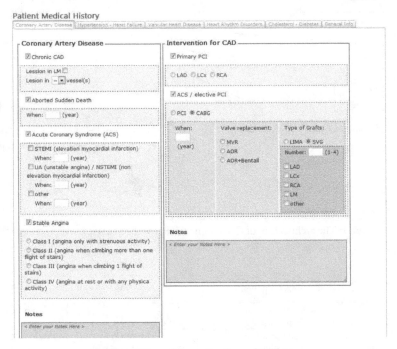

FIGURE 4: Recording patient's medical history.

A patient's medical history is created in detail the first time the patient visits the cardiologist in his/her office or clinic. Cardiologists have full access to this information and can notify it to general doctors who perform physical examinations in cases of emergency, if it is necessary (read only access permissions). Medication is updated by patients or cardiologists. This information would also be updated directly by pharmacists, as future potential end users of CardioSmart365. Information about laboratory examinations is recorded and stored into CardioSmart365 by patients or cardiologists and in the future directly by clinicians.

Information about a new cardiovascular examination is stored by the cardiologist or general doctor who performs it. Periodical measurements of vital signs are performed at home, are imported by patients, and are available to cardiologists for a more comprehensive patient monitoring and decision making. Demographic information is stored along with the medical history during the patient's first visit to a cardiologist, or by a patient at any time and is updated by patient or cardiologist.

Most of the information described above is also stored in Microsoft HealthVault, including medication, laboratory examinations, periodical measurements, and demographics. This way, the information will be available to third parties after patient's approval. Information characterized as more specific to cardiology, such as the detailed medical history, is stored only in CardioSmart365 database.

5.2.3. Cardiologic Patient Modules. Knowledge from experts, in this case cardiologists, is incorporated in separate modules, focused on the most common heart diseases. The cardiologic patient modules (CPMs) are in fact enhanced cardiologic patient profiles that comprise decision support systems (DSSs) based on fuzzy logic. Fuzzy Logic is used because it offers solutions when a system is so complicated that cannot be mathematically modeled, or when it presents fuzziness. In the case of a cardiology patient and a cardiologist that needs to take therapeutic decisions for him/her, decisions should not be based on rules like the following.

FIGURE 5: Patient's Medication History and Details from cardiologist's interface.

(1) If *Aortic Stenosis* is 2.5–2.9 m/s AND *Blood Pressure* is 140/90–160/95 mmHg Then *Decision* is ...

(2) If *Aortic Stenosis* is 3.0–4.0 m/s AND *Blood Pressure* is 140/90–160/95 mmHg Then *Decision* is ...

It is obvious that different *decisions* result from minor changes. For example, a difference of 1 m/s in the *aortic stenosis* of 2.9 m/s to 3.0 m/s may be the reason for a surgery intervention or not. Therefore, fuzzy sets are designed and fuzzy rules are developed, which imitate better the way MDs think and act. For example, the above decision rules are transformed to fuzzy rules in the form of the following.

(a) If *Aortic Stenosis* is MILD AND *Blood Pressure* is LITTLE HIGH Then *Decision* is ...

(b) If *Aortic Stenosis* is MODERATE AND *Blood Pressure* is LITTLE HIGH Then *Decision* is ...

The system includes five discrete patient modules:

(I) the coronary artery disease patient module,

(II) the hypertension patient module,

(III) the heart failure patient module,

(IV) the valvular heart disease patient module,

(V) the heart rhythm disorders patient module.

CPMs contain Alert messages and Critical messages automatically arisen when the MD imports data in the DSS.

Some decisions from the DSS result deterministically while others require the use of qualitative variables. The qualitative variables are transformed in fuzzy sets used to create fuzzy decision rules. For example, in the valvular heart disease CPM the form of the fuzzy rules is the following.

(1) If *mitral regurgitation* is ASYMPTOMATIC AND *LVESd* is HIGH then *surgery intervention* is HIGH.

(2) If *aortic regurgitation* is ASYMPTOMATIC AND *ef* is SMALL then *surgery intervention* is HIGH.

In the Hypertension CPM, Fuzzy Logic is used to help in drugs regulation. The form of the fuzzy rules in this case is:

(1) If *age* is HIGH AND *blood pressure* is LITTLE HIGH AND *coexisting disease* is Chronic Kidney Disease THEN *Medication* is DIURETIC HIGH.

(2) If *age* is MEDIUM AND *blood pressure* is HIGH AND *coexisting disease* is Myocardial Infarction THEN *Medication* is B-BLOCKERS HIGH.

Table 1 presents the basic criteria used in the decision mechanism for each one of the five CPMs. Some of the criteria are fuzzified into fuzzy variables, while others are better exploited as crisp variables. The decision includes starting, ending, or configuring medication, limitation of activity, and surgery intervention.

The CPMs are designed to be used from medical doctors, cardiologists and general practitioners. Although

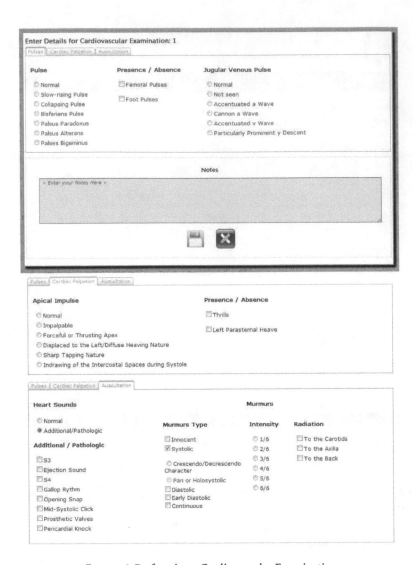

FIGURE 6: Performing a Cardiovascular Examination.

cardiologists are strongly benefited from the CPMs, general practitioners may find CPMs extremely helpful when they are called to manage a cardiologic patient.

5.2.4. Message Management Module. The message management module is a module of CardioSmart365 that optimizes the communication between end users. The module manages inbox and sent messages of all end users and sends automated messages when necessary. The automated messages are formed by customizing specific message templates stored in the system's database. When an automated message is sent or when one user sends a message to another, three actions take place; a message is created internally in the system database and is visible to all recipients, an email is sent to the recipients who have registered their email addresses, and an SMS is sent to the recipients who have registered the numbers of their mobile phones. Through the messaging module interface (Figure 7), the end user can view his/her inbox, edit and send outbox messages, create, save, or send a new message and delete messages.

5.3. Software Framework. The multimodule software architecture is developed in Visual Studio 2010, using the programming language C#. The web services implementation follows the Windows Communication Foundation (WCF) framework that provides a unified programming model for rapidly building service-oriented applications. The mobile application is implemented in Windows Phone 7, the new Microsoft platform for smartphones, specifically version 7.5 Mango, which is an upgraded version of the initial one. The Silverlight toolkit for Windows Phone was used, which allows rapid creation of Rich Internet Application-style user interfaces. The integrated system's database is developed in SQL Server 2008.

A prerequisite for developing applications interconnecting to Microsoft HealthVault is the use of the corresponding library [25]. The library enables encrypted communication among the application and the server of HealthVault. The respective SDK provides supplementary tools for interaction with the platform, instructions for the programmer as well as some standard applications. Each application is represented by a unique ID, which is received through HealthVault

TABLE 1: Cardiologic patient modules and decision support.

Cardiologic patient module	Fuzzy variables	Crisp variables	Decision
Coronary artery disease	Class Duration	Category	Medication
Hypertension	Age Blood pressure	Coexisting disease	Medication
Heart failure	Class	Cause	Limitation of activity
Valvular heart disease	Mitral regurgitation Aortic regurgitation LVESd ef		Surgery intervention
Heart rhythm disorders	Rate control Rhythm control	Type	Medication

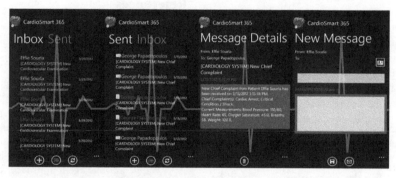

FIGURE 7: The mobile interface of the Message Management Module.

Application Configuration Center. The DSSs based on fuzzy logic are developed in Matlab® Fuzzy Logic Toolbox.

6. Added Value

CardioSmart365 impact is separated to benefits for five categories, which are thoroughly described below:

Every day clinical practice concerns MDs, nurses, hospital staff, outhospital healthcare organisations, and patients. CardioSmart365's patient modules, forms, and DSS can be used as guidelines that are followed for patients with a specific cardiologic disease, standardising in this way the tasks that have to be done for every patient, each day and by whom. In this way, better collaboration is established between all the involved working teams inside and outside the hospital. In addition, the direct interconnection and fast briefing, between different health sectors supported from the system, reduces fraud and optimizes emergency incidents process management.

Medical doctors many times need to act under stress and to take decisions in a fast way. Therefore, speed is important for MDs. cardioSmart365 is a "doctor-friendly" tool that helps recording data in a systematic and quick way, therefore, helping MDs to work faster and in more safety. In addition, CardioSmart365 benefits young cardiologists and general practitioners (GPs) as an educational and decision

support tool, since it provides patient specific guidance in the rapprochement of CPs.

Cardiologic patients dispose a customised EHR. The benefits of EHRs are widely known, but the customised EHR for CPs contains detailed data, formatted in a way that can be easily understood and quickly viewed even from third parties MDs after years. After all, patients suffering from cardiologic diseases, most of the time in reflect chronic pathologies that require medication and followup for the rest of their life. This way, patients receive lifelong advantageous healthcare.

Research and Science strongly benefited towards better monitoring and understanding of cardiologic diseases. CardioSmart365 is a tool for recording and studying scientifically validated data elements of cardiologic diseases. Moreover, CardioSmart365, in the administrator level, can correlate and conclude upon data recorded not only from different places of the same region or country, but from different countries and continents, because it can be accessed from any personal computer connected to the Internet. In this way, maybe for the first time so easily, detailed data from all over the world can be gathered in one database, continuously updated for scientific research.

Healthcare systems are interested in estimating health related economical costs. CardioSmart365 can be used for a reliable estimation of the economical cost that a patient encumbered a healthcare system. CardioSmart365 stores data concerning the examinations of a patient that their cost is usually the higher cost that burdens a healthcare system. Additionally, CardioSmart365 can be used for providing estimations on the cost of every cardiologic disease per patient and to estimate annual costs for every new diagnosed patient.

7. Future Steps

CardioSmart365 was developed to offer advanced added value services for cardiologic patients and physicians into a fast, flexible, and easy-to-use integrated solution. However, many steps towards optimizing the system have to be done. Some direct future evolvements concern (a) healthcare systems and (b) research and science.

7.1. Healthcare Systems. CardioSmart365 is designed to offer an easy way for the incorporation of economic costs customized to different healthcare systems. This future module, apart from the already provided costs of laboratory examinations, will provide costs related to medication, MDs rewards, patients' transportations, and other economic issues important for healthcare systems around the world. Moreover, tools for estimation and various indices used for better monitoring and prediction of health involved costs will be established. For example, questions like "What is the annual cost for a Healthcare system for a patient with a coronary artery disease?" will be answered, or predictions like "How many new diagnosed patients with a coronary artery disease are expected for the upcoming year" will be estimated. AI methods will be closely studied due to the help that they provide in prediction problems.

7.2. Research and Science. Using the web applications and services of CardioSmart365, feedback from institutional centers specialized on cardiologic diseases will be collected and incorporated to future versions of CardioSmart365. The cardiologic patient modules will be continuously updated in an automated way through the tools that will be developed. Knowledge from experts will be further continuously incorporated to the DSS of CardioSmart365, optimizing their support to MDs, leading towards personalized patient profiles and personalized medicine. In this way specialized knowledge and protocols from pioneers in the field of cardiology will be spread all around the world in a direct, fast, and easy-to-follow way.

CardioSmart365 will further adopt clinical data and data involved in healthcare in a greater detail. As a first attempt to collect and group the basic data elements sufficient for a cardiology patient, MDs and the rest staff involved in Healthcare systems, CardioSmart365 will incorporate serious feedback from its end users for optimization and further evolvements.

8. Conclusions

An integrated system based on web applications, Smartphones, and an interconnection to Microsoft HealthVault platform is developed, for (a) monitoring chronic cardiology patients and (b) early notifying and optimizing the process management of an emergency cardiologic incident. The system supports cardiologic patient modules based on common cardiology diseases and customized DSS based on fuzzy logic. The benefits of the system concern patients, MDs, everyday clinical practice, research and science, and healthcare systems.

Acknowledgments

This research has been cofinanced by the European Union (European Social Fund—(ESF)) and Greek national funds through the Operational Program "Education and Lifelong Learning" of the National Strategic Reference Framework (NSRF)—Research Funding Program: Heracleitus II. Investing in knowledge society through the European Social Fund.

References

[1] I. Varlamis and I. Apostolakis, "Medical informatics in the Web 2.0 era," in *Proceedings of the 1st International Symposium on Intelligent Interactive Multimedia Systems and Services*, Piraeus, Greece, July 2008.

[2] E. Faliagka, V. N. Syrimpeis, A. Tsakalidis, G. K. Matsopoulos, J. Tsaknakis, and G. Tzimas, "Diagnosis: A global alignment and fusion medical system," in *Proceedings of the 3rd International Conference on Health Informatics, HEALTHINF 2010*, pp. 21–28, esp, January 2010.

[3] C. H. Liu, Y. F. Chung, T. W. Chiang, T. S. Chen, and S. D. Wang, "Mobile agent approach for secure integrated medical information systems," *Journal of Medical Systems*, vol. 36, no. 5, pp. 2731–2741, 2012.

[4] I. Babaoglu, O. K. Baykan, N. Aygul et al., "A comparison of artificial intelligence methods on determining coronary artery disease," in *Advances in Information Technology*, Communications in Computer and Information Science, pp. 18–26, Springer, Berlin, Germany, 2010.

[5] A. M. Lindquist, P. E. Johansson, G. I. Petersson, B. I. Saveman, and G. C. Nilsson, "The use of the Personal Digital Assistant (PDA) among personnel and students in health care: a review," *Journal of Medical Internet Research*, vol. 10, no. 4, article no. e31, 2008.

[6] M. Prgomet, A. Georgiou, and J. I. Westbrook, "The impact of mobile handheld technology on hospital physicians' work practices and patient care: a systematic review," *Journal of the American Medical Informatics Association*, vol. 16, no. 6, pp. 792–801, 2009.

[7] V. Gkintzou, T. Papablasopoulou, V. Syrimpeis, E. Sourla, G. Tzimas, and A. Tsakalidis, "A web and smart phone system for tibia open fractures," in *ENTERprise Information Systems*, J. Varajão, P. Powell, and R. Martinho, Eds., vol. 221 of *Communications in Computer and Information Science*, pp. 413–422, Springer, Berlin, Germany, 2011.

[8] V. L. Patel, E. H. Shortliffe, M. Stefanelli et al., "The coming of age of artificial intelligence in medicine," *Artificial Intelligence in Medicine*, vol. 46, no. 1, pp. 5–17, 2009.

[9] Y. Peng, Y. Zhang, and L. Wang, "Artificial intelligence in biomedical engineering and informatics: an introduction and review," *Artificial Intelligence in Medicine*, vol. 48, no. 2-3, pp. 71–73, 2010.

[10] T. P. Exarchos, M. G. Tsipouras, C. P. Exarchos, C. Papaloukas, D. I. Fotiadis, and L. K. Michalis, "A methodology for the

automated creation of fuzzy expert systems for ischaemic and arrhythmic beat classification based on a set of rules obtained by a decision tree," *Artificial Intelligence in Medicine*, vol. 40, no. 3, pp. 187–200, 2007.

[11] S. N. Ghazavi and T. W. Liao, "Medical data mining by fuzzy modeling with selected features," *Artificial Intelligence in Medicine*, vol. 43, no. 3, pp. 195–206, 2008.

[12] M. A. Grando, M. Peleg, M. Cuggia, and D. Glasspool, "Patterns for collaborative work in health care teams," *Artificial Intelligence in Medicine*, vol. 53, no. 3, pp. 139–160, 2011.

[13] M. Rowan, T. Ryan, F. Hegarty, and N. O'Hare, "The use of artificial neural networks to stratify the length of stay of cardiac patients based on preoperative and initial postoperative factors," *Artificial Intelligence in Medicine*, vol. 40, no. 3, pp. 211–221, 2007.

[14] A. Chu, H. Ahn, B. Halwan et al., "A decision support system to facilitate management of patients with acute gastrointestinal bleeding," *Artificial Intelligence in Medicine*, vol. 42, no. 3, pp. 247–259, 2008.

[15] X. Zhou, S. Chen, B. Liu et al., "Development of traditional Chinese medicine clinical data warehouse for medical knowledge discovery and decision support," *Artificial Intelligence in Medicine*, vol. 48, no. 2-3, pp. 139–152, 2010.

[16] S. Chemlal, S. Colberg, M. Satin-Smith et al., "Blood glucose individualized prediction for type 2 diabetes using iPhone application," in *Proceedings of the 37th Annual Northeast Bioengineering Conference, (NEBEC'11)*, April 2011.

[17] B. Silva, I. Lopes, J. Rodrigues, and P. Ray, "SapoFitness: a mobile health application for dietary evaluation," in *Proceedings of the IEEE 13th International Conference on e-Health Networking, Applications and Services*, pp. 375–380, June 2011.

[18] F. Sposaro and G. Tyson, "iFall: An android application for fall monitoring and response," in *Proceedings of the 31st Annual International Conference of the IEEE Engineering in Medicine and Biology Society: Engineering the Future of Biomedicine, (EMBC'09)*, pp. 6119–6122, September 2009.

[19] F. Sposaro, J. Danielson, and G. Tyson, "IWander: an Android application for dementia patients," in *Proceedings of the 32nd Annual International Conference of the IEEE Engineering in Medicine and Biology Society, (EMBC'10)*, pp. 3875–3878, September 2010.

[20] M. N. K. Boulos, S. Wheeler, C. Tavares, and R. Jones, "How smartphones are changing the face of mobile and participatory healthcare: an overview, with example from eCAALYX," *BioMedical Engineering Online*, vol. 10, article 24, 2011.

[21] N. Houston, "The best medical Iphone apps for doctors and med students," October 2010, http://blog.softwareadvice.com/articles/medical/the-best-medical-iphone-apps-for-doctors-and-med-students-1100709/.

[22] QxMD, 2012, http://www.qxmd.com/specialty/medicine/cardiology-medical-apps-iphone-blackberry-android.

[23] Webicina—Cardiology in Social Media, 2012, http://www.webicina.com/cardiology/cardiology-mobile-applications/.

[24] Hearth360 Cardiovascular Wellness Center, May 2012, https://www.heart360.org/Default.aspx.

[25] Microsoft HealthVault Development Center, May 2012, http://msdn.microsoft.com/en-us/healthvault/default.aspx.

[26] G. Guidi, E. Iadanza, M. Pettenati et al., "Heart failure artificial intelligence-based computer aided diagnosis telecare system," in *Impact Analysis of Solutions for Chronic Disease Prevention and Management*, M. Donnelly, C. Paggetti, C. Nugent, and M. Mokhtari, Eds., vol. 7251, pp. 278–281, Springer, Berlin, Germany, 2012.

[27] J. W. Wallis, "Invited commentary: use of artificial intelligence in cardiac imaging," *Journal of Nuclear Medicine*, vol. 42, no. 8, pp. 1192–1194, 2001.

[28] P. C. Tang, J. S. Ash, D. W. Bates, J. M. Overhage, and D. Z. Sands, "Personal health records: definitions, benefits, and strategies for overcoming barriers to adoption," *Journal of the American Medical Informatics Association*, vol. 13, no. 2, pp. 121–126, 2006.

[29] NAHIT Report, April 2008, http://healthit.hhs.gov/portal/server.pt/gateway/PTARGS_0_10741_848133_0_0_18/10_2_hit_terms.pdf.

[30] A. Sunyaev, D. Chornyi, C. Mauro, and H. Krcmar, "Evaluation framework for personal health records: Microsoft HealthVault vs. Google Health," in *Proceedings of the 43rd Annual Hawaii International Conference on System Sciences, (HICSS'10)*, usa, January 2010.

[31] A. Sunyaev, A. Kaletsch, and H. Krcmar, "Comparative evaluation of Google Health API vs Microsoft HealthVault API," in *Proceedings of the 3rd International Conference on Health Informatics, (HEALTHINF'10)*, pp. 195–201, Valencia, Spain, January 2010.

[32] L. Liao, M. Chen, J. J. Rodrigues, X. Lai, and S. Vuong, "A novel web-enabled healthcare solution on healthvault system," *Journal of Medical Systems*, vol. 36, no. 3, pp. 1095–1105, 2012.

[33] Microsoft HealthVault, Apps and Devices, May 2012, http://www.microsoft.com/en-us/healthvault/tools-devices/overview.aspx.

[34] S. Nolan, "Microsoft HealthVault Application Connection Recommendations," 2010 http://download.microsoft.com/download/7/4/E/74EA8944-199C-4F56-B3BB-810586942-5BC/HealthVault%20Application%20Integration%20Recommendations%20v1.pdf.

17

Preference Comparison of AI Power Tracing Techniques for Deregulated Power Markets

Hussain Shareef,[1] **Saifunizam Abd. Khalid,**[2] **Mohd Wazir Mustafa,**[2] **and Azhar Khairuddin**[2]

[1] *Faculty of Electrical Engineering and Built Environment, Universiti Kebangsaan Malaysia, 43600 Bangi, Malaysia*
[2] *Faculty of Electrical Engineering, Universiti Teknologi Malaysia, 81310 Johor, Malaysia*

Correspondence should be addressed to Hussain Shareef, shareef@eng.ukm.my

Academic Editor: Thomas Mandl

This paper compares the two preference artificial intelligent (AI) techniques, namely, artificial neural network (ANN) and genetic algorithm optimized least square support vector machine (GA-LSSVM) approach, to allocate the real power output of individual generators to system loads. Based on solved load flow results, it first uses modified nodal equation method (MNE) to determine real power contribution from each generator to loads. Then the results of MNE method and load flow information are utilized to estimate the power transfer using AI techniques. The 25-bus equivalent system of south Malaysia is utilized as a test system to illustrate the effectiveness of the AI techniques compared to those of the MNE method. The AI methods provide the results in a faster and convenient manner with very good accuracy.

1. Introduction

Nowadays, the electric power industry is under deregulation in response to changes in jurisdiction, technology, market, and competition. Regardless of market environment, it is essential to know whether or not, and to what extent, each power system user contributes to the usage of particular system components. This information facilitates the restructured power system to operate economically and efficiently [1]. Moreover, it brings fair pricing and open access to all system users. Because of nonlinear nature of power flow, it is difficult to determine transmission usage accurately. Therefore, it requires using approximate models, tracing algorithms, or sensitivity indices for usage allocation. Methods based on the Y-bus or Z-bus system matrices have recently received great attention since these methods can integrate the network characteristics and circuit theories into line usage and loss allocation. The method reported in [2] is based on Kirchhoff's current law (KCL), equivalent linear circuit that reaches all lines and loads. Based on the stated assumptions, a recursive procedure was used to construct the equivalent circuit for each bus. Moreover, superposition theorem was applied to the bus's equivalent circuit starting from a bus whose injected currents were known. Another circuit concept method was proposed by Chang and Lu [3]. It was based on the system Y-bus matrix and Z-bus modification. Starting from the load flow solution, branch current is determined as a function of generators' injected current by using information from the bus impedance matrix. Similarly, contribution to bus voltages was computed as a function of each generator current injection by decomposing the network into different networks. Using the computed voltages and currents, the power flowing on the transmission lines were unbundled. It uses approximate formulation to calculate the unbundled loss components. This algorithm utilizes the network decomposition concept as proposed by Zobian and Ilić [4] which determines the use of transmission network by individual bilateral contracts. Teng [5] proposed a systematic method, very similar to that presented in [3], to allocate the power flow and loss for deregulated transmission systems. Using similar concept, the authors of this paper introduce a modified nodal equation (MNE) method for real and reactive power allocation [6] in which the load buses powers are represented as a function of the generators' current and voltage.

The tracing methods [1, 7–10] based on the actual power flows in the network and the proportional sharing principles were effectively used in transmission usage allocation. The methods reported in [1, 9] are based on tracing the current and complex power from individual power sources to system loads. Based on solved load flow, the method converts power injections and line flows into real and imaginary current injections and current flows. This method has a clear physical meaning and its results are unique. Bialek [7] proposed a novel power tracing method. However, this method requires inverting a large matrix. Wu [8] proposed a graph theory to calculate the contribution factor of individual generators to line flows and loads and the extraction factor of individual loads from line flows and generators, which is theoretically efficient. This method cannot handle loop flows and losses must be removed initially. Paper [11] was based on the concept of generator "domains," "common," and "links." The disadvantage of this method is that the share of each generator in each "common" (i.e., the set of buses supplied from the same set of generators) is assumed to be same. Furthermore, the "commons" concept can lead to problems since the topology of a "common" could radically change even in the case of slight change in power flows.

Since the meshed and nonlinear nature of power system, the applications of artificial intelligence (AI) to power system become a great potential to explore, especially in power tracing problem. Mustafa et al. [12] incorporated an artificial neural network (ANN) to reactive power allocation in deregulated power system. It uses modified nodal equation [6] results to train ANN. Similarly, research has been carried out by applying feed forward ANN for energy loss problem [13]. This method is relatively simple and easy to apply for loss allocation problem. Optimization technique also has been explored in solving the power allocation problem [14]. The authors proposed a tracing compliant that minimizes overall deviation from the postage stamp allocation. Nevertheless, the approach treats the power tracing problem as a linear constraint optimization problem. In a related work, a continuous genetic algorithm (GA) for real power tracing has been proposed in [15]. The problems of this technique are that it produces multisolution results and requires long time for computation. Paper [16] proposed a support vector machine (SVM) to estimate the contribution of individual generators to loads in power systems. The SVM gives faster results but the accuracy of the result is not promising.

Basically, support vector machine (SVM) is designed to solve the classification problem [17]. Then, it is extended for the case of nonlinear function estimation. Paper [18] uses SVM for detection of abnormalities and electricity theft by incorporating the genetic algorithm to SVM. Using similar concept, the authors of this paper also adopt the hybridization of GA and least square SVM (LS-SVM) into reactive power tracing problem [19]. The new reactive power tracing method is based on manipulation of proportional sharing method [7] and application of GA to tune the performance parameters of LS-SVM.

This paper deals mainly with investigation of two different AI techniques for real power transfer allocation and identifies most appropriate AI technique that can be used in power tracing by critically comparing the qualitative and quantitative performance of the two methods.

2. Modified Nodal Equations Method

The derivation, to decompose the load real powers into components contributed by specific generators, starts with basic equations of load flow. Applying Kirchhoff's current law to each node of the power network leads to the equations, which can be written in a matrix form as in (1) [6]

$$I = YV, \tag{1}$$

where V is a vector of all node voltages in the system, I is a vector of all node currents in the system, and Y is the Y-bus admittance matrix.

The nodal admittance matrix of the typical power system is large and sparse, therefore it can be partitioned in a systematic way. Considering a system in which there are G generator nodes that participate in selling power and remaining $L = n - G$ nodes as loads, then it is possible to rewrite (1) into its matrix form as shown in (2)

$$\begin{bmatrix} I_G \\ I_L \end{bmatrix} = \begin{bmatrix} Y_{GG} & Y_{GL} \\ Y_{LG} & Y_{LL} \end{bmatrix} \begin{bmatrix} V_G \\ V_L \end{bmatrix}. \tag{2}$$

Solving (2) for I_L, the load currents can be presented as a function of generators' current and load voltages as shown in (3)

$$I_L = Y_{LG} Y_{GG}^{-1} I_G + (Y_{LL} - Y_{LG} Y_{GG}^{-1} Y_{GL}) V_L. \tag{3}$$

Then, the total real power P_L of all loads can be expressed as shown in (4)

$$P_L = \mathrm{Re}\{V_L I_L^*\} \tag{4}$$

where $(*)$ means conjugate, substituting (3) into (4) and solving for P_L the relationship as shown in (5) can be found

$$
\begin{aligned}
P_L &= \mathrm{Re}\Big\{ V_L (Y_{LG} Y_{GG}^{-1})^* I_G^* \\
&\quad + V_L ((Y_{LL} - Y_{LG} Y_{GG}^{-1} Y_{GL}) V_L)^* \Big\} \\
&= \mathrm{Re}\Big\{ V_L \sum_{i=1}^{nG} \Delta I_L^{*I_G} + V_L ((Y_{LL} - Y_{LG} Y_{GG}^{-1} Y_{GL}) V_L)^* \Big\},
\end{aligned}
\tag{5}
$$

where

$$(Y_{LG} Y_{GG}^{-1})^* I_G^* = \sum_{i=1}^{nG} \Delta I_L^{*I_G} \tag{6}$$

and nG is number of generators.

Now, in order to decompose the load voltage-dependent term further in (5), into components of generator-dependent terms, (8) derivations are used. A possible way to deduce load node voltages as a function of generator bus voltages is to apply superposition theorem. However, it requires replacing all load bus current injections into equivalent admittances in the circuit. Using a readily available load flow result, the equivalent shunt admittance Y_{Lj} of load node j can be calculated using (7) as

$$Y_{Lj} = \frac{1}{V_{Lj}} \left(\frac{S_{Lj}}{V_{Lj}} \right)^* . \tag{7}$$

S_{Lj} is the load apparent power on node j and V_{Lj} is the load bus voltage on node j. After adding these equivalences to the diagonal entries of Y-bus matrix, (1) can be rewritten as

$$V = Y'^{-1} I_G, \tag{8}$$

where Y' is the modified Y of (1).

Next, adopting (8) and taking into account each generator one by one, the load bus voltages contributed by all generators can be expressed as

$$V_L = \sum_{i=1}^{nG} \Delta V_L^{*I_G}. \tag{9}$$

It is now simple mathematical manipulation to obtain the required relationship as a function of generators-dependent terms. By substituting (9) into (5), the decomposed load real powers can be expressed as

$$P_L = \mathrm{Re} \left\{ V_L \sum_{i=1}^{nG} \Delta I_L^{*I_G} + \sum_{i=1}^{nG} \Delta V_L^{*I_G} \left((Y_{LL} - Y_{LG} Y_{GG}^{-1} Y_{GL}) V_L \right)^* \right\}. \tag{10}$$

This equation shows that the real power of each load bus consists of two terms by individual generators. The first term relates directly to the generators' current and the second term corresponds to their contribution to the load voltages. With further simplification of (10), the real power contribution that load j acquires from generator i is as

$$P_{Lj} = \sum_{i=1}^{nG} P_{Lji}^{\Delta I_L} + \sum_{i=1}^{nG} P_{Lji}^{\Delta V_L}, \tag{11}$$

where $P_{Lji}^{\Delta I_L}$ is the current-dependent term of generator i to P_{Lj} and $P_{Lji}^{\Delta V_L}$ is the voltage-dependent term of generator i to P_{Lj}.

Vector P_L is used as a target in the training process of the proposed SVM.

3. AI Methods Used for Real Power Allocation

The following section describes an overview of the existing artificial intelligence power transfer allocation methods, namely, ANN method [12], and the GA-LSSVM [19].

3.1. Function Estimation Using Radial Basis Function Artificial Neural Network (ANN). The radial basis function (RBF) ANN was first used to design artificial neural network by Broomhead and Lowe [20]. Radial basis function offers several advantages compared to multilayer perceptron (MLP) ANN. Firstly, it can be trained using fast two stages training algorithm without the need for time consuming non-linear optimization techniques. Secondly, the RBFN possesses the property of best approximation [21]. The network consists of three layers, namely, an input layer, a hidden layer, and an output layer. The output of the RBF ANN network simply sums the weighted basis function without using any activation function. Assuming a single neuron at the output layer, the output of the RBF network is calculated using (12) as

$$\eta(x, w) = \sum_{k=1}^{S} w_{1k} \phi_k(\|x - c_k\|_2), \tag{12}$$

where $\|x - c_k\|_2$ denotes the Euclidean distance between the input vector x and the center c_k, $\phi_k(\cdot)$ is a basis function, w_{1k} are the weights in the output layer, and S is the number of neurons (and centers) in the hidden layer.

The output of the neuron in a hidden layer is a non-linear function of the distance. In this work, the functional form of Gaussian basis function is defined in (13) as,

$$\phi_k(\|x - c_k\|_2) = e^{-\|x - c_k\|_2^2 / \beta^2}. \tag{13}$$

Note that the Gaussian basis function is most commonly used where the parameter β controls the width of the RBF ANN and is commonly referred to as the spread parameter. In practice, the value of β that is too big or too small will cause degradation in the performance of the RBFN. The centers c_k are defined points that are assumed to perform an adequate sampling of the input space. Common practice is to select a relatively large number of input vectors as the centers to ensure an adequate input space sampling. RBF ANN performs two major functions which are training and testing. Testing is an integral part of the training process since a desired response to the network must be compared to the actual output to create an error function.

3.2. Function Estimation Using Least Squares Support Vector Machine (LS-SVM). Support vector machine (SVM) is known as a powerful methodology for solving problems in nonlinear classification, function estimation, and density estimation. Least squares support vector machine (LS-SVM) is reformulated from standard SVM [22] which lead to solving linear Karush-Kuhn-Tucker systems. In LS-SVM function estimation, the standard framework is based on a primal-dual formulation. Given N data set $\{x_i, y_i\}_{i=1}^{N}$, the goal is to estimate a model of the following form:

$$y(x) = w^T \varphi(x) + b + e_i, \tag{14}$$

where $x \in R^n$, $y \in R$ and $\varphi(\cdot) : R^n \rightarrow R^{n_h}$ is a mapping to a high dimensional feature space. Then based on model, the following optimization problem is formulated [23]:

$$\min_{w,b,e} J(w, e) = \frac{1}{2} w^T w + \gamma \frac{1}{2} \sum_{i=1}^{N} e_i^2 \tag{15}$$

such that $y_i = w^T \varphi(x_i) + b + e_i, i = 1, \ldots, N.$

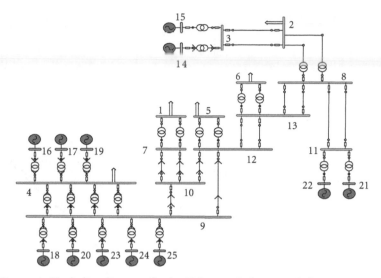

FIGURE 1: Single-line diagrams for the 25-bus equivalent practical power system.

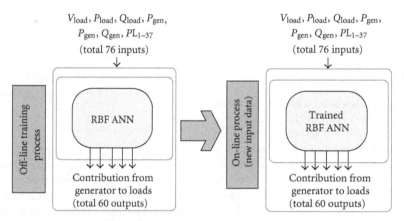

FIGURE 2: Description of inputs and outputs of the training and simulation data for ANN real power allocation method.

With the application of Mercer's theorem [22] for the kernel matrix Ω as $\Omega_{ij} = K(x_i, x_j) = \varphi(x_i)^T \varphi(x_j)$, $i, j = 1, \ldots, N$, it is not required to compute explicitly the nonlinear mapping $\phi(\cdot)$ as this is done implicitly through the use of positive definite kernel functions K [24].

From the following Lagrange function [23]:

$$\zeta(w, b, e; \beta) = \frac{1}{2} w^T w + \gamma \frac{1}{2} \sum_{i=1}^{N} e_i^2$$

$$- \sum_{i=1}^{N} \beta_i \left(w^T \varphi(x_i) + b + e_i - y_i \right), \quad (16)$$

where β_i are Lagrange multipliers. Differentiating (16) with w, b, e_i, and β_i, the conditions for optimality can be described as follow [23]:

$$\frac{d\zeta}{dw} = 0 \longrightarrow w = \sum_{i=1}^{N} \beta_i \varphi(x_i),$$

$$\frac{d\zeta}{db} = 0 \longrightarrow \sum_{i=1}^{N} \beta_i = 0,$$

$$\frac{d\zeta}{de_i} = 0 \longrightarrow \beta_i = \gamma e_i, \quad i = 1, \ldots, N,$$

$$\frac{d\zeta}{\beta_i} = 0 \longrightarrow y_i = w^T \varphi(x_i) + b + e_i, \quad i = 1, \ldots, N.$$

$$(17)$$

By elimination of w and e_i, the following linear system is obtained [23]:

$$\begin{bmatrix} 0 & 1^T \\ y & \Omega + \gamma^{-1} I \end{bmatrix} \begin{bmatrix} b \\ \beta \end{bmatrix} = \begin{bmatrix} 0 \\ y \end{bmatrix}, \quad (18)$$

with $y = [y_1, \ldots, y_N]^T$, $\beta = [\beta_1, \ldots, \beta_N]^T$. The resulting LS-SVM model in dual space becomes

$$y(x) = \sum_{i=1}^{N} \beta_i K(x, x_i) + b. \quad (19)$$

Usually, the training of the LS-SVM model involves an optimal selection of kernel parameters and regularization

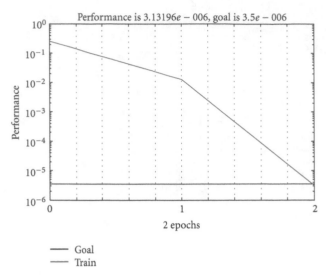

FIGURE 3: Training performance of RBF ANN.

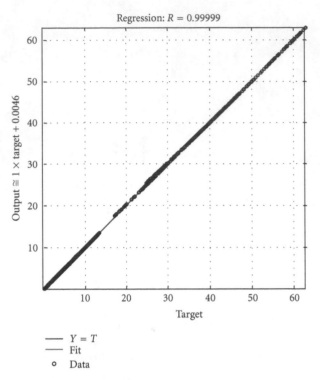

FIGURE 4: Regression analysis between the ANN output and the corresponding target for real power allocation.

parameter. For this paper, the RBF kernel is used which is expressed as

$$K(x, x_i) = e^{-\|x - x_i\|^2 / 2\sigma^2}. \tag{20}$$

Note that σ^2 is a parameter associated with RBF function which has to be tuned. There is no doubt that the efficient performance of LS-SVM model involves an optimal selection of kernel parameter, σ^2, and regularization parameter, γ. Thus by using GA as optimizer, an accurate result can be gained. The hybridization of GA and LS-SVM gives better accuracy and good generalization, especially in power transfer allocation problem [19].

4. ANN Model for Real Power Allocation

In this work, 1 RBF ANN with one hidden layer and one output layer has been chosen. The ANN power transfer allocation method is elaborated by designing an appropriate RBF ANN for the practical 25-bus equivalent power system of south Malaysia region as shown in Figure 1. This system consists of 12 generators located at buses 14 to 25 respectively. They deliver power to 5 loads, through 37 lines located at buses 1, 2, 4, 5, and 6, respectively. The input samples for training are assembled using the daily load curve and performing load flow analysis for every hour of load demand. Similarly the target vector for the training is obtained from the MNE method. Input data (D) for developed ANN contains variables such as load bus voltage magnitude ($V1$, $V2$, $V4$ to $V6$), real power of loads ($P1$, $P2$, $P4$ to $P6$), reactive power of loads ($Q1$, $Q2$, $Q4$ to $Q6$), real power of generators ($P14$ to $P25$), reactive power of generators ($Q14$ to $Q25$) and line real power ($Pline1$ to $Pline37$) flows, and the target/output parameter (T) which is the real power transfer between generators and loads placed at buses 1, 2, 4 to 6. Hence the networks have 60 output neurons. Figure 2 summarizes the description of inputs and outputs of the training and testing for ANN for real power allocation.

4.1. Training. After the input and target for training data is created, it can be made more efficient by scaling the network inputs and targets so that they always fall within a specified range. In this case the minimum and maximum value of input and output vectors is used to scale them in the range of -1 and $+1$. The next step is to divide the data (D and T) up into training. In this case, 100 samples (60%) of data are used for the training.

The training of the RBF ANN consists of two separate stages. The first step is to find the centers parameter by using the k-means clustering algorithm. After a number of trials, k is taken as 14 and the β as 17. These values give reasonable accuracy during training. In the second training stage, the second layer weights in connections between the hidden layer and the output layer are determined using the least squares based on minimization of quadratic errors of RBF ANN network output values over the set of training input-output vector pairs. The training performance is shown in Figure 3. From Figure 3, it can also be seen that the training goal is achieved in 2 epochs with performance equal to $3.13E - 6$. The training time taken by the RBF ANN is 232 msec using an Intel Core 2 Duo, 2 GHz computer.

4.2. Pretesting and Simulation. After the networks have been trained, the next step is to simulate the network. The entire training data is used in pretesting. After simulation, the obtained result from the trained network is evaluated with a linear regression analysis. In real power allocation scheme, the regression analysis for the trained network is shown in Figure 4. The correlation coefficient, (R), in this case is very

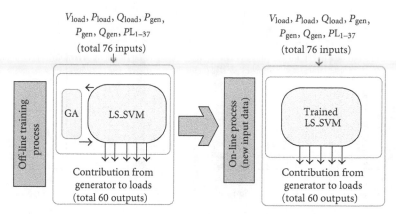

$V_{load}, P_{load}, Q_{load}, P_{gen},$
$P_{gen}, Q_{gen}, PL_{1-37}$
(total 76 inputs)

$V_{load}, P_{load}, Q_{load}, P_{gen},$
$P_{gen}, Q_{gen}, PL_{1-37}$
(total 76 inputs)

FIGURE 5: Description of inputs and outputs of the training and simulation data for GA-LSSVM for real power transfer allocation.

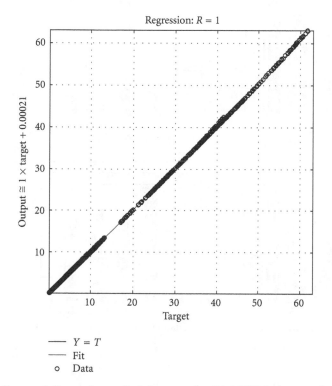

FIGURE 6: Regression analysis between the GA-LSSVM output and the corresponding target for real power allocation.

TABLE 1: Properties of GA to find the optimal γ and σ^2.

Property	Type and values
Selection	Roulette wheel
Crossover	Modified single point arithmetic crossover
Crossover probability	0.9
Mutation probability	0.1
Population	40
Maximum iteration	20

avoid discrimination among all methods considered in this paper. Input data (D) for developed GA-LSSVM contains 76 variables and target (T) contains 60 output parameters which is exactly the same as that used in RBF ANN method, Figure 5 summarize the description of inputs and outputs of the training and simulation stages for GA-LSSVM for real power allocation.

5.1. Training. After the input and target of training data have been created, the next step is to divide the data (D and T) up into training, validation, and testing subsets. Here again, 100 samples of data are used for the training out of 168 hour samples collected for training process.

The property of regularization parameter, γ, and Kernel RBF, σ^2 are decided through the hybrid GA-LSSVM model that has been discussed above. From the testing phase of GA-LSSVM model, the final value of γ is set to 9923.9 and σ^2 is set to 1347.8. It took 210.52 sec to optimize the γ and σ^2 values using the same computer. These LSSVM parameters yield a reasonably accurate output of the predictive model that has been designed. The mean square error (MSE) at pre-testing stage is $2.238E - 5$ which show that the estimation by GA-LSSVM model and the training data are having the similar characteristics.

5.2. Pretesting and Simulation. After the hybrid GA-LSSVM model has been trained, the entire 168 samples of data are used in pretesting. After simulation, the obtained result from the trained model is evaluated with the linear regression analysis as shown in Figure 6. The correlation coefficient, (R),

close to the one which indicates perfect correlation between the proposed method and the output of the neural network.

5. GA-LSSVM Design for Real Power Allocation

In order to find the optimal value of LS-SVM parameters, namely regularization parameter, γ and Kernel RBF parameter, σ^2, the continuous GA is used. The properties of GA to find the optimal γ and σ^2 are set as shown in Table 1.

The GA-LSSVM design for real power allocation is further elaborated for the same 25 bus system shown in Figure 1. Here again the same input and target data sets used in the previous AI power transfer allocation are used to

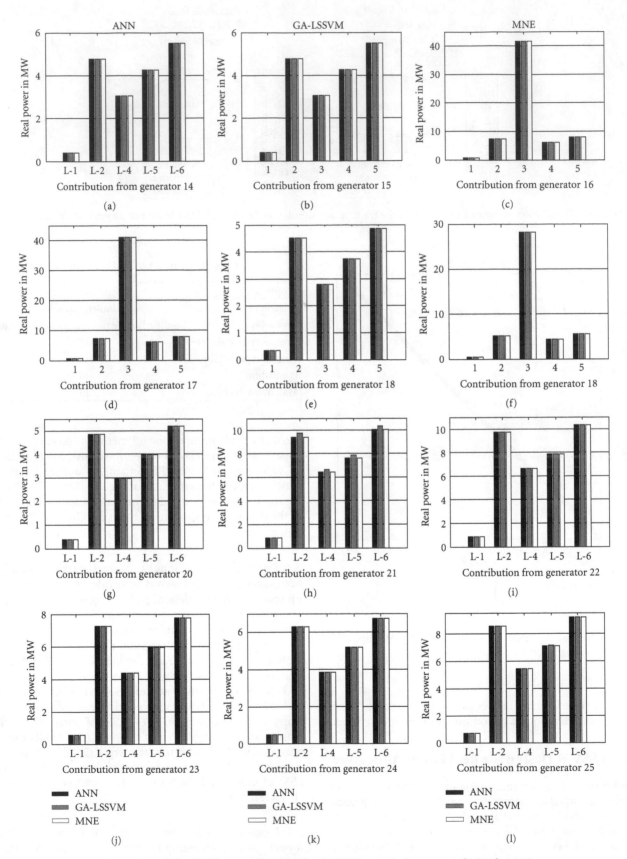

FIGURE 7: Analysis of real power allocation for the 25-bus equivalent system during hour 33.

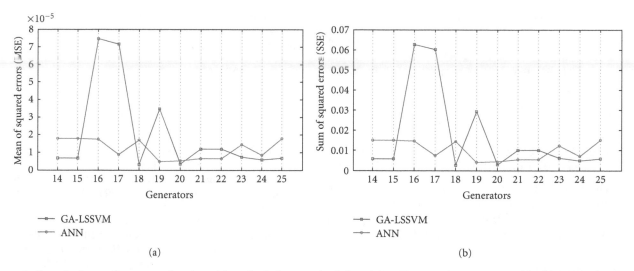

FIGURE 8: Quantitative performance of various AI methods for untrained data, (a) MSE errors in power transfer allocation of individual generators (b) SSE errors in power transfer allocation of individual generators.

in this case is equal to 1 which indicates a good correlation between MNE method and GA-LSSVM.

6. Results and Analysis

A number of simulations have been carried out to exhibit the accuracy of the developed AI power transfer allocation methods with the same 25-bus equivalent system of south Malaysia. The scenario is a decrement by 5% of the real and reactive load demand from the nominal trained pattern for 1 week (168 hours). Besides it also assumed that all generators also decrease their production proportionally according to this variation in the load demands. This assumption is being made to ensure that all real power generation of generator at buses 14 to 25 varies in respond to the varying daily load pattern of the loads. The allocation of real power to loads using proposed AI methods on hours 33 out of 168 hours is presented in Figure 7 along with the result obtained through MNE method. From Figure 7, it can be noted that the result obtained by the AI methods output in this paper is well comparable with the result of MNE method. The difference of real power between generators in both AI methods and MNE method is very small during this hour which is less than or equal to 0.400 kW. The consumer located at bus 4 consumed the highest demand compared to other consumers in this hour. Consequently, the contribution of real power due to generators 16, 17, and 19 located at the same bus provides more real power to load at bus 4 by all AI methods and MNE method as well. This result also justifies the physical meaning of MNE method as these generators are the nearest to load at bus 4.

To further evaluate the quantitative performance, mean square error (MSE) and sum of square error (SSE) observed by individual generator allocations and overall MSE and SSE encountered by each AI method are obtained. Figure 8 shows the MSE and SSE values introduced by each AI method they are subjected to untrained data. It can be observed that

MSE and SSE errors for both GA-LSSVM method and ANN method are comparable. In addition, it can also be noted that error differences between generator allocations in case ANN method is minimum which ranges between $1.71E - 05$ and $4.86E - 06$ for MSE error and 0.0147 and 0.0041 for SSE error.

The overall comparison of two AI methods that is used in power transfer allocation is exhibited in Table 2. It can be noted that mathematical model type (MNE) takes much longer time for training compared with multioutput model types like ANN and SVM. When comparing with overall MSE and SSE errors encountered during data simulation, the best performance is provided by ANN method whose MSE and SSE are found to be $1.19E - 5$ and 0.1203, respectively. All in all, it can be concluded that ANN method is the best to use for power transfer allocation because it takes very short training time in model development and provides more accurate results in less simulation time as shown in Table 2.

7. Conclusion

This paper has presented two preference AI methods that can be used to identify the real power transfer between generators and load. The developed AI method adopts real power allocation outputs determined by MNE technique as the trainer during the model development phase. The robustness of the two AI methods has been demonstrated on the 25-bus equivalent system of south Malaysia. From the results, the following conclusions can be attained.

(1) The AI power transfer allocation methods provide the results in a faster and convenient manner.

(2) Among two AI methods, ANN method provides the most accurate results while GA-LSSVM method also gives an acceptable result.

(3) In terms of training, ANN and GA-LSSVM require comparably small training time.

TABLE 2: Qualitative and quantitative comparison of two AI power transfer allocation methods.

Method	Model type	Training time (sec)	Simulation time (msec)	Overall MSE error for new data	Overall SSE error for new data
ANN	Multioutput	0.2321	21.99	$1.19E-05$	0.1203
GA-LSSVM	Multioutput	0.2388	23.89	$2.05E-05$	0.2064
MNE	Mathematical	—	360.00	—	—

(4) The ANN-based method is the most suitable to be adapted in true application of real power allocation.

(5) The proposed AI method can resolve some of the difficult real power pricing and costing issues to ensure fairness and transparency in the deregulated environment of power system operation.

Acknowledgments

The authors wish to acknowledge the Ministry of Higher Education, Malaysia (MOHE) for the financial funding of this project, and Universiti Teknologi Malaysia and Universiti Kabangsaan Malaysia, for providing infrastructure and moral support for the research work.

References

[1] H. Shareef and M. W. Mustafa, "Real and reactive power allocation in a competitive market," *WSEAS Transactions on Power Systems*, vol. 1, pp. 1088–1094, 2006.

[2] R. Reta and A. Vargas, "Electricity tracing and loss allocation methods based on electric concepts," *IEE Proceedings: Generation, Transmission and Distribution*, vol. 148, no. 6, pp. 518–522, 2001.

[3] Y. C. Chang and C. N. Lu, "Electricity tracing method with application to power loss allocation," *International Journal of Electrical Power and Energy System*, vol. 23, no. 1, pp. 13–17, 2001.

[4] A. Zobian and M. D. Ilić, "Unbundling of transmission and ancillary services Part I: technical issues," *IEEE Transactions on Power Systems*, vol. 12, no. 2, pp. 539–548, 1997.

[5] J. H. Teng, "Power flow and loss allocation for deregulated transmission systems," *International Journal of Electrical Power and Energy Systems*, vol. 27, no. 4, pp. 327–333, 2005.

[6] H. Shareef, M. W. Mustafa, S. Abd Khalid, A. Khairuddin, A. Kalam, and A. Maung Than Oo, "Real and reactive power transfer allocation utilizing modified Nodal equations," *International Journal of Emerging Electric Power Systems*, vol. 9, no. 6, article 4, 2008.

[7] J. Bialek, "Tracing the flow of electricity," *IEE Proceedings Generation Transmission & Distribution*, vol. 143, no. 4, pp. 313–320, 1996.

[8] F. F. Wu, "Power transfer allocation for open access using graph theory—fundamentals and applications in systems without loopflow," *IEEE Transactions on Power Systems*, vol. 15, no. 3, pp. 923–929, 2000.

[9] M. W. Mustafa, H. Shareef, and M. R. Ahmad, "An improved usage allocation method for deregulated transmission systems," in *Proceedings of the 7th International Power Engineering Conference (IPEC '05)*, pp. 406–411, December 2005.

[10] S. Abdelkader, "Efficient computation algorithm for calculating load contributions to line flows and losses," *IEE Proceedings: Generation, Transmission and Distribution*, vol. 153, no. 4, pp. 391–398, 2006.

[11] D. K. Ron and A. G. Strbac, "Contributions of individual generators to loads and flows," *IEEE Transactions on Power Systems*, vol. 12, no. 1, pp. 52–60, 1997.

[12] M. W. Mustafa, S. N. Khalid, H. Shareef, and A. Khairuddin, "Reactive power transfer allocation method with the application of artificial neural network," *IET Generation, Transmission and Distribution*, vol. 2, no. 3, pp. 402–413, 2008.

[13] N. B. Dev Choudhury and S. K. Goswami, "Artificial intelligence solution to transmission loss allocation problem," *Expert Systems with Applications*, vol. 38, no. 4, pp. 3757–3764, 2011.

[14] A. R. Abhyankar, S. A. Soman, and S. A. Khaparde, "Optimization approach to real power tracing: an application to transmission fixed cost allocation," *IEEE Transactions on Power Systems*, vol. 21, no. 3, pp. 1350–1361, 2006.

[15] M. H. Sulaiman, M. W. Mustafa, and O. Aliman, "Transmission loss and load flow allocations via genetic algorithm technique," in *Proceedings of the IEEE Region 10 Conference (TENCON '09)*, pp. 1–5, November 2009.

[16] H. Shareef, A. Mohamed, S. N. Khalid, M. W. Mustafa, and A. Khairuddin, "Real power transfer allocation utilizing support vector machine," in *Proceedings of the International Conference of Electrical Energy and Industrial Electronic Systems (EEIES '09)*, pp. 1–7, Penang, Malaysia, December 2009.

[17] J. A. K. Suykens and J. Vandewalle, "Least squares support vector machine classifiers," *Neural Processing Letters*, vol. 9, no. 3, pp. 293–300, 1999.

[18] J. Nagi, K. S. Yap, S. K. Tiong, S. K. Ahmed, and A. M. Mohammad, "Detection of abnormalities and electricity theft using genetic support vector machines," in *Proceedings of the IEEE Region 10 Conference (TENCON '08)*, pp. 1–6, November 2008.

[19] M. W. Mustafa, M. H. Sulaiman, H. Shareef, and S. N. Abd. Khalid, "Reactive power tracing in pool-based power system utilising the hybrid genetic algorithm and least squares support vector machine," *IET Generation, Transmission and Distribution*, vol. 6, no. 2, pp. 133–141, 2012.

[20] D. S. Broomhead and D. Lowe, "Multivariable functional interpolation and adaptive networks," *Complex System*, vol. 2, pp. 321–355, 1988.

[21] F. Girosi and T. Poggio, "Networks and the best approximation property," *Biological Cybernetics*, vol. 63, no. 3, pp. 169–176, 1990.

[22] V. N. Vapnik, *The Nature of Statistical Learning Theory*, New York, NY, USA, 2nd edition, 1995.

[23] J. A. K. Suykens, T. V. Gestel, J. De Brabanter, B. De Moor, and J. Vandewelle, *Least Squares Support Vector Machines*, World Scientific, Singapore, 2002.

[24] M. Espinoza, J. A. K. Suykens, and B. De Moor, "Fixed-size least squares support vector machines: a large scale application in electrical load forecasting," *Computational Management Science*, vol. 3, no. 2, pp. 113–129, 2006.

18

A Novel Method for Training an Echo State Network with Feedback-Error Learning

Rikke Amilde Løvlid

Department of Computer and Information Science, Norwegian University of Science and Technology, Sem Sælands vei 7-9, 7491 Trondheim, Norway

Correspondence should be addressed to Rikke Amilde Løvlid; rikke-amilde.lovlid@ffi.no

Academic Editor: Ralf Moeller

Echo state networks are a relatively new type of recurrent neural networks that have shown great potentials for solving non-linear, temporal problems. The basic idea is to transform the low dimensional temporal input into a higher dimensional state, and then train the output connection weights to make the system output the target information. Because only the output weights are altered, training is typically quick and computationally efficient compared to training of other recurrent neural networks. This paper investigates using an echo state network to learn the inverse kinematics model of a robot simulator with feedback-error-learning. In this scheme teacher forcing is not perfect, and joint constraints on the simulator makes the feedback error inaccurate. A novel training method which is less influenced by the noise in the training data is proposed and compared to the traditional ESN training method.

1. Introduction

A recurrent neural network (RNN) is a neural network with feedback connections. Mathematically RNNs implement dynamical systems, and in theory they can approximate arbitrary dynamical systems with arbitrary precision [1]. This makes them "in principle promising" as solutions for difficult temporal tasks, but in practice, supervised training of RNNs is difficult and computationally expensive.

Echo state networks (ESNs) were proposed as a cheap and fast architectural and supervised learning scheme and are therefore suggested to be useful in solving real problems [2]. The basic idea is to transform the low dimensional temporal input into a higher dimensional *echo state*, and then train the output connection weights to make the system output the desired information. The idea was independently developed by Maass [3] and Jaeger [4] as liquid state machine (LSM) and echo state machine (ESM), respectively.

LSMs and ESMs, together with the more recently explored Backpropagation Decorrelation learning rule for RNNs [5], are given the generic term reservoir computing [6]. Typically large, complex RNNs are used as reservoirs, and

their function resembles a tank of liquid. One can think of the input as stones thrown into the liquid, creating unique ripples that propagate, interact, and eventually fade away. After learning how to read the water's surface, one can extract a lot of information about recent events, without having to do the complex input integration. Real water has successfully been used as a reservoir [7].

Because only the output weights are altered, training is typically quick and computationally efficient compared to training of other recurrent neural networks.

We are investigating how to use an ESN to learn internal models of a robot's motor apparatus. An internal model is a system that mimics the behavior of a natural process. In this paper we will talk about inverse models, which transform preplanned trajectories of desired perceptual consequences into appropriate motor commands.

The inverse model is often divided into a kinematic and a dynamic model. An inverse kinematic model transforms a trajectory in task space (e.g., cartesian coordinates) to a trajectory in actuator space (e.g., joint angles), and an inverse dynamic model transforms the joint space trajectory into the sequence of forces that will actually move the limbs. The robot simulator in our experiments is controlled by the joint angle velocities directly, thus we are only concerned with kinematics.

It is common to use analytical internal models, and deriving such a model for our simulator would be easy. Despite this, we want to explore using an ESN as an inverse model, because as robots become more complex, with springy joints, light limbs and many degrees of freedom, acquiring analytical models will become more and more difficult [8]. Oubbati et al. also argue that substituting the analytical models with a recurrent neural networks might be beneficial in general, as it can make the inverse model more robust against noise and sensor errors [9].

To acquire an accurate inverse model through learning is, however, problematic, because the target motor commands are generally unavailable. What is known is the target trajectory in task space. Three schemas have been suggested for training the inverse model: directly by observing the effect of different motor commands on the controlled object [10], with a forward model as a distal teacher [11], or with an approach called feedback-error learning (FEL) [10]. Direct modeling was excluded because it cannot handle redundancies in the motor apparatus and therefore will not scale to real problems [11]. FEL was chosen over distal teacher because it is a natural extension of using an analytical model, and because it is biologically motivated due to its inspiration from cerebellar motor control [12]. Another advantage, which we will not exploit here, is that FEL can be used for control during learning.

The objective in this paper is to investigate how an ESN can be trained within this FEL scheme. The traditional ESN learning method falls short in this setup due to inaccurate teacher forcing and target estimation. We propose a novel training method, which is inspired by gradient decent methods and shows promising results on this problem. Preliminary studies of this training method can be found in a related work [13]. The current paper includes further studies of why this new method works so well.

2. Learning to Imitate YMCA

In this paper an ESN is trained to execute an arm movement on a simple robot simulator by computing the inverse kinematics of that movement. The ESN is only tested on the movement it was trained on, which means that we do not verify whether the ESN has actually learned the inverse model or merely to execute this particular trajectory. We have earlier investigated the benefit of learning the inverse model by training on one movement with certain properties [14]. Here we have a slightly more complex inverse problem and encountered a problem when trying to learn the training sequence itself. The solution to that problem is the main point in this paper.

2.1. Training Data. The movement data is a recording of the dance to the song YMCA by the Village People. It was gathered with a Pro Reflex 3D motion tracking system by Tidemann and Öztürk [15]. The system is able to track the position of fluorescent balls within a certain volume by using five infrared cameras. The sampling frequency of the Pro Reflex is 200 Hz. In the experiments we used every fourth sample, meaning the position trajectory consisted of 50 samples/sec, resulting in a sequence with 313 steps.

The tracking of the balls yields cartesian coordinates of the balls in three dimensions. The result was projected down to two dimensions, and the position of each arm was expressed as the x and z coordinates of the elbow relative to the shoulder and the wrist relative to the elbow. The coordinates were normalized to be in the interval $\langle -1, 1 \rangle$. The position in each time step was thus represented by 8 signals, that is, $(x_{elbow}, z_{elbow}, x_{wirst}, z_{wrist})$ for each arm.

2.2. Simulator. For the simulations we used a fairly simple 2D simulator with four degrees of freedom (DOFs), one in each shoulder and one in each elbow. The simulated robot was controlled by the joint angle velocities directly, which means that the problem of translating the velocities into torques was not considered. The ESN was trained to output the joint angle velocities that would keep the elbows and wrists on the desired trajectory. The velocities were scaled to be in the interval $\langle -1, 1 \rangle$ and will be referred to as the *motor commands*.

The range of motion was constrained to be between $0°$ and $180°$ for all 4 DOFs, and if the motor command implied moving the limb further, the limb stopped at the limit and the overshooting motor command was ignored.

The maximum joint angle velocity for each DOF was set to twice the maximum velocity registered in the recorded movement, which meant that a joint angle velocity equal to 1 moved the joint less than 180 degrees. Limited joint velocity is realistic, and it also makes large errors in motor commands lead to smaller position errors, making the movements look smoother.

2.3. Control Architecture. The ESN is trained to compute motor commands that will move the simulated arms from the current position to the next position in the target trajectory. The target motor commands needed for training are not available; what is available is the target positions.

The FEL scheme, illustrated in Figure 1, includes a feedback controller that estimates the error in motor command from the position error. The motor error computed by the feedback controller is used both to train the ESN and to adjust the motor command from the inverse model before it is sent to the arm simulator. In the current setup the transformation from position error to motor error is simple enough to be done analytically, but using the result will still not be perfect as the simulator is noisy and the calculation does not take into consideration any excess motor commands that were potentially ignored if the limbs were moved to their limits.

How much influence the feedback controller has on the final motor command is regulated by the feedback gain, K. To facilitate learning and force the feedback controller to become redundant, the feedback gain was linearly reduced from 1 to 0 during several rounds of training.

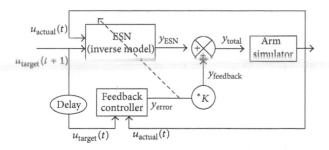

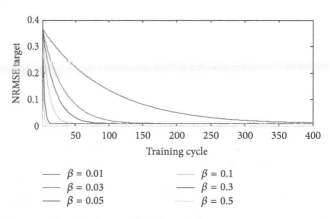

$\beta = 0.01$ $\beta = 0.1$
$\beta = 0.03$ $\beta = 0.3$
$\beta = 0.05$ $\beta = 0.5$

FIGURE 1: The figure illustrates the feedback-error-learning (FEL) architecture used to training the ESN. The input to the ESN is the actual position at the current time step ($u_{\text{actual}}(t)$) and the next position in the target position trajectory ($u_{\text{target}}(t + 1)$). The ESN learns to calculate the motor command which will move the simulated arms from the current position to the next position in the target trajectory. The motor command from the ESN is called y_{ESN} and is adjusted by the motor command from the feedback controller, y_{feedback}, before it is used to move the simulated arms. The feedback controller estimates the error of this total motor command (y_{error}) by comparing the resulting position with the corresponding target position. This error is used to train the ESN and to compute the feedback motor command in the next time step. The feedback gain, K, determines how much the feedback controller can influence the total motor command.

FIGURE 3: The plot shows the difference between the true target and the used target in each training cycle for different values of β when target estimation and teacher forcing are perfect. The result is used to deduce how many extra cycles of training are needed for different values of β. Note that with $\beta = 1$, the used target and the true target will be equal from the start, and only one cycle of training is needed.

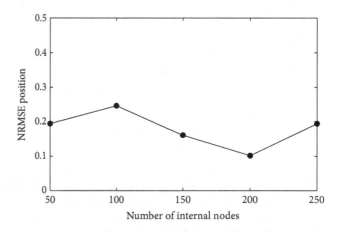

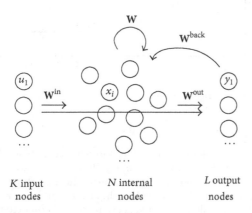

K input N internal L output
nodes   nodes   nodes

FIGURE 2: The figure illustrates a basic ESN.

FIGURE 4: To determine the optimal reservoir size, ESNs with different numbers of internal nodes were trained with the original training method within the FEL scheme. The YMCA movement was repeated 5 times in the training sequence, and the internal noise level was 0.02. The figure shows the mean position errors during testing for 10 repetitions of each experiment.

3. Training an Echo State Network

A basic echo state network is illustrated in Figure 2. The activation of the internal nodes is updated according to

$$\mathbf{x}(t) = f\left(\mathbf{W}^{\text{in}}\mathbf{u}(t) + \mathbf{W}\mathbf{x}(t - 1) + \mathbf{W}^{\text{back}}\mathbf{y}(t - 1)\right) + \nu(t - 1),\tag{1}$$

where f is the node's activation function, and ν are white Gaussian noise. The output of the network is computed according to

$$\mathbf{y}(t) = f^{\text{out}}\left(\mathbf{W}^{\text{out}}\left(\mathbf{u}(t), \mathbf{x}(t)\right)\right).\tag{2}$$

A general task is described by a set of input and desired output pairs, $[\langle\mathbf{u}(1), \mathbf{y}_{\text{target}}(1)\rangle, \langle\mathbf{u}(2), \mathbf{y}_{\text{target}}(2)\rangle, \ldots, \langle\mathbf{u}(T), \mathbf{y}_{\text{target}}(T)\rangle]$, and the solution is a trained ESN whose output

$\mathbf{y}(t)$ approximates the teacher output $\mathbf{y}_{\text{target}}(t)$, when the ESN is driven by the training input $\mathbf{u}(t)$.

3.1. Original Training Method. Training the ESN using the original training methods is done in three steps. First, a random RNN with the echo state property is generated [4]. Second, the training sequence is run through the network once. If there are feedback connections, teacher forcing is used, meaning $\mathbf{y}(t)$ is replaced by $\mathbf{y}_{\text{target}}(t)$ when computing $\mathbf{x}(t + 1)$ and $\mathbf{y}(t + 1)$. After the first T_0 time steps, which are used to wash out the initial transient dynamics, the states of each input and internal node in each time step are stored in a state collection matrix, $\mathbf{M}$. Assuming tanh is used as output activation function, $\tanh^{-1}(\mathbf{y}_{\text{target}}(t))$ is collected row-wise

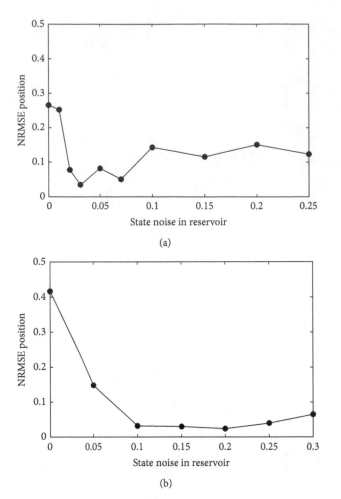

(a)

(b)

FIGURE 5: The optimal choice for the level of internal noise in the reservoir was significantly different for the two training methods. The figures show the mean position error during testing for different noise levels. (a) The networks were trained with the original method with the training sequence consisting of 5 repetitions of the YMCA movement. (b) The corresponding results when the networks were trained with the new method with $\beta = 0.1$ and the movement sequence repeated once. All experiments were run 10 times, and the number of internal nodes was 200 in all the networks. Based on the results we chose noise level 0.03 for the original method and 0.2 for the new method.

into a target collection matrix $\mathbf{S}$. Equation (2) can then be written as

$$\mathbf{S} = \mathbf{M}\left(\mathbf{W}^{\mathrm{out}}\right)^T. \tag{3}$$

Third, the output weights are computed by using the Moore-Penrose pseudoinverse to solve (3) with regard to $\mathbf{W}^{\mathrm{out}}$:

$$\left(\mathbf{W}^{\mathrm{out}}\right)^T = \mathbf{M}^+\mathbf{S}. \tag{4}$$

3.2. New Proposed Training Method. In the original training method the training sequence is run through the network once, and the output weights are updated based on the target collection matrix and the state collection matrix as shown in

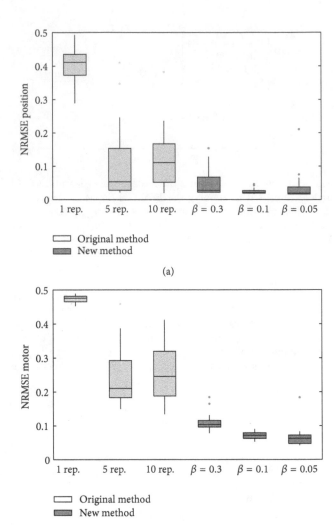

(a)

(b)

FIGURE 6: The figures show a box and whisker plots for 20 runs of each of the 6 experiments. Plot (a) illustrates the position error during testing and plot (b) the motor error during testing. On each box, the central mark is the median, the edges of the box are the 25th and 75th percentiles, the whiskers extend to the most extreme data points not considered outliers, and outliers are plotted individually.

(4). This does not work well with our training architecture, because teacher forcing and target estimation are far from perfect. We therefore suggest *running the training sequence through several times* for each value of the feedback gain. For each of these cycles the output weights are calculated based on the state collection matrix and something in between the estimated target and the actual output from the ESN model. One has

$$\mathbf{y}^i_{\mathrm{used\ target}}(t) = \beta\mathbf{y}_{\mathrm{estimated\ target}}(t) + \left(1 - \beta\right)\mathbf{y}_{\mathrm{ESN}}(t). \tag{5}$$

The vector $\mathbf{y}^i_{\mathrm{used\ target}}(t)$ is the target used to generate the target matrix $\mathbf{S}$ for computing $\mathbf{W}^{\mathrm{out}}$ in cycle i, and $\mathbf{y}_{\mathrm{estimated\ target}}(t)$ is an estimate of the target, as the true target is not available. Note that $\beta = 1$ corresponds to the original training method.

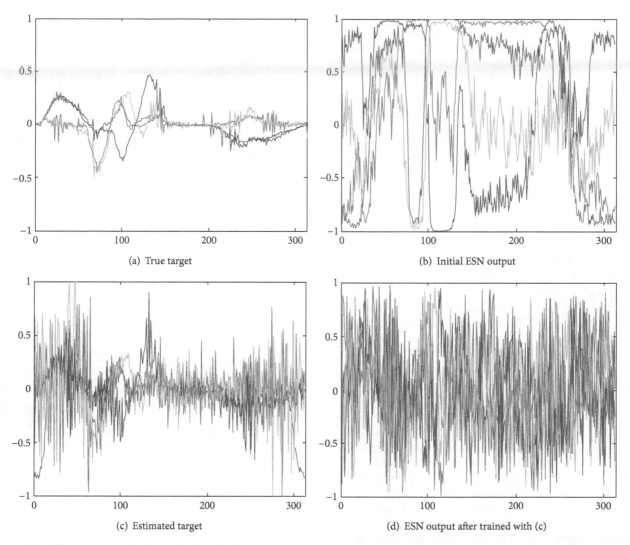

(a) True target

(b) Initial ESN output

(c) Estimated target

(d) ESN output after trained with (c)

FIGURE 7: The plots illustrate why the original method without repetitions (experiment 1) fails. Compared to the true target (a), the estimated target in the first epoch (c) is very noisy. It has the general shape of the true target, but when training the initial, random ESN (b) with this noisy estimate, the result is a network which outputs mostly noise (d). This only gets worse in the succeeding epochs. Plotted are motor commands (joint angle velocities) for the 4 DOFs at each time step in the training sequence.

We hypothesize that this new proposed training method will improve learning. However, the training time increases as β decreases because additional cycles of training are needed. To test how many cycles are needed to converge for each value of β, the network was trained with the true target and perfect teacher forcing for 400 cycles. The true target was found by using an analytical inverse model. Figure 3 illustrates the difference between the true target, $\mathbf{y}_{target}$, and the used target, $\mathbf{y}_{used\ target}$, in each cycle, i. To compensate for this extra computation time, we will try reducing the length of the training sequence when applying this training method.

4. Experiments

The performance of the new proposed method is compared to the performance of the original method through different experiments. Our main hypothesis is that the new method will provide the same or better performance as the original at a smaller computational cost.

In all the experiments the ESN was trained to execute the YMCA movement. It was trained with feedback-error learning with the feedback gain linearly being decreased from 1 to 0 during 10 epochs of training. During testing the ESN was run without the feedback controller and the performance was measured as how accurately the ESN was able to reproduce the training sequence.

The original training method was used on training sequences with varying number of repetitions of the YMCA movement. We hypothesize that training on longer sequences, where the movement is repeated several times, will increase the performance. However, a longer training sequence leads to longer training time.

The new training method was investigated by conducting experiments for three different values of β. All trained

TABLE 1: The table summarizes the experiment details, including the value of β ($\beta = 1$ means the original method), the number of cycles per epoch, and the number of repetitions of the YMCA movement constituting the training sequence. In all the experiments the ESN was trained for 10 epochs with decreasing feedback gain.

Experiment number	β	# cycles per epoch	# rep. movement
Exp. 1	1	1	1
Exp. 2	1	1	5
Exp. 3	1	1	10
Exp. 4	0.3	2	1
Exp. 5	0.1	3	1
Exp. 6	0.05	10	1

on just one repetition of the YMCA movement, but the sequence had to be presented several times for each epoch to make it possible for the used target to converge during the 10 training epochs. The number of cycles used for each epoch was the approximate number of cycles needed for convergence according to Figure 3, divided by the number of epochs.

Table 1 holds the details of the different experiments.

4.1. Parameters. The ESN had 8 input nodes, corresponding to the x and z coordinates of the shoulders and elbows, and 4 output nodes, one for each DOF of the simulator. We used 200 nodes in the internal network, which was optimized for the original training method as illustrated in Figure 4.

When implementing the ESN, we used the simple matlab toolbox provided by Jaeger et al. [16]. The spectral radius was 0.5 and tanh was used as output function. The reservoir noise level was set to 0.03 when using the original method and 0.2 when using the new method. These noise levels are justified in Figure 5. All other network parameters used were the default in the toolbox. Gaussian noise with mean 0 and standard deviation 0.01 was added to the output from the arm simulator.

4.2. Training and Testing. The feedback controller was only used during training, and the feedback gain was reduced from 1 to 0 during 10 epochs. Before each epoch the ESN was reinitialized by setting the internal states to 0 and running the training sequence through once without learning. The epoch continued with one cycle of training when using the original training method and several cycles of training when $\beta < 1$. One last circle without training (but with use of the feedback controller) was run in each epoch to evaluate the performance at that stage.

After training the network was again reinitialized and tested on the training sequence by running it through once without the feedback controller.

To evaluate the performance we use the Root Mean Square Error (RMSE) of the resulting position sequence normalized over the range of the output values:

$$\text{MSE}\left(\mathbf{y}, \mathbf{y}_{\text{true target}}\right) = \frac{\sqrt{\text{MSE}}}{y_{\max} - y_{\min}} = \frac{\sqrt{\text{MSE}}}{2}. \qquad (6)$$

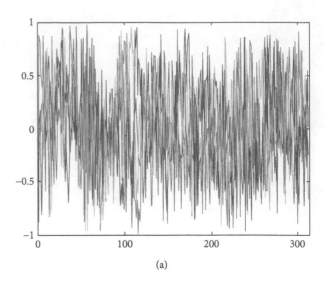

(a)

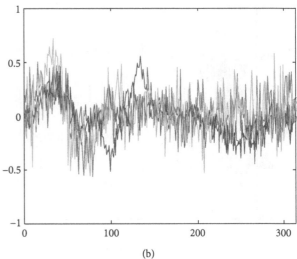

(b)

FIGURE 8: Adding more repetitions of the movement in the training sequence makes the output of the ESN seem less noisy. Plot (a) shows the output of the ESN after training with one repetition and plot (b) the ESN output after training on 5 repetition of the YMCA movement.

The NRMSE for each run was averaged over all time steps and DOFs. A NRMSE = 0 means no error, a random solution would have NRMSE $\approx$ 0.5, and NRMSE = 1 means opposite solution.

5. Results

Each of the six experiments were repeated 20 times, and the results are summarized in Table 2 and illustrated in Figure 6.

The motor error of experiment 1 is close to 0.5, which means that using the original training method on one repetition of the YMCA sequence results in a network that does not perform better than a random network. Repeating the movement in the training sequence (experiments 2 and 3) helps, but note that the variance is pretty large.

Using the new training method makes a larger improvement with a lower additional computational cost. From the box and whisker plot in Figure 6(b) we see that the worst ESN obtained by using the new method with $\beta = 0.1$ (experiment 5) performed better than the best ESN obtained with the original method trained on 5 repetitions of the YMCA (experiment 2). Due to the computation time of the pseudo-inverse calculations, the training time of a sequence of length $m * n$ is longer than training a sequence of length m n times [17]. This implies that the running time of experiment 5 (sequence of 313 steps run $3 * 10$ times) is also shorter than the running time of experiment 2 (sequence of $5 * 313$ steps run 10 times).

5.1. Why the New Method Outperforms the Original. To understand the effects of the different experimental setups we trained the same initial network with the setups in experiments 1 (original, 1 rep.), 2 (original, 5 rep.), and 5 (new, $\beta = 0.1$) and studied how the ESN output, the actual position sequence, the estimated target, and the target used for weight calculation evolved during the training epochs.

Figure 7 shows why experiment 1 fails. The estimated target sequence is too noisy, and with the short training sequence without any repetitions, the output from the ESN becomes even noisier.

The output from the ESN after training becomes significantly less noisy when the movement is repeated several times in the training sequence, as illustrated in Figure 8. In this setup the target sequence does have a repeating pattern, and since the error in each repetition will differ, the weight calculation will average over these slightly different representations.

When using the new training method, the approach for making a smoother target is different. The new method is apparently able to keep the smoothness of the output of the first, random network and just gradually drives that solution toward the target. As illustrated in Figure 9 the used target, that is, the best target estimate combined with the previous ESN output, appears much less noisy than the target estimate alone.

The new method also results in better teacher forcing. Figure 10 illustrates the quality of the teacher forcing for the three selected experiments.

6. Discussion and Conclusion

This paper investigates using feedback-error learning to train an ESN to learn the inverse kinematics of an arm movement. When applying feedback-error learning, teacher forcing is not perfect, and joint constraints on the simulator make the feedback error inaccurate. A novel training method is suggested, which uses a combination of the previous ESN output and the estimated target to train the network. This presumably keeps much of the smoothness of the output from the initial, random network and avoids the unstable output obtained when training with the estimated target directly.

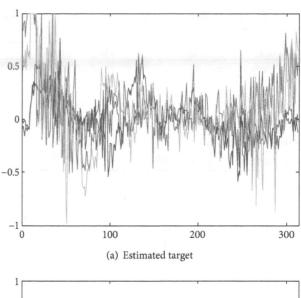

(a) Estimated target

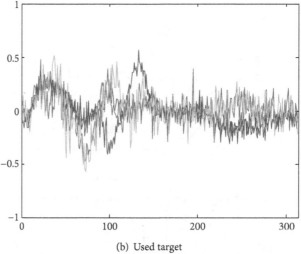

(b) Used target

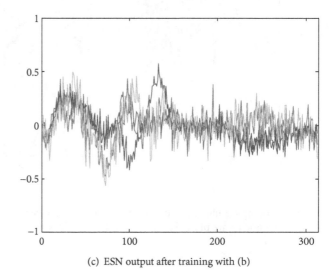

(c) ESN output after training with (b)

FIGURE 9: In experiment 5 the network is trained on one repetition of the YMCA movement with $\beta = 0.1$. The plots show (a) the estimated target, (b) the used target, and (c) the ESN output after training with (b). All the plots are from epoch 5, where the used target is starting to look like the true target. Notice that the used target appears less noisy than the estimated target.

TABLE 2: The mean NRMSE and variance for 20 repetitions of each experiment. All the networks were tested on one repetition of the YMCA movement.

Experiment	Position error	Var	Motor error	Var
1 Orig. method, 1 rep.	0.4000	0.0024	0.4737	$1.4E-04$
2 Orig. method, 5 rep.	0.1088	0.0125	0.2435	0.0071
3 Orig. method, 10 rep.	0.1193	0.0081	0.2500	0.0066
4 New method, $\beta = 0.3$	0.0494	0.0018	0.1100	$6.9E-04$
5 New method, $\beta = 0.1$	0.0245	$7.0E-05$	0.0717	$1.4E-04$
6 New method, $\beta = 0.05$	0.0385	0.0020	0.0669	$9.2E-04$

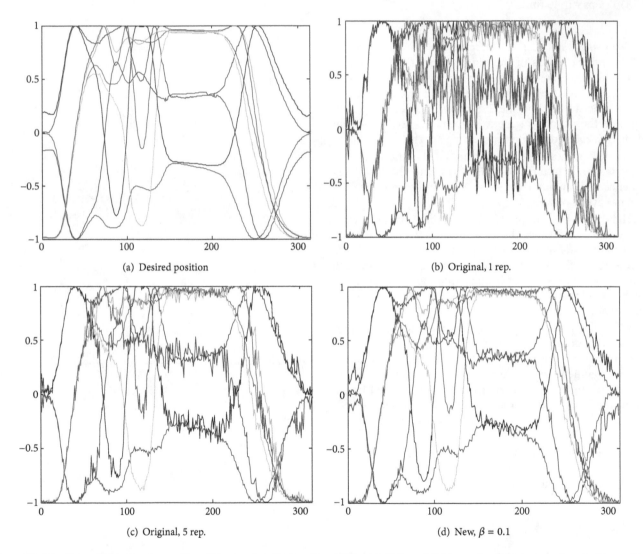

FIGURE 10: The figure illustrates the quality of the teacher forcing in experiments 1, 2, and 5. For each of these experiments the position sequences in epoch 5 are plotted as the 8 coordinate values at each time step for one repetition of the YMCA movement.

The new method requires extra training cycles to converge, but we showed that this can be compensated by using a shorter training sequence.

For benchmark sequences like generation of the figure-eight [18] or a chaotic attractor like the Mackey-Glass system [19], it will be interesting to see whether this new method could be faster than the original method, as it can get the same performance by training on a shorter training sequence. Preliminary results on the generation of the figure-eight verify that a shorter training sequence is needed with the new method, but the potential computational benefits are not yet extensively tested.

References

[1] K. Doya, "Universality of fully connected recurrent neural networks," Tech. Rep. University of California, San Diego, Calif, USA, 1993, Submitted to: *IEEE Transactions on Neural Networks*.

[2] M. Lukoševičius and H. Jaeger, "Reservoir computing approaches to recurrent neural network training," *Computer Science Review*, vol. 3, no. 3, pp. 127–149, 2009.

[3] T. Natschläger, W. Maass, and H. Markram, "The "liquid computer": a novel strategy for real-time computing on time series," *Special Issue on Foundations of Information Processing of TELEMATIK*, vol. 8, no. 1, pp. 39–43, 2002.

[4] H. Jaeger, "A tutorial on training recurrent neural networks, covering bppt, rtrl, and the echo state network approach," Tech. Rep., Fraunhofer Institute for Autonomous Intelligent Systems, Sankt Augustin, Germany, 2002.

[5] J. J. Steil, "Backpropagation-decorrelation: online recurrent learning with O(N) complexity," in *Proceedings of IEEE International Joint Conference on Neural Networks (IJCNN '04)*, pp. 843–848, July 2004.

[6] B. Schrauwen, D. Verstraeten, and J. van Campenhout, "An overview of reservoir computing: theory, applications and implementations," in *Proceedings of the 15th European Symposium on Artificial Neural Networks*, vol. 4, pp. 471–482, 2007.

[7] C. Fernando and S. Sojakka, "Pattern recognition in a bucket," in *Advances in Artificial Life*, Lecture Notes in computer Science, pp. 588–597, Springer, Berlin, Germany, 2003.

[8] D. Nquyen-Tuong and J. Peters, "Model learning for robot control: a survey," *Cognitive Processing*, vol. 12, no. 4, pp. 319–340, 2011.

[9] M. Oubbati, M. Schanz, and P. Levi, "Kinematic and dynamic adaptive control of a nonholonomic mobile robot using a RNN," in *Proceedings of IEEE International Symposium on Computational Intelligence in Robotics and Automation (CIRA '05)*, pp. 27–33, June 2005.

[10] M. Kawato, "Feedback-error-learning neural network for supervised motor learning," in *Advanced Neural Computers*, R. Eckmiller, Ed., pp. 365–372, Elsevier, Amsterdam, The Netherlands, 1990.

[11] M. I. Jordan and D. E. Rumelhart, "Forward models: supervised learning with a distal teacher," *Cognitive Science*, vol. 16, no. 3, pp. 307–354, 1992.

[12] M. Kawato, "Internal models for motor control and trajectory planning," *Current Opinion in Neurobiology*, vol. 9, no. 6, pp. 718–727, 1999.

[13] R. A. Løvlid, "Learning to imitate YMCA with an ESN," in *Proceedings of the 22nd International Conference on Artificial Neural Networks and Machine Learning (ICANN '12)*, Lecture Notes in Computer Science, pp. 507–514, Springer, 2012.

[14] R. A. Løvlid, "Learning motor control by dancing YMCA," *IFIP Advances in Information and Communication Technology*, vol. 331, pp. 79–88, 2010.

[15] A. Tidemann and P. Öztürk, "Self-organizing multiple models for imitation: teaching a robot to dance the YMCA," in *IEA/AIE*, vol. 4570 of *Lecture Notes in Computer Science*, pp. 291–302, Springer, Berlin, Germany, 2007.

[16] H. Jaeger et al., "Simple toolbox for esns," 2009, http://reservoir-computing.org/software.

[17] F. Toutounian and A. Ataei, "A new method for computing Moore-Penrose inverse matrices," *Journal of Computational and Applied Mathematics*, vol. 228, no. 1, pp. 412–417, 2009.

[18] F. Wyffels, B. Schrauwen, and D. Stroobandt, "Stable output feedback in reservoir computing using ridge regression," in *Proceedings of the 18th International Conference on Artificial Neural Networks, Part I (ICANN '08)*, pp. 808–817, Springer, 2008.

[19] H. Jaeger, "The echo state approach to analysing and training recurrent neural networks," Tech. Rep., GMD, 2001.

QUEST Hierarchy for Hyperspectral Face Recognition

David M. Ryer,[1] **Trevor J. Bihl,**[1] **Kenneth W. Bauer,**[1] **and Steven K. Rogers**[2]

[1] *Department of Operational Sciences, Air Force Institute of Technology, 2950 Hobson Way, Wright Patterson Air Force Base, OH 45433-7765, USA*
[2] *Air Force Research Laboratory, Sensors and Information Directorates, 2241 Avionics Circle, Wright Patterson AFB, OH 45433, USA*

Correspondence should be addressed to Trevor J. Bihl, trevor.bihl.ctr@afit.edu

Academic Editor: Weiru Liu

A qualia exploitation of sensor technology (QUEST) motivated architecture using algorithm fusion and adaptive feedback loops for face recognition for hyperspectral imagery (HSI) is presented. QUEST seeks to develop a general purpose computational intelligence system that captures the beneficial engineering aspects of qualia-based solutions. Qualia-based approaches are constructed from subjective representations and have the ability to detect, distinguish, and characterize entities in the environment. Adaptive feedback loops are implemented that enhance performance by reducing candidate subjects in the gallery and by injecting additional probe images during the matching process. The architecture presented provides a framework for exploring more advanced integration strategies beyond those presented. Algorithmic results and performance improvements are presented as spatial, spectral, and temporal effects are utilized; additionally, a Matlab-based graphical user interface (GUI) is developed to aid processing, track performance, and to display results.

1. Introduction

Social interaction depends heavily on the amazing face recognition capability that humans possess, especially the innate ability to process facial information. In a myriad of environments and views, people are able to quickly recognize and interpret visual cues from another person's face. With an increasing focus on personal protection and identity verification in public environments and during common interactions (e.g., air travel, financial transactions, and building access), the performance capability of the human system is now a desired requirement of our security and surveillance systems. Face recognition is a crucial tool being used in current operations in Iraq and Afghanistan by allied forces to identify and track enemies [1] and effectively distinguish friendlies and nonenemies [2]. The human recognition process utilizes not only spatial information but also important spectral and temporal aspects as well.

Utilizing only visual wavelengths for computer vision solutions has significant downsides, where features evident to humans are too subtle for a machine to capture. Prior research has shown deficiencies in computer vision techniques compared to human or animal vision when detecting defects in parts [4] or biometric identification [5]. By increasing the spectral sampling to include nonvisible wavelengths it might be possible to detect some of these subtle features included in the facial data. However, incorporation and handling of features in multispectral or hyperspectral imagery have not been fully investigated or subsequently extended to commercial applications [6].

The design of a biometric identification system should possess certain attributes to make it an effective operational system. These attributes include universality, distinctiveness, permanence, collectability, performance, acceptability, and circumvention [7]. Unfortunately, face recognition modality suffers from weaknesses in the areas of uniqueness, performance, and circumvention [8]. The ability to mitigate these weaknesses and ultimately match or exceed the recognition capability of a human is the performance benchmark for computer-based face recognition applications. By incorporating additional information inherently present in HSI,

| 550 nm | 650 nm | 750 nm | 850 nm | 1000 nm |

FIGURE 1: Spectral layer example from a CMU HSI Face [3].

the vulnerabilities of uniqueness, performance, and circumvention can be mitigated.

The Carnegie Mellon University (CMU) hyperspectral imagery (HSI) face database, graciously provided by Dr. Takeo Kanade, was used for this research [3]. Figure 1 depicts an example of this data over several sampled wavelengths. The utilization of HSI and the contextual information contained within these image cubes provide the tools to create a hierarchal methodology to address the challenges face recognition systems must overcome.

In this paper, various algorithms are used to exploit the inherent material reflectance properties in HSI to detect, segment, and identify subjects. A closed loop fusion hierarchy is applied to a suite of facial recognition algorithms to produce a cumulative performance improvement over traditional methods. A GUI tool is introduced which facilitates responsive operation as pictorial, numerical, and graphical results from the various algorithms are displayed. Experimental results are presented and recommendations for further research are suggested.

2. Face Recognition Architecture

There are three main focus areas for this research, the application of facial recognition algorithms to HSI, the use of feature and decision fusion for improved results, and adaptive feedback to re-examine and confirm the most difficult matches. This discussion starts with a review of the dataset to understand the dimensionality of the data and exploitation potential.

2.1. Database Description. Hyperspectral imagery involves collecting narrow spectral band reflectances across a contiguous portion of the electromagnetic spectrum. The CMU database images contains 65 spectral bands covering the visible and near infrared (NIR) from 450 nm to 1100 nm with a 50 nm spectral sampling and a spatial resolution of 640×480 pixels [3].

By taking advantage of fundamental properties of HSI (different materials reflect different wavelengths of light differently), skin, hair, and background materials are relatively easy to detect. The advantages of using higher dimensional data compared to grayscale or 3-band "true" color image includes the ability to detect skin segments since the spectral reflectance properties are well-understood [9]. The segmented portions of the image can be used to provide context that aids traditional face recognition algorithms.

Leveraging the signatures available through HSI, features such as skin and hair can be detected using a straightforward method similar to the Normalized Difference Vegetation Index (NDVI) used in remote sensing to detect live vegetation [9]. A Normalized Differential Skin Index (NDSI) can be computed easily through the sum and difference of key spectral bands [9]. Applying this technique and a variety of edge detection methods, several contextual layers of an individual's face can be extracted automatically from an HSI as seen in Figure 2 [10]. For individuals attempting to conceal or alter their appearance, it is now possible to detect inconsistencies such as make-up and prosthetic devices due to the differing reflectance properties [11].

Denes et al. [3] noted that the prototype camera used for the CMU data was subject to stray light leaks and optical imperfections as he noted that, "better face recognition clearly requires higher definition through a more sensitive, low noise camera or through higher levels of illumination." Viewed from another perspective, this noisy data provided an ideal environment for the development of an integration strategy for real world applications. The findings from these previous efforts provide a foundation to construct an intelligent hierarchy to address challenges for recognition systems using face recognition biometric as a test bed.

The portion of the CMU database examined herein contains images for 54 different subjects, 36 of whom sat for two sessions on different days. This database subset comprises our gallery and probe sets (subjects to identify and a gallery to search). Additionally, a subset of subjects from the gallery and probe sets were available for multiple sessions; 3 sessions (28 subjects), 4 sessions (22 subjects), or 5 sessions (16 subjects). These additional images are used in the adaptive feedback process to analyze the ability to inject additional images for confirmation of a subject match.

2.2. Previous Hyperspectral Face Recognition Research. Robila [12] investigated using both the visible and NIR wavelengths, as he explored the utility of spectral angles for comparison. Other research investigating NIR and visible wavelength faces include Klare and Jain [13], who examined matching NIR faces to visible light faces. Bourlai et al. [14] presented an initial study of combining NIR and shortwave IR (SWIR) faces with visible for more complete face representation, in addition to comparing cross-spectral matching (visible to SWIR). Kong et al. [15] delivered an overview of advantages and disadvantages of facial recognition methods with respect to the image wavelengths. Chou and Bajcsy [16] used hyperspectral images and experimented with segmenting

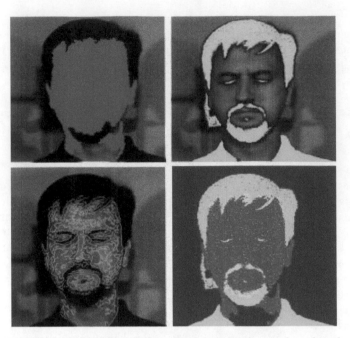

FIGURE 2: Contextual layers of a hyperspectral image: skin, hair, edges, and combined representation.

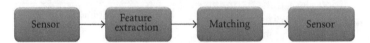

FIGURE 3: Conventional biometric system components.

different tissue types in the human hand. Elbakary et al. [17] used the K-means clustering algorithm to segment the skin surface in hyperspectral images and then measured the Mahalanobis distance between signatures to match subjects. Pan has accomplished the most extensive research utilizing spectral signatures of skin to identify individuals [18–20] and in a subsequent effort [21] explored the benefit of incorporating spatial measurements at various wavelengths. These efforts all produced valuable insight but individually these techniques did not provide the desired performance for this challenging data set.

2.3. Recognition Algorithms.

Traditional biometric systems are often open loop, comprised of four basic components, sensor, feature extraction, matching, and decision making, illustrated by the block diagram in Figure 3 [22]. However, such systems do not typically incorporate feedback from the feature extraction, matching, or decision making processes.

The sensor module acquires the biometric data, in this case a hyperspectral image, from the intended subject. The feature extraction module processes the captured data from the sensor and extracts features for detection. The matching module compares the extracted features against stored features saved in memory and generates comparisons called match scores. Match scores are comparisons made in a multidimensional comparison space and are a measure of distance between two images. The decision-making module

takes these scores and determines the user's identity by selecting the stored features (identification) associated with the smallest match score or by evaluating the obtained match score against a threshold for the claimed identity's features (verification). Feature extraction algorithms, including hair and face detection, are considered as part of preprocessing, while matching algorithms (Table 1 lists specific algorithms considered) are divided into spatial, spectral, and interest point variants; since some functions calculate scores relative to the entire gallery, those are annotated as well.

2.3.1. Preprocessing and Feature Extraction Algorithms.

The face recognition methodology presented employed a variety of techniques and methods to preprocess and segment data. Many applications use images accompanied by the manually selected coordinates of the eyes that are subsequently used for alignment and sizing. This upfront effort can be time consuming and assumes the involvement of human recognition and participation at the onset of the process. Typical manual preprocessing techniques [23] include selecting eyes coordinates, geometric normalization, and masking. For the CMU dataset and the process presented, an automated centroid detection based on hair or skin segmentation, face elliptical mask cropping, and or subsequent histogram equalization was employed. Following this process, two separate algorithms were used to locate face and hair surfaces through NDSI [9].

TABLE 1: Algorithms Examined.

Algorithm name	Underlying method	Recognition type	Score relative to gallery
Face	Eigenface	Spatial recognition	Yes
Hair	Eigenface	Spatial recognition	Yes
Skin	Eigenface	Spatial recognition	Yes
Spectral hair	Spectral angle mapping using an average hair signature	Spectral Recognition	Yes
Spectral face	Spectral angle mapping using k-means on an average face signature	Spectral recognition	Yes
Spectral face Matching	Spectral angle mapping using an average face signature	Spectral recognition	Yes
Soft	Mahalnobis distance for face area, eccentricity, and major and minor axes	Spatial recognition	Yes
Sift	SIFT using an averaged true color face image	Interest point recognition	No
HF Sift	SIFT using a hair and face composite image	Interest point and spatial recognition	No
Face using HF	Eigenface using shape of hair and skin segments	Spatial and spectral recognition	Yes
Face using HF pix	Eigenface using an image comprised of hair and skin segments only	Spatial and spectral recognition	Yes

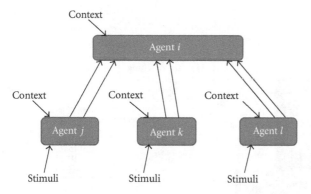

FIGURE 4: Agents, information, and levels of abstraction.

2.3.2. Spatial Recognition Algorithms. Following the preprocessing functions, the image data is ready for recognition algorithms. The first area explored was the spatial domain of the hyperspectral data in the form of grayscale face images. The skin and hair segments were subsequently fed to supporting algorithms of increasing detail for matching. The first and most straightforward method was to use face measurements such as size, length, width, and eccentricity to create a string of parameters for comparison. These images either can be the spatial face segments, hair segments, or combined representations.

The method used for hair and face image matching was the eigenface method devised by Turk and Pentland [24]. Eigenface is a holistic approach developed as an attempt to replicate the human recognition process and also as an alternative to many feature-based methods that utilized specific attributes but unfortunately discarded much of the surrounding image and contextual information. An important aspect of this algorithm is the creation of the comparison space or face space. In the eigenface algorithm

all probes are projected into a face space for comparison, eigenface then computes distances between faces in a face space of the gallery of potential candidates [24]. The composition of the gallery's subjects has a direct impact on the comparison scores and quality of the matches. The creation and dimensionality of the face space are an active area for research [25]. In the final architecture, the gallery will be tailored based on the progression of matches and will play a role in the adaptive selection of matches.

2.3.3. Spectral Recognition Algorithms. In addition to spatial recognition algorithms, spectral recognition can be considered with data that includes multiple spectral dimensions, such as the CMU dataset. For this analysis, spectral signatures of the hair and face segments are compared using spectral angle comparisons [12, 26]. Following methods used by Robila [26], spectral matching capability was evaluated using several variations. The first and most straightforward was by simply using a comparison of the average spectral angle. The variability of the spectral signatures, especially at the sensor wavelength limits, did have an effect on the overall performance. With that in mind, several of the wavelengths at the end of the frequency span were iteratively removed until maximum recognition performance was achieved.

Nunez's [9] research provided a method with NDSI to identify skin surfaces using only two wavelengths from hyperspectral images. The technique and reduction offered an attractive option to a more involved clustering method. Unfortunately, NDSI looked for two key wavelengths 1080 nm and 1580 nm in order to calculate the index. The CMU data only spanned the spectral range from 450 nm to 1090 nm. So only one of the key wavelengths was contained in the data, and the one wavelength included was located at the performance boundary of the Spectropolarimetric camera.

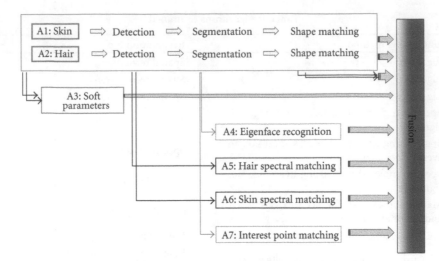

FIGURE 5: Recognition agent interface.

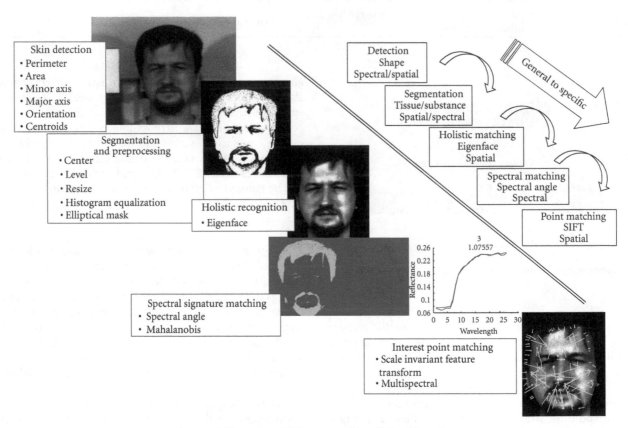

FIGURE 6: Hyperspectral face recognition fusion hierarchy.

With the advice from Nunez, a less effective, but suitable, alternative was devised that used a combination of indexes designed to highlight the unique characteristics of the spectral signature of human skin and eliminate common confusers. By examining the available wavelengths in the data as well as the quality of the information, an alternative approach was designed to sum relevant wavelengths and create indexes similar to NDSI that exploited the spectral characteristics of skin. Seen below.

NDSI Substitute Approach

$$\text{NDSI} \qquad \gamma_i = \frac{\hat{\rho}_i(1080\,\text{nm}) - \hat{\rho}_i(1580\,\text{nm})}{\hat{\rho}_i(1080\,\text{nm}) + \hat{\rho}_i(1580\,\text{nm})},$$

$$\gamma_{Vi} = \frac{\sum_{j=1050\,\text{nm}}^{1080\,\text{nm}} \hat{\rho}_i(j)}{\sum_{k=450\,\text{nm}}^{480\,\text{nm}} \hat{\rho}_i(k)}, \qquad \gamma_{Wi} = \frac{\sum_{j=890\,\text{nm}}^{910\,\text{nm}} \hat{\rho}_i(j)}{\sum_{k=970\,\text{nm}}^{990\,\text{nm}} \hat{\rho}_i(k)}, \qquad (1)$$

$$\gamma_{Xi} = \frac{\sum_{j=1060\,\text{nm}}^{1080\,\text{nm}} \hat{\rho}_i(j)}{\sum_{k=970\,\text{nm}}^{990\,\text{nm}} \hat{\rho}_i(k)}, \qquad \gamma_{Yi} = \frac{\sum_{j=600\,\text{nm}}^{620\,\text{nm}} \hat{\rho}_i(j)}{\sum_{k=540\,\text{nm}}^{560\,\text{nm}} \hat{\rho}_i(k)}$$

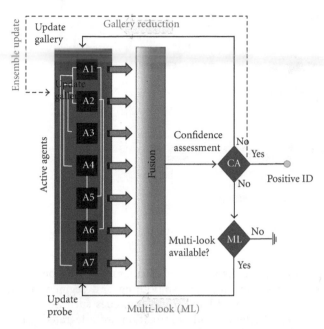

FIGURE 7: Architecture of facial recognition adaptive logic.

is the NDSI calculation and the alternative indices. Below the NDSI equation are four indices used to highlight the increase in reflectivity in the NIR wavelengths versus blue wavelengths (γ_{Vi}), highlighting the characteristic water absorption dip at 980 nm (γ_{Wi}, γ_{Xi}) and a final check to remove potential plant material that can act as a confuser (γ_{Yi}). By combining these indices that indicate the possibility of skin, when the value is greater than one, the skin segment can be identified rather efficiently compared to K means. The most effective implementation of this approach relied on (γ_{Xi}) and (γ_{Yi}) indicators to identify skin potential pixels. All pixels in the hyperspectral image cube that fell near the calculated average of the potential skin pixels were deemed a skin surface. A similar approach was used for the identification of hair segments in the image. This time using a NDVI calculation, (2), and then fine tuning the selected segment using Mahalanobis distance comparison for only the red (650 nm), green (510 nm), blue (475 nm), NIR (1000 nm) wavelengths and the hair segments, including facial hair, was obtained.

NDVI Calculation

$$\text{NDVI} \qquad \gamma_i = \frac{\hat{\rho}_i(1000\,\text{nm}) - \hat{\rho}_i(650\,\text{nm})}{\hat{\rho}_i(1000\,\text{nm}) + \hat{\rho}_i(650\,\text{nm})}. \qquad (2)$$

With the unique ability to segment the skin and hair segments of the image, it was uncomplicated to include a centroid calculation to accomplish the task of automatically centering images for identification. These adjustments include the centering of all face images, leveling in the case of unintended rotation of the face, and resizing the image for a consistent scale across individuals or the population. Once this is accomplished, the removal of background clutter

is accomplished by the application of an elliptical mask. Unfortunately, when this is accomplished, some important information is removed from the image including the relative shape of the head and a good portion of the hair on top of the head. This same approach was initially attempted but as our processing capability matured, we found this step crude in its application.

2.3.4. Interest Point Recognition Algorithms. Finally, the face, hair, and combined representation are feed to Lowe's scale and orientation robust scale invariant feature transform (SIFT) method to compare matching interest points or SIFT keys [27, 28]. SIFT extracts these features or key interest points using a difference of gaussians function. The local minimum and maximum of this function are used to create a feature vectors that describe the orientation and gradient based on neighboring pixels. These features are shown to be invariant to image scaling, translation, and rotation. To establish baseline performance, these methods are initially used in isolation and then used in combination to evaluate a range of fusion strategies.

3. Adaptive Facial Recognition

3.1. Qualia Exploitation of Sensor Technology (QUEST) Motivated Methodology. Ultimately, the performance and computational demands of working with high-dimensional data required a strategy that utilized only the relevant information in a more effective method. Intelligently handling high-dimensional biometric data involves dealing with varying levels of abstraction, learning, adaptation, organization, and exploiting structural relationships in the data [29].

Turning to the qualia exploitation of sensor technology (QUEST) methodology, we attempt to develop a general-purpose computational intelligence system that captures the advantages of qualia-like representations [30]. Qualia can be defined as a representation of the physical environment or a facet included in ones intrinsically available internal representation of the world around them [31]. It is our goal to combine different qualia into a metarepresentation, so sensory inputs can be integrated into a model that is adaptable and efficiently functional and can be deliberated repeatedly. A guiding principle of QUEST highlights the use of qualia that map sensory input to more useful and efficient states that complement the reflexive intuition level of processing. The functional requirement for a QUEST system is to possess the ability to detect, distinguish, and characterize entities in the environment [32].

In order to build a QUEST system for our task, it is important to develop and understand the concept of an agent [31]. An agent takes a subset of stimuli from the environment and processes this into relevant information. Information is defined as the reduction of uncertainty in that agent's internal representation. An agent has knowledge of other agents and of their environmental representation, akin to a theory of mind with insight into their needs. The agent transmits selected aspects of its information representation to neighboring or "aligned" agents. Agents transmit stimuli upward in higher levels of abstraction and can also transmit

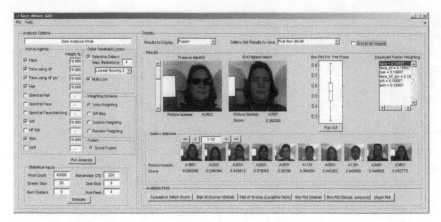

FIGURE 8: HSI facial recognition graphical user interface (with unity weighting).

information downward providing details and context that can influence lower level agents (Figure 4). An entity uses various sets of these agents and their collective knowledge to create an internal representation of its environment.

The relevant information or context is compromised of biometric characteristics and cues across the electromagnetic spectrum. Rogers et al. [32] states that the concept of an agent is to synthesize aspects of its qualia that are provided to it by an "aligned" agent, such that an agent reduces the uncertainty in its internal representation by processing data into information. An agent communicates this context to other agents that use this information to improve their internal representation and reduce their uncertainty. Context can only be transmitted between agents that are aligned as each agent contains a representation of the other's environment. The combination of fiducial features and higher level abstracted characteristics creates this context. In the human recognition system, the mind stores data not so much as sensory numbers but as relative comparisons to prior experiences that can change over time. For a face recognition system, the relative comparisons should serve an equally important role in refining the solution space and guiding the search process. The connections or links in our fusion hierarchy provide the context of the face. There are many links that can connect the internal and external facial features that have proved so important in human recognition research [33]. The links chosen can help incorporate higher levels of abstraction such as important soft biometric [34] cues or can be the connection between spatial and spectral information.

Figure 5 illustrates the links and various identification algorithms employed in our HSI face recognition system. The concept in Figure 5 can be considered as an extension of the general face recognition concept from Figure 3 to incorporate multiple feature extractions, matching algorithms with a fusion decided identity declaration. A combination of score and rank fusion strategies will be evaluated to obtain the best method to synthesize the results of the agent information.

3.2. Fusion Hierarchy. From the field of automatic target recognition, Ando [35] provides a useful hierarchy for processing the hyperspectral face images. At the lowest level, processing includes smoothing and segmenting the image. During mid-level processing, cues such as shading, texture, reflectance, and illumination are integrated. Lastly, high-level processing integrates information that is invariant across different viewpoints for final identification. Using this guide, the initial face recognition hierarchy could be achieved though incrementally applying segmentation, processing, and identification steps. However, a more efficient means involve parallel processing and score fusion of the segmentation, processing, and identification steps, utilizing not only information from the spatial dimension of the image but spectral elements to help assist in the tasks of segmenting, processing, and identification. Figure 6 illustrates the combined and incremental approach, wherein the algorithmic scores are normalized and then fused across algorithms applied through score fusion.

The straightforward fusion approach presented in Figure 6 did not provide the desired performance during initial testing. Subsequent adjustments, such as the implementation of feedback loops would eventually prove necessary, but the general approach of progressing from easily processed general characteristics to more specific and more computationally intensive characteristics would remain apparent through design of the final processing architecture.

3.3. Adaptive Feedback. As alluded to earlier, algorithms used herein, such as the eigenface algorithm, derive scores for a set of faces that remain constant within a static comparison space derived from the gallery of candidates for a situation. Our implementation of the eigenface method counter balances this consistency with an adaptive training set wherein identified poor matches are removed. Eigenface is then rerun with a different training set, resulting in a different set of eigenfaces (principal components of the set of faces) for the next iteration. Additionally, for score fusion, each set of algorithmic scores must be normalized so the set of algorithms employ consistent and fusible scales. The adaptive feedback strategy employed leverages the changing eigenface space and the normalized scores passed to the fusion algorithms, tailored during the matching process by removing the lowest scoring subjects.

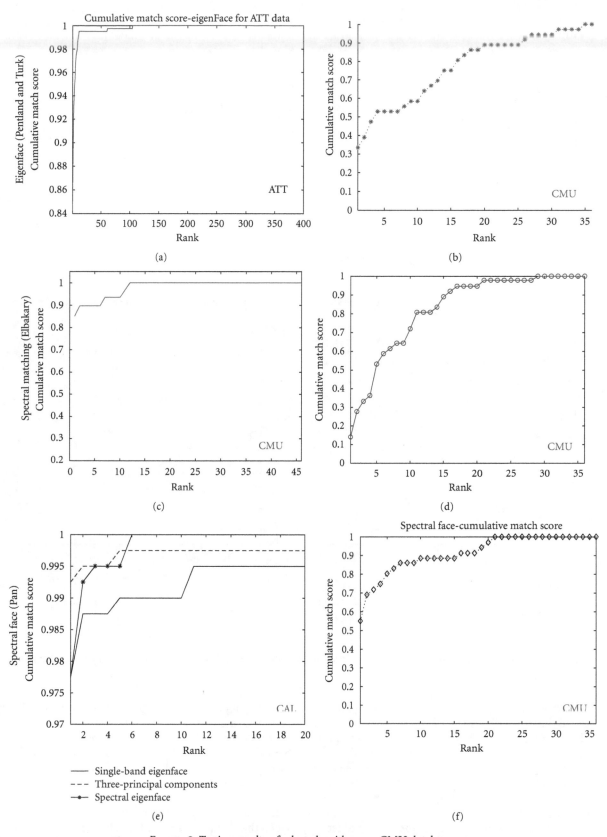

FIGURE 9: Testing results of select algorithms on CMU database.

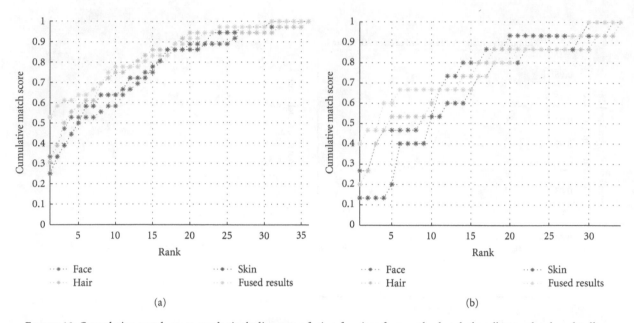

FIGURE 10: Cumulative match score results including score fusion for eigenface methods: whole gallery and reduced gallery.

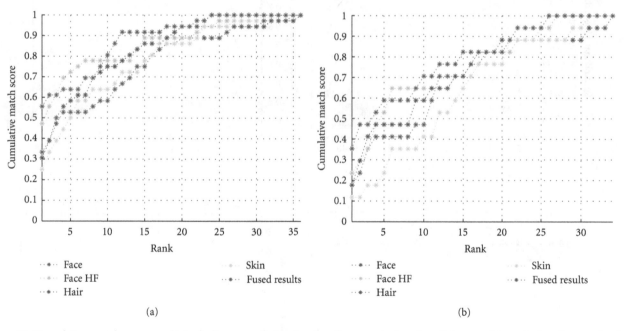

FIGURE 11: Cumulative match score results including score fusion for eigenface, spectral, and spatial recognition: whole gallery and reduced gallery.

To incorporate the ability to make relative comparisons over time, adaptive feedback loops were added to the established facial recognition hierarchy (Figure 3), but within the adaptive fusion framework this approach is depicted in Figure 7. Closed loop systems compare the measurement of the feedback with the desired output [36]. By incorporating feedback of decision making results, refining the decision-making accuracy is possible.

For the biometric system presented, there are two feedback loops. The first feedback loop is included to examine the improvement potential of changing the dimensionality of the candidate gallery, thus changing the relative scores of some algorithms. This procedure involves reducing the gallery size by removing the lowest scoring subjects. This process is applied only for subject matching scores that fall below a user-specified threshold. The second feedback loop incorporates multi-look functionality, adding the capability to test additional probe images if and when they become available. This facet represents a temporal dimension that comes with multiple probe images or with hyperspectral video that obtains a series of face images over time.

Both feedback loops can be active or applied individually. Finally, there are several control variables for the selection and weighting of the agents used in the fusion process.

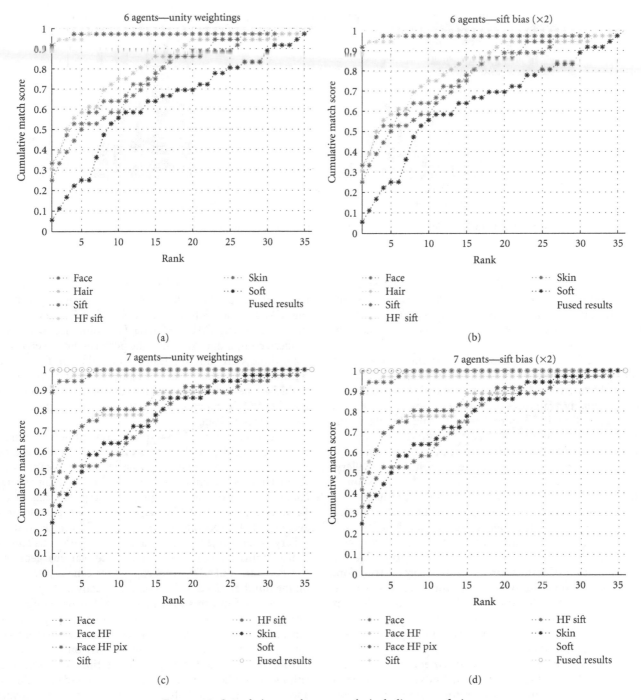

FIGURE 12: Cumulative match score results including score fusion.

Research by Chawla and Bowye [25] and Kuncheva [37] has highlighted the importance of randomness and diversity in the creation of classifier ensembles, so the controlled and random selection of these active agents is a current area of research.

At any stage of the hierarchy presented earlier in Figure 6, a Libet level answer similar to intuition is created and is integrated at the higher or metarepresentation levels of the hierarchy. The incorporation of qualia occurs as deliberation is made over the combined evidence from prior agents. The qualia-based Cartesian theater that is created through the fusion representation provides an engineering advantage in the confidence assessment.

4. Graphical User Interface Tool

To facilitate interpretation of data analysis and assist with the visualization of results, a Matlab-based GUI tool was designed to operate and test the facial recognition software.

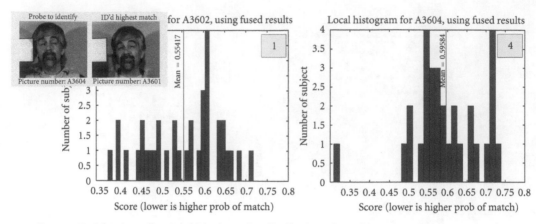

FIGURE 13: Adaptive gallery/multi-look results, distribution of matching scores for poorest match.

The GUI tool, pictured in Figure 8, is a direct parallel to the architecture presented in Figure 7. A user can select the active agents, enable feedback loops, and select from either a score or rank fusion approach while simultaneously analyzing results.

The GUI displays the probe to be matched and the best current match is directly opposite. Below these displays, the top ten matches are displayed in thumbnail depiction along with their relative rankings and scores. Viewing the results of each algorithm is permitted by selecting the algorithm of interest in the "Results to Display" drop down menu. If feedback loops are employed, a user can select which result set to view, accompanied by the dimensionality of the gallery, in the "Gallery Set Results to View" menu. The pictorial results can be viewed in either grayscale or color images.

A box plot is displayed for each probe under consideration to provide continuous score distribution feedback when viewing results for each face and method. Additionally, gallery matches for each probe are scrollable to enable the visual evaluation of results for the entire score distribution. To review the quantitative results, the user can choose from cumulative match score plots, box plots, or histogram depiction of the relative scores and statistics.

For processing purposes, Matlab's multiple processor pooling was employed on a dual quad core computer with 16 GB of RAM. The processing requirements of the hyperspectral data along with the chosen methods benefit from the use of parallel processing. However, for computational ease, an additional utility tool allows the user to view saved results of any prior run by simply loading a results file. This file will display the algorithms used, type of feedback loops used, and weighting schemes and permit a user to view all results and face matches. The user is notified if the selected computer can support running the complete suite of software tools by viewing the status bar.

5. Performance Assessment

5.1. Algorithm and Fusion Performance. During the initial testing of the CMU data, many of the same algorithms were utilized from previous HSI research [12, 17, 18, 21].

The results confirmed some of the challenges present in the CMU data. The difference being the quality between the CMU data and the grayscale AT&T data [37] or the more recent CAL HSI data [18] obtained with more modern equipment. Although the performance level of these algorithms were not replicated, the value of the various techniques is not diminished. A comparison of the previously published performance versus that obtained through our initial testing is shown in Figure 9, to establish a preliminary performance threshold.

Data processing starts with common but now automated preprocessing step, followed by the extraction of basic face features and then a matching step where face features and characteristics are compared for subject matching. Average computation time for the preprocessing of each face is 14 seconds. Face matching algorithms take an additional average of 13 seconds to process each face against the gallery of 36 subjects for an algorithm suite consisting of 6 algorithms including SIFT, eigenface, various geometric comparisons, and NDSI. Processing time can vary depending on the number of algorithms or agents activated by the user.

Findings from this initial round of testing reinforce the need for a fusion framework that combines complimentary aspects of these algorithms to enhance the performance capability regardless of data quality or environmental setting. Taking into account the processing time of some algorithms, a method to accomplish effective data reduction and processing should also be considered to reduce overall computational time. The next section will briefly describe the results of integrating the separate algorithms into a hierarchy for a robust face recognition system.

5.2. QUEST Hierarchy Results and Findings. A combination of score and rank fusion strategies were tested with the most effective being a weighted score fusion strategy, wherein the overall matching score is a combination of weighted individual matching scores. Figure 10 illustrates a cumulative match score result using three eigenface-based methods ("hair," "face," and "skin") and unity weighting; the right-hand figure illustrates the changes to the comparison space through dropping the two lowest performing faces from the gallery and reexamining only the lowest scoring half of the probe set. The cumulative match score plots depict the number of correct matches for the rank along the horizontal access. The scores of "1" in the following figures indicate the ability to correctly identify all images during the first attempt. These figures should not be confused with ROC curves or a summation of match scores.

Figure 10 displays score fusion improving the cumulative results over any one method. The reduced gallery included 15 probes to identify against a gallery of 34. Of particular interest is the rank at which the fused results reach 1 indicating that through the reduced gallery method; all subjects are identified within 30 matches improving over 31 matches for the full gallery.

Figure 11 incorporates spectral and spatial recognition to the algorithms presented in Figure 10, the improvement is seen through reaching a cumulative match of "1" by 24 matches. The reduced scores converge to "1" slower than the full gallery (26 versus 24 matches); however this is for a gallery space of the 17 most difficult subjects to identify for this algorithm set. Both results show a distinct improvement over fusion for only the eigenface method in Figure 10.

Continuing the fusion methodology to incorporate interest point matching produces Figure 12, which depicts cumulative match score results obtained using unity weighting for all agents compared to double weighting for the SIFT algorithms using either 6 agents or 7 agents. While the SIFT algorithm contributes a majority of the contribution, it is only through the inclusion of other identification methodologies, and inherent segmentation capability, that the overall identification accuracy is increased to 100%.

Enhancing this fusion strategy with the addition of the adaptive gallery feedback loop and the multi-look functionality allows us to continually process the results until a chosen threshold or confidence level is achieved. Figure 13 depicts an example, using the "6 Agent" framework with unity weighting from Figure 12, where the poorest scoring match distribution is shown after initial matching and then after four feedback repetitions, during which the gallery size was reduced by 10 percent, and a new probe image was injected each time. Through this repetitive process, matches with the lowest matching scores are rechecked as poor candidates are removed from the gallery, and additional probe images are inserted into the process to confirm the correct identification.

6. Conclusion

Even with the distinctiveness that comes with every human being, no single metric or feature has demonstrated the ability to identify all individuals in both controlled and uncontrolled environments across large populations using a single modality. This challenge frequently leads to solutions that incorporate multiple modalities that require close proximity and permission that accompany the selected biometrics not to mention the additional equipment and complexity. An alternative to this challenge may be to fuse contextual or complimentary spatial, spectral, and temporal information in an efficient architecture that enhances effectiveness and efficiency. The use of hyperspectral imagery and a fusion hierarchy similar to the one presented in this paper offers many opportunities for the improvement of current face recognition systems and can be applied to a wider array of object recognition problems.

References

[1] K. Osborn, "U.S. ugrades biometrics gear to spot terrorists," *Defense News*, vol. 24, no. 7, p. 30, 2009.

[2] M. T. Flynn, M. Pottinger, and D. Batchelor, "Fixing intel: a blueprint for making intelligence relevant in Afghanistan," Center for a New American Security, 2010.

[3] L. J. Denes, P. Metes, and Y. Liu, "Hyperspectral face database," Tech. Rep. CMU-RI-TR-02-25, Robotics Institute, Carnegie Mellon University, 2002.

[4] T. Verhave, "The pigeon as a quality-control inspector," in *Control of Human Behavior*, R. Ulrich, T. Stachnik, and J. Mabry, Eds., pp. 242–246, Scott, Foresman and Company, Glenview, Ill, USA, 1966.

[5] P. J. Phillips, W. Scruggs, T. O'Toole et al., "FRVT 2006 and ICE 2006 large scale results," Tech. Rep. NISTIR 7498, National Institute of Standards and Technology, 2007.

[6] D. Shastri, A. Merla, P. Tsiamyrtzis, and I. Pavlidis, "Imaging facial signs of neurophysiological responses," *IEEE Transactions on Biomedical Engineering*, vol. 56, no. 2, Article ID 4599232, pp. 477–484, 2009.

[7] A. K. Jain, "Biometric recognition: how do i know who you are?" in *Proceedings of the IEEE 12th Signal Processing and Communications Applications Conference (SIU '04)*, pp. 3–5, April 2004.

[8] A. K. Jain, A. Ross, and S. Prabhakar, "An introduction to biometric recognition," *IEEE Transactions on Circuits and Systems for Video Technology*, vol. 14, no. 1, pp. 4–20, 2004.

[9] A. Nunez, *A Physical Model of Human Skin and Its Application for Search and Rescue*, Air Force Institute of Technology (AU), Wright-Patterson AFB, Ohio, USA, 2009.

[10] D. Ryer, *QUEST Hierarchy for Hyperspectral Face Recognition*, Air Force Institute of Technology (AU), Wright-Patterson AFB, Ohio, USA, 2011.

[11] I. Pavlidis and P. Symosek, "The imaging issue in an automatic face/disguise detection system," in *Proceedings of the IEEE Workshop on Computer Vision Beyond the Visible Spectrum: Methods and Applications*, pp. 15–24, 2000.

[12] S. A. Robila, "Toward hyperspectral face recognition," in *Image Processing: Algorithms and Systems*, vol. 6812 of *Proceedings of SPIE*, 2008.

[13] B. Klare and A. K. Jain, "HeTerogeneous face recognition: matching NIR to visible light images," in *Proceedings of the 20th International Conference on Pattern Recognition (ICPR '10)*, pp. 1513–1516, August 2010.

[14] T. Bourlai, N. Kalka, A. Ross, B. Cukic, and L. Hornak, "Cross-spectral face verification in the Short Wave Infrared (SWIR) band," in *Proceedings of the 20th International Conference on Pattern Recognition (ICPR '10)*, pp. 1343–1347, August 2010.

[15] S. G. Kong, J. Heo, B. R. Abidi, J. Paik, and M. A. Abidi, "Recent advances in visual and infrared face recognition—a review," *Computer Vision and Image Understanding*, vol. 97, no. 1, pp. 103–135, 2005.

[16] Y.-T. Chou and P. Bajcsy, "Toward face detection, pose estimation and human recognition from hjyperspectral imagery," Tech. Rep. NCSA-ALG04-0005, 2004.

[17] M. I. Elbakary, M. S. Alam, and M. S. Asian, "Face recognition algorithm in hyperspectral imagery by employing the K-means method and the mahalanobis distance," in *Advanced Signal Processing Algorithms, Architectures, and Implementations XVII*, vol. 6697 of *Proceedings of SPIE*, August 2007.

[18] Z. Pan, G. Healey, M. Prasad, and B. Tromberg, "Face recognition in hyperspectral images," *IEEE Transactions on Pattern Analysis and Machine Intelligence*, vol. 25, no. 12, pp. 1552–1560, 2003.

[19] Z. Pan, G. Healey, M. Prasad, and B. Tromberg, "Hyperspectral face recognition for homeland security," in *Infrared Technology and Applications XXIX*, vol. 5074 of *Proceedings of SPIE*, pp. 767–776, April 2003.

[20] Z. Pan, G. Healey, M. Prasad, and B. Tromberg, "Hyperspectral face recognition under variable outdoor illumination," in *Algorithms and Technologies for MultiSpectral, Hyperspectral, and Ultraspectral Imagery X*, vol. 5425 of *Proceedings of SPIE*, pp. 520–529, April 2004.

[21] Z. Pan, G. Healey, and B. Tromberg, "Multiband and spectral eigenfaces for face recognition in hyperspectral images," in *Biometric Technology for Human Identification II*, vol. 5779 of *Proceedings of SPIE*, pp. 144–151, March 2005.

[22] A. Ross and A. K. Jain, "Multimodal biometrics: an overview," in *Proceedings of the 12th European Signal Processing Conference*, pp. 1221–1224, September 2004.

[23] R. Beveridge, D. Bolme, M. Teixerira, and B. Draper, *The CSU Face Identification Evaluation System User's Guide: Version 5.0*, Computer Science Department, Colorado State University, 2003.

[24] M. Turk and A. Pentland, "Eigenfaces for recognition," *Journal of Cognitive Neuroscience*, vol. 3, no. 1, pp. 71–86, 1991.

[25] N. V. Chawla and K. W. Bowye, "Random subspaces and subsampling for 2-D face recognition," in *Proceedings of the IEEE Computer Society Conference on Computer Vision and Pattern Recognition (CVPR '05)*, pp. 582–589, June 2005.

[26] S. A. Robila, "Using spectral distances for speedup in hyperspectral image processing," *International Journal of Remote Sensing*, vol. 26, no. 24, pp. 5629–5650, 2005.

[27] D. G. Lowe, "Object recognition from local scale-invariant features," in *Proceedings of the 7th IEEE International Conference on Computer Vision (ICCV '99)*, pp. 1150–1157, September 1999.

[28] D. G. Lowe, "Distinctive image features from scale-invariant keypoints," *International Journal of Computer Vision*, vol. 60, no. 2, pp. 91–110, 2004.

[29] W. H. Fleming, *Future Directions in Control Theory, a Mathematical Perspective*, Society for Industrial and Applied Mathematics, Philadelphia, Pa, USA, 1988.

[30] S. K. Rogers, "Qualia Exploitation of Sensor Technology," Web log post, Quest Discussion Topics, 2010 http://qualellc.wordpress.com/2010/06/17/quest-discussion-topics-june-182010/.

[31] S. K. Rogers, Types of Qualia, Presentation, November 2009.

[32] S. Rogers, M. Kabrisky, K. Bauer, M. Oxley, and A. Rogers, *QUEST: QUalia Exploitation of Sensor Technology*, 2008.

[33] I. Jarudi and P. Sinha, "Recognizing degraded faces: contribution of internal and external features," in *Department of Brain and Cognitive Sciences, Massachusetts Institute of Technology, Artificial Intelligence Memo 2003-004 and Center for Biological and Computational Learning Memo*, p. 225, 2005.

[34] A. K. Jain, S. C. Dass, and K. Nandakumar, "Can soft biometric traits assist user recognition?" in *Biometric Technology for Human Identification*, Proceedings of SPIE, pp. 561–572, April 2004.

[35] H. Ando, "ATR human information processing laboratories," in *Proceedings of the International Media Technology Workshop on Abstract Perception*, Kyoto, Japan, January 1994.

[36] R. Dorf and R. H. Bishop, *Modern Control Systems*, Prentice Hall, Upper Saddle River, NJ, USA, 9th edition, 2001.

[37] L. Kuncheva, *Combining Pattern Classifiers, Methods and Algorithms*, Wiley and Sons, Hoboken, NJ, USA, 2004.

Permissions

The contributors of this book come from diverse backgrounds, making this book a truly international effort. This book will bring forth new frontiers with its revolutionizing research information and detailed analysis of the nascent developments around the world.

We would like to thank all the contributing authors for lending their expertise to make the book truly unique. They have played a crucial role in the development of this book. Without their invaluable contributions this book wouldn't have been possible. They have made vital efforts to compile up to date information on the varied aspects of this subject to make this book a valuable addition to the collection of many professionals and students.

This book was conceptualized with the vision of imparting up-to-date information and advanced data in this field. To ensure the same, a matchless editorial board was set up. Every individual on the board went through rigorous rounds of assessment to prove their worth. After which they invested a large part of their time researching and compiling the most relevant data for our readers. Conferences and sessions were held from time to time between the editorial board and the contributing authors to present the data in the most comprehensible form. The editorial team has worked tirelessly to provide valuable and valid information to help people across the globe.

Every chapter published in this book has been scrutinized by our experts. Their significance has been extensively debated. The topics covered herein carry significant findings which will fuel the growth of the discipline. They may even be implemented as practical applications or may be referred to as a beginning point for another development. Chapters in this book were first published by Hindawi Publishing Corporation; hereby published with permission under the Creative Commons Attribution License or equivalent.

The editorial board has been involved in producing this book since its inception. They have spent rigorous hours researching and exploring the diverse topics which have resulted in the successful publishing of this book. They have passed on their knowledge of decades through this book. To expedite this challenging task, the publisher supported the team at every step. A small team of assistant editors was also appointed to further simplify the editing procedure and attain best results for the readers.

Our editorial team has been hand-picked from every corner of the world. Their multi-ethnicity adds dynamic inputs to the discussions which result in innovative outcomes. These outcomes are then further discussed with the researchers and contributors who give their valuable feedback and opinion regarding the same. The feedback is then collaborated with the researches and they are edited in a comprehensive manner to aid the understanding of the subject.

Apart from the editorial board, the designing team has also invested a significant amount of their time in understanding the subject and creating the most relevant covers. They scrutinized every image to scout for the most suitable representation of the subject and create an appropriate cover for the book.

The publishing team has been involved in this book since its early stages. They were actively engaged in every process, be it collecting the data, connecting with the contributors or procuring relevant information. The team has been an ardent support to the editorial, designing and production team. Their endless efforts to recruit the best for this project, has resulted in the accomplishment of this book. They are a veteran in the field of academics and their pool of knowledge is as vast as their experience in printing. Their expertise and guidance has proved useful at every step. Their uncompromising quality standards have made this book an exceptional effort. Their encouragement from time to time has been an inspiration for everyone.

The publisher and the editorial board hope that this book will prove to be a valuable piece of knowledge for researchers, students, practitioners and scholars across the globe.

List of Contributors

Iman Sadeghkhani
Department of Electrical Engineering, Islamic Azad University, Najafabad Branch, Najafabad 85141-43131, Iran

Abbas Ketabi
Department of Electrical Engineering, University of Kashan, Kashan 87317-51167, Iran

Rene Feuillet
Grenoble Electrical Engineering Lab (G2ELab), Grenoble INP, BP46, 38402 Saint Martin d'Hères Cedex, France

Víctor Uc-Cetina
Facultad de Matem´aticas, Universidad Aut´onoma de Yucat´an, Perif´erico Norte Tablaje 13615, Apartado Postal 192, C.P. 97119 M´erida, Yucat´an, Mexico

Alireza Rowhanimanesh and Sohrab Efati
Center of Excellence on Soft Computing and Intelligent Information Processing (SCIIP), Ferdowsi University of Mashhad, Mashhad, Iran

Shiva Kumar
Department of Mechanical Engineering, MIT, Manipal 576104, India

P. Srinivasa Pai and B. R. Shrinivasa Rao
Department of Mechanical Engineering, NMAMIT, Nitte 574110, India

Amarda Shehu
Department of Computer Science, George Mason University, Fairfax, VA 22030, USA
Department of Bioengineering, George Mason University, Fairfax, VA 22030, USA

Brian Olson, Irina Hashmi and Kevin Molloy
Department of Computer Science, George Mason University, Fairfax, VA 22030, USA

Kieran Greer
Distributed Computing Systems, Belfast, UK

Dora Melo
Iscac, Instituto Polit´ecnico de Coimbra, Quinta Agr´ıcola-Bencanta, 3040-316 Coimbra, Portugal
Centre for Artificial Intelligence (CENTRIA) and Departamento de Inform´atica, FCT/UNL, Quinta da Torre, 2829-516 Caparica, Portugal

Irene Pimenta Rodrigues and Vitor Beires Nogueira
Centre for Artificial Intelligence (CENTRIA) and Departamento de Inform´atica, FCT/UNL, Quinta da Torre, 2829-516 Caparica, Portugal
Departamento de Inform´atica, Universidade de ´Evora, Rua Rom˜ao Ramalho, No. 59, 7000-671 ´Evora, Portugal

Zoran Majkić
International Society for Research in Science and Technology, P.O. Box 2464, Tallahassee, FL 32316-2464, USA

Salvador E. Barbosa and Mikel D. Petty
University of Alabama in Huntsville, 301 Sparkman Drive, Huntsville, AL 35899, USA

F. Hosseinali and A. A. Alesheikh
Faculty of Geodesy and Geomatics Engineering, K.N. Toosi University of Technology, ValiAsr Street, Mirdamad Cross, Tehran 19967-15433, Iran

F. Nourian
School of Urban Planning, University of Tehran, Enghelab Avenue, Tehran 14155-6135, Iran

Manoj Tripathy
Department of Electrical Engineering, Indian Institute of Technology Roorkee, Roorkee 247 667, India

Solvi Arnold, Reiji Suzuki and Takaya Arita
Graduate School of Information Science, Nagoya University, Furo-cho, Chikusa-ku, Nagoya 464-8601, Japan

Anis Zouaghi
LATICE, ISSAT, University of Sousse, Cit´e Ibn Khaldoun, Taffala, 4003 Sousse, Tunisia

Mounir Zrigui and Laroussi Merhbene
LATICE, FSM, University of Monastir, Avenue de l'Environnement, 5000 Monastir, Tunisia

Georges Antoniadis
LIDILEM, University of Stendhal, BP 25, 38040 Grenoble Cedex 9, France

Pier Luigi Mazzeo, Marco Leo, Paolo Spagnolo and Massimiliano Nitti
Istituto di Studi sui Sistemi Intelligenti per l'Automazione, CNR, Via G. Amendola 122/D, 70126 Bari, Italy

E. Chatzimichail and A. Rigas
Department of Electrical and Computer Engineering, Democritus University of Thrace, 67100 Xanthi, Greece

E. Paraskakis
Department of Pediatrics, Democritus University of Thrace, 68100 Alexandroupolis, Greece

Efrosini Sourla and Athanasios Tsakalidis
Computer Engineering & Informatics Department, University of Patras, 26500 Patras, Greece

Spyros Sioutas
Department of Informatics, Ionian University, 49100 Corfu, Greece

Vasileios Syrimpeis
General Hospital of Patras "Agios Andreas", 26335 Patras, Greece

Giannis Tzimas
Department of Applied Informatics in Management & Economy, Faculty of Management and Economics, Technological Educational Institute of Messolonghi, 30200 Messolonghi, Greece

Hussain Shareef
Faculty of Electrical Engineering and Built Environment, Universiti Kebangsaan Malaysia, 43600 Bangi, Malaysia

Saifunizam Abd. Khalid, Mohd Wazir Mustafa and Azhar Khairuddin
Faculty of Electrical Engineering, Universiti Teknologi Malaysia, 81310 Johor, Malaysia

Rikke Amilde Løvlid
Department of Computer and Information Science, Norwegian University of Science and Technology, Sem Saelands vei 7-9, 7491 Trondheim, Norway

David M. Ryer, Trevor J. Bihl and Kenneth W. Bauer
Department of Operational Sciences, Air Force Institute of Technology, 2950 Hobson Way, Wright Patterson Air Force Base, OH 45433-7765, USA

Steven K. Rogers
Air Force Research Laboratory, Sensors and Information Directorates, 2241 Avionics Circle, Wright Patterson AFB, OH 45433, USA